When a Dream Dies

When a Dream Dies

Agriculture, Iowa, and the Farm Crisis of the 1980s

Pamela Riney-Kehrberg

UNIVERSITY PRESS OF KANSAS

© 2022 by the University Press of Kansas
All rights reserved

Published by the University Press of Kansas (Lawrence, Kansas 66045), which was organized by the Kansas Board of Regents and is operated and funded by Emporia State University, Fort Hays State University, Kansas State University, Pittsburg State University, the University of Kansas, and Wichita State University

Library of Congress Cataloging-in-Publication Data

Names: Riney-Kehrberg, Pamela, author.
Title: When a dream dies : agriculture, Iowa, and the farm crisis of the 1980s / Pamela Riney-Kehrberg.
Description: Lawrence, Kansas : University Press of Kansas, 2022. Includes bibliographical references and index
Identifiers: LCCN 2021058927
ISBN 9780700633555 (cloth)
ISBN 9780700638048 (paperback)
ISBN 9780700633562 (ebook)
Subjects: LCSH: Agriculture—Economic aspects—Iowa—History—20th century. | Farm tenancy—Economic aspects—Iowa—History—20th century. | Farmers—Iowa—Economic conditions. | Iowa—Economic conditions—20th century.
Classification: LCC HD1775.I8 R56 2022 | DDC 338.109777—dc23/eng/20220225 LC record available at https://lccn.loc.gov/2021058927.

British Library Cataloguing-in-Publication Data is available.

For my graduate students,
past and present.
You are my inspiration,
and this book is for you.

For my graduate students,
past and present.
You are my inspiration,
and this book is for you.

Contents

Acknowledgments ix

Introduction 1

1 The Go-Go Seventies 14

2 From Fencerow to Fencerow to Failure: 1979–1983 36

3 The Year of Realization: 1984 66

4 From Penny Auctions to a Declaration of Emergency: 1985 96

5 From Fears of Violence to Glimmers of Hope: 1986 132

6 From Crisis to Chronic: 1987–1993 163

Epilogue: Last-Generation Farmers 196

Notes 223

A Note on Sources 263

Bibliography 265

Index 277

Acknowledgments

This book has its roots in my years as a graduate student at the University of Wisconsin, where I learned about the history of farms and took a stab at my first agricultural crises, the Dust Bowl and Great Depression. During those years, I was only dimly aware of the crisis going on in the countryside around Madison (in spite of John Mellencamp's *Scarecrow* album, which I owned and loved). When I was teaching agricultural and rural history to graduate students at Iowa State, my students began to ask why there wasn't any recent scholarship on the farm economic crisis of the 1980s. Even so, this book might not have been written had it not been for a special issue of the *Middle West Review*, guest edited by Jenny Barker Devine and David Vail. It was with that call for contributions that I began thinking of what I might write about the 1980s.

There are so very many debts I have accrued in the process of writing this book. Many people have shared their expertise with me, helping me to find materials, understand concepts, and improve my writing. I am deeply indebted to the archivists and staff at the State Historical Society of Iowa, in Des Moines; at Special Collections, Parks Library, Iowa State University; at Special Collections, Rod Library, University of Northern Iowa; at Special Collections, Drake University; and at the Iowa Women's Archives at the University of Iowa. There are also numerous librarians in small places who may—or may not—have understood why I wanted to look through their yearbook collections, but were gracious, nonetheless. Speaking of yearbooks, I am deeply indebted to Nate Buman, who introduced me to the collection at the Shelby County Historical Museum, and one of the most important sources in my research. Thank you, too, to the people who helped me understand different aspects of the Farm Crisis and were willing to share their stories. I especially appreciate the help I received from Cheryl Tevis, Paul Lasley, Mike Duffy, David Ostendorf, Joe Harper, Maynard Hoberg, Leah Tookey, and Edie Hunter.

I am ever so grateful for the people who read this manuscript for me. First and foremost are my two colleagues, Julie Courtwright and Stacy Cordery. For more than two years, we participated in a writing group, and they have shared in the development of this book. I cannot thank them enough. I also want to thank a large band of friendly critics: Joe Anderson, Jenny Barker Devine, Marv Bergman, David Danbom, Paul Lasley, Debra Reid, and Scott Riney, each of whom brought unique perspectives and expertise to the project. Thank you so much—and please realize that where you contradicted each other, I had very difficult decisions to make about *whose* advice I would follow. I wish to thank the two anonymous reviewers for University Press of Kansas, who provided excellent feedback. There are also many colleagues within the Rural Women's Studies Association and the Agricultural History Society who have helped me to refine my ideas.

Numerous individuals helped me with the illustrations for the book. Cheryl Tevis and Kevin and Steven Hill shared family photographs. Lisa Hovis made those family photos publishable. Charlie Langton and David Peterson allowed me to use their beautiful and moving photographs from those terrible years. Archivists helped me to find materials in the Denise O'Brien, PrairieFire, Bill Gillette, and Bob Kisken collections.

For financial assistance, I wish to thank the State Historical Society of Iowa for a research grant and the Dirksen Center for a Congressional Research Grant.

Various parts of this book have been published in other forms. The following journals have graciously given their permission to use those materials in this book: *Annals of Iowa*, *Middle West Review*, the *Journal of the History of Childhood and Youth*, and *Agricultural History*.

I am particularly aware of familial debts I accumulated as I completed my manuscript. My son and husband, the two Ricks, have been my rocks and incredibly patient with my research travel, hours of writing, and endless musing about the Farm Crisis. We also were locked up at home together, along with two cats, while I was in the final stages of preparing the first complete draft of the manuscript. The COVID-19 pandemic provided the backdrop to that work and continually reminded me how fortunate I was in my family, and in the security we enjoyed, even in the midst of a crisis. If I had to be locked up with two people and two felines for months, I am so glad it was with them. The pandemic has also added another layer of understanding to this book. It has given me a tiny taste of the incredible stress and insecurity that families faced in the hard times of the 1980s. Not knowing, and having so little control, over what tomorrow will bring has been a learning experience—and one I hope never to repeat.

This book, initially, was to be dedicated to Margaret Beattie Bogue and Diane

Lindstrom, two of my mentors at the University of Wisconsin. Neither lived to see the book finished, but I hope both of them would have understood how much their influence has shaped my work, and how grateful I am. I think they would also understand why, with the graduate programs in history at Iowa State facing termination, I have decided to dedicate this book to my students. It was the graduate students who wanted to know, time and again, why this book hadn't been written. They put up with my endless dissection of the 1980s and provided astute suggestions. Two of them shared their memories of those years, and the ways in which their experience of hard times continues to shape their lives. This book is for my graduate students, past and present, with both respect and love.

Pamela Riney-Kehrberg
Ames, Iowa

When a Dream Dies

Introduction

December 9, 1985, dawned like any other winter day in rural Lone Tree, Iowa. By noon, four people were dead: three murdered and their killer a suicide. Dale Burr, an area farmer, shot his wife, Emily, in the kitchen as she baked cookies. He then drove to the Hills Bank and Trust. He tried and failed to cash a check from his overdrawn account. Before he left town, he killed a banker, John Hughes. After leaving the bank, he drove by the farm of neighbor, Richard Goody, shooting and killing him, while also shooting at, but missing, Goody's wife and six-year-old child. Burr drove away; about five miles east a Johnson County deputy sheriff stopped but did not approach his truck. By the time backup arrived, Burr had shot himself in the chest. He left a note that said, "I'm sorry. I can't take the problems anymore."[1]

At the time of his implosion, Burr was a farmer under stress. He had accumulated more than $500,000 in debt, although the bank's representatives denied that there was any foreclosure underway. Burr and Goody were involved in an ongoing legal dispute over land. Burr had a further dispute with the Agricultural Stabilization and Conservation Service over a check they should have written to his bank but wrote to him, and which he cashed. The stress was showing in his work; he failed to complete the fall's harvest, leaving crops in the field. But despite Burr's problems, no one was expecting violence. While his wife evidently knew that their economic troubles were mounting, other relatives had only recently become aware of Burr's substantial debts. What happened left them in disbelief. The events shocked bank employees, too. Hughes was not even Burr's loan officer. Iowa's governor, Terry Branstad, was also stunned. The news came while he was in Delaware, at a governors' conference. He knew the Hughes family. One of the daughters had babysat his children. He rushed to console Iowans, telling them that this situation was an "aberration" and urged everyone to care for their neighbors: "Give them reassurance and help. If you think they really have a problem, get them professional assistance." Newspapers across the state swung into action, providing information on when, how, and why to provide aid to distraught friends and neighbors.[2]

As the story continued to sink in, people who knew Burr reacted with shock. His situation was not one that they expected to spin out of control. Keith Forbes, Emily Burr's brother, knew that tight finances were stressing the couple and that their indebtedness embarrassed them. He commented, "He was afraid of what the people were going to think," noting that "Emily was concerned about what her neighbors would say." Floyd and Betty Hotz could see the Burr farm from their front window. Floyd commented, "You sit over here and look over there and think it's a dream." His wife corrected him: "A nightmare."[3] The situation literally rattled another local farmer. He commented, "I was skinnin' a deer when I heard it over the radio and my hand got to shakin' so I had to quite if I didn't want to cut myself. . . . It reminds me of when President Kennedy got shot—this really shook me." John Ramsey, a store owner in Lone Tree, reflected, "When I stop for coffee, 65 percent of the conversation you hear is farmers in trouble. . . . The thing is, it's not just here in Lone Tree, it's everywhere." Larry Culver, the mayor of tiny Hills, a town of only 550 people, told a reporter, "You hear about this kind of thing from time to time and you never think it could happen to your town."[4] In the estimation of many, Burr was "strapped" but not beyond hope—but he could only extricate himself by selling his five hundred acres in order to retire his debt.[5] People were astonished that such an explosion of violence could happen in rural Iowa; perhaps they underestimated just how painful farm debt had become and how attached some farmers were to every last acre of land.

Years into an agricultural crisis, farm families were watching their lives unravel. A central Iowa farm couple, both working second jobs in order to keep their 110-acre farm solvent, noted that they had failed to make a profit in four years and were anticipating another loss. The wife, Linda Fenley, shared, "All our beans are frozen out in the field. . . . Our banker has been very good to us bit it's getting tougher. It makes you wonder sometimes." Another farmer, indebted to the tune of $165,000 and struggling to continue on rented acres, doubted his banker would allow him to keep on planting. He observed, "It's getting to the point where you ask yourself, 'What the hell difference does it make?'" There was no simple answer to his question. Iowa's secretary of agriculture, Robert Lounsberry, was understandably uneasy: "You get to believe the doom and gloom after a while," he remarked.[6] As shocking as the events of December 9, 1985, were, they were part of a much larger pattern of hardship, loss, and dismay beleaguering the state's farmers.

This was Iowa in the 1980s. The state was at the epicenter of a nationwide agricultural collapse unmatched since the Great Depression. While farms failed and banks foreclosed, rural and small-town Iowans watched and suffered, struggling to find ways to cope with the crisis. If families and communities were to endure, they would have to think about themselves, their farms, and their futures in new ways. For many, this would entail either getting out of agriculture altogether or significantly remaking their livelihoods. For the Midwest, and indeed for farm communities all across the United States, it was a decade of relentless challenge.

Outside of communities deeply affected by the crisis, the struggles of those years have faded from the historical consciousness of the American people. And yet, at the time, the Farm Crisis was big news. It was front page and front cover material in the *Des Moines Register*, as might be expected, but also in the *New York Times*, *Washington Post*, *Time Magazine*, and *Ladies' Home Journal*. It also made its way into public consciousness via popular culture, in the form of critically acclaimed movies, best-selling books, massive Farm Aid concerts, and chart-topping songs. Jessica Lange acted it, Jane Smiley wrote it, and Don Henley, John Mellencamp, and Willie Nelson sang it. The average American might not have known a great deal about the origins of the crisis, or the way farm families experienced it on a daily basis, but it was hard to escape the knowledge that something difficult and disturbing was happening in farm country, especially in 1984, 1985, and 1986, the worst years of the crisis. It was a nationwide disaster, and between its eve in 1978 and its ending point roughly in 1992, 15 percent of all of the farms in the United States disappeared. In many states, and especially in the Midwest, the numbers were even more painful.[7]

This book represents an attempt to write the Farm Crisis more thoroughly into the history books. It does so by tackling the story from the perspective of a single state, Iowa. Even though this story is told in Iowa, it is not just Iowa's story but the story of rural communities and families in many places. The Farm Crisis extended from coast to coast and from the Canadian border to Texas. It was a nationwide phenomenon, a huge event. It involved hundreds of thousands of farm families in every state. It made a particularly deep impression in the American Midwest. But telling the story of the crisis in a national context, or even a regional context, in a manner that meaningfully incorporates the stories of average individuals would be a life's work. Take, for example, the way in which residents of farms and rural communities responded, writing their governors about their experiences and needs. In Iowa alone, the letters written to Governors Robert Ray and Terry Branstad ran into the thousands. They came from farm men, women, and children, from small-town school teachers, ministers, and bankers. They came from those who sympathized with farmers in trouble and those who did not. Everyone told a story about how economic disaster was distorting their lives, sometimes in excruciating ways. Telling these stories, multiplied across fifty states, across many different kinds of agriculture and diverse communities, would be a disservice to those many and painful stories, all of which deserve historical attention. The story in Iowa is both big enough, and small enough, for a book of this sort.

But Iowa also provides more than a conveniently sized container to hold a story about the Farm Crisis. In the 1980s the Farm Crisis dominated Iowa and the Midwest. The agricultural downturn smacked the region hard and sent farm communities reeling. Each Midwestern state had a compelling story, but Iowa's was central to the national understanding of the situation. In Iowa in the 1970s, land prices rose to staggering heights, only to crash to dismal lows in the 1980s, taking thousands of farmers down with them.[8] Iowa's story formed many of the impressions that the nation's people had of farmers under siege. The 1984 movie *Country* found its setting in Iowa. The filming took place near Dunkerton, and the Des Moines office of Rural America, a farm advocacy organization, provided the advisors who gave the movie its painfully realistic details. While many acts of violence marked the Farm Crisis, one of the most publicized was the shooting at the Hills Bank and Trust. Other Iowa tragedies also intruded on the nation's consciousness. In 1989, when lightning killed farmer Dixon Terry—one of the leaders of Iowa's Prairiefire, an influential farm advocacy organization—the Reverend Jesse Jackson spoke at the funeral, as did Missouri congressman Richard Gephardt. Both had been presidential hopefuls in the 1988 election. The *New York Times* printed an obituary.[9] The agricultural leaders who called Iowa home were nationally known, and the way the situation played out in Iowa was central to the way in which the American people perceived the nature and depth of the crisis.

What happened in Iowa during the 1980s was devastating, but economic crises can be difficult for people to understand, assimilate, and accept. In the 1930s, for example, middle-class families were especially hard hit by the economic downturn, following a decade of prosperity. They could not fathom how hard-working and successful people like themselves could plunge into poverty.[10] For Iowa's farmers, the 1980s played out in a similar way. During the 1970s large numbers of farmers had cashed in on rising land prices and robust exports to expand their operations. They bought new equipment. Some bought new cars and built new houses.

Throughout American history, to be a farmer had been to be land rich but poor in material possessions. In the 1970s a number of Iowa's farm families tried to join the middle class.[11] For long-suffering farmers, the 1970s had felt good and seemed to provide justification for years, and often generations, of hard work. Unfortunately, it was not to last. With economic collapse came shame and despair.

Compounding the misery was that farmers often felt alone in their suffering. Economists and agricultural professionals recognized that this was a catastrophe in which everyone was decidedly *not* in the same boat, which made the situation quite different from the Great Depression, when every sector of the economy suffered and people in every part of the United States faced real hardship. Farmers, industrial laborers, doctors, lawyers, and teachers all felt the pinch. Not everyone suffered equally, but the pain of hard times was remarkably widespread. In a sad way, that was comforting. During the Great Depression, farm families saw pictures of people standing in bread lines in cities across the United States and knew that they were not alone. That was not the case during the 1980s. While the entire nation faced a recession in the late 1970s and early 1980s, the larger economy recovered. Recovery came slowly, if at all, in farm country.[12]

Not all farmers were in trouble in the 1980s, but the agricultural depression had a fairly broad base. Among farmers in Iowa, there were three rough divisions. A third of farmers, more or less, were in reasonably good shape and not in any significant danger of losing their farms. Another third faced economic troubles. They were endangered, but the experts expected them to pull through somehow. The final third was in imminent danger of losing their land and livelihood.[13] Ultimately, almost a quarter of Iowa's farms would disappear across the decade. This book is largely about the two-thirds of Iowa's farm families who faced the possibility of disaster and the communities that struggled with the loss of farms, families, and resources. Because of this focus, the book does not reflect everyone's experience. Not every family suffered. Most managed to keep their farms. There were even differences of opinion over what this particular crisis was all about—or whether there was a crisis at all. Some people extended little or no sympathy to those who faced economic distress and blamed their neighbors' economic problems on poor management and reckless spending.[14]

By the middle of the decade, as the crisis rolled onward, both professionals who worked with farmers and officials in state government begged to differ with those who called failing farmers poor managers. They argued for the reality of the crisis and labeled the situation an "unprecedented restructuring" of the state's agricultural economy. While there certainly were poor managers, that description could not explain a crisis this deep and persistent. Those farmers who were in dire condition generally fell into one of three categories. Some relied heavily on borrowed money for their operating expenses, such as farmers who purchased cattle on a yearly basis to feed and fatten for market. When interest rates were low to moderate, they could manage. They staggered and often fell, however, under the burdens imposed by double-digit interest rates, and many lost their farms quite early in the crisis.

Another troubled group were young, ambitious farmers, often well-educated. In the 1970s, they had borrowed against the value of their land in order to improve their operations. In the name of progress and modernity they bought silos, tractors, and combines and installed new milking machines and feed-handling equipment. When interest rates rose and land values fell, they faced the very real possibility of forced sales. They gambled on the continuing prosperity of the agricultural economy and lost.

And then there were the older, well-established farmers whose children came of age in the 1970s. They wanted to increase the size of their holdings in order to bring new generations into the family business. To achieve this goal, some went into debt—often quite significant debt. They, too, faced disaster, caught between high interest rates and the falling value of their land. On occasion, this kind of planning for the future destroyed "century farms" that had been in families for one hundred years or more.[15]

One of the barriers to understanding this crisis is that there was no single "ah-ha" moment when everyone knew that there was a problem. Even farm people did not simultaneously acknowledge the existence of a crisis. Iowa State University's Cooperative Extension Service (Extension)—the US Department of Agriculture's representative in the state, which kept a close watch over happenings on the farms—issued a report summing up this problem of perception: "Unlike many disasters in farming where the consequences are readily visible and can often be objectively assessed, such as number of acres lost, number of diseased livestock, and so on, it is very difficult to obtain objective indicators of the extent of current difficulties." Observers had a hard time isolating the causes of the crisis and an even harder time identifying "the true victims of the crisis." It was also a "rolling" disaster that threatened to become a chronic state of agricultural depression. As Extension sociologists explained in the midst of the crisis, "some farm families were adversely affected four or five years ago, while others are just now being impacted." Perhaps worst of all from the point of view of sufferers, "there is a lack of consensus that there is a crisis.... In many areas some people still deny that a farm crisis exists."[16]

A factor strongly influencing this problem of perception was that many farmers were in debt, but not all of their lenders felt the pinch of the credit crisis or began pressuring farmers for repayment at once. The first lender to experience difficulties was the so-called lender of last resort, the Farmers Home Administration (FmHA), which handled the most marginal borrowers and disaster loans. Then the Production Credit Associations (PCA), which provided short-to-medium-term loans to farmers, began to falter. By 1985 the entire federal Farm Credit System (FCS) showed signs of weakening. Throughout all of this, rural banks were in jeopardy and a number would fail. Farmers in a particular community, borrowing from a small-town bank, might believe that they were in relatively good shape, until a bank examiner noticed problems in its books and they suddenly faced foreclosure because the Federal Deposit Insurance Corporation (FDIC), which insured their bank, could not find a buyer to assume their loans. As lenders faltered and fell, so did farmers.

Everyone in Iowa's small towns and rural communities had something to lose. To be sure, with large numbers of farming operations facing liquidation, a few people had the opportunity for gain, buying up acres that their neighbors could no longer afford to farm. They bought land at the lowest prices in more than a decade, and the number of very large farms grew. But inasmuch as the strength of rural communities was important to rural and farming people, the Farm Crisis did serious damage to institutions and structures upon which these people depended. Families left for greener pastures. Small-town banks and businesses failed. Schools consolidated and closed. Industrial workers also lost out. The pressures that restructured Iowa's agriculture restructured industry, too. Agriculture coughed, and John Deere caught the flu. With most of the state's manufacturing tied to agriculture, its health depended on farmers.

In a nation far removed from its agricultural roots, it is worthwhile to contemplate just how difficult agricultural restructuring was for the families caught in the middle. Understanding farm loss means understanding the emotional toll that it took on families, especially on men who saw maintaining their families' lands as an essential part of their identity. Particularly in cases where they inherited land that once belonged to parents and grandparents, it came with a heavy responsibility. They felt a deep obligation to maintain possession of the land their ancestors had worked so hard to acquire and keep, and often an equally deep obligation to pass that land on to their children.[17] In their minds, losing the land made them failed sons, grandsons, and fathers. It stripped them of both their inherited role within the family and their position in the community. Losing the land shamed them deeply; they were no longer men. Women, on the other hand, had more flexibility in the face of the crisis. They, too, experienced depression and anxiety, but their traditional place on the farm gave them a different set of tools with which to fight this kind of crisis. As farm women, their role had always been to bend their own wishes, desires, and work roles to fit the needs of their families. They scrimped, saved, and went out to work when hard times forced adaptation. While they managed the land together with their husbands, the vast majority of the time it did not belong to women or come down through the female line of their families. Economic stress and financial disaster forced them to change, too, but did not challenge farm women's identity in quite the same way as it did men's.

Losing a farm was not a minor embarrassment. It was a deeply personal loss, enmeshed with meaning. It was also a very public humiliation. In spite of efforts to hide what was going on, ultimately everyone knew. Notices of land sales, foreclosures, and bankruptcies made their way into the papers, advertising to the whole community that a family had so miscalculated as to lose their most precious possession. It became gossip at the café, elevator, and feed store. As anthropologist Kathryn Dudley discovered in her study of the shame of farm loss, "Like criminals or outcasts, distressed farmers are made to feel they possess a deeply discrediting character flaw.... like a scarlet letter, it is always visible and always potentially mortifying."[18] Individuals and organizations serving distressed farming families would have to confront the issue of shame as well as the economic stresses of the decade. Losing a farm was a crushing blow. A farmer, on the brink of failure, explained his situation in this way:

> I am 57 years old. My son joined the operation five years ago. I did not feel that I had reached retirement age at 52. It seemed logical to expand the operation enough to accommodate another family.... It was me who signed the mortgages and loan commitments. Yet, if I fail, that young man, his wife and two little girls will pay the price just as surely as if they had signed.[19]

A farm's loss threatened a family and often endangered a multigenerational web of relationships.

The word "shame" appears often throughout this book. Understanding shame is essential to understanding the impact of the Farm Crisis. Shame is not a brief, passing emotion. A person who is ashamed usually believes they have violated deeply held community norms, and also that their family and peers are judging them for that violation. Shame envelops the person and is incredibly difficult to escape; it causes deep suffering. It can cause paralysis. It can also cause those experiencing it to destroy themselves.[20] The weight of this emotion bore down on farmers in crisis.

While outside observers tended to think of farmers as stoic people—and indeed, they generally did not like to share their troubles—this was an exceptionally emotional decade, and that emotion did not always manifest itself in constructive ways. The most glaring and painful way in which the crisis revealed itself was in a rash of farmer suicides. In its first five years, 281 Iowa farmers killed themselves. This is probably an artificially low number, though, since suicide carried a profound religious and social stigma. Authorities may have recorded a number of suicides as accidents. The suicide rate remained high throughout the decade, with farmers killing themselves twice as often as men in Iowa's cities. And suicide was not the only kind of trouble that blossomed in hard times. Alcoholism, depression, and domestic abuse all resulted from the mental health crisis that accompanied the Farm Crisis.[21]

One of the goals of this work is to convey to readers some sense of what this decade felt like—what it was like to live day-to-day and week-to-week with the anxieties embedded in the Farm Crisis. Reading letter after letter from suffering people is a painful process. Living with the circumstances that inspired those letters had to have been excruciating. Being the aide in the governor's office who read and responded surely led to sleepless nights. Living with personal losses and witnessing those of other people in one's community meant stress for practically everyone, whether a person sympathized with bankrupt farmers or not. Farm and business failures threatened everyone in small places. Plummeting land values affected everyone's bottom line, not just the those of the indebted.

The stress of the 1980s is still apparent decades later. People look back on those years with trepidation. A woman whose work took her nowhere near Iowa's farms or farmers described her memories of that decade as "scary." Men who worked with farmers in trouble had difficulty finding words when describing the hardships their clients faced. Governor Terry Branstad choked up remembering that decade. At best, for those whose farms and families were not in trouble, the 1980s were uncomfortable and uncertain. Mental health professionals working in and studying

Even in hard times, the work continued for farming families. Note the crosses, representing lost farmers. By permission of David Peterson.

Iowa late in the decade described the state's people as being in shock, reeling from hardships. Iowa's farmers lost their optimism. Bad things, they now knew, could and did happen to good people. Even at the decade's end, the pain remained.[22]

But this is not just a story about things falling apart—or about lives and communities ripped to shreds by a decade of hard times. It is also a story of coping. One of the amazing things about the worst of times is that, somehow, people live through them. Life continued, and people found the wherewithal to negotiate with their troubles. The population did not simply succumb to depression; people acted and came together to fight what they saw as injustice. Farm groups organized. They set up hotlines, enrolled the needy in the food stamp program, and lobbied the state and national government. They organized penny auctions and protests. Ministers serving tiny congregations made sure that there were food pantries in their churches and implored the haves to care for the have-nots. Catholic bishops sat down with farmers to talk about what could be done. The state's Cooperative Extension Service, the educators and agricultural professionals who took information to the fields, answered emergency calls, helped families to make sense of their economic situations, and developed mental health programs. Even though they were not, on the whole, trained to do this, they did it anyway. The governor's staff read letters and provided referrals and reassurance. Farm women dusted off skills sometimes unused since high school and went out to find jobs to support their families. Fear immobilized some people and some people killed themselves, but others leapt into action. This book tells Iowa's story, from the heady days of the 1970s through the floods of 1993, which formed an ending of sorts to the long decade of the 1980s.

But has the Farm Crisis actually ended? Some have argued that the situation simply moved from "crisis to chronic." Farmers continue to be caught in a squeeze between the costs of production and the value of their crop. Drought follows flood, follows drought. When operating costs are painfully high, it becomes even more difficult to meet the challenges imposed by nature. And then there are problems like trade wars and pandemics that may have a significant economic effect on farmers, sometimes in unexpected ways. The result is the same as it was in the 1980s: more farmers leave the land. More young people choose other careers. Extension professionals have a name for a phenomenon they are seeing in Iowa's countryside: last generation farmers. With tumultuous decades in back of them, nothing certain ahead, and sons and daughters who would rather go off to college and work in urban areas, the average age of Iowa's farmers has increased significantly. Many will retire—or die—without having anyone to whom to leave their family's acres. Or, rather, they will have heirs who will inherit the land, but never work it. There is a growing rural/urban divide, with residents of rural communities believing that they have been forgotten, and equally believing that they have no reason to trust government. The hard times of the 1980s reverberate.

Questions about those years also linger. In the case of an economic disaster, it is natural for people to want to lay blame and find fault. They want to know who, or what, was responsible. Some, at the time and since, chose to blame the farmers for their predicament. They signed the loan papers and spent the money, which is, in fact, true. At the same time, it is also true that bankers, economists, farm management experts, and the United States Department of Agriculture (USDA) encouraged farmers to expand their operations and buy land, even at very high prices. They encouraged farmers to modernize their equipment and acquire debt. In the 1970s, under a particular set of conditions, those decisions were sensible. In the 1980s, under a completely different set of conditions, particularly Federal Reserve Chairman Paul Volcker's 1979 decision to raise interest rates to staggeringly high levels, expansion and debt became, in retrospect, both dangerous and foolish. It was exceptionally easy for farmers to lose their footing and fall because of decisions made with the best of intentions. The only way to pass through the 1980s without a hint of trouble was to enter and end the decade without debt, either through existing wealth or extreme frugality, and a commitment to the old-fashioned values of making do and doing without.

Laying blame and finding fault also apply to the other side of the question, the government response. Because of the regular and significant ups and downs in the agricultural economy, it was unlikely that anyone in government would immediately jump to the aid of farmers when the situation began to erode in the late 1970s. Even so, farmers had to wait until the middle of the 1980s before there was anything approaching a systematic response to a very deep agricultural depression. Many in Washington remained wedded to the idea of farmers "getting big or getting out" and were willing to preside over a significant winnowing out. Volcker's 1979 interest rate hike had serious repercussions and very few in Washington seemed to care that farmers, as a group, could not bear the weight of a significant increase in the cost of doing business. No one seems to have anticipated, or cared, that rising interest rates would drive down the value of land, stripping farmers of their collateral. Given prevailing attitudes in the USDA about the direction in which agriculture should move, toward fewer farmers on larger farms, it is rather unlikely that Washington would have chosen differently. Policy decisions made elsewhere cascaded into a decade of troubles for farmers.

In the 1980s, when economists, agricultural professionals, and government officials talked about an "agricultural restructuring" taking place, that expression was somehow sterile. It failed to reflect adequately the pain, anxiety, and hopelessness that gripped many families and communities. This book is about the pain inflicted by a decade of wrenching change. There is a story of losses and resulting transformation to be told that has, to this point, been largely neglected. The Midwest—the Iowa—that entered the agricultural downturn was not the one that emerged a decade later. The agriculture-dependent Midwest would never be the same. Too many farms were lost and too many small towns gutted. What happened in Iowa happened in Minnesota and Wisconsin, too. Different versions of this story played out in Kansas, Oklahoma, and Texas. Large portions of the nation's agricultural heartland are not what they were in 1979. The resentments nurtured by a decade of pain linger. Americans need to know what was lost in those years and how those losses shaped—and continue to shape—lives in the nation's farming communities.

CHAPTER ONE

The Go-Go Seventies

In the 1970s the word that best described Iowa agriculture was expansion. Confident farm families were making investments to accommodate the next generation. The Schwennens of Bristow, a tiny place in the north central part of the state, had raised two sons who wanted to join them in the family business. As Elizabeth Schwennen remembered, "my husband & I bought more land to get them started."[1] The Schwennens were not the only parents borrowing to bring children into the family business. In Rutland, Gerald Pedersen did much the same for his two sons. He recalled, "When my sons decided to farm, I bought some extra land. To do so, I had to borrow money; which at that time was at a low interest rate and thus cash flowed."[2] The Drahos family, in Mount Vernon, also expanded to accommodate the desires of a son. The young man was twenty-three, with experience in managing hog production, and ready to join the business. Lorna Drahos recorded the project's evolution: "At this time we went to Federal Land Bank to help us make a decision on what would be the most feasible, to expand our hog operation or to buy more land. They advised us to expand our hog operation as our son had 3 years of hog management, so they gave us a loan of $145,200.00." Money in hand, the family increased the size of their swine operation: "It was used for a hog confinement, remodeling our old machine shed for a farrowing house and building a new larger machine shed. Other outstanding debts were also paid which is a custom of Federal Land Bank to gain first mortgage on the farm. We successfully operated the confinement together for 2 years."[3] The Reicherts, in New Hampton, also expanded hog facilities to make room for children within the family business: "Our son, wife & 2 children farm with us since 1975. They had a few pretty good years. We built a mini-complex hog unit in 1978. Has worked out very good. Is a lot of work & management but we all make a little money from it even above a lot of interest to build it."[4] Like generations of Iowa families before them, parents made sacrifices to enlarge their farms, hoping another generation would work beside them.

Other young couples began building farms of their own. In 1972 the Urbans of Cherokee, Iowa, decided to end the waiting and buy some land. Michael Urban had grown up on a livestock farm but had been working in construction to save money to purchase equipment. His wife, Ardythe, worked as a medical technologist. That year, they bought 260 acres near Cherokee, paying $300 per acre. Five years later, they bought Michael's father's farm of two hundred acres. The PCA "encouraged the purchase as added grain potential to our operation." The land had been in the family for close to eighty years, and the young couple was happy to continue the tradition. About six months later, a neighboring farm they rented came up for sale. Although the PCA was uncertain about the purchase, the Federal Land Bank encouraged it, saying that they "couldn't see how we could go wrong." When times got a bit tighter in the late 1970s, the PCA "urged finding more income.... A hog confinement to increase capacity was planned, approved, and built in 1980."[5] Working hand in hand with their lenders, the young couple established a crop and livestock operation of considerable size.

The Urbans were not alone; the Van Der Pols were also starting their own farm close to Oskaloosa. Sondra remembered: "We started farming in May of 1976, by buying 110 acres with the help of my father. In 1977 we bought a small tractor, small herd of stock cows and haying equipment. The following year we were advised we needed to tile our farm ground, by FHA [Farmer's Home Administration, also FmHA].... those were our capital expenses other than an occasional new bull." Although they economized, farming did not pay all of the bills. "My husband has worked for my father taking care of livestock and field work since 1977 starting out at minimum wage," Sondra wrote. "We paid my father machine hire for 3 to 4 years and wasn't able to the others. Our farm has only 60 acres tillable the rest is pasture and farm and house buildings. Our 110 acres cost us $139,000 of which we've only missed one payment."[6] Keeping costs low and working for family on the side, Jerry and Sondra Van Der Pol believed they had done what they needed to create a small but successful livestock operation.

Similar developments were happening all over Iowa. Parents were making sacrifices to bring their children into their operations. Young people were striking out on their own, investing in what they hoped would be a bright future. They studied the situation, consulted with advisors, and pressed ahead, believing that conditions justified their investments and optimism. Late in the decade, however, expectations collided with changing conditions, catching many farming families off guard. Each of these families—and many others—would find themselves challenged when their hopes and dreams clashed with an unexpected set of unfavorable circumstances.

Farmers, scientists, inventors, bureaucrats, and others planted the seeds of the Farm Crisis in the 1970s—and earlier. Since the end of the nineteenth century, farmers had produced more than the population of the United States could eat. The country had an abundance of land and an abundance of tinkerers and inventors interested in agricultural innovation. When the lands of the prairies challenged the capabilities of wooden plows, inventors delivered steel plows. When farms expanded in size and farmers lacked the labor to harvest their many acres, companies like McCormick marketed a mechanical reaper. There were moments when the nation's leaders worried that the American farmer would not be able to keep up with the needs of a rapidly growing urban and industrial population, but by the time the United States reached the twentieth century, farmers could easily produce as much as the population could consume. During both world wars, those same farmers proved that, when asked, they could also feed the nation's allies and starving refugees, even with a reduced number of farmers on the land.[7]

After World War II, agricultural change accelerated in Iowa, especially in the form of technological and scientific innovations. Iowa farmers of the first half of the twentieth century had worked in ways that their great-grandparents would have recognized, reliant on the labor and muscle of humans and animals. They raised a variety of crops and animals, diversifying their income streams. In the postwar years, the tools and ways of farming changed. Although milking machines were available before the war, few farmers at the time had the electricity to power them. Rural electrification proceeded quickly at the war's end, and milking machines and on-farm refrigeration became ubiquitous. New herbicides increased the farmer's ability to control weeds. New pesticides made it possible to decrease insect damage. Chemical fertilizers, such as anhydrous ammonia, promised to restore the fertility of tired fields. Farmers turned to these innovations in the hope of improving yields, thereby improving their incomes.

All of these new technologies, however, came at a cost. Tractors, combines, hybrid seed, and chemicals were expensive. In order to justify and meet the cost, farmers planted and harvested more acres. In doing so, they increased their production, which ultimately had the effect of driving prices down even further. As historian R. Douglas Hurt succinctly put it, "Contrary to other businesses, farmers

This Boone County farm's layout indicated the kind of diversification common before 1945. In addition to a substantial farmhouse, the property included a chicken house, corncrib, barn, silo, hog barn, machine shed, and cattle barn. By permission of Cheryl Tevis.

were penalized in the marketplace for their efficiency."[8] Put another way, the market penalized farmers for doing what they wanted to do, which was produce. They wanted to adopt new technology, try new crops, and make their acres work for them. They saved themselves labor but did not generally see substantial financial returns. In fact, they often produced to their own detriment, driving down prices further. Still, Iowa's farmers pursued efficiency relentlessly. In 1945 they produced 462 million bushels of corn and 10.9 million hogs; by 1970 they produced 858 million bushels of corn and 17.8 million hogs.[9] Farmers experienced what has been called the cost-price squeeze, caught between low prices for the items they produced and high prices for machines, land, and other supplies; they increased production attempting to overcome the pressure. Unlike other forms of business, farmers did not set the price for their products; it was determined by markets external to them.

Wanting and needing to produce more, farmers demanded machines, chemicals, and other innovations. Historian J. L. Anderson called this "an industrial ethos" in agriculture. He argued that farmers "accepted and demanded new machines and chemicals and used them to meet their needs.... Farm families were the ones who allocated resources to invest in new technology, and who lived with the anticipated and unanticipated consequences of using it."[10] The physical demands of traditional agriculture were significant, and few farmers wanted to return to older ways that required long hours of back-breaking labor. Few wanted to continue to care for and feed horses in all seasons, for example, when they could put away tractors for the winter. Participating in the technological revolution, however, meant that farmers adjusted their attitudes toward farm finance, becoming increasingly more comfortable with the idea of debt. Pre–World War II farm families lived in a culture of making do and doing without. They scrimped, saved, and struggled to avoid going into debt.[11] But the new machines of the postwar era tempted farmers, and given the need to farm on an ever-larger scale to use those tools efficiently and economically, debt grew to massive proportions. Over the course of the 1950s, farm debt doubled from $4 billion to $8 billion. The 1960s saw it grow by $3 billion each year.[12] By the 1970s many farmers accepted debt as a necessary part of doing business. When Myron Ortman began farming in the Lone Rock area in the late 1970s, for example, he expected that the per day cost of interest on his farm debt would be roughly $100. He built it into his financial planning.[13]

Government policy fed the farmer's problem of overproduction. Since its founding in 1862, scientists at the USDA helped American farmers grow more and better crops, leading over time to excess. During the Great Depression, the federal government began paying farmers to take land out of production, in the hope of creating artificial scarcity, which would (in theory) push up the incomes of farmers. During World War II and after, the government provided price supports in order to keep America's farmers producing adequately to meet the needs of a world at war, and then a world that was rebuilding. The government also began purchasing surpluses to use in domestic food programs such as school lunches, or for foreign policy purposes, to sell at a discount or give to allied or strategically important nations experiencing food shortages. All of these approaches were in play at one time or another during the years from 1933 to 1979, resulting in even greater surpluses. In particular, when the government paid farmers to take land out of production, the measure led to greater yields. Farmers chose to idle their worst acres while working their better lands more intensively. Government action helped to support farm families' income but did little to stem the problem of overabundance.[14]

Rural and Agricultural Depopulation

One of the results of the cost-price squeeze was that the numbers of farmers drifted downward throughout the twentieth century, but this was not the only factor driving this phenomenon. Technology certainly played a part. It was no longer necessary for large numbers of laborers to plant, cultivate, or harvest the crops. Additionally, the price of land and machinery made it increasingly difficult for young people who wanted to farm to establish themselves. Major events played a role in driving down the number of farmers as well. Two world wars encouraged young people to leave farming communities, taking young men and women off the farm to serve in their nation's armed forces or to take advantage of civilian job opportunities and high wartime wages. The jobs the wars created often paid far more, with far less risk, than agriculture. Farm-raised youth, increasingly educated, had skills that allowed them to leave home and secure employment in cities, near and far, in wartime and in peace.[15]

The number of farms peaked in the early twentieth century, falling thereafter. Because of lands being put into production in the western United States, the growth in farms continued longer than it might have otherwise. In 1920 the number of farms reached its highest point, more than 6.4 million. By 1969, though, this had more than halved, to just over 2.7 million.[16] In Iowa the number of farms peaked earlier, and the pace of farm loss was slower. In 1900 there were 228,622 farms, a number that declined every decade across the century. In 1969, however, Iowa still had 140,354 farms, or roughly 60 percent of the number the state had boasted at the beginning of the century. Iowa remained an agricultural state long after much of the United States had become urban and industrial.

As the number of farms fell, those who remained on the land absorbed the acres of others who, one way or another, left. The average Iowa farm in 1900 had been just 151 acres, usually worked by a farming family: husband, wife, and children. They used few machines and relied heavily on neighbors and themselves. By 1945 the size of the average farm had only grown to 165 acres, reflecting both the similarity in modes of agriculture across the intervening forty-five years and the poverty of the long agricultural depression that lasted from 1920 to 1940. By 1969 the size of the average farm had jumped to 239 acres, and machines and chemicals did more of the work compared to farming families and their animals. Farmers realized economies of scale as farm size grew. In the early 1970s, a small farmer working 160 acres paid thirty-two dollars per acre for expenses such as machinery, power, and fuel. If a farm doubled in size, those expenses fell to twenty-five dollars an acre. At six hundred acres, the expense would only be nineteen dollars an acre.[17] *Successful Farming*, one of the farm management magazines that Iowa's farmers most trusted, counseled farmers to buy more land in order to use their machinery more efficiently, thus lowering their costs.[18]

Rising Incomes and Rising Hopes

In the early 1970s, conditions seemed to be improving; farmers appeared to be closing in on the rest of the nation, at least as far as income was concerned. While per capita income for farmers had been only 50 percent of nonfarm per capita income in the 1960s, in the 1970s it was 75 percent.[19] The $6,544 a year (on average, equivalent to nearly $30,000 in 2019) coming into Iowa farms from off-farm sources helped to explain the narrowing earnings gap.[20] Additionally, in the early years of the 1970s, surpluses were down while prices rose, caused by a change in policy. For years, the US government had refused to allow trade with its Cold War enemy, the Soviet Union. In the early 1970s, however, government officials decided to take advantage of poor harvests in the USSR with grain sales.[21] The USDA encouraged farmers to avail themselves of this situation. Earl Butz, secretary of agriculture under Presidents Richard Nixon and Gerald Ford, believed that the only way to farm, and the only way to cash in on the Soviet market, was on a grand scale. He counseled the nation's farmers to "get big or get out" and to plant from "fencerow to fencerow." Export markets offered farmers an opportunity to improve their economic situation, and many jumped in with both feet.[22] As Hurt explained, "Unable to control prices or to organize and bargain collectively, farmers believed they had no choice other than to increase production in order to lower unit costs and thereby maintain a profitable business."[23] Sales to the USSR and the booming market they created masked some of the costs of doing business.[24]

Even so, Iowa's farmers were living with uncertainty. The cost-price squeeze was ever present and became even more of a concern with the Arab oil embargo in 1973 and 1974. The Arab member states of the Organization of Petroleum Exporting Countries (OPEC) placed an embargo on the United States because of its support of Israel in the Yom Kippur War. The price of oil rose by 400 percent, causing the price of gasoline to skyrocket. This was particularly difficult for farmers because of their strong reliance on fuel for their tractors and combines. Synthetic fertilizers also rose in cost because of the increase in petroleum prices.

There appeared to be no end in sight to increases in the cost of production, and yet farmers' return on their investments fell, in part because of the US commitment to cheap food. More than ever, farmers grappled with the expectations of consumers. Americans emerged from the Great Depression and World War II with a desire for and expectation of inexpensive food. Most of the cost of food came in the processing, but consumers perceived farmers as the authors of rising food costs. Farmers, returning the favor, believed that the attitudes of consumers were one of their biggest problems, with a 1975 poll identifying being "misunderstood by consumers" as a major drawback to their job.[25] While farmers made up a small and shrinking proportion of the American public, everyone was a consumer, and increasingly, the USDA catered to the needs and wants of the majority. From the 1970s onward, agricultural legislation took seriously the desires of the nation's people for a cheap, safe food supply. Farmers no longer had the more or less exclusive ear of the USDA.[26]

In the 1970s rising land values masked some of these realities for Iowa's farm families. Land values, in many ways, represent people's expectations. When land values are high, it means that farmers (and others hoping to purchase land) expect that the land, and what can be grown or developed on it, will be profitable and increase in value. When land prices fall, it usually means that people's expectations have fallen as well. In the 1970s expectations were apparently high. Land values soared across the state. In 1970 the average acre of Iowa farmland was worth $419. Its value would peak in 1981 at $2,147 dollars an acre, a whopping 512 percent increase. Not all land was equally suited for agricultural purposes, and some acres were more valuable than others. For example, Allamakee County in far northeast Iowa is hilly. It is beautiful country, but hilly and scenic do not often coincide with prime agricultural uses. In 1970 an average acre of land there was worth $233, only slightly more than half of the state average. Even so, by 1981, an acre of land in Allamakee County was worth $1,300. In Boone County, in central Iowa, the land is flatter and more suitable for intensive cultivation of corn and soybeans. In 1970 an acre of Boone County land was worth more than the state average, a substantial $545 an acre. By 1981 it would be worth $2,685, again in excess of the state average. In 1970 the most expensive land would be in Scott County, close to the industrial city of Davenport along the Mississippi River, at a healthy $664 an acre. By 1981 an acre in Scott County would be worth $3,484. Iowa's least valuable land was in

Decatur County, at $197 an acre, reflecting the county's location on the southern border of the state. It was rolling, and on the whole, less prosperous. Land values there would rise to a relatively slim $922 an acre.[27] Nevertheless, the picture across the state was of high land values and high expectations.

What rising land values meant for an individual farmer was highly variable. If a family wanted to get out of farming and timed their exit for the right moment, they could leave as millionaires. Because the tax code allowed farmers to keep a large portion of their capital gains, not much would be lost to Uncle Sam.[28] If a family wanted to improve and upgrade their farm operation, perhaps replace an older tractor with a newer model, or build a new farrowing house for their pigs, they could borrow against the increased value of their acres, counting on their investment to pay for itself. Agricultural economists, such as the University of Illinois' Folke Dovring, encouraged farmers to take advantage of the unprecedented "market power" given to them by the farmland values of the 1970s.[29]

The equity in land made it possible to think expansively. Often, improvements around the house are the very last a farm family makes. Consequently, Iowa's farming families of the 1970s lived in houses their parents and grandparents had built. Fewer than 20 percent lived in a home that was less than twenty years old. An even larger percentage lived in a house that had been built in the previous century. After all, a new house, unlike a new tractor, would not help with the chores, but in the 1970s, rising land values made it possible to consider home improvements. Many a farm woman wanted to upgrade the family home and replace the old frame farmhouse, built with profits from World War I, with a new ranch house with all of the modern conveniences.[30] While some farm families dreamed of more comfortable homes, others contemplated snowmobiles and vacations. All of that was possible, given the equity landowners held in their farms. But, as historian Mark Friedberger has argued, even though many Iowa farmers were now millionaires, they did not act as if they were millionaires, because their wealth was tied up in their land: "The stereotypical Iowa farm millionaire wore bib overalls, drove a pickup, went to church, and had a daughter who taught Sunday school." Some were upgrading their homes, cars, and lifestyles, but many were not.[31]

While older, established farmers might have been reaping the benefits of land ownership, the situation was more complicated if a young person wanted to get into farming, especially if they wanted to do so on their own, rather than in partnership with a parent. Soaring land prices made purchases less and less possible. Some young farmers could rely on the generosity of prosperous parents who were willing to mortgage their own acres in order to buy land for their children. After all, "they weren't going to make any more," and land looked like a good investment, as prices rose, and then rose again. Those with parents unwilling or unable to invest faced a more difficult situation. In 1975 160 acres of Boone County farmland would have cost approximately $237,600, before equipment, buildings, and animals.[32] In the twenty-first century, this represents an investment of more than a million dollars. Robert Lounsberry, Iowa's secretary of agriculture in the late 1970s and early 1980s, provided an estimate of costs for beginning farmers. To a hopeful young man, he wrote,

> Statistically, about 3,000 young people (men and women) enter farming in Iowa each year. As you are aware of, it is not easy as the average sized farm in Iowa is now 286 acres and the capital outlay averages in excess of $600,000. Obviously, unless there is family or other help, a young man or woman just out of high school is not very likely to get started on his own.[33]

Renting, or working and saving, were the only options for a young person without significant wealth or generous parents, and when land prices were high, rent tended to be high as well. By the end of the decade, the state would decide to imitate Minnesota and create a loan program just for beginning farmers in need of a helping hand.[34]

Young farmers sometimes ran afoul of the expectations of the go-go 1970s. If a couple wanted to farm on a smaller scale, rather than go big, establishing their farm could also be an uphill climb. Lenders wanted to see plans ambitious enough to guarantee a large profit. Dixon Terry, an Iowa farmer and agricultural activist, hoped to purchase land for a small dairy farm. He commented, "I was working as a hired hand on my parents' dairy farm in the mid-seventies, and my wife and I were trying to borrow money to buy our own farm. But our goal of starting a traditional moderate-sized Iowa farm went against the grain of the expansion minded lenders. We had great difficulty in finding financing because our plans were too modest—we weren't thinking big enough."[35] They eventually found less expensive land in southwestern Iowa, hilly and less suitable for row crops but workable as a dairy farm. Terry was not alone in his perspective. Darrah Roberts, who farmed near Iowa Falls, worked a small farm of 186 acres and raised 150 hogs a year. That was what he and his wife wanted, and Roberts proclaimed that "you can make a darn good living on 160 acres if you own the ground." The experts agreed, and argued that with good management, little to no debt, some hogs, and judicious use of technology, a small farm could provide its owners with a satisfactory living. But the

Many Iowa farmers raised hogs, like this handsome Hampshire boar. By permission of Cheryl Tevis.

key, they argued, was to avoid debt at all costs. A small farmer who owed money on land or machinery faced a long, uphill climb.[36]

Beyond a certain point, rising land values failed to make sense. By the middle of the 1970s, agricultural income was falling. In the early 1970s American exports grew phenomenally. The dollar's value was relatively low, and the US government's agricultural policies encouraged production. The United States became the "bargain supplier in world export markets."[37] Farmers put more money into land and machinery. In constant dollars, the value of capital investments grew by 73 percent between 1969 and 1978, and much of that investment went into land. Farmers had good reason to put their money into land. Laws at the time limited the tax liability for capital gains. Inflation was high throughout that decade, and farmers looked for a safe place to store their wealth as a hedge against inflation; they believed land was that place. Nevertheless, the continuing high value of farmland, climbing "closer to the sky," was a bit of a surprise to experts. Some economists dubbed what was happening the result of "upward trend psychology," meaning that as values moved upward, farmers continued to buy land and to expect that the price would be higher than the year before.[38] Given conditions, their borrowing appeared to be sensible.

While buying expensive land was not necessarily a problem, borrowing in order to do so could become one. Throughout much of the 1970s, the inflation rate and the interest rate were quite similar, which meant that in real terms, the cost of borrowing money was low. At times, the inflation rate was greater than the interest rate, which meant that the interest rate, in real terms, was negative. This encouraged a cavalier attitude toward borrowing.[39] In the 1970s farmers borrowed differently than their fathers and grandfathers had two decades earlier. When farmers purchased land in the 1950s, 42 percent of those purchases took place without borrowing. By the end of the 1970s, only 11 percent of farmers made land purchases with cash. Farm mortgage debt grew from $71.4 billion in 1970, to $113.2 billion in 1980. Debt had not played such a large role in agricultural investments since 1915–1919—and the economic reckoning that came when prices fell at the end of World War I led farmers into the Great Depression a full decade before the rest of the country.[40]

While farmers were busy making investments in high priced land, the value of the crops that could be grown on that land was slipping. In constant dollars, farmers' income in the last four years of the decade was 25 percent lower than it had been in the first four. Farmers got big and plowed fencerow to fencerow, leading to a vast oversupply of agricultural commodities. In spite of the value of their land, farmers struggled to keep their heads above water. It was an odd situation. As agricultural economist Barry Barnett explained, "Many agricultural producers who owned land found that their wealth was increasing dramatically, while at the same time they were experiencing cash-flow difficulties. This problem was overcome by refinancing with lenders on a periodic basis, perhaps annually, to reflect the increased value of the land that was being used to collateralize the loan."[41] As long as interest rates remained low, these farmers could continue to juggle their debts and remain solvent. In 1979, however, interest rates soared and while land values remained high after that, they suddenly crashed in 1981. The value of land had continued to rise for a good five years beyond the point when that increase coincided with strong farm incomes and realistic expectations.

Looming Trouble

By 1977 signs of distress were sneaking into the pages of farm publications. That year, a two-page spread in *Successful Farming* addressed the problems of "how to adjust an out-of-balance debt load," and "coping with financial crisis." The cash flow problem created by low prices for crops and heavy debts was already causing headaches for some farmers. A USDA survey of Midwestern bankers showed that a third of farmers with borrowed funds were incapable of easily repaying their loans. Lenders were increasing their financial counseling services and telling farmers that it was time to refinance. Bankers directed farmers with cash flow problems to the FmHA for loans and refinancing. The FmHA had historically operated as the lender of last resort and offered farmers lower interest rates and longer repayment periods. It could also loan to farmers experiencing emergency situations, such as droughts.[42]

Given the problems looming on the horizon, experts offered a number of suggestions, such as belt tightening, living with older equipment, diversifying, and abandoning expansion plans. They also suggested cutting out frills: "Park your pickup on your farm instead of in front of a local restaurant."[43] For a large subset of farmers, it was time to put on the brakes, if they had not done so already. Even so, the vision of the agricultural good life would persist for a few more years. Just in time for Christmas 1977, Kawasaki took out a single page spread in *Successful Farming*, and Caterpillar a two pager, to advertise their newest snowmobiles. Kawasaki promised farmers that their machines were the "hottest thing on snow," while Caterpillar used sex to sell their Panther model. The countrified copy read,

> Well, I asked her if she wanted to take a ride on my Panther. And without too much coaxin,' she hopped on behind me and off we went. And then she whispers something in my ear that's still got my engine racin.' She says, 'I think we're made for each other.' And I don't know whether she meant me and her . . . or me and the Panther. I still don't know.[44]

While their neighbors dined at home, some couples indulged in cold-weather fun.

For Iowans, 1977 had been a mixed year, with the central and southern parts of the state suffering from drought. As a writer for the *Des Moines Register* put it, drought had "ripped the heart out of the Iowa corn crop," with losses to farmers at $776 million. The *Farm Journal* depicted the situation just as poetically, describing what farmers saw in central Iowa fields as looking more like pineapple than corn. Instead of seeing tall, green stalks, the observer saw corn that was short, spiky, and brownish-yellow. It was supposed to be farmers' turn to prosper, but the rains failed. The less droughty portions of the state experienced enormous yields, fueled by the decade's rush to agricultural intensification, pushing down prices for everyone.[45] On the other hand, 1978 was a record-breaking, bin-busting year statewide.

The elevators were overflowing as farmers had, again, produced far more than the demand.⁴⁶ What all of this meant, unfortunately, was that 1978 looked more like leftovers in the kitchen than supper at the café for increasing numbers of farm families.

The prices for farm products were in a downhill slide, although no one was sure how far they would fall, or for how long. The price of corn slumped, and the likelihood of good crops in both the United States and abroad added to the gloom. Large harvests in other places suppressed prices in Iowa. The USDA also forecast soybean prices to fall, anticipating stiff competition from overseas producers. With consumers eating less red meat and more chicken, the price of beef plummeted. The USDA forecast the biggest crop of pigs since 1971, again a predictor of falling prices.⁴⁷ Very high levels of production became very low incomes. Additionally, the cost-price squeeze, fueled by high rates of inflation, continued to cause problems for farmers. Their purchasing power was falling, declining significantly since the beginning of the decade. Analysts compared the purchasing power of farmers in 1973 to that of 1978 and found serious deterioration: a "four-year plunge of more than 50%. This means when you go to the store your dollar bills are like fifty-centers—you can buy only half of what you could in 1973."⁴⁸ In Iowa, gross farm income looked reasonable, but net farm income was falling, due to the high cost of production. While gross income was $59,027, a number that looked quite healthy, net income was only $5,769 per farm.⁴⁹ According to surveys conducted by the Iowa Corn Growers, only 25 percent of their members expected to break even in 1978, and they expected conditions to be worse in 1979.⁵⁰

Agricultural suppliers continued to push increased production as the way to improve farm income. Perhaps none was more aggressive with this message than Harvestore, a company that sold enormous blue silos that the company promised would turn corn and cornstalks into cattle-pleasing silage. The four-page spread the company ran in the March 1978 *Farm Journal* called on farmers to unleash their check books in the fight against falling profits. "When you're up against the wall," the ad exhorted,

> You're ready. Fight back. It hurts. You borrow a big wad of money to buy feeder cattle. Work like a private in boot camp. Feed up a crop that cost you a bundle to produce . . . and end up the year looking at red ink. If it happened, no one would blame you for washing your hands of the whole mess. Yet, you won't. You like feeding cattle and backing down doesn't sit right with you.

Those who fought, invested, and refused to give in, Harvestore argued, would make it. And although the copy writer slipped in a few equivocal words about profits, they still pointed to those big blue bins as the sign of success, if not prosperity: "So although no one is completely satisfied with the return on their investment in the cattle business today, you should know that there are some cattlemen still making money. Harvestore forage system owners feed more of what they grow, buy less store-bought protein and reduce the cost of a balanced ration.... You're Ready."[51] Buying a Harvestore system was a huge investment, but the company argued that with the right equipment, farmers could win the war against the bottom line.[52]

The Politics of Farming

Despite such sales pitches, investing and improving one's way to prosperity was looking less and less possible. Across the country, farmers anxiously watched slumping profits. By the mid- to late 1970s, a tide of concern was rising. Organization, advocacy, and protest were not novel ideas for Iowa's farmers. In the economic turmoil surrounding the agricultural depression of the 1920s and 1930s, farmers had used their organizational skills to try to find answers to their problem of producing much and earning little. Many larger farmers joined the Farm Bureau, which emphasized planning and science as a means of increasing farm incomes. Others found solace in the Farmer's Union, which encouraged the federal government to use its power to keep smaller farmers on the land.[53] When times became particularly tough, militancy flared. Farmers organized protests against mandatory bovine tuberculosis testing and the destruction of infected animals that followed. Fearing the loss of their livelihoods, dairy farmers waged a "cow war" against the authorities, including the veterinarians from Iowa State who did the testing. In northwest Iowa, farmers violently protested against sale auctions, including the near lynching of a judge. In the early 1930s, Iowan Milo Reno created the Farmers Holiday movement, calling for a farm strike. Reno asked farmers to buy, sell, and produce nothing until the price of farm goods rose enough to meet the costs of production. This farm strike, as well as other moments of militancy, gained attention for struggling farmers but produced little in the way of results.[54]

Organizing continued in the 1950s, 1960s, and 1970s, with farm associations challenging what they perceived as both political and economic attacks on agriculture. There were those, for example, who thought of rural depopulation and the loss of farms as a positive good. In 1962 the Committee on Economic Development (CED), a nongovernmental organization created by business leaders in tandem with economists at the University of Chicago, issued a report claiming that farmers were leaving the land too slowly. The problem in agriculture, the council claimed, was inefficiency; by keeping prices low, the government could force uneconomical producers out of agriculture. The report commented, "The movement of people from agriculture has not been fast enough to take full advantage of the opportunity that improving farm technology and increasing capital create for raising the living standards of the American people, including, of course, farmers." The CED envisioned the displacement of two million farmers over the next five years.[55] Not surprisingly, this led to protests. Theodore O. Yntema, chairman of Ford Motor Company's finance division, headed the CED, and members of the National Farmers Organization (NFO) picketed Iowa Ford dealerships, demanding a retraction of the report. Protestors in Fort Dodge carried signs saying "Repudiate C.E.D. or no more Fords."[56] Protestors also camped out in front of Sears stores across the Midwest, as Theodore Houser, director of Sears, Roebuck and Company, was vice chairman of the committee. Within days, both Ford and Sears had repudiated the report, and the NFO had launched a new holding action, keeping cattle off the market for more than a month in order to push up prices. While the move gained attention, it ultimately failed to improve prices.[57]

Other efforts were more successful. These decades saw an increased presence of Iowa's farm women in advocacy. One of the best examples was the women's auxiliary of the Iowa Pork Producers, otherwise known as the Porkettes. Hoping to change American attitudes about pork, which in the 1950s and 1960s had a reputation as a low-quality meat, the Porkettes undertook a major campaign to sell their product to the nation. Through a variety of strategies, including positioning themselves in grocery stores with pork chops and electric skillets, the women worked to change attitudes to improve their families' incomes. Their activities resulted in a more robust market for pork.[58] This was emblematic of the "responsible hell" (as a writer for *Successful Farming* put it) that farm women raised in order to challenge low prices, legal disabilities, and consumer-, rather than farmer-, oriented lawmakers and bureaucrats.[59]

The American Agricultural Movement

Agricultural organizing was well underway in the mid-1970s. Rural America, an advocacy group based in Washington, DC, took up the business of investigating rural housing, rural poverty, and numerous other issues related to the quality of life in the countryside. In 1981 Rural America would open an office in Des Moines.[60] On the more militant side, farmers organized the American Agricultural Movement (AAM). In September 1977 a farmers' group that had been meeting over coffee in a diner in Campo, Colorado, decided that the time had come to fight against the economic forces strangling agriculture. Taking their cues from the NFO, the AAM decided to call a farm strike. The protestors demanded parity. As political theorist Michael Stewart Foley defined it, "Parity essentially measures the prices of farm products against other commodities, and in relation to the prices of items farmers have to buy; in 1977, farm prices stood at 67 percent of parity, their lowest level since 1933."[61] The AAM wanted to meet suppliers on a level playing field. The National Farmers Union president agreed, arguing, "Who says Americans have a God-given right that farmers will subsidize them with a cheap food policy?" Certainly not the Farmers Union, which also argued in favor of 100 percent parity.[62] The NFO, whose president was Iowan Oren Lee Staley, also endorsed the strike.[63]

Not everyone in the agricultural community agreed with their perspective. The Farm Bureau, which often took a conservative political line, opposed parity guarantees because members believed "guaranteed controls and guaranteed federal supervision of farming" would result. "Free choice in agriculture," argued the national Farm Bureau president, "could not survive."[64] Iowa Farm Bureau president Dean Kleckner professed to be glad that the threatened strike was bringing attention to the problems facing farmers, but he and his membership did not support the initiative. He commented, "I think most Farm Bureau members realize that farm strikes in the past haven't been effective," perhaps referring to the Farmers Holiday movement of the 1930s and more recently, the NFO.[65] Nevertheless, the editor of *Farm Journal* took a relatively gentle line while writing about the strike. Lane Palmer praised the strikers for raising the consciousness of the American public. He wrote, "Whatever its final effect, if any, on farm prices, the Farm Strike has been a highly effective dramatization of the real farm problems: your never-ending struggle to cope with uncertain weather, with highly variable markets, and with the relentless climb in your costs." Even so, he questioned the efficacy and wisdom of the AAM's actions: "The tragedy of the Farm Strike at this writing is that it has accomplished little for the relief of those who so obviously need help. We fervently wish that we could see a way that all farmers could achieve parity in the marketplace. Not only does that appear politically impossible, but as Secretary Bob Bergland points out, government-created parity would put farmers in a regulatory straight jacket."[66]

The strikers did not find much support in President Jimmy Carter's administration, either. While Agriculture Secretary Bob Bergland and his chief economist, Howard Hjort, claimed they supported the strike, they did not support the federal government promising parity to farmers. Bergland told Carter that the idea was too expensive and that it was the farmers' responsibility to devise ways to achieve parity without a government guarantee.[67] For his part, Carter gave qualified verbal support to the idea of a farm strike. While he believed that farmers had cause and asserted that he would, if he was still peanut farming, join the protests, he would not stop planting and harvesting.[68] Neither the USDA nor the president, it seemed, supported striking farmers.

Nevertheless, some Iowa farmers heeded AAM's call. In October of 1977, AAM supporters opened the state's strike office in Council Bluffs. In November, farmers organized small local rallies.[69] On December 10, farmers gathered in Des Moines in support of parity. The event was not the powerful spectacle for which organizers had planned and hoped. They had envisioned a parade of fifty machines and attendance by five hundred farmers. In Kansas, farmers formed a tractorcade seven miles long. And while six thousand farmers rallied in the president's home state of Georgia, the turnout was considerably smaller in Iowa. The weather was terribly cold, so much so that only about 150 farmers attended. Some stayed home because they feared that the frigid temperatures would make it impossible to start their diesel tractors. The small tractorcade had an undignified experience: a car collided with the last and smallest tractor. The frost-covered contingent came to express their discontent and to lobby. In addition to parity, they asked that Congress pass legislation requiring food processors to label their products to show the percentage of the cost farmers received. They also came to tell their stories. "If this strike doesn't work, I'll be a lot better off selling out this winter," said Bob Marckmann, who farmed just outside Adair. Another protestor decorated his tractor with a sign proclaiming, "Farming has no future."[70]

The next week, striking farmers met with Iowa's unenthusiastic governor, Robert Ray. While he told protesters that they could do what they wanted with their own land, he would prefer that they plant, saying, "What I'd like to see you do is market more, not less of your product."[71] The farmers told the governor about their increasing problems with credit; in return, he reminded them that the state was proceeding with research in ethanol fuels and looking for more effective ways to market Iowa's agricultural products. Iowa's secretary of agriculture, Robert Lounsberry, also voiced disapproval of the idea of a farm strike. He was afraid that farmers would abuse the promise of parity prices with even greater overproduction. He also echoed Ray, saying that what Iowa's farmers really needed were new and diverse uses for the crops they already produced. Ray and Lounsberry told strikers to go away and "form a committee to work directly with legislators and state officials on agricultural issues."[72] But even the farmers seemed less than completely committed to pleading their case. After the meeting one of them commented about the governor, "I don't know what I'd do if I were in his shoes."[73]

Small towns witnessed some protests. In the southwest Iowa town of Tabor, a group of farmers disrupted Christmas shopping, cramming their vehicles onto Main Street. Bloomfield, on the other side of the state, experienced a similar scene, with fifty farmers parking their tractors and trucks in the town square, to the dismay of local merchants. At the farmer's cooperative in Ralston, business was slow, as many farmers were holding onto their corn and soybeans. The co-op's manager, however, did not blame the strike for slow business. Farmers in this central Iowa community often sold their crops throughout the year, he explained, waiting for the moment when the price was right. In other places, however, the strike was having no apparent effect. In Algona, trucks were backed up at the Cargill elevator, waiting to make their deliveries. This was in stark contrast to strikers shutting down potato processing in Oregon and California, closing dairies in Texas, and bringing business to a halt in Plains, Georgia, President Carter's home town. The strike's organizers in Bloomfield, by contrast, promised that they would not block access to stores again. Respectability in small town Iowa required a person—even a protestor—not to inconvenience the neighbors.[74]

In the spring, representatives of AAM continued their efforts to drum up support in Iowa. Strike organizers asked farmers to plant just 50 percent of their corn crop in the spring, arguing that if they did, prices would rise to 150 percent of parity. AAM also asked farmers to support the movement in other ways, in particular by reducing their purchases of supplies and machinery. Farmers needed to sacrifice anything nonessential until that day when their goals were achieved. The organizers claimed that a healthy farm economy would make a healthy nation: "What farmers really need is a good price out of their crops. When this happens, it will create wealth, let us farmers pay income tax and help keep our government from being so broke."[75] Yet, despite extra attention from AAM activists, Iowans continued to take a relatively low profile in the strike.

In the spring of 1978, with planting in full swing, the editorial page of the *Cedar Rapids Gazette* announced, "Farm strike *flops.*" A quick visual survey of neighboring farm fields revealed that "few rural Iowans, if any, are angry enough to leave cropland unplanted." The editor mused that participating in a farm strike was just not Iowan. "Iowa farmers' dissociation from the Westerners' mind-set is not surprising. As observed here last winter, this region's farmer is too taciturn and independent a soul to align with angry group tactics such as tractorcading through Washington or leaving fields unplowed." In the shadow of looming debt, it also became almost impossible to strike; farmers had mortgages to pay. With Iowa's farmers operating at full speed, the *Gazette* observed, it would behoove the federal government to develop the nation's export markets; control over price-depressing surpluses depended on it.[76]

In April, what Kansas Senator Bob Dole called a "flexible parity bill" failed in Congress, and with it, the 1977–1978 farm strike. The sponsors designed the bill to provide farmers a guaranteed price, reduce surpluses through scaled down production, and increase federal purchases of food for humanitarian purposes.[77] Despite support from the Senate Committee on Agriculture, Nutrition, and Forestry, the measure failed in the House. President Carter's Council on Wage and Price Stability, which was responsible for inflation-fighting measures, declared the bill would lead to higher food prices, and the president came down on the side of consumers, threatening a veto.[78] The AAM called off the strike without achieving parity. *Successful Farming*'s postmortem was bleak. "There was no strike; there was not a 50% reduction in plantings; winter wheat was not plowed under." On the bright side, "the consuming public of the United States became more aware than ever of some of the economic problems facing farmers. That itself may have made the whole movement worthwhile." The publication damned the AAM's efforts with faint praise. For their part, the strike's organizers held out a faint hope of regrouping and continuing their efforts in the fall.[79]

Iowa's Farmers on the Edge of Disaster

Iowa's farmers trudged on. For most the situation continued much as it had for the previous five years. Prices for corn, beans, hogs, and cattle moved downward, while the price of land remained high. Although some farmers felt the pinch of debts they could not pay, the factors were in place to maintain the status quo—just as long as nothing dramatic happened. Given this situation, farmers continued to hold many of the same attitudes that they had held throughout the century. They wanted what they considered a fair price for their products, and they wanted government to intervene on their behalf to meet this goal, but they rejected the idea of excess regulation. Mostly, they wanted the United States to sell their products abroad more aggressively so that they could enjoy the benefits of their investments.[80] Farmers would keep trudging onward, as long as the situation did not change significantly.

Unfortunately, things were about to change, and in most unpleasant ways. Seeds sown in previous decades were about to bear ugly fruit.[81] Beginning in 1979 life on Iowa's farms would cease to be business as usual. Farmers had responded to economic forces in ways that made sense to them, not to mention to most agricultural economists, using their abundant equity to purchase land and improvements. Even after the economy began to cool off, low interest rates combined with high land prices continued to make it possible for indebted Iowa farmers to stay afloat. It might not be pretty, but they were getting by. The Federal Reserve, however, was about to make war on inflation, and in doing so, make war on Iowa's farmers. Interest rates would rise to new and painful heights, wringing the inflation out of the economy and ripping the safety net out from under anybody who owed money. And Iowa's farmers owed.

Parents who had borrowed to bring children into the business would watch their hopes and dreams crumble. As lenders took land and equipment, Elizabeth Schwennen lamented, "Who will be left for young men to do the farming in the future?" Gerald Pedersen, facing floodwaters and even higher interest rates, begged the governor's office for relief: "The high interest rates are my number one problem. I have to renew the notes every six months, and it's killing me." Wesley and Lorna Drahos were in deep financial trouble, and the son who had wanted to run a hog confinement had lost his taste for the business after disease took seven hundred of his animals. Their debts were twice as great as their assets, but they still wondered if it would be possible, somehow, to get the money to bring yet another of their sons into the business? The governor's office was not encouraging.[82]

Younger farmers were in trouble, too. Myron Ohrtman, who had begun his operation planning to pay $100 a day in interest, could no longer continue when the bank projected those interest payments rising to $370. For the thirty-five-year-old, getting out of farming was sensible, but crushing. He wrote, "There is no way to go back into farming, but I want to be an active participant of agriculture. I have more to offer than being a hired man." Jerry and Sondra Van Der Pol faced the same reality; they, too, needed to get out, because the weight of the farm had become unbearable. Sondra wrote, "Jerry and I were once on the Iowa Farm Bureau Young Ranchers and Farmers Committee and really thought we were going to have a good life farming and to raise our two kids, But that's not true any more we just want to exist now working and trying to pay our bills." The Urbans struggled to hang on, even though their lenders told them the time had come to quit their operation.[83] Families that had worked and sacrificed to fulfill dreams of a life in agriculture were discovering that work and sacrifice were not enough.

CHAPTER TWO

From Fencerow to Fencerow to Failure: 1979–1983

In May of 1980, a large envelope arrived at Governor Robert Ray's office. Inside was a letter and a petition with nearly fifteen hundred signatures. The packet came from a group of "concerned citizens from all walks life, occupations, and businesses" who were worried about the state of agriculture in Iowa. The letter writers assured the governor that there was no political agenda in this petition, just a plea for help:

> We cannot stress enough how concerned all these people are and how difficult and frustrating it is. Farmers are losing money before they *ever* go to field, and losing money on livestock; therefore every business is suffering loss of business, more people are getting laid off every day, some small businesses are closing and the distinct probability that many more will be forced to; as well as many farmers, will have to sell out—this is not in the best welfare of our nation.

The petitioners reassured the governor that they were not demanding anything extravagant. "These people who we contacted WANT to work and take great pride in their accomplishments. They will be happy with the cost of production plus a REASONABLE profit."[1]

The petitioners were reacting to the dramatic turn of fortune the state's farmers experienced at the end of 1979 and the beginning of 1980. While many had been managing to get by on the basis of money borrowed against the value of their land, events beyond their control dramatically reduced their options. In the course of 1981, things would go from bad to worse. At some point, the "farm problem" became a farm crisis. While a few people had adopted that terminology in 1978 with the AAM farm strike, it did not become a common expression until around 1982. Stray references appeared, such as Republican congressman Jim Leach's appearance in Belle Plaine to talk about the "family farm crisis," but such comments were relatively rare.[2] By 1982 people familiar with Iowa, such as Iowa's then Representative

Tom Harkin, would label the problems that farmers were facing a "farm crisis," a term that implied an urgent situation, in need of immediate attention. And yet that attention was slow to come. While the indicators of crisis were abundant, the nation had yet to notice serious trouble in farm country. Instead, most Americans focused their attention on what were to them larger problems, such as a nationwide economic recession. In 1982, unemployment hit the 10 percent mark for the first time since the Great Depression, and 1.9 million workers lost their jobs.[3] And yet, while most Americans kept their eyes on urban troubles, the crisis in the countryside intensified.

Between 1979 and 1983, the situation on farms across Iowa went from difficult to critical and the number of foreclosures mounted. The first four years of the crisis revealed myriad cracks in Iowa's agricultural foundations. It would soon be evident that the borrowing and spending of the 1970s had been a mistake. Before long, families would be tightening their belts and contemplating off-farm jobs as they scrambled to remain solvent. They were also going to have to confront very old habits of individualism, which might have worked well in times of prosperity but left them vulnerable to depression when hard times destroyed their image of themselves. Even those who were feeling pretty good in 1979 were going to be worried by 1983, when a rolling disaster enveloped a significant portion of Iowa's countryside.

New Challenges

The situation dramatically worsened on October 6, 1979, during the confirmation of hearings of Paul Volcker to chair the Federal Reserve. At the hearings, President Jimmy Carter's Fed nominee declared his intention to bring inflation under control, a position Carter endorsed because inflation had eaten into his popularity throughout his term in office. If Congress had been willing to impose taxes, the government could have used that tool to fight inflation. Lacking that resource, the Federal Reserve raised interest rates significantly. While inflation had been hard on farmers because it increased the price of all of their inputs, high interest rates proved to be their undoing. Many farmers ended the 1970s with significant debt. As long as inflation remained high, they repaid that debt with dollars that were lower in value than those they had borrowed, making repayment easier. Reducing inflation meant higher valued dollars, however, which farmers struggled to repay. High interest rates also drove up the cost of doing business and interest payments became for many their largest outlay. A stronger dollar did not just affect farmers as borrowers, it affected them as they tried to market their crops in an environment where American corn, beans, and wheat suddenly became more expensive abroad. Overseas purchasers sought new sources of agricultural commodities, and exports fell. High interest rates also added another wrinkle to the farmers' troubles: they made land a less attractive asset for investors. Farmland had a rate of return of 3 to 4 percent, which looked less and less desirable as interest rates rose. Certificates of deposit, and even many savings accounts, had a higher rate of return than land. Investors no longer wanted it, as land prices would peak in 1981, and then fall rapidly. Ultimately, farmland in Iowa would lose 60 percent or more of its value. And when their debts became greater than the collateral they held in their land, farmers became vulnerable to forced sales.[4]

And then another blow fell, this one more psychological than actual. On December 24, 1979, the USSR invaded Afghanistan. The Soviet invasion of a remote nation was an unlikely cause of unrest in farm country. Yet that unrest surfaced in January of 1980, when President Carter retaliated with a grain embargo against the USSR. The Soviets had been a major importer of American grain, and farmers felt as if they had been punched in the gut. They had experienced embargoes before. Both Presidents Richard Nixon and Gerald Ford had placed embargoes on the export of specific products to guarantee domestic supplies, but Carter had promised that he was different. During his campaign he courted the farm vote and pledged never to inflict an embargo on America's farmers, and yet, now seventeen million tons of American grain were awaiting delivery to the USSR and going nowhere. Other nations stepped into the breach and sold when the US government was unwilling. Ultimately, the United States would sell grain meant for the USSR to nations that had overestimated their ability to sell for export and meet domestic need. Exports, it turns out, rose during the embargo.[5]

In the embargo's early stages, this outcome was unclear. Instead, it seemed like another economic insult. While the editor of *Wallace's Farmer* did not come right out and condemn Carter's action, he did ask why farmers were bearing the burden of this foreign policy decision. He wrote, "It would seem if foreign policy demands a really effective economic squeeze on the USSR, it should be a broad based action covering industrial goods, technology, services, credit, the Olympics, etc. Again, such action would carry more weight if it were imposed in concert with free world nations."[6] He asked that everyone, not just farmers, carry the weight of economic sanctions. Farmers, as might be expected, were deeply distressed by these developments. A president with his roots in agriculture had broken a promise and used their livelihoods as a foreign policy weapon. Iowa's farmers shared their disapproval with the editors at *Wallace's Farmer*. When Carter announced the decision, 63 percent of Iowa's farmers disapproved. Seven months into the embargo, 75 percent disapproved. A Benton County farmer commented, "I didn't approve of the embargo to begin with, but I tried to understand. It was a weak move. US agriculture took the rap."[7] For people who were already living on the edge, it was yet another sign of the precariousness of their position.

While blaming their woes on the embargo may well have been misplaced, farmers were not wrong to feel uncertain about the future. Early in 1980 farm publications were already calling the situation "the worst economic recession agriculture has suffered since the Great Depression of the 1930s. Depressed prices, credit refusals, and foreclosures are increasingly commonplace."[8] Rural banks were short on money, making it difficult for farmers to secure operating loans. Other lenders were also in trouble. Because of budget cuts, the FmHA exhausted its funds. In the face of the capital crunch, President Carter released an extra $2 billion in loan money to the FmHA, but it was gone in days. Advisors informed farmers of this reality and offered little hope: "If you've tried to borrow operating money this year you know high interest rates are your *second* concern. The first is where to get money, no matter what it costs."[9] Two other associations of lenders, the Production Credit Associations and Federal Land Bank Associations, took out a full-page ad in *Wallace's Farmer* encouraging their borrowers to think soberly and carefully. Part of the densely packed copy read, "Your first interest should be your family. Your second interest should be existing debt obligations. Next comes paying for your plans for modifying or expanding your farming operations. You may have to decide between what you really need and what you only want. Be cautious if your net worth has increased largely because of inflation." If debts became too pressing, downsizing might be a good idea, they counseled. "It's not a sign of failure, but of good business sense. Much like a livestock man culling his herd of unproductive animals."[10] Some farmers were beginning to wonder if they were the ones being culled.

Looking ahead to 1980, farmers were expecting bad, or worse. Robert Dircks, a Cedar County farmer, explained it this way: "Rather than planning for profit, we see it minimizing losses. We made a lot of decisions last fall that are totally wrong now. We didn't foresee 20% interest, or a grain embargo either. After 2 years of local drouth, we needed a healthy grain market to bring us back."[11] The pain farmers were feeling was increasing, or, as a writer for *Successful Farming* graphically phrased the situation, "the jaws of a Vise Grip around your throat couldn't hurt any more than the squeeze of sagging commodity prices and rising production costs on your financial windpipe." Because of the combination of low commodity prices and higher interest rates, farmers were going to have to run faster just to stay in place.[12] The cost of other inputs was going up, too. University of Minnesota agricultural economists predicted that in 1980, the cost of corn production would run 40 percent higher than it had in 1979. The cost of diesel fuel was primarily the culprit.[13] In a letter to Governor Ray, a farm woman from Neola, Iowa, demanded help for folks like herself who were "going broke" and suffering from a droughty spring. "Why are you not going 'to bat' for us now with your depressed prices and high interest rates?" In her opinion, it was his responsibility as a farm state governor to combat misunderstandings about agriculture: "People have no idea what it is like on a farm and how much our expenses are. Just because meat, bread & corn flakes are high, they blame it all on the farmers."[14] The price of food might be up, but the returns to the farmers who grew the raw ingredients were falling. It was processors who were making the profits.

In fact, the price of food sometimes precluded farmers from purchasing what they needed. The first news stories about farmers qualifying for food stamps appeared in 1980, when an astonished writer for the *Des Moines Register* reported on the phenomenon.[15] Dave Gergen, a northwest Iowa farmer who lived near Orange City, had seen his net worth fall from around $120,000 to just over $18,000, due to "disastrous" cattle and hog prices. In shock, he reported, "It doesn't make sense . . . I'm getting food stamps and I've got all that livestock out there." He was one of fourteen farmers in Sioux County who qualified for food stamps that year, and it hurt. Said Gergen, "I'm losing everything else; now I'm losing my pride."[16] Gergen might have felt alone in his predicament, but not for long. The numbers of farmers relying on food stamps multiplied rapidly in the first half of the decade.

Farmers and Stress

The stress on the farm was showing. A *Wallace's Farmer* poll published in mid-1980 disclosed that because of high levels of uncertainty and debt very few farmers were feeling good about their situations.[17] Life had been hard before, but these times seemed peculiarly bad and things were looking more uncertain by the day.

In the face of this uncertainty, 1980 saw the beginning of mental health campaigns aimed at farming people. Both *Successful Farming* and *Wallace's Farmer* devoted space to features discussing stress. Writers for both publications acknowledged that stress was unusually high and that farmers, particularly young ones, needed to be conscious of their reactions and choose healthy responses. Extension professionals (the USDA's employees who took agricultural research to the farming public through the nation's land grant universities) also emphasized stress mitigation. The 4-H program developed a new curriculum to help teens understand and cope with stress, at the same time as Iowa State University began promoting a program for adults. The 1980 Farm Progress Show featured a display called "New Ways to Manage Stress," designed by Randy Weigel, an Extension employee who had done research on farm families and mental health. He had adapted new research on corporate stress management to farmers, who he believed were, under a certain set of circumstances, one of the most pressured occupational groups. Weigel promoted a "stress management formula," which called for "recreation + exercise + good nutrition + positive outlook." It was the beginning of what would become a much more comprehensive approach to mental health as the crisis deepened.[18] Mental health was not something that people readily discussed in the early 1980s, and especially not among farm people. In communities where everyone knew everyone else, and where mental illness carried a serious stigma, seeking help could be difficult and embarrassing.

The research showed that older farmers were feeling the pressure, but younger farmers were feeling it even more acutely. In January of 1980, *Wallace's Farmer* published the results of a poll about their prospects. While a quarter of respondents thought that beginning a farm would be "difficult but not insurmountable," 55 percent believed that it would be almost impossible for a young farmer to get started. Finding land and financing were the two greatest problems standing in their way.[19] In response to concerns such as these, the state legislature voted to create the Iowa Family Farm Development Authority (IFFDA) in July of 1980.[20] With this legislation, the state defined a beginning farmer as one with a net worth of $100,000 or less. A beginning farmer had to be at least eighteen years of age, unless married, and a permanent resident of Iowa. Under the IFFDA, the state would arrange for loans at 4 to 5 percent below market rates for purchases such as property, agricultural improvements, and land. The farmer could not use the loans to purchase land from family. The first beneficiary of the IFFDA was Brian Luse, of Moravia, who received a loan of $100,000 for a hog confinement system. The nineteen-year-old owned thirty acres of his own while also working for his father. He hoped to market up to twenty-five hundred hogs per year. The program made possible a loan at 14 percent, rather than 18 or 19 percent. Even a 14 percent loan represented a significant expense for a beginning farmer, and while the state could arrange the financing, it could not guarantee anyone's success.[21]

Individual problems meshed with political concerns in 1980. It was a presidential election year, and Iowans needed to know how the candidates stood on agricultural issues. Richard Krumme, editor of *Successful Farming*, worked hard to secure interviews with Jimmy Carter, Ronald Reagan, and independent candidate John Anderson but found himself unable to get anything beyond promises of written answers to written questions, provided by advisors. In disgust, he gave up, telling his readers, "I'll tell you what's wrong with that proposal. Bob Bergland [Carter's Secretary of Agriculture] didn't decide to embargo Russian grain sales. Jimmy Carter did. The next big farm decision which will have an impact on the *total* US economy will *not* be made by the Secretary of Agriculture or the president's farm advisors." That reality made it necessary for farm people, and farm publications, to hear direct candidate statements. Krumme continued, "We realize that the candidates are busy people, but it appears there is a blatant disregard for agriculture in this campaign. The platforms barely mention this industry. . . . The candidates' general disdain for interviews with the farm press indicate a lack of concern for agriculture."[22]

In 1980 the United States would elect Ronald Reagan president, a man who promised less government, which presumably meant less government support for agriculture. He touted the benefits of market-determined prices and less support for farm programs. While a number of Iowa's farmers believed that having government in agriculture was what was wrong with the business, others wanted government to take a strong hand in supporting and regulating agriculture in order to make the business profitable for smaller farmers. For the time being, Reagan would push for less government support of agriculture, a position that became increasingly unpopular in Iowa.

The state began 1981 on a sober note. When Lieutenant Governor Terry Branstad introduced Governor Ray for the January 12 Condition of the State address, Branstad waded right in, telling his audience that "we are in the midst of what may be the most difficult economic time since the depression days of the 1930s." The nation was in a recession, and Iowa was in the thick of it. In his speech, Governor Ray tried to put a brighter spin on the situation, but it was a struggle. He called on Iowans to remember the dark days of the Great Depression and how an earlier generation had climbed out of that pit to develop an "agri-business economy second to none." Ray continued, "All of this will pass, and the Iowa we know and love will go on, with some cloudy days, yes, but always with the prospect of a bright, new dawn.... Will we succumb to circumstances beyond our control? We will not! Will we turn our backs and walk away from urgent problems? We will not! Will we let special interests chart our course? We will not!" With the state staggering under the weight of a nationwide recession and a particularly fraught farm situation, Iowans found it difficult to look ahead with optimism.[23]

Probably the biggest "event" of 1981 was not an event at all; land prices reached their apex in 1981 and then tumbled. Paul Volcker's interest rate hike was having an effect, ushering in what economic historian Peter Lindert called "the most unstable period" in the history of land values in the United States. "Neither the Civil War decade, nor the famous bust in farmland speculation in 1920, nor the Great Depression, brought as sharp a change in trend as that since 1980," he wrote. In 1981, largely in response to the dramatic rise in interest rates, they began a sharp reversal, taking the equity of many of Iowa's farmers with them.[24]

Indeed, rising interest rates made farmland a less appealing investment compared to certificates of deposit. Iowa's bankers knew this about as well as anyone and shared their concerns with Governor Ray. Morris Neighbor, president of Farmers State Bank in Marion, wrote to the governor, describing the situation in stark terms. Although he termed the recent "era of inflation" as "repulsive," what had come next was even worse. His borrowers were in an untenable situation: "A good many of our borrowers, especially the cattle and hog feeder, cannot possibly endure the continuation of *high interest rates*, high energy costs and no profits. Our livestock feeders cannot continue to provide low-cost food to the consumer and continue to lose money." While his agricultural customers had been surviving on their equity, "*this well is running dry!*" The cure for inflation, in his opinion, was worse than the disease itself: "I don't believe this nation can afford to sacrifice the backbone of small-town America to have a hurry up control of inflation. Interest rates must be lowered and soon."[25] Morris Neighbors's borrowers were already feeling pressure, and with a collapse in land prices imminent, the situation would deteriorate rapidly.

Another sign of growing concern for the countryside was that Rural America opened a Des Moines office in July 1981. With its primary office in Washington, DC, Rural America provided education and advocacy in the areas of rural low-income housing, energy, land, and health. When David Ostendorf, the organization's associate director, moved to Des Moines, he imagined that he would be spending most of his time on rural housing issues, such as financing and economic development. Soon, however, he and his staff would be sitting in church basements throughout the state, visiting with farmers and listening to their troubles, as Rural America shifted its focus to the credit and foreclosure crisis in the countryside.[26]

Farm Women and Off-Farm Employment

Another sign that all was not well was the increasing number of women seeking off-farm jobs. For many farm families, new sources of income were becoming a necessity. Women facing the prospect of taking jobs off the farm were remaking themselves and their role in agriculture. In the Iowa of the 1980s, very few farm women identified themselves as farmers. Instead, most called themselves farm wives and farm women, who helped their husbands with the many tasks involved in running an agricultural operation. The scope of those tasks was broad and could involve anything from keeping a garden, to vaccinating piglets, to running a combine and keeping the books. Surveys done in the 1970s and early 1980s revealed that most did between 45 and 50 hours of housework per week, and an average of 690 hours of agricultural labor per year, largely during the busy seasons of spring and fall.[27] Their working lives within the context of the farm and family were varied and often involved a great deal of independence and managerial prowess. Even so, most farm women in Iowa and throughout the United States defined themselves as "helpers." Leaving the farm to bring in a wage was also being a helper, but a helper with far greater autonomy and a work life no longer circumscribed by family.[28] Women's jobs would increasingly provide families with insurance, money for groceries, and the wherewithal to keep farming less and less profitable acres.

In the 1980s off-farm work for women was not entirely new. By the late 1970s, half of all borrowers in the Federal Land Bank's Omaha office (which covered Iowa, Nebraska, South Dakota, and Wyoming) had off farm income, and women earned 37 percent of it. On average, these women had an annual income of $7,400 a year. From the perspective of the twenty-first century, this may not sound like much of a contribution, but in the early 1980s, most Iowa farm families spent between $12,000 and $20,000 a year on living expenses. A woman's off-farm income could make the difference between bare cupboards and relative comfort.[29]

Taking a job off the farm was not a simple matter. According to anthropologist Deborah Fink farm women often balked at the idea of moving outside of the family circle to work. They did an enormous amount of work at home, between domestic chores and farm labor, especially in the spring and fall. Additionally, in conservative rural communities, off-farm work had a bit of a taint, since it often involved doing low-wage, low-skill work for people who were not kin.[30] In the midst of an economic crisis, it took on another potential taint, that of airing dirty laundry. If a farm woman had never worked off the farm previously and suddenly sought employment in town, it was practically an admission of problems on the farm, visible to the whole community. Additionally, off-farm work could create stress between husband and wife and cause upheaval for a family's children. Seeking off-farm employment was not something women did lightly, or easily, but times were hard, and necessity overrode other considerations. Farm women's most important traditional role had been to do what was needed, when it was needed, no matter the personal and social strictures.

During the Farm Crisis, farm women would take jobs off the farm in ever increasing numbers. Those who had education and training were in a better position to find jobs. Mary Ann Reinsche, of Jesup, was a nurse and able to work on-call to cover sick days, vacations, and staff shortages at the local hospital, retaining the freedom to work on the farm around the busy months of May, June, October, and November. Bev Hupp, of Webster City, picked up work at the city library. Others went to work not just for the money but for needed benefits. Mickie Cairns, of rural Story County, worked for a company in Ames in order to receive both life and full medical insurance for her family. Farm women like these found working off the farm a balancing act. Some things, like the fine details of housework, went undone, and most women found that the men in their lives were either unwilling, or seemingly unable, to cover more than a small share of the chores. Since the vast majority of farm women did some sort of farm labor, from plowing to livestock care and bookkeeping, taking a job in town involved a juggling act. Deciding whether or not the job was worthwhile was a matter of balancing the potential wages and benefits against the commute, the availability and cost of child care, and the ability of others to cover the work a woman normally would have done on the farm.[31]

Farmers Air Their Grievances

Farm families were facing many adjustments and having to confront many new realities. The evidence of their pain showed up in letters to the statehouse and minutes of farming organizations. Venting stress was a central element in farmer correspondence. Robert Steinke, of Gibson, Iowa, looking at a year of low yields, lamented "every thing us farmers buy goes up in price and every thing we sell goes down aspecially grain corn and beans at todays price is below what it cost to produce [sic]."[32] He protested his continued pain, caught as he was in the cost-price squeeze.

The stress that families were feeling was both real and significant and could show up in unexpected places. The minutes of the Omega Township Women's Club, a northwest Iowa institution, generally reflected little emotion. Sometimes, however, the recording secretary let the facade slip. On April 14, 1981, she noted, "Our program was on 'Stress'.... We came to the conclusion that being a farmer's 'partner' is indeed a stressful occupation."[33] It was an understated, but heartfelt, comment. Cheryl Tevis, who edited the "Woman Interest" page for *Successful Farming*, also noted the many stressors that farm women were experiencing. They ranged from sources that farm families felt in any year, such as weather and a lack of time to complete the chores, to those that were at the top of everyone's list at the moment—cash flow and heavy debt.[34]

A west central Iowa farm woman wrote to Rural America's David Ostendorf about the emotional burdens the crisis placed on everyone, even those who were managing. "The financial pinch is accompanied by questioning God's providence, anxiety, tension, strained family relations, and depression. Fear deepens as the bills pile up, a sow has only three pigs, a calf looks sick, the water pump breaks, needed rain doesn't fall, or hailstones plink on the roof. God can seem very far away. Fear begets fear and depression sets in," she wrote. Part of her sorrow was not knowing whether acquaintances, friends, and family were suffering, too. "Many of those whose backs are against the wall are hurting inside but say nothing." She asked, "How can we 'bear one another's burdens' if we don't know what they are?" In farm communities, stoicism—and shame—kept people from admitting to their troubles. In many ways, it was a problem of not knowing what to do, and for whom. "Are words and prayers enough? Besides praying for those who are hurting are there more tangible ways to help them, to let them know we care, to reassure them of God's promises?" She did not know. Her postscript read, "This is unfinished—so is our search for the answers."[35]

Still, despite the sobering times in which they were living, there was no shortage of young farmers who wanted into the business. The idea of being one's own boss and working on the land continued to appeal to some young people, particularly those raised on farms. Given that in the 1980s parents were increasingly unable to help their children who wanted to farm, state aid was in great demand. The IFFDA continued its work in 1981, and the response to the idea was overwhelming. The authority held five meetings in January. The turnout was so great that "it was impossible to obtain an accurate count of those people attending each meeting." Organizers estimated attendance at the Ames meeting at one thousand, while those at Janesville and Storm Lake may have drawn as many as twelve hundred. In Washington and Atlantic, eight hundred attended each meeting. The IFFDA received thirty-nine completed applications and approved thirty-seven.[36] Many of the projects included land purchases. Some parcels were small, under one hundred acres, while others were quite large. Other young farmers proposed to raise livestock, such as one who applied to purchase twenty-five cows. Several wanted to get into the hog confinement business and applied for money for farrowing stalls, manure pits, and other essentials. Some would use their money for tractors and implements.[37] In one case, the state approved Tom and Sandy Heiar of rural Zwingle. He was the farmer in the family, while she worked as a dental assistant. They received a loan of $40,000 at a reduced interest rate in order to place a down payment on fifty-five acres of land. The Heiars were optimistic. Tom commented, "Prices are going to get better." They needed to, since the Heiars planned to invest $150,000 in their project.[38]

While the Heiars were beginning the year with optimism and resources, most Iowans in agriculture faced 1982 with pessimism. Governor Ray's 1982 Condition of the State address attempted to balance the bad news with the good, but the bad won out. He stated, "Here in Iowa we have felt the full force of this recession. Farm prices have yet to rebound. Adjusted farm income last year was the lowest of any year since the Great Depression." Balanced against the bad news was the fact that "Iowa farmers harvested a record corn and bean crop, tops in the country."[39] Bumper crops, however, only added fuel to the fire, driving down prices. Iowa's citizens were still suffering the worst economic stress in nearly fifty years. There was little cause for optimism.

Throughout 1982 the news would be dismal in farm country. In a January story for *Successful Farming*, Tom Anderson, a Cedar Rapids farm manager, predicted nothing but losses for grain producers: "I can't see great hope for corn and soybeans because of the mammoth supply, plus the fact that most of the Corn Belt has excellent subsoil moisture going into 1982."[40] In February the magazine reported that the previous year's low prices had wiped out ninety thousand hog farms nationwide, mostly smaller operators with fewer than one hundred animals.[41] The predictions were no more positive in the fall. In September, *Successful Farming* reported on the "State of the Farm Economy," and began with the dire comment, "Agriculture is in a severe financial crisis. For the first time in history production expenses as measured by the USDA may very likely exceed farm cash receipts in 1982." Farmers had "lost control of their debt. They are essentially bankrupt. Many of these we've talked to were blindsided by their debt loads." Farmers had planned on paying their bills with commodities selling at mid-1970s prices, but those days were gone. The writer ended his analysis on a gloomy note: "It is not certain that the 'glamour days' of agriculture are over. But, certainly the ag economy has been tarnished. And, it may take some time to restore the former glitter that dazzled us so in the '70s."[42] In other words, 1982 was bad and farmers should not expect 1983 to look any better. The continued downward drift in land prices made an already untenable situation worse, as farmers needing to sell were unable to find buyers. Many who had borrowed against the value of their land stood on the brink of ruin.[43]

The pundits were not the only ones predicting disaster. Farmers, themselves, were saying the same things. *Wallace's Farmer* regularly polled its readers, and the results were grim. When they asked farmers in April "How would you describe your current farm financial outlook for the year ahead," 47 percent of them said, "The worst ever." A Linn County farmer shared, "I've farmed for 20 years and 1982 shapes up to be a financial disaster." A Greene County farmer was equally pessimistic, noting, "I just don't see much hope for farm income to recover this year." Young farmers were particularly pessimistic, with more than 50 percent expecting 1982 to be their worst year ever. Those over sixty-five were more philosophical, given the greater financial stability and lower debt that often came with age. About a third thought that the year would be fine. But not all older farmers agreed. One from Sac County commented, "I can't afford to keep farming. I'm glad I own the farm, it's a nice place to live. My wife teaches so we can stay here."[44] A survey later in the year revealed that 45 percent were in their worst economic condition ever, with two-thirds of those in the large thirty-five to sixty-four age bracket asserting that their financial condition was between somewhat and far worse than ever before. Additionally, 44 percent knew someone whose financial condition had forced them out of farming, while 49 percent expected more families they knew to suffer the same fate, if conditions did not improve quickly.[45]

Strategizing Survival

The question, of course, was what to do. When the general public sought to provide the answers, they could border on the absurd. A Des Moines woman, looking for ways to help with the state's overabundance of corn, had a novel suggestion: "Has anyone come up with a good corn-wine? How about a corn-wine contest at the Iowa State Fair 1982?"[46] Corn wine, however, was not the solution. Farmers needed practical strategies. These were not the years of getting bigger. Instead, they were the years of cutting the coat to fit the cloth. More than a third of farmers planned on reducing capital purchases, and more than 20 percent were trimming their living expenses.[47] The survival measures experts suggested took farmers right back to those their parents and grandparents had employed in the 1930s. Experts told them to think about cost control and efficiency, rather than growth. They needed to lower their cash outlays and practice preventive maintenance. Repairing machinery became more important when it became impossible to replace. They could even trade work and equipment with neighbors, a strategy that had been common before World War II. They might have to consider liquidating some of their assets now, to avoid losing them all later. They needed to think about the farm household, as well.[48] Home economists counseled budgeting and the use of cash rather than credit cards. One touted a slogan from World War II: "Grandma's advice long ago is still pretty good—make it over, wear it out, make it do, or do without."[49] It was unclear, however, that the advice met the magnitude of the situation.

State officials mulled over the crisis, trying to figure out just what sort of trouble Iowa faced, who was responsible, and how the problem should be resolved. State Statistician Duane Skow's analysis was particularly useful and clear. Asked by the governor's office to compare the current situation to that of the 1930s, Skow explained the difficulty in doing so; the farms of the 1980s were not the farms of the 1930s. Skow observed, "Many of the variables are completely different. In the 30's, most farms were diversified with farm labor being one of the larger inputs to a crop and livestock operation, utilizing year-round employment." By comparison, "Today, because of the high cost of equipment, specialization has become a reality . . . When you look at some of the larger expenditure items for a current farmer such as farm services, fertilizer, fuels, and machinery, the makeup of expenditure is entirely different than 50 years earlier."[50] In his opinion, farmers more easily economized in the 1930s, when a family's largest expense was labor. When times were tough, everyone pitched in and met the demand for workers. The economic problems of the 1930s, in many ways, had been easier to resolve.

In the atmosphere of the early 1980s, Skow explained, a farmer's success or failure depended entirely on their level of indebtedness. As he noted, "If land is paid for and most of his machinery, the farmer is generally in a profit situation." Not so for others: "For the newer operator who has borrowed, the situation is entirely different. Interest rates have doubled from two years ago and is one of the larger expenditure items and the largest increase in expenditures from earlier times." Servicing debt absorbed all of the resources of many young farmers. Skow, unlike others, did not make moral judgements about that fact. Times had changed. "Many of the things that are now viewed as bad management decisions several years ago would not have been viewed as bad management at that time." The economic downturn and skyrocketing interest rates were "beyond the control of the individual operator." The situation was not easily comparable to the Great Depression. "The monthly obligated overhead has created the current serious economic situation and differentiates the current condition from that of the mid-1930 period. Agriculture is one of the few industries, if not the only industry, that is selling many of its products at the same cost of 5–7 years earlier." In other words, there were no simple answers, placing blame was unproductive, and encouraging people to pursue cost-cutting strategies would not necessarily solve debt problems that were this unwieldy. Old responses could not be recycled to fit this situation.[51] Trimming a few cents off a grocery bill would not pay the interest on a farmer's loans.

The Iowa Farm Unity Coalition

Continuing problems sparked the creation of one of the most active advocacy groups of the Farm Crisis, the Iowa Farm Unity Coalition (IFUC). It grew out of meetings held in a bank basement in Atlantic led by thirty-three-year-old southern Iowa farmer Dixon Terry. The coalition brought together a number of politically liberal Iowa farm groups, including the U.S. Farmer's Association, the American Agriculture Movement, the Farmers Union, and the National Farmers Organization. By mid-decade, it would also include Rural Iowa, Catholic Rural Life, Iowa

Citizens for Community Improvement, the Iowa Inter-Church Agency for Peace and Justice, the Iowa United Autoworkers, and the Iowa Citizen Action Network. The organization worked side by side with Rural America, which would at mid-decade dissolve and become PrairieFire.

The coalition promoted an agenda that looked very similar to New Deal farm policy. They wanted higher price supports, stronger production controls, a large national grain reserve, and a moratorium on farm foreclosures. Terry's position was this: "We have to get away from the idea that the free market levels things out and makes everything all right. It just ain't so." The organization led protests during President Reagan's February visit to Des Moines, where he failed to mention agriculture at all, and protests at the state capitol.[52] In October, IFUC sponsored a Farm Crisis Day rally at the Story County Fairgrounds in Nevada, drawing attention to the lack of concern given agriculture by national leaders. Roughly 300 farm families attended the meeting, which included speakers such as Catholic Bishop Maurice Dingman, and James Riordan, a Boone County farmer who was running for Iowa's secretary of agriculture. Attendees predicted that the agricultural situation was only going to get worse.[53]

In the face of crushing difficulties, members of the IFUC looked for concrete ways to aid struggling farmers. The creation of the Farm Survival Hotline was one of the organization's most significant actions in this regard. It was a free service, paid for by donations and staffed by trained volunteers. The hotline served those who were distressed and feared the loss of their farm. Volunteers did not have money to lend; they were there to talk strategy and provide emotional support. They encouraged farmers to find out exactly what their situation was and not "wait for the roof to cave in." They advised farmers to write letters to their lenders and get everything in writing. They asked them to involve their friends and neighbors and not keep their troubles to themselves. The organization also offered "direct action" to "forestall foreclosure and machinery repossession" when all else failed. Involving neighbors meant that distressed farmers could bring allies to negotiations and potentially deploy them to block farm sales. The IFUC wanted to make sure that lenders were following the rules, since the government was scrutinizing the FmHA for failure to follow its own foreclosure guidelines. Above all, the volunteers offered reassurance: "Be supportive and be sure to stress that it is not the farmer's own personal failure. That at $1.80 corn no one can be a good manager. That many other people are facing similar situations. That their family and health are of greater importance than loan procedures. Be sensitive to callers that exhibit severe emotional distress and be prepared to refer those calls to qualified mental health personell [sic]."[54] Given the propensity of farm people to keep their troubles to themselves, what the IFUC was doing was remarkable. Telling people that they should share their woes flew in the face of centuries of conditioning that said that failure was shameful and that problems should be kept within the family. The IFUC contended that it was the system that was shameful, not individual failures.[55]

Hotline volunteers worried about the mental health of farm people, as did professionals. In 1982 the level of concern skyrocketed. The Greene Township Women's Club brought in the county home economist, Nancy Beyer, to talk about "Stress on the Farm." The secretary recorded, "Farmers are in a situation that their job is very stressful by the fact that they are managing large sums of money, rapid technological advances, events occurring in foreign countries, and inflation.... A very interesting lesson given by Nancy."[56] The 1982 Iowa Power Farming Show featured a "Program for the Ladies—'Stress in the Family Farm.'"[57] And when the National Corn Growers Association met in Des Moines in August, the organization offered a special program for "farm wives" on such topics as estate planning and father/son working relationships, but especially "coping with stress on the farm."[58] Organizers of such events perceived maintaining the family's emotional health as women's work. They would be attuned to their families' needs and perhaps more willing to listen to the mental health message than men.

Getting farm people to accept help in the face of crisis could be difficult. Cheryl Tevis, who edited and wrote on family issues for *Successful Farming*, reflected upon the mental health problems that hard times brought and the shame surrounding them. Many individuals who needed assistance, she commented, refused to seek it because someone might see them parked outside a mental health clinic.[59] As an alternative, both *Farm Wife News* and *Successful Farming* took the mental health message to their subscribers in print, to be read in the privacy of the home. Beginning in 1982, *Farm Wife News* hired South Dakota therapist Val Farmer to write a regular column of mental health advice. Farmer's column covered a variety of topics, from the noncontroversial—such as networking and how to argue constructively—to the far more difficult, such as "ending the hurt and danger of violent relationships," in which he encouraged farm women to leave abusive spouses.[60]

Farm Wife News largely confined its mental health discussions to Val Farmer's regular column, but *Successful Farming*, interestingly enough, took its efforts further. As early as 1979, Cheryl Tevis was writing about stress on farms, asking the question, "Where does SHE go to let off steam?" She touted a peer counseling program developed at the University of Wisconsin-Stout, called Women Helping Women.[61] In 1980 she cast a broader net, writing for both men and women, encouraging farm families to talk about their problems without fear or embarrassment. In 1982 the magazine published an eight-page spread on stress, leading with the story of a farmer's suicide. It is unclear who the editors thought would be reading this material, but it is likely that farm women were the primary consumers, who then used the information to aid the distressed people in their homes, churches, and neighborhoods. Taking care of the mental health of families was as much a woman's job as cooking the meals and caring for the children.[62]

In March 1982 Democratic members of Congress, including Iowa's Berkley Bedell and Tom Harkin (at that point a representative for Iowa) pushed for the passage of the Farm Crisis Bill, which included increased price supports, emergency credit for struggling farmers, payments for idling land, and a ban on agricultural embargoes. They used the word "depression" to describe the state of the farm economy, likening the situation to that of the 1930s.[63] One of the features of the bill was a national referendum, which would have allowed farmers to decide if they wanted mandatory land retirement, coupled with a 10 percent increase in price supports. Farmers would be expected to take land out of production in order to get larger support payments from the federal government. The idea of the referendum, however, proved unpopular and a barrier to the bill's passage. Secretary of Agriculture John Block even called it "dumb."[64] The bill failed to make it out of the House Agriculture Committee.[65]

In 1982 Iowa was voting for both a new governor and a new secretary of agriculture. In the course of the election, a Depression-era measure resurfaced and became a cause for debate. Congressman Jim Leach tipped off the director of Rural America that there was an interesting provision in Iowa law. In 1933, at the height of the Great Depression, the state legislature had responded to the large number of farm bankruptcies by enacting a moratorium on foreclosures. Under the law, the owner of real property on the verge of foreclosure had the right to apply to the court for a continuance of up to two years on the basis of two conditions. The first was environmental: if drought, flood, heat, hail, storm, other climatic conditions, or pests could be proven to be the cause of the owner's default, then the court would have grounds to act. The other condition was more interesting, given the ongoing situation. If a governor declared a state of economic emergency, then the court could also grant continuances. The state legislature renewed the measure in 1935 and 1937. The Iowa Supreme Court struck down the legislation in 1937, which resulted in the passage of a revised law in 1939. Although rarely used, in 1982 it became part of the election-year discussion.[66]

The idea intrigued the public. Mrs. Garrett Schreur, a farm woman from Kanawha, took Governor Ray to task for failing to consider a moratorium. She had listened to him on the radio, where he had declared that the state should not interfere with agreements made in good faith between farmers and lenders. She responded,

> You think the state government should not interfere with signed financial agreements. Perhaps that is undemocratic. The fact is that the federal government did interfere with the farmers' ability to market their produce (embargo) and the results are that the farmer is either "breaking even" or "operating at a loss." As a small landowner, mother of two beginning farmers, member of a family who "loves the soil," may I ask you to be patient with us farmers?

She urged him to reconsider his position: "We do not favor handouts, we only want the opportunity to keep trying to make ends meet. We do not want to be unemployed. We want to live and help others have food, too."[67] Farmers were not the only group asking for consideration. The Quad Cities Unemployed Association also requested that the governor support a moratorium. His failure to do so, the organization's secretary asserted, meant that Ray "agree[d] with and endorse[d] foreclosures on homes, farms, and small businesses in Iowa."[68] In spite of the calls by individual citizens and farm groups to declare a moratorium in advance of October's Farm Crisis Day, Ray refused to go along, commenting to the press that it would create "some very serious problems" and wasn't "a very satisfactory solution."[69]

The governor was listening to the people in his administration, rather than the activist groups and citizens writing letters. Aides in the governor's office pointed out that he might be on somewhat shaky ground making a disaster declaration since the law "does not define depression and there exists no technical definition of a depression by either the state or the federal government." The state's secretary of agriculture, Robert Lounsberry, also disagreed with the idea of a moratorium. Although his opponent in that fall's race, Jim Riordan, argued that a moratorium would help save thirty to forty thousand endangered farms, Lounsberry disagreed, pointing to the many hoops, including court supervision, that farmers would have to jump through to benefit from such a measure.[70] His position on the moratorium evidently did not hurt him, as he remained in office until his retirement in 1987.

Lieutenant Governor Terry Branstad, who was making his first run for governor, was of the same mind as Ray: no moratorium. Branstad believed that the level of foreclosures did not yet warrant such drastic action. However, if foreclosures reached 10 to 15 percent, he would be willing to reconsider.[71] Roxanne Conlin, his Democratic challenger, stated during the gubernatorial debate that she was considering declaring an emergency and triggering a moratorium immediately.[72] In the end, Branstad would prevail, although it was not a clean sweep for the Republicans, as a Democrat, Robert T. Anderson, became lieutenant governor. While the lack of movement on the farm debt moratorium may have pushed a few voters away from Branstad, they were unlikely to have been Republican voters anyway. The issue would remain in abeyance, but the farmers would remember, and so would Branstad.[73]

While state officials did not always agree with activists' assessments of what was needed, that did not mean that they were ignoring the problems in the farm economy. When Terry Branstad became governor in early 1983, he cast about for solutions to the agricultural slump. One possibility was agricultural diversification. In mid-February 1983, the governor convened a meeting to discuss the issue. Leading the effort was Edward Stanek, director of the state's Office for Planning and Programming. The initiative came to public attention as "Project Apple Corps," an effort to revive the sagging agricultural economy by way of an apple industry. At the turn of the century, Iowa had been one of the nation's largest apple producers, but by the 1980s, apples had gone by the wayside. Stanek touted orchards as a way for young couples to get into farming and to absorb a large number of agricultural laborers. By midyear, the diversification task force had made its report, suggesting a wide range of potential fruit and vegetable crops for the state, including an expansion of Christmas tree farming.[74]

Farmers with operations of various sizes jumped on the idea. Kenneth Nollen, who farmed on a small scale near Pella, wrote to inquire about "these potential new crops." He wrote that he "would be interested in the planting, cultivation, and care of such crops, land and facility needs, markets, income potential, etc. Any information which you have, or could direct me to, would be most appreciated." The Burrows, who farmed roughly seventeen hundred acres of corn and beans in northeast Iowa, wanted to get into the apple business, too, as a way of managing risk. They hoped to divert "as much as 40 acres of that land to fruit and/or vegetable production. We have been especially interested in growing apples."[75] For his part, Dennis Juhl appealed to the governor in hope of getting started. He wrote, "I grew up on a farm in western Iowa, and it has been my dream and goal to own a small farm of my own. My wife and I are a young couple and are very interested in starting a fruit and vegetable business of our own. We would be willing to work very hard at this and make it succeed." They anticipated that the state would be able to help them develop their farm.[76]

As appealing as the idea was, it almost immediately stalled. The publication of the task force's report led to cautionary comments from horticultural experts in the state department of agriculture, warning that without new markets these efforts would fail. There were other reasons for caution, too. The executive secretary of the Iowa Christmas Tree Growers' Association wrote to Stanek, providing a reality check. Even if Iowa's farmers began planting Christmas trees immediately, it would be another eight to twelve years before they would be marketable, and "new growers rarely produce premium trees on their first attempt." Even more important was the skepticism about the whole project from within the Iowa Development Commission (IDC), the state agency tasked with economic development. A May 23 internal memo suggested that cooperation on this issue would not be enthusiastic, if forthcoming at all. It read, "Please review this and then let's discuss.... IDC is not committed in the short term.... I do not necessarily agree with all that has been stated in this report, nor do I feel it is how I would go about a market development project. But we may be fighting a losing battle here. Do we want to cover ourselves with the Governor in case this blows up in the future?" A further July memo reinforced the agency's stand: "The IDC has never been comfortable with the project and have alerted the Governor to our hesitancy."[77] The IDC's hesitancy became the governor's hesitancy, and the Apple Corps and other diversification ideas died untested.

More pressing issues may have killed the diversification push, such as the adverse weather conditions that hit the state's farmers. Iowa began the growing season exceptionally wet. In April there was so much rain that instead of losing the usual five percent of their newborn calves, farmers were losing 15 percent. In some feedlots, the mud was eighteen inches deep. Older animals were losing weight slogging through the mud; calves were drowning. Cool temperatures and wet weather continued into June, and farmers fell behind. They finished planting their corn in mid-June, and their soybeans at the end of June, far later than usual. Then the drought began. In July, nearly all of the state, except for a few counties in far western Iowa, was in drought, and the southeastern corner was in extreme drought. Temperatures far above normal compounded the problem. The assessment of the governor's office was that the drought was extremely serious, and that any farmer feeding livestock was in a precarious position. The assessment from *Successful Farming*'s editor was mournful. Most of the state's corn had produced mere "nubbins," and livestock raisers were making hard decisions. As he put it, "What do you say to a cow who's cranked out a calf every year for the past decade and is now heading up the chute on her way to the packer because the pasture and hay are drought burned?"[78] It all seemed terribly unfair. The slowness of disaster relief made the situation even more difficult. Applications for disaster loans flooded FmHA offices, so much that the processing ran months behind. Facing a mountain of requests, the organization tightened up on its requirements. Not everyone was going to get the disaster funds they wanted, or needed.[79]

Payment-in-Kind

Even if the weather had been the only factor in play, 1983 would have been a complete disaster. This, however, was the year of the PIK program, or payment-in-kind, which helped some farmers while devastating others. Late in 1982 Secretary of Agriculture John Block and administrators in the USDA realized that they had a significant problem. The government held huge stocks of commodities, market prices were low, and it looked like 1983 was likely to be another good growing year. The answer to this dilemma was payment-in-kind, trading farmers grain for land that they promised to take out of production. The USDA planned to idle millions of acres across the nation, allowing farmers to improve their land through conservation. Planners assumed that even with more than eighty million acres out of production there would still be sufficient crops for domestic needs. They based this prediction on past performance; previously, farmers had responded to government programs idling land by taking their worst acres out of production rather than their best.

In the month after the program's announcement, nearly half of all Iowa farmers thought it was a good idea, and another 32 percent thought the idea had some merit. As a Buchanan farm woman said, "We'll go in the program if it just lets us break even." A Union County farmer commented, "It's too bad they didn't think of this two years ago."[80] In the end, Iowa had one of the largest PIK enrollments in the country, with 42 percent of its acres idled. Only Minnesota had a greater percentage of land in PIK. The calls to the Iowa Farm Unity Coalition's hotline slowed.

David Ostendorf, director of the Des Moines office of Rural America, commented, "The PIK program has lulled [farmers] into thinking everything is going to be okay."[81]

Not everyone planned on joining the PIK program, however. Livestock producers, in particular, were wary. A Benton County farmer commented, "I've got a lot of hogs and want my own corn, so I'm not interested." In particular, farmers with large numbers of cattle and hogs needed to be sure of the quality of the corn they fed their animals. Said one, "I want my own corn. There's a lot of difference in the feed value—too much to gamble on getting corn from an unknown source."[82] Unfortunately, the combination of the drought and PIK ended up being disastrous for these farmers. PIK, as planned, reduced surpluses and pushed the price of grain up. The drought, however, left livestock producers and dairy farmers with nothing for their cattle and hogs, and very high prices for feed. By the time the fall harvest season rolled around, nearly 60 percent of Iowa's farmers believed that PIK had provided short-term relief to grain farmers but had been unfair to livestock producers.[83]

Livestock and dairy farmers were not the only unhappy constituents. The program jeopardized a number of rural businesses. Acres diverted into PIK meant that farmers did not need to spend as much on fertilizer, fuel, machinery, and repairs, a situation that was good for farmers but bad for their suppliers. In Shelby County, for example, the extension service estimated that agribusinesses had lost $6.8 million dollars. Losses statewide ranged from $540 to $600 million. Machinery dealerships were already hurting before PIK. Owners had hoped that when the price of corn and beans went up, their business would improve, but they had not counted on PIK. Before the summer was over, the USDA realized it was going to have to act to avert serious economic problems across agricultural America. And so the agency provided disaster loans for a disaster it had created. Eligibility extended to any county with at least fifty thousand acres or 20 percent of its productive land in the program. The government limited the funds and made the requirements stringent. Many small businesses did not qualify.[84] PIK's ripples extended throughout the countryside.

PIK was an experiment, and the USDA was unlikely to ever try exchanging crops for idled acres again. Even before Congress approved funds for PIK disaster loans, the program was phenomenally expensive. Many signed up, and moving crops around the country was pricey. In September 1983 the USDA estimated the cost of the program at a whopping $21 billion. Senator Bob Dole of Kansas commented that PIK payments had "the dubious distinction of exceeding farm income this year." It was also highly unpopular with the general public, which could not understand why the government was giving grain to farmers, let alone trying to prop up grain prices. Some called it "welfare for farmers," a comment that was highly unpopular in farm country but a predictable reaction on the part of the nation's nonfarming population. In the end, officials at the USDA indicated that although they were uncertain about the future direction of farm policy, they would not repeat PIK.[85]

Lenders—and Borrowers—in Trouble

On the whole, 1983 was not shaping up to be a very satisfactory year. Interest rates had declined, but they still were well above ten percent. Bad news about land values more than offset the good news on interest rates. Early in the year, land values plunged to a twenty-year low, and continued to fall. While lower land prices promised to make it easier for some to purchase land, it made life much harder for individuals who had used land as collateral. As a result, increasing numbers of farmers who got their loans from Production Credit Associations were getting bad news. A third of PCA borrowers had fallen into the "high risk" or "problem" category, and if they had no co-signor or additional property to mortgage, the PCAs told them to pay up or face a sale. As the year progressed, the situation worsened. Another lender, the Federal Land Bank Association (FLBA) announced more delinquencies, and the president of the Harlan office noted the highest level in thirty years. The U.S. Farmers Association started counting advertisements for farm auctions and claimed that the numbers were "outrageous." They had seen 488 auctions advertised in February, with 95 in a single day, and 506 auctions advertised in March. Farm families predicted a year of just getting by. Leon Harms, of Grundy County, told *Wallace's Farmer*, "We just plan to survive in 1983. I don't think we'll change our farming operation at all." Harms also planned to work off the farm, selling real estate, to keep his farm afloat. In April, the editors of *Successful Farming* wanted to declare the farm recession over—but they could only do so in the most cautious of terms. After explaining the many signs of hope on the horizon, they ended on a less optimistic note: "The fact is, many farmers are still battling to stay in business. And even in the best of circumstances it will be some time before they can breathe easily again." Agricultural economists were looking ahead with trepidation, telling

Vehicles jamming a country road were a sure sign of an auction underway. By permission of Charlie Langton.

farmers that they would have to "farm smarter" in 1984, due to lower levels of government support, and more problems finding financing.[86]

The uncertainties of 1983 meant continued efforts in agricultural advocacy. Early in the year, American Agri-Women (AAW) and Women Involved in Farm Economics (WIFE) held their meetings, and both groups encouraged women to join the cause and lobby for their interests. Tough times called for cooperation and a united front. Some of the latter were more local in nature. When in March the United Central Bank in Algona cut off the credit of a local family, the Zeimets, thirty of their neighbors, friends, and the members of the IFUC gathered at the bank to show their support. While the Zeimets had to meet the bankers alone, the protestors remained outside the bank, carrying signs saying, "Farmers Need Cash, Not Crash" and "Stop Foreclosures." Bank officials allowed the couple to fill out loan forms, but to no avail. The bank refused to extend credit, and the Zeimets planned their sale. Jerome Zeimet began looking for alternative employment. The protests and meetings continued.[87]

In July a group gathered in Irwin to discuss "saving farms and rural communities." A Council Bluffs attorney joined them to discuss the rights of those facing foreclosure. In October a number of groups, including the Iowa Inter-Church Forum and Catholic Rural Life, sponsored a meeting in Des Moines to give farm and rural people the opportunity to educate urban Iowans about the problems of the previous year. They intended to build a larger pool of allies for farm people. Another protest, also in October, aimed to create a coalition between the unemployed in urban areas and Iowa farmers. Farmers donated sixty-eight hogs, and workers at the Rath packing plant in Waterloo processed them into more than eight thousand pounds of sausage to be distributed to needy families at Waterloo's United Auto Workers (UAW) Union hall. The growing crisis had closed the John Deere plant in Waterloo, which explained both the location of the event and the choice of allies in the UAW. The UAW and IFUC cooperatively organized the event, which also featured a soup kitchen serving a "Depression-style" lunch.[88] The state was experiencing a rolling call to action, in big events and small, in rural and urban areas, as groups sought solutions to their problems. Sometimes, as in the case of the sausage protest, farm groups joined with urban churches and organized labor, not organizations that they might normally see as allies: hard times demanded creative thinking and dialogue across the rural-urban divide.

Advocacy groups, and especially the IFUC, continued to put their faith in the idea of a foreclosure moratorium. In March several hundred protestors showed up at the state capitol to demand an end to forced sales. They urged anyone in trouble because of weather emergencies to apply to the courts for individual assistance as the law allowed, but what they really wanted was for the governor to declare a state of economic emergency, making it possible for more people to apply. The governor's office replied with a report. In April the Office of Planning and Programming sent to the governor a twelve-page document, which ended with the sentence, "More farmers would be hurt by loss of credit and higher interest rates than could possibly be helped by the moratorium." Upon publication of the report, fifteen members of the IFUC met with Branstad, hoping to change his mind. While they were happy that Branstad met with them, they were not happy with the meeting's outcome. The governor echoed the report but asked the farmers to study it and prepare a reply. When the IFUC sent their reply in May, they emphasized that the report only speculated about a moratorium's results and underestimated the trouble that farmers were facing. Nevertheless, the governor had yet to be convinced that the situation was dire enough for such drastic action.[89]

The farm groups knocking on the governor's door were soon to have an unexpected ally: Hollywood. In 1983 the movie *Country* was in production, and producer and actor Jessica Lange, who had grown up in rural Minnesota, was committed to confronting the troubles of Midwestern farms. A news photograph from New London, Ohio, had inspired her. The picture showed farmers reacting in anger and sorrow at an FmHA auction.[90] She, along with director Hal Ashby and writer-producer Bill Wittliff, turned to Iowa as the setting for their story. Lange, Ashby, and Wittliff toured the state on a fact-finding mission, hoping to build an authentic picture of a farm family facing foreclosure. They met with farm women in several locations. The women spoke to the film's creators about the competition involved in modern agriculture and the pain of having neighbors pass judgment on their situations. One woman told Lange, "I just scream and yell in the house by myself if there's no one to listen." Another explained the trouble the crisis was causing in her marriage: "It's a constant stress. All he thinks about 24 hours a day is the farm."[91] The Iowa connections of the film went even deeper. In addition to tapping the state's farm women for ideas, the producers called on Rural America for help. Iowa staff served as technical advisors on the film, reading the script for accuracy, and developing a budget for the film's fictional farm. Lange set and filmed her story near Dunkerton, and Iowans eagerly awaited its release.[92]

Self-advocacy was also an important tool for suffering farmers. Writing to their elected officials allowed distressed individuals to vent while asking for help for their families. Both were important functions of the hundreds of constituent letters flowing into Iowa's statehouse. Farmers crammed Terry Branstad's mailbox with stories of broken dreams. One of these came from Myron Ohrtman, "a 35 year old [sic] ex-farmer." Ohrtman had twenty years of experience in agriculture, including a decade's work with cattle and four years with hogs. He was also proficient in using a computer to manage his operation. He said, "I like watching things grow and am innovative." High interest rates forced Ohrtman to give up his farm, and with neither a farm nor a college degree, Ohrtman was stuck. "I have been actively searching for employment since the first of the year, and I'm at a loss as to where to go for help now." Ohrtman had plenty of experience, but no credentials, and the governor's office had little to offer in the way either help or encouragement.[93]

The FmHA was foreclosing on a farm near Cherokee, and the family turned to the governor out of frustration. While waiting for the auction, FmHA rules left the family little in the way of sustenance. The farm woman wrote, "For the past 3 months every hog or grain of corn we have sold has gone directory to FMHA. We have *tried* to survive on $35.00 a week I make as a waitress. This FMHA expects us to buy groceries, utilities, gas to go to work, insurances, plus any other non-related

Auctioneers at work selling equipment and land were an increasingly common sight. By permission of Charlie Langton.

farm expenses we incur." Keeping themselves and their livestock alive and fed was a trial. "The most disgusting part of this is when Mr. Taylor [of the FmHA] asked if we had enough feed for the hogs, when we had gone without groceries for 3 weeks." When the couple held their equipment auction, they had to give all of the money to the FmHA, which left nothing for living expenses or bills. Their lender also told them not to discuss their problem in public, "but it is sure hard to keep your mouth closed when your stomach's growling." They were at the end of their rope. "The criminal has more rights as does an FMHA borrower. Our crime was to try to buy an 80-acre farm. Governor Branstad can you help us?" All the governor's office could do was suggest contacting their congressional representative.[94]

Farmer Ralph Engelken, of Greeley, wrote to Branstad to plead for a moratorium on foreclosures. He wrote, "Being our Govenor [sic] we know you have the sole power to enforce a moratorium on these farm foreclousures [sic] and give these people a second chance." The Engelkens were on the verge of losing their long-established organic farm (they preferred the term "bio farm") to the Federal Land Bank. The Engelkens enjoyed a bit of celebrity status in the organic farming world, having published a book in 1982, *The Art of Natural Farming and Gardening*. By 1983, however, they had a debt of approximately $350,000 on their 480-acre farm, and no lender willing to assume their loan. Engelken pleaded with the governor for the debt moratorium. While Branstad was willing to think about the idea, he was not yet willing to act. As his aide wrote to the Englekens, "you can be assured that Governor Branstad will keep your recommendation in mind should there be a rash of farm foreclosures in the coming months."[95] Unfortunately, Ralph Engelken was not going to live long enough to see the moratorium. In December 1984, at age fifty-eight, he succumbed to pneumonia and a blood clot. Rita Engelken would see her family's acres auctioned off in late June 1987, with two hundred supporters looking on helplessly.[96]

The Path of the Crisis in the Early Years

The conditions of the early 1980s dashed the dreams of many farming families. For every family in trouble, there was a unique set of circumstances that led to the loss of their farm. Many of those whose operations failed early in the crisis were young and their farms were fragile. The story of one Audubon County couple helps to illustrate the pressures that confronted many of those who lost farms between 1979 and 1983. It also highlights the difficult situations these families faced once the farm was gone. Leah Tookey and her husband began farming in western Iowa in 1977. She was just out of high school, and he was in his early twenties. They were tenants, and owned equipment and cattle, rather than land. They rented 160 acres from her husband's father, in addition to farming some land with him.

Not far into the 1980s they realized that many around them were facing serious trouble. Tookey remembered, "I wasn't living in a cave, I watched the news, I listened to what was going on in the news. And, of course, Audubon County was hard hit with the Farm Crisis. There were auctions. All the time. We would go to auctions, [my husband] would go and buy equipment from these auctions and farmers who were going out of business. There were suicides. There were sad stories." Before long, the sad story became theirs. They had an operating loan and the interest rate rose to 23 percent. Their bank would not continue to carry their loan without a cosigner, and Tookey's husband was uncomfortable asking his father for help. Tookey's father-in-law believed that his son should pull himself up by his own bootstraps. They were out of options. "We owed about $80,000, which doesn't sound like a lot when we look back at what other farmers owed. But we really had very little. We had some cattle, we had some hogs. We didn't hardly have any equipment because he mostly used his dad's equipment, and so we thought, well, there's nothing we can do, we're going to have to get out of farming."

They found an attorney and added up their assets. They owed $80,000 but owned only about $60,000 in property. The bank demanded that the debt be paid in full, which would mean finding another lender or declaring bankruptcy. They began to plan. Their attorney told them to take any money they had out of the bank; if the bank learned of the pending bankruptcy their assets would be frozen. They could lose everything. Tookey remembered, "It was a Saturday morning, I had the kids in the car. We drove up to the bank, Landsman's Bank in Kimballton. And a little girl came to the window. I remember I was praying, please let it be a high school girl. And this high school girl came to the window. And I had $800 or something like that, a lot of money for us, and I had written a withdrawal slip, but I'd left $50 in the bank, so it wouldn't look suspicious." The waiting began: "She walked off, and she didn't come back, and it was quite a while.... I remember that whole time I was just thinking, oh, my god, she's checking. They're not going to give us our money. But she brought it back, and she counted it out to me, and it was the best feeling in the world that I got this money out of the bank before they could take it away from us." She took the money home and hid it, relieved that she had saved some of the little they owned.

In the end, her husband's grandparents stepped in, unwilling to let them declare bankruptcy. They paid off what remained of the loan and bought them a small house in Exira. After five years of farming, Tookey and her husband were living in town, her husband pumping gas, making three dollars an hour. She would take minimum wage work at the local grocery store once their children began school. All they had ever wanted was to farm, and the farm was gone. Her husband suffered from depression. Under the weight of his depression and her resentment, the marriage eventually ended, another victim of the Farm Crisis.[97]

Tookey and her family were representative of a group of young farmers whose enterprises failed early in the 1980s. Poorly capitalized and dependent on operating loans, they had little in the way of collateral and no way of continuing to secure the funds they needed in the face of ruinous interest rates. Farms around which young couples had built their dreams could not withstand the economic rigors of the decade. Their farms were among the first to go, but they would not be the last.

CHAPTER THREE

The Year of Realization: 1984

Early in 1984, a news story broke that angered, horrified, and bewildered Iowans. Around the New Year, the Humboldt County sheriff's office received an anonymous tip. Something was terribly wrong at Warren Wood's farm. The tipster also called a local bank, which relayed information to the First American State Bank in Fort Dodge. When Sheriff Marvin Andersen and First American president Joseph Lawler arrived at the farm on a bitterly cold day, they found the carcasses of 167 cattle, starved and frozen, some badly decomposed, others recently dead. Merle Lange, Iowa's state veterinarian, called it the worst case of animal cruelty he had ever seen. The Wood family was nowhere to be found. Several weeks earlier, they had packed a van and left for a vacation. They told friends and family that they were planning to watch the University of Iowa Hawkeyes in the Gator Bowl, followed by an additional two weeks in Florida. No one knew exactly where they were, or why they had left their cattle to die.[1]

Nothing about the situation made sense. Wood's pigs were alive and well in a confinement building on the property, and he had arranged for his brother to feed them while the family was gone. Wood had asked no one to care for his cattle, but when Lawler turned on the auger on the silo, he found feed in it. Wood had eight thousand bushels of corn and six thousand bushels of soybeans at a local elevator. The preceding fall, the bank had released $18,000 to Wood to feed livestock and meet other farm business expenses. Investigation showed that Wood, who had been worth approximately $2.7 million at the beginning of the decade, was now $763,000 in debt. By the time his cattle died, he had thirteen loans outstanding with ten different lenders, the most important being the bank in Fort Dodge and a John Deere dealership. The dealer planned to repossess several pieces of machinery. The First American State Bank was demanding payment and had notified local businesses that when Wood sold crops or livestock, the checks should be made out to the bank, in addition to Wood. The bank had not released money for living expenses and expected the family to tap Mrs. Wood's inherited savings and the cash value of his life insurance. When Wood sold several cattle and hogs just before the trip to Florida, he did so in his wife's name, circumventing the bank and its lien on his property. The community was baffled. The most charitable conclusion was that he had given up, and realizing that he would earn nothing from the sale of the cattle, let them die of starvation and exposure.[2]

When Wood returned to Bode, he faced arrest and twenty-five counts of animal cruelty, in addition to twenty-five counts of failure to properly dispose of dead animals. In his defense, Wood claimed that his creditors were hounding him and that they had left him no way to feed his cattle. The court disagreed. Wood eventually served forty-seven days of a sixty-day sentence, with time off for good behavior. The law only allowed sixty days, which frustrated the judge. The situation appalled rural Iowans; a farmer had gone on vacation while his animals starved. A farm woman from rural Story City wrote the *Des Moines Register*, commenting, "The horror of the situation at Bode is unfathomable." If she ever found herself in the same situation, she wrote, "we'll sell our cattle. A thin cow on a poor market is worth a lot more to our banker than a dead one in the rendering truck."[3]

The situation that played out on the Wood farm disgusted all but Wood's family, who tried to defend his actions, although those defenses fell on deaf ears.[4] Yet, in some ways, it was surprising that versions of this tragedy had not occurred on other Iowa farms. There was evidence that other distressed farmers were either having to reduce their animals' rations or feared having to do so.[5] The combination of the debt crisis, the drought, and the PIK fiasco hit livestock farmers hard. Many were struggling to find the money to buy feed for their cattle and hogs while trying to fight off bankruptcy. What happened on this Humboldt County farm illustrated (in a drastic form) a truth played out often in the course of this agricultural depression: people facing extreme levels of economic and emotional stress did not always choose rational solutions to their problems. Although the details of the situation were in question, with Wood claiming abuse and his lenders claiming otherwise, it was clear that a crisis was unfolding and that many situations would arise in its course to dismay and dishearten Iowans.

Dismay and downheartedness were reasonable reactions to Iowa's condition. In 1983 the vast majority of the state had suffered from serious drought. Statistics showed that many counties had experienced the hottest, driest weather since the terrible 1930s. There were less than half as many bushels of corn to harvest as there had been in 1982.⁶ The situation in 1984 was different, but not much better. When it came time to plant the fields were awash with mud, and conditions remained wet from April through June. The weather prevented some farmers from planting and washed out those who made it into the field. Water pooled and drowned the corn. It also eroded terraced fields and damaged drainage ditches. The wet weather forced farmers to abandon thousands of acres. Western Iowa took the brunt of the damage; in Shelby County alone storms damaged over eighty thousand acres. As the months went by, the situation did not improve. Tornadoes, lightning, hail, and high winds filled the summer. A June tornado outbreak caused property losses in seventy-five of ninety-nine counties. In September, there was a hard freeze, killing much of the bean crop. Then it started to rain again. While 70 percent of the corn would normally have been harvested by late October, farmers could only get into the fields and harvest 20 to 30 percent of the crop. The governor's office succeeded in getting disaster declarations and assistance for every county in the state, but the funds would not cover all losses. Nor would they alleviate the anxiety caused by a year of continuous environmental stress.⁷

A July 1984 letter to the governor illustrated the kinds of problems farmers were experiencing. Ray Hodde farmed on the Missouri River bottom west of Hamburg, Iowa. He had been there all his life, farming land that his grandfather and father had farmed before him. He and his brother worked roughly twelve hundred acres, part of which was rented. He was carrying a heavy debt load. Because of three straight years of poor weather conditions, his burdens were worsening. Nothing had prepared him for 1984: "At present time, out of the 1200 acres, only one-third is planted with the rest being flooded. It looks like it is going to be impossible to plant the remaining two-thirds." He pleaded with the governor, "We need governmental help in the form of grants or acreage payments for the acres not planted due to flooding to preserve our future as farmers."⁸ Disaster declarations made assistance in situations such as this one possible, but whether Hodde and his neighbors would be able to fend off financial collapse as well as the Missouri River was yet to be determined. In his own letter to the governor, a Hamburg banker bolstered Hodde's claims. Dan Boatman, president of the Iowa State Bank, believed that the situation was critical. He wrote, "Many of our customers have borrowed to our legal lending limit, $200,000.00. We are now faced with the problem of being unable to provide additional funds for continued operation. This situation has already caused some bankruptcies and will be followed by many more." In his assessment, "many of our farm families are desperate and have nowhere to turn." He asked the governor for help with the water and for further funds for his community.⁹

The Debt Situation

The situation in far western Iowa was grim, and state officials were still trying to estimate the dimensions of the troubles facing the state's farmers. Early in 1984 agriculture officials carried out an intensive survey of debt on Iowa farms. They discovered that the farmers fell into three categories: 31 percent debt-free, another 29 percent carrying heavy but theoretically manageable loans, and 40 percent with dangerous debt to asset ratios. The condition of the bottom 40 percent had worsened for three years, and most farmers traced their problems back to 1979's rate hike. Almost 10 percent of farmers believed that they were within a year of failure. Robert Lounsberry admitted in a news release that the state might lose up to 10 percent of its farmers and ruminated on the meaning of those statistics: "I am asked, is it as serious as the Great Depression? Then we had 222,000 farms and 17,316 farms were foreclosed. In 1981, by contrast, 71 of 118,000 farms were foreclosed.... I would say that agriculture in general in Iowa can not [sic] be compared to the Great Depression, but for a segment of our farmers it is about as bad in terms of being forced off the farm."¹⁰ Lounsberry, however, was comparing a single year of farm foreclosures to a whole decade of depression, and in the three years since 1981, land prices had continued to fall, each year placing more farmers at risk. His numbers also did not reflect the "lag time" involved in bankruptcy filings. Many of the farmers pushed to the wall by the drought of 1983 did not file for bankruptcy until after the new year. The number of bankruptcies filed in the first six months of 1984 exceeded the 1983 total.¹¹

While Lounsberry attempted to comfort his readers, he was worried. In addition to the public news release, he produced a report meant for a narrower audience of government officials. He thought that adverse economic conditions would force eleven hundred farmers out of business in the next two years, decreasing Iowa's farm population by roughly sixty thousand people. Although he had mentioned these numbers in the press release, he had chosen not to expand upon their meaning. The internal document indicated that such substantial losses would severely damage the state's industry, too, since farm-related businesses accounted for more than 50 percent of Iowa's manufacturing. He predicted that many companies involved in agricultural supply, such as seed and implement dealers, would face enormous losses. Land values would continue their downward slide, causing rural banks to fail. Potential buyers would wait for land values to bottom out before making purchases, causing the price of land to tumble even farther. The situation might not yet be as bad as the Great Depression, but hard times were far from over.[12]

Lounsberry was not alone with his worries. An Iowa State University task force of individuals who were both agricultural economists and Extension personnel were now certain that there was a crisis. Farm operators and lenders were reaching the breaking point. In their report, the economists acknowledged the strangeness of the situation. "The flow of grain and meat has not diminished and will not diminish. In spite of large losses of farm equity, the corn will be planted, the pigs will be fed, the fertilizer applied and the grain trains loaded. The flow to consumers will continue. The financial crisis brings loss of wealth, but there is very little effect on production or price." This was a disaster for farmers and for members of the rural community who served farmers, but it was unlikely to have much effect on the average citizen, who was an agricultural consumer, rather than a producer. This did not make the crisis any less real for the farm families facing ruin. The task force predicted that the conditions plaguing farmers in 1984 were likely to continue for the next two years, and that the miserable situation would be compounded.[13] Farmers struggled with a severe reversal of fortunes, caught by an unexpected change in "the rules." As economist Robert Jolly explained, "The rules for farmers changed from a time when debt offered a means to increase wealth—creating strong incentives to expand debt and land ownership—to a time when debt caused loss of equity and expansion by borrowing was unwise."[14]

Up until this point, Iowa's Cooperative Extension Service had been hanging back, not sure whether the situation was a crisis or one of the periodic ups and downs that farmers experienced. By 1984, however, they knew this was not business as usual. Accompanying the task force report was a document outlining the basic features of Extension's ASSIST program, rolled out in the fall of 1984. Extension intended this as a short-term program, from August to December. The reality was that it would be around for years. A central part of the program involved education for farmers, lenders, and communities, but the most important innovation would be FarmAID (not to be confused with Farm Aid concerts), a computer assisted financial planning system that farm families and lenders could use to analyze individual operations. The program allowed farmers to "run the numbers" and find out if their businesses were salvageable. Extension enlisted agricultural publications to spread the word, and *Wallace's Farmer*, for example, began carrying ASSIST updates under the program's logo.[15]

Farmers clamored for the FarmAID program, and in the first few months of operation it reached one thousand individual families, and another ten thousand in informational meetings. For most, taking advantage of FarmAID involved in home, one-on-one financial analysis. Mike Duffy, who worked for the Cooperative Extension Service, was one of the first people in the field. He began at Iowa State University in 1984 and supervised eighteen people with master's degrees who implemented FarmAID. In the first three years of the program, they provided free and confidential consultations to thirty-five hundred families a year. Duffy did not always feel up to the task. He understood farm finance, but families' problems ran deeper than the numbers. The results of his computer analysis had a direct effect upon the economic, and often mental, health of a family. His training was not adequate to the heartbreak. He said, "a lot of the tools that I was trained with worked as far as explaining why and so on and so forth, but sitting across a kitchen table from people that were losing everything.... It was really difficult and it was hard to try to keep people focused on, okay, here's what we need to do." Sometimes, farm wives asked him to deliver bad news to their husbands. Women often kept the books and might know that a farm was failing before anyone else. Unable to bring themselves to tell their husbands, they brought in Duffy. He remembered, "Well, if you want to be in an uncomfortable position, go out to a farm family, seven o'clock at night, sit down at the kitchen table. 'Well, I'm here to talk about your farm and why it's in trouble,' or don't phrase it that way, but ... the wife invites me out to tell the husband they're losing the farm." He was often the bearer of bad news.[16]

Telling couples they had to change strategies could be uncomfortable. When a family needed to rethink their business model, Duffy had to explain to husbands why they could not slash family living expenses to the bone to save their farm. He had to help them understand that while they might be willing to do anything in order to save their land, their wife might not agree. He helped couples clarify their goals and develop plans. He had to steer the conversation away from the issue of fault and toward the future: "My point was always there's plenty of blame to go around, and whose fault it was was relevant to a minor degree ... What was more relevant was what are your goals? What are your assets? How can we combine them to achieve your goals?" Roughly half of the farmers with whom he consulted had little option but to get out. Ultimately, the experience of working with troubled farm families changed Duffy's life: "That period formed the whole rest of my life.

Like I said, I'll never forget a lot of them. I'll never forget the anguish. I'll never forget the murder and suicide and problems that would drive people to that level. I always said and tried to do for the whole rest of my career, was whatever I could to make sure it never happened again."[17]

Extension Personnel under Stress

Mike Duffy was not the only distressed Extension employee. Extension personnel knew how to advise farmers about crops and livestock but generally had no mental health training and had taken their jobs never expecting to provide that kind of service. Eventually, extension began holding workshops for employees who worked with the distressed public, but the situations they faced could be overwhelming. Daniel Merrick was the agricultural director for Cass County. The farmers who worried him the most were ones who had been farming for thirty and forty years: "There were farmers who—59, 60 years old lost everything. Probably had paid very little into Social Security. What do you do? At 59, 60 years old where do you go?" Merrick worked with people who were in a very precarious mental state. "I remember one morning at 3:30 in the morning I got a call from a farmer I had not talked to in five years. And the more I talked the more I became concerned about just what was taking place. But here again, he could not sleep. He wanted somebody to talk to." He worried about the farmer's intentions. Some people were more direct about what they were thinking: "I can remember a farmer coming in and says as I cultivated my corn, I thought 3 or 4 times about killing myself. But then I also knew that I would be leaving that burden on my wife and children." These were not just discussions about corn and beans, but life and death, and as Merrick said, "Most of us did not get that in college."[18]

Even Extension personnel trained in mental health services were shaken by what they encountered. In 1984 the Northwest Iowa Community Health Center in Spencer hired Joan Blundall, a human development specialist, to create a program on "stress education and prevention of emotional problems." Because center staff were seeing so much evidence of crisis-generated marital problems, she developed the group for women who needed help with depression, troubled marriages, and other struggles exacerbated by their families' economic stress. Attendance at the meetings ranged from fifteen to seventy, with some driving more than fifty miles to attend. Blundall also fielded calls from distressed farmers. One woke her in the middle of the night, saying over and over, "I can't hold it anymore." A desperately frightened woman called to tell Blundall that her husband had taken his high-powered rifle and gone for a drive. He told her "I'm a good shot. I'll only get the banker." Blundall called a local minister, who enlisted his parishioners to form a human chain across the road and stop the truck. The man returned home peacefully. Extension personnel in the field confronted grief, sorrow, and their ensuing complications on a daily basis.[19]

As a result, Extension introduced another part of its farm crisis programming, a pamphlet series called Take Charge in Changing Times. Among the first of these was "Managing Farm Family Finances," prepared by Extension economist William Edwards and family environment specialist Cynthia Needles Fletcher. Apparent in this and other initiatives was a desire to give farm families the tools to handle sensitive issues in the privacy of their own homes. Asking for help publicly and attending meetings or even bringing extension personnel into one's home could be difficult and embarrassing. Pamphlets like this one, in workbook form, allowed farm couples to examine their cash flow, household budget, and financial goals on their own, without involving anyone outside the family. As with the FarmAID program, the workbook asked families to determine their goals and set priorities, something that could be difficult when a family was struggling daily with economic survival.[20] Extension also developed self-help material addressing mental health. In 1984 the Extension service rolled out the "Stress on the Farm" home study course. Human development and communication specialists came together to develop a six-part series covering multiple issues of concern to farm people. The pamphlets provided assessment tools, quizzes, exercises, and other action-oriented projects for families.[21]

Extension was working with a client base that was stubborn and resistant to the idea of asking for help. Picking up a pamphlet at the extension office allowed reluctant individuals to sidestep the embarrassment of openly seeking assistance. It was a way to provide aid quietly to people who might not ask for or accept it otherwise. Even so, some rural Iowans dismissed the idea of mental health services entirely. They did not want pamphlets or counseling. Many, at least in part, blamed the system for the problems they faced and did not see the solution in a counselor's office but in changes to the agricultural economy. They wanted reform that would allow them to keep their farms. Donald and Catherine McLean of rural Traer wrote an indignant letter to the governor's office: "You are doing a gross injustice to us by offering psychiatric counseling to Iowa farmers who have lost their farms due to the TERRIBLE economic conditions we are forced to put up with! Counseling will never help the terrible feeling of hopelessness and despair and worst of all the knowledge that NO ONE IN GOVERNMENT CARES ABOUT IOWA FARMERS"[22] To the McLeans, mental health services were an insult layered on top of the injury that economic conditions had already inflicted.

Since the state could not improve the bottom line of families like these, however, it would have to attempt to soften the blow. The heightened attention to mental health issues was overdue. The level of stress in some farm homes was becoming too much to bear. The July 1984 suicide of fifty-six-year-old Kenneth Meisgeier stunned the tiny community of Arlington, just northeast of Waterloo. Meisgeier and his family worked two 160-acre farms. They were longtime community members; the land had belonged to Kenneth's great-great-grandmother. At the time of his death, the farm was in chapter 11 bankruptcy. Troubles began to accumulate in 1981. Meisgeier and his two sons decided to build a new barn for their herd of dairy cattle. The project ran behind schedule and over budget. The cows stood outside in bitterly cold conditions during the work. The stress was hard on the cows, and a mysterious illness killed twenty-eight in just two years. The vet bills climbed. The family needed special protein supplements to fatten their hogs for market, but they had no money for them. Because they had no funds for fuel, Betty Meisgeier walked miles every day to tend the hogs. Their oldest son left the farm to find a job to feed his family, adding to the work of the remaining three. Running out of corn to feed their hogs was the final straw. Bankruptcy was their only option. After beginning proceedings, Meisgeier seemed happier and more at peace. His demeanor, however, masked anguish. One of his sons found him hanging in the machine shed.[23] Meisgeier was in the most endangered group of farmers: those over fifty. They had a lifetime in farming, could see very few options for themselves, and experienced the greatest risk for suicide.[24]

Deborah Bahe, Meisgeier's daughter, reflected on his depression and death. Her father had sunk into a pit of helplessness, not knowing where to turn. He felt a responsibility to his family, past and present, that he could not fulfill. Bahe wrote, "We tried to get dad help, but as dad felt, what could they do? He and mom were overwhelmed with debt, coupled with adversity. He was caught in the middle of his German ancestors settling the farm in 1865 and his next generation wanting to continue farming in the 1980s." His children could see how difficult the situation was and how he and Betty were scrimping and saving, struggling to get by. Then, "he took his life. Did he do it because he was so overwhelmed and depressed, or to access his life insurance to hang on to the farm? When he died there were two waves of shock. The first wave was that he <u>died</u>. The second wave was that he committed *suicide*. Our church, community, and friends, were a great source of support and strength." Although there was deep religious and social stigma surrounding suicide, Joan Blundall convinced the family to share their story, in the hope of helping others. It appeared first in the *Cedar Rapids Gazette*, followed by *Ladies' Home Journal* and the MacNeill-Lehrer News Hour on PBS.[25] The family's decision to share their story meant that thousands of people might be emboldened to ask for help.[26]

The need for support extended beyond the adults in farm families. Children, teenagers, and young adults also suffered. If a farm was under stress, that stress would affect every member of the family. In Iowa, the farmers with the worst debt-to-asset ratio were young, averaging forty-five years of age. Most of them had children at home under the age of eighteen. These families reported high levels of stress on a daily basis.[27] Parents transferred their anxiety to their children, who felt the weight of problems well beyond their control. Adult quarrels had children hiding in their rooms, and threatened repossessions had them running for cover when there were "unexpected knocks on the farmhouse door."[28] They heard what their parents and other adults were saying and responded. A farm woman from Cresco, writing to the governor, described the way in which the crisis was affecting her young son. She wrote, "This morning my son (7 yrs) asked why the President doesn't love the farmers." The youngster had listened to the news and heard that the president was asking Congress for military aid for American allies. The same president was not providing aid for farmers like his parents. Hence, the child had come to believe that President Reagan did not care about people like him. As the boy's mother wrote, "I really don't know what to tell him."[29]

Stress also found its expression in children's behavior. Another mother wrote a nine-page letter to the governor, detailing her family's trouble with lenders. The family had two boys, ages twelve and thirteen, and a girl, age three. The three-year-old was the least affected. Her mother wrote, "Our 3-year-old is a sweetheart. Gets 5 minutes of my undivided attention a day but adjusts to it—although hurt. She's learned her numbers—I know not where or how. I've lost 5 months of the precious third year of my last child." The little girl was oblivious to her parents' problems but missed her mother's attention. The two boys were far more aware of their farm's situation. The thirteen-year-old, faced with parents who had to work off farm to keep the family afloat, had stepped up and taken an adult role. His mother described his efforts: "Our 13-year-old son has done all of the spring field work with the exception of corn-planting, besides being a top student, active in 4-H, band, jazz band, choir, swing choir, Little League baseball—also does the majority of feed grinding for the livestock." The twelve-year old's reactions were less positive. "Our 12-year-old son has gone from being an average student and fantastic livestock man to an absolute horror: failing grades, irresponsibility to chores, discipline problem. . . . This son has been 'pulling' pigs for years, pulled several calves this year when we were gone on farm business, has an uncanny ability to sense 'problems' with animals." Their mother knew that the family crisis was taking a toll: "Each son has shown his way of coping with our situation. One good, one bad—hard to help when we struggle to keep each other going." In the fight to keep the farm alive, the children were falling through the cracks, coping in whatever ways they could with deep family stress. Their parents needed them to be mature beyond their years.[30]

Other young people made their own concerns known. Christopher Siebens, a student at Akron-Westfield community school, wrote to the governor as an assignment for a civics class. He wanted to know what the outlook for agriculture was, and how the federal government was going to address farmers' problems. His interest was personal: "I plan to follow in my fathers [sic] footsteps. My father is currently engaged in farming and is also on the board of directors for the Iowa Farm Bureau. . . . The land we farm and live on was owned and farmed by my grandfather and if I start to farm I would definitely classify our farm as a family farm."[31] He wanted reassurance that he would be able to pursue his dreams.

Some, like Siebens, were concerned; others, however, were distraught. Another young man, a farmer's son from southern Iowa, wrote to tell the governor about his family's troubles. Environmental conditions meant that "our country has been practically destroyed for 3 to 4 years and this year it looks like its [sic] going to be like that again." His father's farm was on the verge of disaster. The youngster wrote, "If we don't get some money one of these days we're going to have to move." His family's pain was his pain. He was working hard and pouring everything he had into his father's acres. He asked the governor to imagine his predicament: "Do you really know what its [sic] like to have to work day after day, and then still not be able to do what you want with your money. I do." Rather than struggling, he wanted, for "once in your life [to] be able to do something you've always wanted to do."[32] Another young man, slightly older, realized he had chosen a bad time to get into agriculture. After high school, he had foregone higher education to begin farming, without access to inherited land. Now twenty-three, he pondered the possibilities: "Is there any helps for a young person who wants to start into farming, and see it as a real life-time reality? This is my 3rd going on 4th year of farming. I guess I am starting to face the facts of what could happen."[33] These were complicated years for young people on farms. They had to think carefully about what they wanted, sometimes with the knowledge that their dreams were out of reach. No matter how hard they worked, they might not be able to achieve their aspirations.

Food Assistance

Farm families' needs extended from the emotional to the material. In 1984 the number of families turning toward food assistance programs multiplied. These were not the farms of the early twentieth century, where families had a primary goal of feeding themselves in addition to producing for the market.[34] In the 1980s, in general, farm families no longer expended a great deal of energy on their subsistence needs. These were farms where families produced primarily, if not entirely, for the market. Some still slaughtered pigs and chickens, hunted, and raised large gardens, but most no longer provided for themselves the majority of their food. In the early 1980s, Paul Lasley, who taught rural sociology at Iowa State University in addition to working for Extension, presented his findings about economic decline in rural communities and the need to be prepared to respond to hungry people to the Iowa Institute of Cooperatives. He told his audience that the time had come to think about food pantries and other emergency measures to combat hunger in the countryside. The response to his presentation ranged from cool to downright hostile. At the end of his talk, Lasley remembered, "two people in the audience came up to me and one started thumping me on the chest with his pointed finger saying, 'We're going to have your goddamned job over this.'"[35] Not everyone wanted to hear about hard times in the countryside and what it might mean at farmers' kitchen tables.

There was something quite shocking about the idea of Iowa's farm people going hungry. At a fundamental level, people believed it could not and should not happen in America's agricultural heartland. Farmers were supposed to grow food, not lack food. They were supposed to be independent, resilient, and self-sufficient, or at least that is what the mythology surrounding agriculture proclaimed. The mythology met reality in the 1980s, and the reality was that many rural people needed food. The reality also was that farm people were reluctant to admit their needs and ask for help.

Volunteer efforts provided food to some families who overcame their resistance and asked. A combination of practicality and humanitarian concern formed the basis of Food for Life. Paul Ehmcke, an O'Brien County pork producer, founded the program in 1981. One of his hogs had separated its shoulder, making it unfit for commercial slaughter and he had already slaughtered his family's meat for the year. The animal needed to be processed quickly. He offered the hog to a local minister who ran an after-school nutrition program for children. Out of those circumstances, Food for Life was born. Farmers contributed animals and donations from churches paid the costs of processing the meat. Local committees, working through community groups, determined eligibility guidelines. By 1984 Ehmke was out doing the rounds of Farm Bureau women's clubs, drumming up support for his program.[36]

Home economists in the agricultural extension service were also thinking about ways in which the gap between income and needs could be met. They suggested the creation of emergency food pantries as a partial solution. Commonplace in the twenty-first century, these pantries were somewhat novel in the 1980s. A 1984 pamphlet from the Take Charge in Changing Times series laid out the process, step by step. A food pantry could be a simple cupboard in a church basement or a clearinghouse for information on assistance. Extension emphasized the importance of building a volunteer base and establishing reliable sources of food within the community. As they suggested, "by involving as many community members and groups as possible, you can ensure regular food contributions as well as a continuous source of volunteer help." They encouraged involving as many community organizations as possible in the publicity network: "A food pantry is worthless if the people who need it don't know about it."[37] It would also be worthless if people were ashamed to ask for help. Going to a food pantry required a family to make their needs known within the community.

If families could get past the shame, they could also stand in line for surplus commodities. One of the federal programs born of agricultural excess was the distribution of foods such as cheese, rice, flour, honey, and dried milk. In the early 1980s, surplus foods became available to needy families. At times, the USDA could not provide the distribution infrastructure for commodities and threatened to cut off the supply. Pressure from members of Congress and state agencies, combined with an extensive network of volunteers, meant that in 1983 and 1984, over $33 million in surplus food flowed into Iowa. The state made use of an army of volunteers, forty-six hundred strong, for all stages of the distribution program. Charles Palmer, deputy commissioner of Iowa's Department of Human Services, commented, "I don't claim the food distribution program has kept anyone from starving... but it does help thousands of Iowans to stretch their budgets and eat a little better than they could otherwise afford to."³⁸ The food went to both urban and rural Iowans.

Standing in line for free government cheese could meet some of the nutritional needs of Iowa's farm families, but not all of them. Another possibility, again if families could bring themselves to do so, was to sign up for food stamps, the USDA's program that provided funds for food to low-income individuals and families. Enrolling needy farming families for food stamps became both a political and a humanitarian act, encouraged by the IFUC and Catholic Rural Life. One of the first food stamp drives for farmers happened in Union and Taylor Counties in 1984, just before Christmas. Hundreds of farmers arrived at courthouses in both counties to pick up the sixteen-page applications. Those at the courthouse in Creston were wearing black armbands and the church bells tolled as the farmers streamed into the courthouse. Chuck Ryan, a spokesperson for Catholic Rural Life commented, "We have the start of an agricultural funeral in Iowa." It was also an opportunity to explain to reporters that times had changed and that hungry farm families were not able to feed themselves in the same ways as they had in the past. As Phil Britten, a local farmer, stated, "We can't kill our livestock as in the old days because it's written down on an inventory note for the bank."³⁹

The emphasis of those who organized food stamp drives was somewhat different than that of Extension. While Extension personnel would refer farm families who needed food aid to the appropriate resources, their larger goal was to get farmers to run the numbers, assess their position, and to make the next step, which might be to reorganize their operation or leave the farm. This was not the route that organizations such as the IFUC, Rural America, and Catholic Rural Life encouraged. These groups hoped to help farm families gather enough resources to hang on and fight to keep their farms.

Denise O'Brien, a farmer and activist who helped to organize the IFUC, recalled attending meetings that included Extension speakers:

> There was a meeting in particular that I remember in Elk Horn, Iowa, where I gave my presentation about how the tables had been turned and the farmers had become the victims only to be followed by an Iowa State Extension expert who told people that there is life after farming. One can imagine my frustration with this message after I had spent the previous forty-five minutes trying to rally people to actively protest.

Denise O'Brien worked through the Iowa Farm Unity Coalition to encourage farmers to fight to keep their land. Denise O'Brien Papers, Iowa Women's Archives, University of Iowa Libraries.

Extension had undermined her position. O'Brien walked the walk. Her own farm's computer assisted financial analysis for 1984 showed a negative income of $607. Numbers of that sort did not necessarily demonstrate that a farm was recoverable; she and her husband, however, took food stamps and kept on fighting.[40]

Speaking Up for Farmers

Organizing farmers to sign up for food stamps publicly was but one form of agricultural advocacy. Voices being raised on behalf of beleaguered farmers increased in 1984, and sometimes came from unusual sources. Someone, and it is entirely unclear who, decided to organize a letter drive by northwest Iowa bankers and business people on behalf of local farmers. That spring, they wrote to any elected official who would listen, asking that they take "immediate action" to stop the bleeding. J. Mark Dominy, a bank official from Larchwood, told the governor that farmers in his community "are in the worst financial conditions since the great depression." Arlan Draayer, president of the Sioux Feed Company and director of the Iowa Grain and Feed Association, pleaded for lower interest rates, saying, "We need your help desperately!" His business was on the line: "This past six months, I have lost $19,000 to uncollectable debt and I know there is another $12,000.00 that might be uncollectable. These people have lost or are losing their farms. Again, Please consider *all* alternatives to lower interest rates." John De Groot, a realtor and auctioneer from Hull, expressed his bewilderment.

> I am sorry I can't give you a solution to this catastrophe. It would seem to me that something could be of help. More farm land has been put on the market in the last six months, then [sic] we had listed in the past three years. I usually don't write letters to the people that represent us. However, I feel the time has come to appeal to you people, because we are in deep trouble.

Bette Hanson, owner of Hanson's Fabrics in Inwood, was also feeling the pain and asking for help. "Big business does not walk through my doors, farm wives do. As president of Inwood Commercial Club, I am concerned about our town. Most of our business comes from farm people. Farm people do not have money to spend. SO GO THE FARMERS, SO GOES THE TOWNS."[41] Every letter writer reinforced a single message: a farm crisis affected more than farms. Its ripples extended to bankers, implement dealers, fabric shop owners, and anyone who did business in rural communities.

Farm groups papered the offices of their elected officials with petitions. In northwest Iowa, 384 citizens affixed their signatures to a petition calling for interest rates to be lowered to 5 to 6 percent, a measure the signers believed "will offer us an opportunity to make a comeback."[42] In Bedford, in far southern Iowa, ninety-nine citizens came together to share their ideas. They asked, "Why is talk so cheap? We cannot continue to ignore this problem, like the ostrich who sticks his head in the sand. Our rural economy will not improve until State government, Federal government, and the Federal Reserve Board change policies." They asked for lower interest rates and more lenient disaster loan policies for farmers in their community. The leaders of the Bedford group also polled those at their meetings to find out just how difficult their economic situations were. No one said their condition was good. The vast majority, 73 percent, said their circumstances were serious, while another 7 percent said they were in imminent danger of foreclosure or forced (involuntary) sale. When asked about the sources of their problems, 69 percent refused to pinpoint one particular problem but said that their troubles resulted from a combination of low commodity prices, high real estate taxes, high interest rates, weather, and deflation of land and machinery values. Tucked into the bottom of the survey was a tellingly worded question: "If you were in a position to issue farm policy and legislation, where would you start? (Be realistic—we cannot bomb the Secretary of Agriculture's headquarters!)"[43] The farmers of Bedford were not fans of Agriculture Secretary John Block.

Farming people also engaged in individual activism, making the difficult choice to lay bare their situations and confess their difficulties to people in government. Letters came from men, women, and children, but women's letters were particularly long, detailed, and passionate. While on one hand, these letters can be viewed as statement of conditions and difficulties, they can also be read in a different way. In the face of disaster, women took on the role of spokesperson for their families. They kept the books and were laying open their troubles to people in government. In many ways, the farm women who wrote these letters were attempting to justify themselves against possible criticism, demonstrating their adherence to a set of agrarian values that prioritized endurance, thrift, and above all, hard work. For these women, letter writing served as a form of last-ditch farm advocacy, an important part of their caretaking roles in their families. Their letters were an attempt to make sense of difficult family situations and to fight emotional battles. In the midst of an economic crisis that only seriously affected a portion of Iowa's farmers, writing letters allowed women to wage war against rumor and innuendo, justifying the choices they and their families had made both in better and crisis times.

Typically, the women's letters began with recitations of hardships. They were desperate and had hit bottom before asking for help. For example, the Urbans, of rural Cherokee, had been through years of negotiations with lenders, and were now facing the possibility of a forced sale, despite their hard work both on and off the farm.[44] Another central Iowa farm woman wrote the governor that she and her husband had been tussling with high interest rates (up to 24 percent at times) that had pushed them into a possible foreclosure with Norwest Bank. Their predicament was compounded by her arthritis and his severe depression, which required hospitalization. She wrote, "I believe we need time to make these major decisions." Appealing to the governor was her last option, but "I don't feel we can submit until we have exhausted every possible source of help."[45] The Swestka family, of Cresco, had faced bad weather and low prices and were now unable to get their loan officer to meet with them. Joyce Swestka provided dates of cancelled appointments, documenting a situation that had spiraled out of the family's control.[46] These women told stories that would have been familiar to many Iowans.

The letter writers did not stop with tales of woe. Women also were careful to include evidence of their frugality, establishing their families' worthiness and virtue. These discussions served several purposes. Tales of thrift located these women's stories firmly within older traditions of rural Iowa. These women, like generations of farm women before them, knew how to tighten their belts and pinch pennies. They knew how to make do and do without. What their mothers and grandmothers had done during the Great Depression, they were willing to do a half-century later.[47]

Their discussions also served to counter another narrative of the Farm Crisis: that those facing hard times were doing so because of their lack of frugality. Many, including some farmers, believed that families in trouble had frivolously spent themselves into catastrophe. Not so, the women argued. By telling the governor about the extremes to which they were willing to go to save money, they reinforced their view of themselves and buttressed their claims to aid from the state. Mrs. Raymond Anderson, of Boone, prefaced her discussion by telling the governor that in thirty-eight years of farming, she and her husband had "*never* [been] able to even have a vacation—*not one.*" She balanced this against the evidence of her husband's virtues: "My husband has been a survivor. He survived the '30s depression, Pearl

Harbor, the D-day invasion when he landed on Omaha Beach 40 years ago, last year he had quintuple by-pass heart surgery and now this farm debt crisis is about to take its toll on our way of life."[48] Mrs. Anderson laid claim to aid by emphasizing thrift in tandem with service to the country.

The Urban family did not tell a tale of persistence in the face of depression and war, but they did demand credit for a level of frugality that they believed was less common to families in cities and towns. Mrs. Urban wrote, "We were (and still are) on our second used car in 16 years of marriage. In that time our only new furniture we'd bought were a chair and a cheap [Montgomery Wards] bedroom set for our 2 young sons as they outgrew cribs. Our one indulgement [sic] was for a fold down camper in 1974 . . . We now eat out once every 3–4 months at a fast-food place." The list went on: they never bought clothing at more than half price, their home had only a total of four rooms for five people, and Mrs. Urban "never had less than an acre garden, canning and freezing all season long." Her husband worked the farm and a part-time job, while she did the bookkeeping, helped outside, and held an off-farm job as a caterer.[49] Joyce Swestka's story was similar. She wrote, "I raise chickens and also work for an insurance agency. I help my husband with field & farm work. We do all the work ourselves. We have 2 children 7 and 4. I've always taken [them] with me in the field in spring and fall to save money by not getting a babysitter to watch them." The couple had also opened a feed store, hoping to bring in some additional funds. She asserted, "As you can tell we work, work, work, we love our farm and we hope and pray we'll be one of the few that will survive."[50]

These letters to the governor were symbolic acts. Unfortunately, the responses that flowed from the office of the governor back to the writers were largely symbolic as well. The state had limited resources and ability to aid farm families facing foreclosure. Most of the return letters from the governor's office followed a formula: an expression of sadness and acknowledgment of the writer's pain, a discussion of the attempts the governor was making to bring the state's problems to the attention of the federal government, and a discussion of what he hoped to do in the future to improve the agricultural economy. There was reassurance that the governor understood that their problems were real and that he did not blame them for their situations. The governor's special assistant, Keith Heffernan, often closed with words such as these: "Please know that the Governor is very much aware of the current problems that many farm operators are facing and is doing everything he can to alleviate the problem. When the Governor speaks in regard to the farm situation, he is speaking from his heart because of his agriculture background and his deep commitment to the people of Iowa."[51] The notations on the return letters sometimes showed further action. In one case, the governor asked the state FmHA director to review and report to his office about a couple's problems with the loan office. In another, the governor called the family to listen and talk. An aide scrawled across the correspondence, "Talk to Gov—Is there something Minnesota is doing we should be?" This may have been a reference to the Minnesota legislature's 1983 vote in favor of a mortgage foreclosure moratorium, or perhaps its 1984 creation of a Farm Advocate Program, which provided farmers help with budgeting and understanding their legal rights, in addition to providing representatives to accompany them to meetings with lenders.[52]

Historian Jenny Barker Devine has written about the economic activism of Iowa farm women in the post–World War II era who were willing to step outside of their traditional roles to fight for the survival of their family enterprises.[53] In the 1980s letters flowing out from Iowa's farm women were also activism on behalf of the family farm. With little left to lose, they wrote their governor to ask for mercy. Sometimes they demanded it. They took on the emotionally difficult work of explaining to public officials their needs, often with little hope of aid. The governor's office, having little to give in return, reassured them that they had been heard, acknowledged their pain, and passed no judgement on their circumstances. Essentially, the response was a recognition that these letters were an integral part of the emotional work that farm women did on behalf of their struggling families.

Penny Auctions in the '80s

Activism also took the form of protests at farm auctions. The 1980s saw a sharp rise in forced auctions, undertaken when a bank or other lending agent required a family to sell its property. These were unlike other auctions, which happened when a farmer voluntarily quit the business, usually at the end of a career in agriculture. Taking their cues from the "penny auctions" of the 1930s, protestors planned to attend involuntary farm sales in order to disrupt them and prevent significant bidding. Historian William Pratt identified the first of the decade's penny auctions, which took place in Westbrook, Minnesota, in August 1982. Citizens Organizing Acting Together (COACT) organized the protest, although other groups joined. Activists promoting the use of penny auctions consciously modelled their actions on those of 1930s protesters. Pratt argued that they did this as a means of

This farmer held a cross at an auction to indicate that he was attending in support of the family and would not be bidding. Photograph by Bill Gillette, by permission of the State Historical Society of Iowa.

legitimizing their action. He wrote, "They wanted to publicize that farmers had protested before, and that those protests had helped."[54] The idea moved south, from Minnesota to Iowa.

In June 1984, 200 people gathered at Orville and Joan Luedtke's farm in Lucas County, and many of them were there to protest rather than purchase. Rural America and the IFUC worked out a strategy in advance, and hoped to keep the bidding to a minimum. They divided into committees, each covering a different part of the sale, but all with the goal of forcing a failed auction. Some would meet auction-goers at the gate. Their job would be to explain the Luedtke's situation, and to ask that attendees "(please)" not bid. People who had agreed not to bid wore red armbands. Members of the watch committee observed the crowd and discouraged bidding, but politely. Their instructions included the following: "*PLEASE*, make *NO INTIMIDATING* or *THREATENING* remarks of *ANY KIND*. Attempt to have non-threatening manner at all times!" The media committee worked with the television and newspaper reporters. The bidding committee hoped to be alone in placing bids, since the IFUC discouraged everyone else from obtaining an auction number. They planned to shame anyone making serious bids with calls to identify and explain themselves. The law and order committee discouraged violence and escorted disorderly people from the auction. Meanwhile, the undercover committee circulated through the crowd, assisting in any way possible. The goal was a sale where only the protestors made exceptionally low bids.[55]

The day of the auction began hopefully. The farm was south of Des Moines, but some protestors came all the way from Minnesota. At the beginning of the auction, the Luedtkes announced that this was a forced sale. They read a statement to the assembled crowd which began, "We are gathered here today to witness the death of a family farm." While the IFUC aimed for a penny auction, the auctioneer and some of the assembled buyers did not agree. Auctioneer Wilbur Veenstra refused low bids. He told the crowd that they would hurt the Luedtkes more than help them. One of the family's sons was able to purchase about 40 pieces of his father's machinery for $25,000, less than half of its worth, but much more than he had anticipated spending. Orville Luedtke planted that spring, and hoped to work out an agreement with his creditors that would allow him to remain on his farm. He told a reporter, "We're still here, fighting the obstacles."[56] Protesters could not save farms if auctioneers and all those attending declined cooperation.

Agriculture at the Movies

The fall of 1984 offered Iowans many opportunities to reflect on the struggles happening throughout the state. In October the state enjoyed a much-anticipated event, the release of *Country*. Farm movies flooded the screen in 1984. *The River*, starring Sissy Spacek and Mel Gibson, told the story of a couple fighting against economic conditions and the environment to save their Tennessee farm. In *Places in the Heart*, set in the Great Depression, a Southern widow, played by Sally Field, battled the elements, a cotton merchant, and a banker to hold on to her land.[57] *Country*, however, was Iowa's film. The movie even premiered in Des Moines. Starring Jessica Lange and Sam Shepard, *Country* followed the fictional fortunes of the Ivy family, with wife, Jewell, and husband, Gil, and revolved around the downward spiral of the farm. The couple had taken out significant loans in the 1970s, when the farm was worth $2,500 an acre. In the early 1980s, with the farm worth half as much, the FmHA gave them thirty days' notice and called in their $96,000 loan.

The film followed Gil's implosion, as he gave in to paralysis, alcohol, and anger, as well as Jewell's decision to fight for her family's farm. Indeed, it was *her* family's farm, as her husband had married into the 180 acres they worked. There were four climactic scenes in the film. In the first, a neighbor, distraught over his farm's impending foreclosure, killed himself. In the second, the pressures eating Gil Ivy led to a fistfight with his son, as well as his wife, ending with her smashing him over the head with a board and throwing him off her land. The third was the farm auction, shut down by angry neighbors and cries of "no sale." In the final scene, the couple apparently reconciled. From the cost-price squeeze, to indebtedness, to the mental health concerns and family stress accompanying hard times, *Country* led its viewers through the pressures pushing so many farmers toward economic collapse, in an unglamorous way.[58]

The movie's unvarnished look certainly appealed to Iowans. In *Country*, they saw themselves. Some drove many miles to attend the premier. Verlan Rouw of Macksburg proclaimed the movie "more than fair" in its portrayal of families and their struggles. Rouw's son, a recent high-school graduate who farmed with his father, praised the film for its realistic treatment of the pressures facing farm children.[59] *Country* moved the reviewer for *Farm Journal* to tears. He wrote, "Men and women alike cried, including this reviewer, who has never cried at a movie in his life." What appealed to him was the movie's true-to-life view of the circumstances facing many farm people. He interviewed the Schweins, who farmed just twelve miles from the film's location. They commented, "We know exactly what the Ivys were going through, except to us it's the real thing." The only problem with *Country*, in their estimation, was its happy ending: "It made you feel like the Ivys' troubles were over when they weren't. I know our troubles are far from over."[60]

Filmed at an abandoned farmhouse near Dunkerton, the setting was muddy and appropriate to a family living on $9,000 a year. Roughly one hundred people in the film were, in fact, Black Hawk County farm people. The young man who played the Ivys' son, Levi Knebel, was a local who gave up his place on the football team to appear in the film. Jim Ostercamp, who played a neighbor's developmentally disabled son, was a Waterloo resident, as were the twin girls who played the Ivy family's baby daughter. The craggy, weather-beaten folks who nearly turned over the auctioneer's car were also local and acted the scene with vigor.[61] The film, like the situation, as one reviewer put it, was "far from being happy or upbeat." This was no escapist version of the crisis but an immersion in the pain bombarding farm families and communities. Only the Iowa countryside, in a bleak and wintry way, was beautiful.

Despite its grim content, Iowans loved the movie, and reviewers from farm publications were cautiously optimistic about what it might do to help resolve the crisis. As Eleanor Jacobs of the *Farm Wife News* put it, "Perhaps what's best about *Country* is the effect it will have on millions of city people who view it—it will help them understand the hard work and long hours that farmers and ranchers put in to produce the food many people take for granted. And on a more current basis, it will help them understand the financial plight being faced by many of today's families." The reviewer for the *Des Moines Register* was equally hopeful that the movie might hit home with urban audiences. "Moviegoers in these parts no doubt will watch it with typical Midwestern defensiveness, wondering whether urban brethren, tuned in to car chases and fast street life in movies and only dimly aware of the connectedness of farm life with city survival, will be reached by this powerful, low-key, true film." She concluded, "A city audience that isn't reached by the unromanticized realities of *Country* probably cannot *be* reached."[62] The movie ended with Gil and Jewell reconciling, and just as importantly, with white words on black film. Viewers read that in 1984, a North Dakota judge had certified a class action lawsuit against the FmHA for, among other things, its failure to allow farmers to apply for loan deferrals under existing FmHA rules.[63] This was, in fact, true, and the court had given beleaguered farmers facing FmHA foreclosures a tool to forestall auctions. Thus, *Country* allowed its viewers to walk away from a grim film on a vaguely hopeful note. The Ivy family had a fighting chance to hold onto their farm.

NOW THAT YOU HAVE SEEN *Country*
WHAT SHOULD YOU DO?

Join the Fight for America's Family Farmers!

America's farmers and rural communities are in a period of serious economic and social crisis, unparalleled since the Great Depression. The deteriorating farm economy of the 1980's has already forced thousands of farm families off the land, ruined many small town businesses, and contributed to high unemployment in our cities, for America's farmers are the hub of the largest sector of our nation's economy. As more families are driven from the land, the possibility for greater control over food and marketing by the relatively few looms on the horizon. Whether we live in the city, the suburbs, or the countryside, we must realize that the continuing tragedy of rural America — the erosion of our fields and small communities, the destruction of family farming, the forced sale of family farm operations and the growing concentration of land ownership — should concern us all.

Help Support a Grassroots Solution to the Farm Crisis...

RURAL AMERICA, INC. is proud to have served as technical advisor to "Country". For 15 years we have supported farmers and rural citizens with housing, transportation, & health care needs. Now, in response to the rise in farm foreclosures, a Midwest "Farm Crisis Project" is in operation. When farmers lose their farms, they lose more than their jobs. RURAL AMERICA is committed to keeping agriculture diversified and the productive family farm alive in America.

The North American Farm Alliance is a coalition of farm, church, trade unions and community groups from the United States and Canada. The Alliance provides a variety of services to its member organizations including research, advocacy and referrals. With your support and help the Alliance will continue to be a clear, strong voice for family farm agriculture.

For More Information and to Send Your Tax-Deductible Contributions Contact:

RURAL AMERICA — Farm Crisis Project
550 11th Street, Suite 200
Des Moines, Iowa 50309

North American Farm Alliance
3255 Hennepin Ave. South, Suite 252
Minneapolis, Minnesota 55408

Printing and Distribution of this flyer has been made possible through the help of Clergy and Laity Concerned. Contact CALC, 198 Broadway, New York, NY 10038.

Country became a rallying cry and educational tool for organizations of various types, including activist, farm, and educational groups. PrairieFire Collection, by permission of Iowa State University Library Special Collections and University Archives.

Between Hope and Despair

Iowa's farmers were hovering somewhere between hope and despair in the fall of 1984. As the leaves turned, Paul Lasley at Iowa State University carried out his biannual "Farm and Rural Life Poll." In a random selection of 1,585 farm families, the results were a mixed bag. There was uneasiness in the air, but not everyone was willing to admit uneasiness about their own operations. When asked "how do you feel about the current financial condition of Iowa farmers," 67 percent felt there was a serious problem, and 25 percent a moderate problem. They also perceived that agribusiness was in trouble, with 79 percent gauging it as moderate to serious trouble; 47 percent believed that lenders were in an equal amount of distress. When asked specifically if they were concerned about their own farm, 42 percent were very much so, and 24 percent moderately. Those with the highest debt levels were more likely to be worried about themselves, other farmers, agribusiness, and lenders. Debt, for good reason, created doubt and anxiety. Given high levels of stress, the poll revealed a surprising fact: farmers were still glad to be farmers. A majority were satisfied with their jobs and 72 percent said that, given the choice again, they would continue to farm. On the other hand, 44 percent indicated that they would not recommend farming to a friend, and another 27 percent was undecided.[64]

Unfortunately, as the year progressed, farmers had seen numerous new wrinkles in their confusing situation. One of the first lenders to experience trouble had been the FmHA. By the middle of 1984, the Production Credit Association was pushing customers for repayment.[65] Farmers in trouble who planned to sell part of their assets in order to forestall their creditors discovered yet another problem: taxes. The sale of land, livestock, or machinery might result in significant capital gains taxes, even if all of the receipts from the sale went to creditors. Getting off the farm, or scaling back, could mean owing money to the government, rather than (or in addition to) the bank or another lending institution.[66] This realization could cause desperation. Radical groups, such as the National Agricultural Press Association (which actually had nothing to do with the mainstream agricultural press), were muddying the waters, arguing that farmers could thwart their lenders with "common law liens." In essence, they told farmers that their labor and time constituted a legal claim on the land that creditors could not overcome. Desperate farmers then went to court and discovered that the legal system did not recognize these claims.[67] As the number of indebted farmers rose, the number of desperate appeals also rose. Without greater skills in finance and risk management, surviving on the farm was going to be a precarious proposition.[68] As conditions deteriorated, some farmers got a bit of grim satisfaction from the situation of Agriculture Secretary John Block. Earlier in 1984 the news reported that Block, too, faced significant trouble. He and various of his partners in agricultural businesses owed millions of dollars. The editors at *Wallace's Farmer* hoped that Block's situation would help him to better understand farmers' need for relief, but they were not counting on it.[69]

The Election of 1984

In 1984 Iowans had to decide whom to support in a presidential election. It was not an easy choice. Although many had turned their back on Carter and voted for Reagan in 1980, they were less sure they would support him again in 1984. They had issues they wanted addressed first. While farmer Philip Britten of rural Creston wrote to Reagan to thank him for what he had done to turn around "the economic chaos" that the nation had endured under Carter, he was suffering so much that he was unable to come up with the $15 to become a sustaining member of the Republican National Committee. In a letter he wrote to Reagan but gave to the governor to deliver, he made a demand: "If I may quote yet another phrase from your letter, 'I am counting on you to stand by me,' and initiate some action from your office directed at correcting this injustice so that I may remain a productive member of society and continue my all important work of producing food for the people of our nation, on the land that my forefathers homesteaded."[70] His letter demanded action, rather than providing support. Donald Albert, of tiny Randalia, population 101, invited the president to visit his farm when he came to Iowa. He had grown weary of waiting for the president to notice there was a problem in agriculture. "I am aware that you have been unable to devote much time to the farm issue so it is necessary to channel the responsibility to a committee or a cabinet or to the Sec. of Agriculture. By this procedure our needs are not being met. The time has come for you to get personally involved. You must get a first hand [sic] report by visiting with these farmers." Albert offered to escort the president, so he would have the opportunity to visit with his neighbors, "many of whom are facing foreclosure, bankruptcy or liquidation of much of their property."[71] David Noller, of rural Sigourney, was more direct in his criticism. He wrote to the governor, "Having suffered through four export embargoes during the 1970s I felt that President

Ronald Reagan and his people would be our salvation but I was wrong. In the past three years I have watched a malignant indifference toward agriculture set in in our government and unless it is corrected in the near future all the philosophies I have worked for in my lifetime will have been for naught."[72] Charges of malignant indifference did not sound like an endorsement of the president's policies, or a vote in his favor come November.

A farm woman, who had many questions for her governor, also wanted to know for whom she should vote. She noted that she had "nothing but praise for our local Congressman and Senator, they care not whether we are Republican or Democrat." While she supported her Republican governor, she was not planning on voting for Reagan. Her commentary on his politics was brief: "He has no time or inclination to help the farmer. Recognizes not that it was government borrowing and deficit spending that forced our interest rates up and lost the small amount of profit left in farming. The cost of one missile would help many of us." She also disapproved of John Block, condemning him because he "refuses to take a stand for the farmer in need—claims those in trouble got there by 'greed.' . . . The PIK program only helped the wealthy and the large grain farmers in our area . . . the livestock farmer is never included in programs anyway." Her choice in the election would have been easier if she believed that the Democratic candidate offered more. She dismissed Democratic hopeful Walter Mondale: "Promises all to everyone. To keep all promises, there goes government spending again."[73] Like many rural Iowans, she was examining her choices but felt little confidence in any of them.

As the election drew closer, both Reagan and Mondale turned their attention to farm country. Both included debt relief measures in their campaign promises. Reagan's plan, which looked remarkably like one introduced in the House of Representatives by Iowa congressman Jim Leach, entailed rescheduling and deferral of some debts, forgiveness of portions of some private loans in exchange for FmHA guarantees, and formation of assistance teams at the county level to help farmers and lenders restructure debt. Reagan also took out full-page ads in agricultural publications such as *Wallace's Farmer*, reminding farm voters that "Mondale was an active full-time partner in the failed policies of the prior administration that pushed farmers to the ground," while on the other hand arguing that he was committed to agriculture. In bold, the ad proclaimed: "His leadership is working for farmers." Not everyone was buying the message. Cy Carpenter, president of the National Farmers Union commented, "The same president denied the use of $600 million in FmHA emergency funds appropriated by Congress." For his part,

Mondale also proposed the use of management teams at the county level to work with farmers with credit problems, in addition to calling for a 180-day moratorium on FmHA foreclosures, a measure that would have affected 80,000 of approximately 280,000 borrowers.[74] Agricultural economist Neil Harl called the attention to farm troubles "heartening." The significance of Reagan's attention to debt relief was "that it sends the message to Congress and the American people that agriculture does indeed have a serious problem. As recently as July, there wasn't a person in the entire USDA or elsewhere in the administration who would admit that a problem exists."[75] Indeed, in July, one of Iowa's Republican senators, Roger Jepsen, had ripped into USDA Deputy Under Secretary Kathleen Lawrence for claiming in hearings held in Indianola, Iowa, that the current agricultural situation was no worse than normal, simply business as usual.[76]

Agriculture was also front and center in the senate race, which pitted Jepsen against Tom Harkin, who hoped to move from the US House to the Senate. Harkin campaigned hard on agricultural issues and even took Sally Field, star of farm movie *Places in the Heart*, with him on the campaign trail. In a June 1984 speech, Harkin laid out his plan for improving the agricultural situation. He called for disaster assistance, a program to restructure debt, both in the short and the long term, and increased attention to conservation. He also asked that the government support "family-farm agriculture" instead of large farmers, commenting that "future programs must concentrate on those we truly want to help." He argued that Iowa should focus on combining agriculture and technology: "If we do so, we in Iowa are more likely to have a vital and dynamic economy in the future—one that will maximize our agricultural advantage and insure [sic] that our children can stay and prosper in Iowa."[77] Both Harkin and Jepsen courted the farm vote, but Jepsen was vulnerable. In the course of the campaign, the news broke that in 1977 Jepsen had joined a club in Des Moines that offered sex for sale. Harkin prevailed in an overwhelming win against Jepsen and received strong support from farm voters.[78] Reagan also won in Iowa, as part of a nationwide landslide, but Iowa voted for Reagan in proportionally lower numbers than the rest of the nation. This, perhaps, reflected the discomfort among farmers.[79] After four bad years, with no end in sight, farmers were splitting their tickets and choosing not to put their faith entirely in either party.

1984 Winds Down

It was an eventful fall, and a busy end to a difficult year. In November a service of "celebration, remembrance and hope" took place at the Church of the Land at Living History Farms in Urbandale, a suburb of Des Moines. It was the same place where Pope John Paul II had led worship in 1979. Leading this service was Bishop Maurice Dingman of the Catholic Diocese of Southwest Iowa, the Reverend Charles Morrow of the United Methodist Church, the Reverend David Ostendorf of the United Church of Christ and Rural America, and the Reverend Suzanne Peterson of the Episcopal Diocese of Iowa. They made an ecumenical call to support farms and farmers. The assembled worshippers recited:

> We seek to stand side by side with our neighbors who suffer personal loss as a result of the economic crisis on the land, and to bring to a halt once and for all the demise of family farm agriculture by supporting actions and policies that will bring about peaceful change in rural America. We seek to change institutions and conditions that contribute to the current tragedy of rural America—the erosion of our fields and small communities, the demise of family farming and the liquidation of family farm operations, the growing concentration of land ownership.[80]

The congregation paused, gave thanks, and prepared themselves for the coming year. Nineteen eighty-four had tested Iowa. It had begun with a barnyard full of dead cattle and ended with more questions than answers. Unfortunately, 1985 was going to be just as difficult, perhaps even worse.

CHAPTER FOUR

From Penny Auctions to a Declaration of Emergency: 1985

For the Book family of rural Story County, the year began on a terrible note. On January 3, eighty acres of their farm went on the auction block. They were the first Iowans of 1985 to lose land in a forced sale. Before the auction, the Books decided to make their situation public. The Iowa Farm Unity Coalition organized a protest and arranged for the *Des Moines Register* to cover the sale. Loren and Ruth Book appeared on the front page of the *Register*, clutching white crosses. A picture of a weeping Ruth Book appeared next to the story on page 6. The Books did not face their loss alone. A crowd of seventy people accompanied them. They gathered at Nevada's Presbyterian Church to pray before moving to the county courthouse to witness the sale. The protestors carried white crosses, which they pounded into the lawn at the courthouse, symbolizing families who had lost their land. The Story County sheriff prefaced the bidding with the comment, "This is kind of a tough situation. I realize that. Ruth Book grew up across the street from me." It was a virtually silent auction. There were no buyers among the crowd. The sheriff pulled an envelope from his pocket containing the single bid. The sale was over in minutes, with the Federal Land Bank paying $136,000 for the Book's acres.[1] The protestors lent emotional support, but they could not save the family's land.

Less than a week later, Ruth Book wrote to Governor Branstad, asking for a favor. "I heard you are going to Washington tomorrow," she wrote. "I'm a farm wife—I don't know how to solve the agriculture problems. But I do know the people in Washington can't feel the hurt that Iowa farmers are going through. Please take this copy of the January 4 *Register* to show them the anguish that farm families are going through." She continued, "One picture is worth a thousand words, right? The *Register*'s picture of us represents so much more than we could write. And we represent *many, many* hurting farm families. Since January 3 farm wives have been calling me, asking where to turn to get help." She pleaded with the governor, "Can you *please take the pictures to President Reagan?*" The governor did take the paper to Washington and showed it to the president, Paul Volcker, Bob Dole, and John Block. He hoped it would soften some hearts.²

Days later, on Tuesday, January 14, 1985, Governor Branstad went before the Iowa legislature to give his Condition of the State address. The IFUC transformed what was normally a humdrum event into a protest. Three hundred members of the organization packed the gallery, carrying signs and white crosses. The signs read "foreclosure moratorium now" and "stop forced farm sales." As at the Book protest, the crosses represented family farms lost to the debt crisis. The crowd stood silently throughout the governor's address. David Ostendorf, director of PrairieFire, held his breath. The success of the protest depended upon its solemnity. One shouted interruption would have destroyed its silent witness, but the quiet held. More than thirty years later, the governor remembered the gathering with a sense of awe.³

On that January day, Governor Branstad tried to reassure the gallery: "In Iowa, we are all tied to the land. When a tractor grinds to a halt in the farm field, the wheels of commerce move more slowly on Main Street. During the past year, many Iowans have shared with me their hardships and their fears. And looking at the galleries today, I can see, that many of these people are here who share those concerns with us." He wanted them to know that even though they were silent in their protest, he had been listening.

> My heart goes out to the families who have lost their farms and to the businesses who have seen their doors closed. A western Iowa farmer recently told me how federal liquidators had refused him the authority to purchase the feed needed to complete his hogs to market weight. I have heard from workers laid off by Caterpillar, Rath, and International Harvester—many of these Iowans are confused and they are afraid for their family's future.

Unlike others, he did not blame them for their economic condition. He described the crisis not as a set of personal failures but as the result of a system that had failed, saying, "These are good people, innocent victims of an economic storm which, although brewed elsewhere, struck here." He hoped to be able to do something to help them and shared details of his efforts: "I have put forward a comprehensive plan for an agricultural recovery. We need federal action to bring down interest rates and help farmers get through this immediate credit crunch—a situation that will only get worse between now and March first. The federal government should do for farmers what they did for Chrysler—provide loan guarantees to allow them to work out of this immediate credit crisis." The year was beginning on a somber note, and the distance between the situation farmers were experiencing and the improvements they wanted and needed was very wide indeed.

What the governor did not tell either Ruth Book or the assembled protestors was that his meetings in Washington had not gone well. While Douglas Gross, an aide to the governor, had reassured Book that "as a result of his trip, people in Washington are now at least aware of the serious agricultural crisis now affecting the heartland of America," the truth was that the president and other officials had not listened. In particular, the president's budget director, David Stockman, remained unmoved. In spite of a display of anger on Branstad's part, which included picking up and slamming down a chair for emphasis, he received a "brush-off" from Stockman. Stockman told the Iowa delegation that farmers had caused their own problems and that he had no intention of helping. And although President Reagan had promised farmers debt relief on the campaign trail, it would not be immediately forthcoming. If Stockman had his way, it would never come at all. At the end of January, John Block told farmers not to count on Washington for solutions—they were going to have to "tough it out."[4] It was looking more and more like Iowa's farmers were going to be struggling through 1985 without any commitments or support from the Reagan administration. If they were going to get help, it was going to be homegrown, or come from Congress.

The Rural Concern Hotline

Homegrown help meant different things to different groups. In the new year, a quarrel erupted with the governor's office and Extension on one side and the IFUC and its allies on the other. The central issue in the dispute was who spoke for farmers: the agricultural establishment or the activist groups that had been struggling for five years to aid farmers in distress?[5] The disagreement broke out over the decision by the Branstad administration to support Extension's creation of the Rural Concern Hotline. While the initial plan for the hotline had included cooperation with the IFUC, the final plan did not. The announcement in the new year of a project run by Extension alone caused the activists to bubble over with anger. Roz Ostendorf, director of the Iowa Interfaith Human Needs Council, penned the initial volley, in a letter to the governor. She had attended several meetings with the governor's Advisory Committee on Commodity Foods and Shelter and had been under the impression that funds for the IFUC's own volunteer hotline would be forthcoming. Instead, the Extension project cut them out. In spite of two years of experience fielding twenty-five hundred calls, the state had excluded the Farm Survival Hotline. She wrote, "I would like your answer as to why they have not been consulted and why do you think there should be *two* farm/rural Hotlines in Iowa?"[6] David Ostendorf, on behalf of the IFUC board, also wrote the governor, saying, "We interpret your move to establish this hotline in cooperation with the Extension Service as a blatant political act designed to supplant or replace the Coalition's Farm Survival Hotline. There is real irony in your decision and action." In 1984 IFUC and Rural America had asked for state aid and received a negative answer. There was, supposedly, no money available for both the Extension FarmAid program and a hotline. Now, there was money for an Extension hotline, but not for their existing one. They wanted to know why.[7]

The administrative discussion that went on before the governor's office responded to this criticism did, in fact, indicate that the decision was political. The governor's office gave credit to the IFUC for its work but was uncomfortable with the organization—which it viewed as being comprised of "the lower economic strata of farmers" and sitting on "the left side of the political spectrum"—managing a hotline on behalf of the state. Additionally, the coalition tended "to view the Extension Service as a part of the problem, as having advised farmers to become overextended." The coalition and the Farm Bureau were also on different sides of the political fence, and "the differences should not be glossed over." On the one hand, the governor's office believed that both the Farm Bureau and Extension were necessary to developing a state-funded hotline. On the other, the administration also argued that, given the coalition's political leanings, not every farmer would be comfortable calling its hotline for advice and support. The same would be true of an Extension hotline. The analysis continued: "If the real issue is avoiding a narrow political base for the Hotline, then it must be said that the Coalition's view of farm problems and solutions is attractive to some, scary to others, and a turnoff for others. The same is true of any one political perspective." Even with a difference in politics, the governor's advisors believed that nine times out of ten, both the IFUC and Extension hotlines would give farmers the same advice. The answer was to have two hotlines. The state would provide the Extension Rural Concern Hotline the lion's share of the funding, while giving the IFUC Farm Survival Hotline a much smaller sum. The governor's office viewed this as a win/win situation. The IFUC and its allies did not agree. In retrospect, however, David Ostendorf regretted the aid from the state and wished he had never accepted it. The reporting requirements for state funding were such that, in terms of time, it cost more than it was worth. There were benefits to running an all-volunteer organization.[8]

As this dispute illustrated, Iowa's farmers were not a single, undifferentiated mass. Their operations ranged from small to large, and their operators from poor to wealthy. Their political leanings were not uniform, either. Those who cast their lot with the IFUC supported an interventionist federal farm policy, which would provide price supports and production controls in an attempt to keep farmers with modest-sized operations on the land. In essence, they embraced the continuation of a New Deal approach to agriculture. They sought support from labor unions, such as the UAW, and the social justice-oriented Catholic Rural Life. Farm Aid, the nationwide, celebrity-driven fund-raising organization was, in general terms, aligned with the activist organizations such as the IFUC. Those who joined the Farm Bureau tended to farm more acres and be in favor of limited government controls and supports. They believed that government's role in agriculture was more of a problem than a solution, except in the case of the research emanating from the USDA and Extension and trade agreements that benefitted agriculture. This was not entirely the case, however, since many families joined the Farm Bureau in order to get insurance and other benefits.

People tended to lump the Farm Bureau and Extension together. The two organizations had formally split in the mid-1950s, but between World War I and World War II, the Farm Bureau had done much of the fund raising for Extension, and the two often shared an office. Farmers could be uncomfortable with Extension, given its position as an arm of the USDA, the agency that had in the 1970s told them to "get big or get out." Nevertheless, in the 1980s, Extension continued to offer its services to everyone, and in the midst of the crisis, many Extension employees worked as intermediaries between various competing groups. Quarrels, such as that over the hotline, often involved Extension personnel such as Paul Lasley as mediators. In truth, at any given moment, if anything was to be accomplished, the problems facing the state's farmers required the input of multiple sources of advocacy, the state, and Extension.[9]

The Crisis Deepens

Farmers' needs were growing. A survey taken by Extension in the spring of 1985 showed just how deeply the Farm Crisis was cutting into their cash flows. While only 10 percent of respondents had been unable to pay their property taxes, more than 70 percent had postponed major farm purchases. When it came to purchases associated with family living, the reductions were also significant. More than 70 percent had cut back on entertainment and social activities, and 65 percent had postponed major household purchases. Nearly 60 percent had dipped into their savings to meet day-to-day expenses. Fifty-six percent had changed their food shopping or eating habits in an attempt to save money. Some types of spending, however, families endeavored to maintain. They were far less likely to have cashed in their life insurance or postponed medical care.[10] Not surprisingly, the same poll found that stress levels among farmers had grown over the previous three years: 71 percent indicated that their stress levels had increased, and 32 percent said that they had increased significantly.[11]

Food remained a central problem for farm families struggling with debt. In the early months of 1985, the demand at Iowa's food banks was increasing and some rural food banks were having difficulty maintaining their supplies.[12] Administrators remained perplexed by farmers who were unable to feed themselves and their families. As Patrick McClintock, an administrator for Legal Services Corporation of Iowa commented, "Never in our wildest dreams did we think that we would have to deal with the [food] problems of farmers."[13] In general, Iowa's government and its people were in a reactive state—the crisis had caught them unprepared and it took some time to work out solutions.

Economic stress affected the food purchases of close to 60 percent of the state's farmers. Charities gave out more food than ever before. In 1985 in Pocahontas County, home to roughly ten thousand people, the Food for Life committee distributed more than four thousand pounds of meat to 572 families.[14] Other food charities opened their doors in 1985, such as Loaves and Fishes of Story City. In May 1985 Story City suffered a bank failure, another casualty of the agricultural collapse. A church project to provide food baskets to needy families blossomed into multichurch sponsorship of a food pantry to serve Story City, Roland, and Gilbert. Despite church involvement, the founders located the pantry at the Lakes Machinery building in Story City, so anyone in need would feel comfortable coming to the site.[15] It was but one of many food pantry projects inspired by the tribulations of the 1980s. Another was in tiny Ledyard. The Reverend Victor Vriesen wrote to President Ronald Reagan about the food pantry he was developing in his community and pled for assistance: "Please help us. I never thought I would see the day when we would have to begin a food shelf for farmers. Our local food shelf opens next week and we're asking retired people who haven't gone down financially with their children to contribute to it. No one else can."[16]

Other organizations also struggled to fill the food gap. The Iowa Inter-Church Agency for Peace and Justice and the Iowa Inter-Church Forum sponsored the Iowa Rural Crisis Fund. Contributions to this fund went directly to services and supplies for rural families. The fund provided money to rural food pantries, to help them stock their shelves and provide grocery store vouchers to their clients. They also provided cash to a program called "Neighbor Helping Neighbor." Iowans in need could receive financial help through their local United Methodist pastor, who doled out funds to help pay for utility bills, food, medical care, clothing, and housing, regardless of the denominational affiliation of the needy person.[17] Some of the money for these efforts came from the proceeds of the Farm Aid concerts that began mid-decade. Led by country singer Willie Nelson, musicians performed benefit concerts for beleaguered farmers. The 1985 concert raised $900,000, $100,000 of which Farm Aid distributed for hunger relief. The Iowa Rural Crisis Fund received $10,000, which it distributed to thirty-three food pantries throughout the state. The balance went to similar programs across the United States.[18]

At the same time, private efforts could not meet the growing needs of Iowans on their own. The number of children qualifying for free and reduced-price school lunches increased considerably. In the Woodbury Central Community Schools, for example, the number of children using the program had grown by 75 percent in just three years.[19] Between 1984 and 1985, Iowa farm families receiving food stamps grew from 493 to 1,557. Those 1,557 families represented approximately four thousand individuals in need of food assistance.[20] The Sindt family, of Everly, Iowa, was one of those receiving aid. Norman Sindt reacted to his predicament with anger and sorrow, commenting that farmers "didn't want to go out of the house, things are so bleak."[21] The Sindts had lost more than $40,000 in the previous three years and were doing everything they could to make their money stretch, which included growing a garden full of potatoes, sweet corn, onions, beans, cauliflower, lettuce, tomatoes, cabbage and squash. They bought generic brands and day-old bread and chopped wood to keep themselves warm. Beyond the vegetables, however, they could eat nothing else they raised, since it had to be sold in order to pay lenders. As Linda Sindt noted, "Nothing on this farm goes back into this house at all." The situation forced them to apply for food stamps, although the process was long, arduous, and full of frustrations and humiliation.[22]

In 1985 the Iowa Bureau of Economic Assistance prepared a guide for farm families applying for food stamps. The formula was deceptively simple: gross farm income, minus the cost of producing the income, plus capital gains, plus depreciation, and divided by twelve to determine monthly income and eligibility. But it took more than three pages of explanation to define what farm income was, what costs were allowable, and what allowable and disallowed resources the family owned. Because circumstances could change radically from month to month and year to year, a family could shift from ineligible to eligible quite quickly.[23] While the Sindts persisted and eventually received aid, Norman Sindt commented of the process, "I know two or three other farmers who have just thrown up their hands and said to heck with it."[24]

The Sindt family's story appeared in the *Des Moines Register* as part of an August 1985 article about farmers receiving food stamps. The story was front-page news and set off a three-week-long avalanche of commentary. One of the first letters came from Karen Peters, a resident of rural Clear Lake. Her response was a strong endorsement of farmers doing whatever they needed to do in order to survive. She emphasized, "Farmers are very independent and most refuse to admit to trouble they can't work their way out of unless it has really become unbearable. Many have gone without medical help, dropped insurance, cashed in life-insurance policies . . . I'm glad to know the Department of Human Services is responding to this need of recognizing a rural crisis here in Iowa. Now if we can just get through to President Reagan."

Others, however, were not so understanding. Susan Erickson, a Des Moines resident, wrote that she "truly sympathize[d] with farm families who earn so little money that they must apply to food stamps" but qualified her sympathy with a long statement about what farmers should be able to do for themselves.

> It seems to me that a farmer should be able to grow just about all the food that his or her family would need. A large garden, a milk cow, a few pigs and a couple head of cattle (which could feed on last year's corn) should supply most of the food an average family would need in a year. A large dose of self-sufficiency would solve a lot of our problems in today's world.

Wynn Phipps, who had farmed with her husband near Pleasantville, declined to express any sympathy at all. She and her husband had survived the 1930s when "dry weather, grasshoppers and chinch bugs . . . took our crops." They had suffered through the economic stringencies imposed by hogs sold at two dollars per hundredweight, and corn sold at eight to twenty cents per bushel. Phipps commented, "How did we manage? We milked cows, and always had cream, milk and butter. We had hogs for meat that we fed corn to. Also, chickens for eggs. We would butcher a fat calf and I would can the meat ... Food stamps? Pah! You should have lived from 1929 to 1938."[25] Erickson and Phipps failed to notice the time the Sindts put into self-sufficiency or the bank's restrictions on their efforts. Lending restrictions could not be ignored. Many mortgages covered all of the livestock on a farm, and killing an animal carrying a lien was a crime. Rule-breaking could threaten a family's ability to continue to get financing, or even send a farmer to jail. The loan requirements facing farmers thwarted self-sufficiency.[26]

And if Phipps was asserting that all Iowa farm families had made it through the 1930s without needing food aid, she was wrong. Although the problems in that decade had been somewhat different, Iowa's farm families had faced hunger then, too. The 1930s saw catastrophically low prices for corn and hogs, and two major droughts in 1934 and 1936. Grasshopper plagues rounded out the tale of woe. It was hard to keep a family fed when field crops and gardens were first baked, then eaten by insects. Many of Iowa's poorest farm families at the time turned to the federal Farm Security Administration (FSA), which aided low income and tenant farming families by providing what were called rehabilitation loans, which could be used for family living expenses, such as food.[27] Additionally, farmers made use of federal work programs such as the Civil Works Administration and the Works Progress Administration, which provided a plethora of low wage jobs. The level of poverty facing Iowa's farm families during the Great Depression had surprised even seasoned Extension personnel. Louise Rosenfeld, who had worked in the 1930s both for Iowa's Extension service and the FSA recalled the conditions she saw on farms: "Whatever the drought didn't take, the grasshoppers did. I never thought I'd ever see that a farm family wouldn't have food. It never occurred to me that that could happen.... But there were people that if there hadn't been rehabilitation grants they would have had no food." The drought years, in particular, robbed many families of their self-sufficiency.[28] Farmers in that era turned not to food stamps but to government work relief programs and the FSA.

The letters flooded in to the *Register* the next week, criticizing both Erickson and Phipps, under the banner "Farmers Tired of Hearing about the Bad Old Days." The message in these letters was that farming had changed. Farmers in the 1980s struggled with a new set of challenges. The writers "knew very well about the dry weather, grasshoppers and low prices of the 1930s." What was different in the 1980s was the incredible cost of running an agricultural business. The farmers of the 1980s faced far more expenses, in the form of "repairs and maintenance, seed, fertilizer, fuel, rent, insurance, veterinary and medicine, equipment, conservation, supplies, etc."[29] Belt-tightening was not going to take these families very far.

This was also a new world where young farmers were having to do more to survive than work the land. As one commenter wrote, "After being taught for generations that a successful farmer has his wife working by his side, many of our busy, young farmers' wives (and also even our farmers) have had to take on extra jobs to survive. Drive out into the country sometime, and see all the empty cattleyards that have turned to weeds because of sick farm prices." One writer addressed the tug of war between these jobs and the ideal of self-sufficiency: "Many farmers, as well as many town dwellers, have gardens, of course. Many farmers and their spouses also have full- or part-time non-farm jobs along with their farming operation. This leaves precious little time for the weeding, watering, and later, food preservation, necessary to maintain a garden." A farm wife from Boyden commented, "Do those who recommend farmers raise a few chickens, a milk cow, and a hog or two realize these creatures need care every day?"[30] Those who were working a full day off the farm, followed by a long night with the crop in the field, had little time for subsistence activities. A letter that came in a week later, from a farm woman from Inwood, took issue with the idea that farm families should accept a lower standard of living than urban Iowans in order to survive: "It seems the farmer's problems started when he wanted electricity, indoor plumbing, and all the other things our town and city friends took for granted."[31] Among urban Iowans, let alone urban Americans in general, the understanding of the rural situation was limited.

Still, even though farm people had a better grasp of the depths of their troubles, applying for food aid was difficult and shameful. It violated many people's most fundamental beliefs about who they were and what they should be able to do for themselves. The state was well aware of the shame surrounding food aid. A public service announcement featuring Governor Branstad, Senator Harkin, and Senator Grassley promoted a compassionate—and bipartisan—vision of these programs. The sixty-second spot began with the governor: "Iowa food-producers feed the world. Ironically, some Iowans are unable to provide well-balanced meals for their own families. However, help is available." Senator Grassley chimed in, urging Iowans to take advantage of food pantries: "Iowans always help one another—raising a barn, threshing, or responding to danger. Overcoming hunger and poor nutrition is no exception. All across Iowa local communities have established food pantries. Donated food is distributed to those in need. No hassle. No, fuss, and no need for embarrassment. Just neighbors helping neighbors." Senator Harkin plugged the food stamp program: "Government can be a neighbor too. The federal Food Stamp Program is an example. Food stamps help people stretch their food dollars and get the well-balanced meals they need. As a US taxpayer you support this program and help feed your neighbors. You should have no qualms about receiving food stamps when your family needs them." The PSA ended with Branstad directing listeners to the Iowa Department of Human Services for the location of pantries and help applying for food stamps.[32]

Unfortunately, there were enormous hurdles to leap. While the ad may have convinced some, it failed to overcome the resistance of many. Historian Mark Friedberger, in his analysis of farmer response to the Farm Crisis, termed this a desire "to be independent even in adversity," while at the same time acknowledging the stigma of asking for aid. He believed that a tiny fraction of the total number of farmers who might have qualified for food stamps actually applied.[33] Friedberger's assertion would appear to be correct, since the USDA estimated that one third of Iowa's farms were in dire circumstances, yet at the height of the crisis, only 2,316 out of more than 100,000 families received food stamps.

When it came to the shame associated with poverty, circumstances had remained unchanged since the 1930s. During the Great Depression, many families had suffered almost to the point of starvation because of the deep shame evoked by admitting their poverty and asking for help.[34] Their children and grandchildren suffered the same shame fifty years later. Those who worked with newly poor rural people struggled to get them to accept help. Correspondence between aid workers about a farm client illustrated this problem: "I talked to her about applying for food stamps and she said they would *never* apply for them because everyone in the county knows them and they talk." If food stamps were unacceptable, so was going to the local food pantry. "I suggested the food pantry and she really hit the roof and said 'Listen lady, I *work* for the pantry, I don't *take* from it.' I asked her if the pantry people knew she had a need (the pantry is in their church) and she replied, 'They don't know and they aren't going to know.'"[35] In the same vein, one farm woman commented that despite four years of hard times, she and her husband could not bring themselves to apply for aid: "The pride that he holds and that I share have kept us from signing up for the food stamp program."[36] In some cases, husbands refused to allow their wives to apply for food stamps or other government programs, and wives frequented food pantries without their husbands' knowledge.[37]

A letter between farm women addressed the many complexities of the issue of poverty and food insecurity on the farm, and the role that food stamps played in many farm families' lives. A conversation in the grocery store led to a letter from farm woman Lois (no last name provided) to her friend and farmer/activist, Denise O'Brien. Lois wrote, "It was very comforting to hear that other people face many of the same day-to-day struggles that we face—Loren [her husband] & I have a strong tendancy [sic] to think that we're the only ones in the whole world who are having such difficult times." Pride and shame kept people from sharing their pain. Lois continued,

> I don't know if you could tell by my attitude, but we are also receiving food stamps. I didn't come right out and say it because my mom was with me, and Loren & I decided we didn't want to cause our folks extra worry by telling them. A part of Loren feels ashamed for needing help to feed our family and so he would feel embarrassed if our folks knew.

Accepting food aid was, in the case of this couple, something that could not be discussed, even with family.

The decision to apply for and accept food stamps set off a whole round of deliberation. In her letter, Lois made clear that her acceptance of food stamps was not done without careful thought and deep emotion. She wrote, "Mostly I feel like screaming to the gov't, 'Look, you guys are making us pay for all your mistakes ... so you can just darn well buy our groceries so we don't starve to death while working our 18–20 hour [sic] days!'" She chose the foods to buy with stamps deliberately: "I make the gov't support the dairy industry by buying *all* the dairy products we need with food stamps, instead of using our own precious milk for our family." Using food stamps meant that Lois had more time and energy to devote to income generating tasks on the family's dairy farm. She commented, "Actually, I'm *very* thankful for the food stamps because we need all our money to help pay bills, plus it freed me from having to garden so much this summer and I was able to put my time into calf & cow care and to do all those 'detail jobs' that Loren would always just as soon leave to me anyway."[38] The difficult choice to accept help came with the added bonus of being able to exchange the time that might have been spent on gardening on more lucrative work on the family dairy farm.

Denise O'Brien, the letter's recipient, was an Iowa farmer and farm activist who worked extensively with the IFUC.[39] Over time, she came to believe that accepting food stamps was integral to the survival of her own farm and of many others. Families facing stubborn debts often weighed multiple options while formulating their survival strategies. One approach to relieving the debt burden was for women to take off-farm jobs, and in fact, some lenders advised the farmers with whom they worked that their wives needed to find jobs. But as O'Brien argued, a wife working off the farm did not necessarily solve a family's money woes. Small businesses across rural Iowa were failing just as large numbers of women began looking for work. Finding employment often involved driving forty or fifty miles, just to work at minimum wage. As O'Brien commented, "By the time they take out money for gas and child care, there isn't going to be hardly enough left to buy groceries." Instead, they would be "better off quitting that job and getting food stamps or using the pantries."[40] That realization, however, did not make accepting food aid easy. In the early days of the Farm Crisis, O'Brien had done her grocery shopping at midnight, hoping that nobody she knew would see her using food stamps.[41] While shopping at midnight eventually went by the wayside, the feeling of shame remained. In a 1985 interview, she reflected on the discomfort of accepting aid from the government: "I still feel guilty about wearing decent clothes and driving a car, although I had the clothes already and don't know how else I could get around.... Being on food stamps, I feel I ought to be in rags."[42]

In an effort to help farm people overcome feelings of shame to care for their families, activist groups organized small food stamp drives in 1984. The next year, the idea spread. In March, the IFUC, in cooperation with other farm groups, held its first food stamp drive on Ash Wednesday. They asked farmers across the state to toll church bells at 10:00 a.m. to call people in stress together to talk about their troubles.[43] They held a second drive in March 1986. The purpose of the drives was multifaceted. On the one hand, there were many hungry people in Iowa who needed the resources food stamps would provide. On the other hand, many of those hungry people were too embarrassed to take advantage of the program, or unsure how to fill out the long, complicated forms. A food stamp drive, which brought together large numbers of needy people and connected them with trained individuals who could help, might provide the encouragement people needed to take care of themselves and their families. The organizers asked everyone, not just the needy, to take part: "Farmers, clergy, and community leaders are being asked to participate in the March 3rd Food Stamp Drive in order to bring relief and dignity to those who are without adequate resources to meet their own family needs." Maybe if the mayor, the minister, and the president of the Kiwanis Club all applied for food stamps, more people would feel comfortable asking for the help they needed. The drives were also political, drawing attention to the Farm Crisis in a dramatic fashion. Many of the men involved in organizing the drives saw them, first and foremost, as a measure meant to alert everyone to the painful irony of hungry farmers. They wanted the public to absorb the astonishing fact that many of the state's farmers were poor enough to qualify for food stamps.[44] For the women, like O'Brien, the political message seemed to be secondary to the very real problem of feeding their families.

Off-Farm Employment

Food aid was one way to deal with tight budgets. Seeking a job in addition to farming was another. While some farm women, like O'Brien, rejected the idea of off-farm work, more and more were looking for jobs. Some took jobs that allowed them to work from home, combining work with child care and farm labor, but those jobs tended to be low income, and usually carried no benefits.[45] When they looked for jobs in town, they often discovered that rural communities did not have a great deal to offer.[46] Looking did not necessarily meaning finding work, or finding work that would pay enough to make the trouble worthwhile. Iowa State's Extension provided women the vocabulary to sell themselves and their experience so that they could do their best in the job market. An Extension pamphlet listed the skills of farm wives that "translated to job skills." Running errands demonstrated an "ability to follow detailed instructions" and being an "expert at managing a variety of responsibilities simultaneously." "Borrowing money with husband" was really "financial planning." And "planting/harvesting" demonstrated skills as a "large equipment operator." Finding work would involve selling farm-honed skills in a new marketplace.[47]

Men would have to wait nearly two years before Extension published a similar pamphlet for them. Perhaps that was because the problem of finding alternate work for displaced farm men seemed so intractable. They were used to being their own boss and organizing their own time. Most had been in farming all their lives and had never applied for a job. They were deeply invested in their land and their work and often could not, as one observer put it, "distinguish the failure of the farming business from the personal integrity of the farmer himself." They had never thought they would find themselves in this position. They also suffered from enormous fears about what they would find in the job market: "While any worker is fearful of what might happen to them and their family if they lose their job, the farmer is fearful of being able to find a job which compares to the job he has. That is nearly impossible, because there are not many jobs like farming."[48] Being a parts store salesperson, mail carrier, or janitor, all jobs the Extension pamphlet suggested were appropriate to a farmer's skill set, had to have seemed like dismal options to a displaced farmer who had run his own operation.[49] Women looking for off-farm work were in a somewhat different position. Part of being a farm woman was doing whatever might be necessary, whether it was actually "her job" or not. They lived with somewhat flexible gender roles and work responsibilities. Farm women might not have expected to work off the farm, but many knew those who did. As far back as the 1950s better roads, access to automobiles, and the cost-price squeeze had led more and more women to do so. Taking an off-farm job may not have seemed like a step so far for many women.

In 1985 farm woman Mrs. Dan H. Witt wrote to Governor Branstad about her role on her family's farm. In the middle of the crisis she had become a wage earner. She and her husband cultivated a fairly large parcel of land, largely rented, totaling roughly six hundred acres. Hard times had sent her off the farm for employment in 1982. She wrote, "To make things easier ... I went to work for a finance company in Clinton. Now its [sic] not by choice I am working, it's a necessity." Hard times were about to interfere with her family's plans, yet again. The finance company for which she worked was filing for bankruptcy. She was about to lose her job. Her family was about to lose their farm. She had no idea what to do, except to write the governor. She elaborated, "It is a fight from year to year just to survive. We need help and soon. We love living in Iowa and farming the land. Whats [sic] even worse, if we quit farming, what will Dan do? Jobs are very scarce in this area. Please listen to this cry for help from the heart of America."[50] Her letter expressed many of the frustrations and problems facing Iowa's working farm women. Many needed off-farm jobs, rather than wanting them, and given the economic problems facing rural businesses, maintaining a job could be difficult.

Young People in Hard Times

The Farm Crisis belonged to everyone, young people included. When a family lost a farm, it could be particularly hard on the children. A psychologist in southwest

Iowa commented, "Farm families are a unique population. There are no clear boundaries between job and family." The work of the farm extended to everyone in the family—men, women, and children—and happened in the place they called home. Children's activities intertwined with farm finances; calves and pigs might be their 4-H or Future Farmers of America (FFA) project but remained vulnerable to repossession in the event of problems with lenders. Youngsters might imagine themselves inheriting the family farm one day. If a farm faced financial difficulties, they could also imagine themselves homeless and without a future. A young woman who ran away from her farm home described her reasons why: "You're wondering if the farm is going to be there tomorrow and if you're going to be there tomorrow . . . It's nerve wracking. I just couldn't handle the stress."[51]

The evidence of the effect of hard times on rural youth could appear in unexpected places. In the fall of 1984, Harlan high-school senior Beth Ellsworth and her yearbook staff faced a tough task: how to tell the story of the good things that were happening at Harlan Community High School, while at the same time acknowledging the pain that they and their classmates were feeling. Harlan Community High School was located in a small, county seat town of just over five thousand residents. It was a consolidated school, serving families throughout the southern half of Shelby County. By 1984 western Iowa was deep in crisis, and both Harlan and Shelby County were suffering.[52] The yearbook staff decided to address the situation head-on: "The way things were going at that time were really not so great, so instead of shying away from that we opted to tell it like it was."[53] The result was a remarkable Farm Crisis yearbook, evidence of the confusion and pain the downturn created for a community's young people.

The yearbook staff titled their work "Something's Missing." Throughout the text, they invited their peers to reflect on conditions throughout the county. They began with a somber shot of a dark and empty school hallway, and the words "Something's Missing." The narrative pulled no punches: "Population growth has staggered and fallen in the Midwest as there are few jobs to keep people here. In the past year we have seen many of our own businesses close down . . . Over 150 houses were for sale in Harlan and things don't look much brighter in the near future."[54] The writers mourned the friends and teachers who had left and noted that "there were no new faculty members this year."[55] The narrative asked their peers to consider their situation. "Are we missing out here in 'Small town' Iowa? Is it all toil, humdrum and drudgery? Is this 'no where [sic] city' occupied only by corny farm folk? Do we occupy these seats only in anticipation of 'getting out of this hole' and on to other things? Life is sometimes what you make it. Is something missing? You decide."[56] While other yearbooks gave occasional glimpses into teenagers' perceptions of the Farm Crisis, the 1985 *Harpoon* provided compelling evidence that some young people were thoroughly and painfully aware of the decade's troubles.

One of the most interesting, and perhaps even daring, commentaries appeared deep in the volume, on page 147. Between two sets of senior pictures were the words, "Seniors Going . . . Gone." The writer noted, "In recent years, Shelby County has lost many youth. Many of the seniors intend to leave both Shelby County and Iowa. They find their home-town boring and have discovered they can make more money and find more opportunities in other parts of the country." The author concluded, "These seniors may be the exception. They seem quite adamant about leaving and staying away."[57] They juxtaposed this commentary with Iowa's advertising slogan from the 1980s, "Iowa: A Place to Grow." The yearbook staff had confronted one of the most debilitating problems facing small communities throughout the state: the loss of their young people.

According to editor Beth Ellsworth, the yearbook staff carefully considered this approach to the year's events. Given the seriousness of the crisis, reporting only the news from inside the high school did not seem appropriate. Harlan's persistently powerful football team was not the biggest story of the year. These were "tough times," and peers' families were suffering. One of their biggest concerns was to represent as much of their community as possible. The divisions ran deep at Harlan Community High School, existing from the years when smaller communities lost their schools and students boarded buses for Harlan. According to Ellsworth, people still talked about the "townies versus the colonies," "colonies" being a derogatory term for the outlying farm communities. In spite of this, the yearbook staff wanted their project to provide a single vision, reflecting the high school motto, "joined as one, we get the job done." They also believed it was important to allow their peers to come to their own conclusions about the community and its future. They preferred not to be completely negative and repeatedly circled back to the refrain, "you decide." They hoped to lead their readers to the "position that there are always positive things . . . but in the end, it's you. I guess that was our focus on the literary, trying to get people to think from their own perspectives about their own year in school." This approach emerged from long discussions between the staff and their sponsor, biology teacher Jim Tiller. It was the only honest approach they could imagine, given the circumstances of this year at the height of the Farm Crisis.[58]

The "Something's Missing" yearbook answered the question of whether or not young people, on the farm or off, were aware of and troubled by the economic disaster going on around them. The more difficult question facing parents, educators, and others, was how to mitigate the anxieties of children and teens. Even the editors of an agricultural journal such as *Wallace's Farmer* realized that these issues had to be addressed, publishing an article entitled, "When Financial Problems Occur . . . Should You Tell Your Children?" The answer was yes. Parents should be open and honest in explaining to their children why certain purchases, such as a dress for prom, were impossible. Professionals believed that giving children enough information so that they could understand the family situation, as well as a limited role in discussions about money, was appropriate. One of the experts, however, suggested that teenagers should look on deprivation as a growth experience, and that "you can learn integrity by going without occasionally."[59] This kind of advice was more likely to be appreciated from a great distance, rather than at the moment when a teenager attended prom in a borrowed dress.

A flurry of youth programming occurred in 1985. Extension developed a packet of materials, including a videotape entitled "The Rural Crisis Comes to Schools," meant for use by educators. The printed material that accompanied the videotape included an important observation: "Often when there is a crisis in the home, adult members of the family may stop being involved in community affairs. Children attending school may be the only contact the family has with the outside world." It was another burden rural youth were carrying, but it also made it possible for them to get help more readily than the adults in their families. Washington High School, in Vinton, rolled out a support program for stressed students. The school social worker was seeing a lot of suffering: "It's real clear to us, the administrators and the teachers, that the kids aren't concentrating, they're having a really rough time." The adults often had no idea why a youngster was struggling until a bankruptcy or foreclosure occurred and the behavior suddenly made sense. At the request of parents and students, the school social worker, guidance counselor, principal, teachers, and a group of students at Washington High put together a plan. The first phase involved a teacher in-service on the Farm Crisis. The following day, the entire student body watched *Country* and discussed it in their homeroom classes. Then came the student-run support group, meant for everyone: "We want the students to be sure and know that this isn't just for kids who have lost a farm, it's for town kids, for everybody. It's about supporting each other and sharing information, and it's about kids taking an active role in what's going on around them."[60]

Beyond Vinton, other young people also helped themselves by helping others. FFA members in Mapleton assisted the local farm crisis committee with a fund-raising bingo tournament to raise money for a lobbying trip to Washington. The peer counselors at Norway Community School went to a local community college to learn about the situation. Students at Morningside College, in Sioux City, organized a "Phone-A-Rama," to raise money to assist students "whose families are caught in the farm crisis, with scholarships, work-study jobs . . . and in other ways."[61] Young people did what they could for suffering friends and more than likely improved their own outlook in the process. Helping others gave them some agency in a situation where individuals often felt out of control.

Dismissal from Washington

Although there were many different ways of experiencing the crisis, many rural Americans felt as if they were under siege. The economic troubles facing two-thirds of the state's farming families were deep and pervasive, and the frequency with which they were fighting either flood or drought added to the urgency of their situations. If they had believed that someone in power at the national level was listening to their concerns and taking them seriously, they might have felt less threatened. This, however, was not the case. Those at the pinnacle of power did not seem to either take their troubles seriously or believe that there was anything that they should do to correct the problem. President Reagan regularly dismissed calls for debt relief and rejected any sort of aid for farmers. In March 1985, both farmers and their legislators were appalled when, at the annual Gridiron Club dinner and political roast, Reagan joked that he had found a solution to the crisis in agriculture: "I think we should keep the grain and export the farmers." The silence in the room was deafening, and calls from Iowa's congressional delegation for an apology and retraction came quickly. None, however, was forthcoming. Reagan merely remarked that he wished he had not told the joke, because it failed to get a laugh.[62] The editor of *Wallace's Farmer* fired back angrily, "We'll tell him something else that isn't funny, like watching your family farm sold at public auction. You don't laugh about the suicides, attempted suicides, the mental depression, divorces, and family stress brought about by agriculture's economic problems."[63]

Reagan's budget director, David Stockman, was equally dismissive. When the governor had visited Washington in January, Stockman had been, at best, uninterested, and at worst, hostile. In February, he announced that the United

States had too many farmers and needed a "shakeout." He disdainfully referred to them as "consenting adults" who were solely responsible for their troubles.⁶⁴ Some Iowans agreed with Stockman. A Des Moines woman wrote to the governor, "Let the 'farmers' wallow, if they must, it is not our concern when they subject themselves to such 'borrowing.' Let them get back of a team of horses—it is much cheaper and less expensive."⁶⁵ Attitudes such as these, however, did not predominate. A dentist from Ida Grove wrote Stockman to ask for a reassessment because of the dire condition of his community. Fewer and fewer patients were walking through the door, and he had lost more than $4,000 in a three-month period. He wrote, "How long do you feel that small business and health care providers can survive with this type of depressed money flow?" A Lake City man wrote to the chairman of the Republican National Committee to protest "Stockmanomics" and his "ill-conceived attitude towards the farmers." Wayne and Miriam McDonald, who farmed near Clemons, wrote Stockman to protest his "consenting adults" comment: "Our net worth 1/1/81 was $1,003,782. On 1/1/85 it was $248,894. 1981–1985 we purchased NO land, NO car, NO pickup, NO machinery, No vacations, for the house a gas kitchen stove. Is this extravagance? Our net worth changed only because of high interest, land devaluation, and government action and inaction that affected profits." Ronald Hall's letter began similarly to the McDonalds's, with the facts about his farm operation, and ended with passion: "I'm saddened and overjoyed about two things. That you have the stoney [sic] cold heart of a Bookkeeper, and you'll never have enough Heart to hit the field come spring. MAY YOU NEVER HAVE A MOMENTS PEACE." There was plenty of anger to spare for members of the Reagan Administration, but Stockman in particular drew Iowans' ire.⁶⁶

The needs created by the crisis, in tandem with the anger generated by comments of individuals such as Reagan and Stockman, motivated 1985's constant round of protests, meetings, and benefits. As the months rolled by, the activity just kept coming. Mid-January saw the creation of the Western Iowa Farm Crisis Committee and meetings at St. Mary's Catholic Church in Mapleton and the Methodist Church in Denison. The committee advertised the gatherings as "not just for farmers, but for anyone who is concerned about the crisis in rural communities. We urge our pastors, lenders, and all local business people to attend." The group prided itself on its broad base. Committee members were both Republicans and Democrats and members of a wide variety of farm organizations. There was action in addition to organizing. In the first week of January, protestors gathered for the

Book family's auction in Story County. In the last week, protestors in Chariton, including members of the IFUC and UAW, forced the Central Iowa PCA to call off an auction. The PCA gave the farmer involved another fifteen days to work out a repayment plan.[67]

In February fifteen thousand people gathered at Iowa State University's Hilton Coliseum for the National Crisis Action Rally. The list of organizations and individuals sponsoring the event was long and cut across the political spectrum. The American Agriculture Movement and Rural America/PrairieFire were there, but so was the Iowa Farm Bureau Federation. WIFE sponsored the meeting, as did the IFUC, Catholic Rural Life, and the National Farmers Union. The Farm Crisis Committee was a sponsor, together with the National Grange. Iowa's politicians chipped in as well, with the state legislature, Governor Branstad, Lieutenant Governor Robert Anderson, and Iowa's congressional delegation all acting as sponsors. The governor declared February 27 Agricultural Crisis Awareness Day and encouraged citizens from across the state to attend. As *Wallace's Farmer* commented, "Perhaps one of the most significant things to come of the rally was that it was a rare display of cooperation by a cross section of farm groups. As one speaker warned, 'Mr. President, you have awakened a sleeping giant!'" Communities across the state sponsored participation. The newspaper in Mapleton exhorted its readers: "IT IS NECESSARY FOR YOU TO ATTEND." Mapleton residents could travel to Ames for just five dollars, since two local banks paid most of the costs of renting buses. Many other locations followed suit. At least a dozen states, mostly Midwestern, sent delegations, and more than one hundred buses crammed the parking lot.[68]

The speakers came from many different walks of life. Some were farmers in foreclosure. Another was a factory worker from Moline, Illinois, who spoke about farm machinery plant closures. Jon Wefald, chancellor of Minnesota's university system and former commissioner of agriculture, challenged David Stockman to a debate. The crowd responded most enthusiastically to Bishop Maurice Dingman, who held up a white cross for all to see. He told the audience that 250 like it stood in Lafayette Park, in view of the White House, representing the number of American farmers going broke every day. Inside the coliseum were numerous visual displays of anger. Some protestors wore "Endangered Species" T-shirts, available for purchase. One held up a sign that said, "For Sale: Rural Iowa, Call: 1-800-HELP." Someone hanged David Stockman in effigy from a railing—an action that received surprisingly little comment, given most Midwesterners' propensity to avoid controversy. Lest it seem like everyone at the rally was in agreement with everyone else,

Outside Hilton Coliseum at Iowa State University, organizers created a number of displays, including white crosses commemorating farms lost, on the right side of the picture. Farwell T. Brown Photographic Archive, Ames Public Library, courtesy of Ames History Museum.

a farmer from South Dakota hoisted a sign saying, "Farm Bureau Doesn't Speak for ME."[69]

There was no pause in the action. The Maple Valley Concerned Citizens rang the church bells at 2:00 p.m. on Sunday, March 3, to remind everyone to pray for the forty-nine Iowans traveling to Washington, DC, to lobby for rural communities. In Adair County, farmers raised $1,200 to send three of their own, Dixon Terry, John Vogl, and Stan Kading. Neighbors pitched in to help all three, so their chores would not be neglected. Even though there was plenty of support in Iowa, the lobbying effort foundered. Before the delegation had even left Washington, President Reagan rejected a debt relief plan that would have subsidized lower interest rates on restructured farm loans. Reagan referred to the plan as "completely unacceptable and unnecessary." On March 20, the IFUC marched to the Federal Building in Des Moines, to "foreclose" on the federal government and to build support for a congressional override of Reagan's action. The IFUC announced, "The President doesn't seem to care about farmers, rural communities, workers, cities, the poor, or anyone but the Defense Department. WE ARE FIGHTING FOR OUR LIVES, OUR LAND AND OUR LIVELIHOODS."[70]

The protests inside Hilton Coliseum included hanging in effigy David Stockman, President Reagan's budget director. Farwell T. Brown Photographic Archive, Ames Public Library, courtesy of Ames History Museum.

In April, a Women's Farm Crisis Committee organized at St. Mary's Catholic Church in Mapleton. The women brainstormed about ways to keep themselves and their communities "alive and vital" even in the midst of a crisis. They encouraged letters and phone calls to Congress, especially to urban representatives and senators. They planned to get their children involved with letter writing, so that they could tell government officials "how they feel about living in a rural community—what they understand about the Farm Crisis." Schleswig School was the first to participate "with the hearty support of their administration." The women's group hoped to keep up the publicity through all media outlets, especially their churches, and encouraged each other to remain positive: "Let us know how you're keeping the farm issues in the forefront in your communities.—You're the heartbeat of America because you make things happen." The women mapped out a plan of regular meetings and ongoing political action.[71]

Homegrown women activists got a boost from those in Hollywood. Both Sally Field and Jessica Lange agreed to appear at the Farm Crisis Committee rallies and events throughout the Midwest. In May, Lange, along with Jane Fonda and Sissy Spacek, went to Washington for an informal hearing sponsored by the House Democratic Caucus's agriculture task force. Although Sally Field could not attend, she sent a prepared statement. These actors, who had starring roles as farm and rural women, pleaded for legislation to improve the circumstances of beleaguered farm families. Lange commented, "We understand that there are no simple answers to farm policy, but there are simple values that never lose meaning." A contingent from WIFE, dressed in red, joined the actresses. While the event did not impress Senator Jesse Helms, chairman of the Senate Agriculture Committee, the publicity was not meant for him but for ordinary Americans who might be impressed by star power and demand that their representatives do something for farmers. It certainly lifted the spirits of Iowa's rural women.[72]

As the spring gave way to summer, meetings continued around the state. In early June, organizers gathered at the Woodbury County Fairgrounds for a Farm Crisis Expo. In July, Emmanuel Congregational Church in Des Moines hosted a benefit for farm families at Valley High School. The evening featured a dinner and a special showing of *Country*. All of the funds went to the Farm Relief Fund of the Congregational Church, which provided farm families short term emergency aid. The churches were able to afford the event because Walt Disney Studios lent a special print of the movie to PrairieFire for fundraising and other events. Late in July, the Farm Crisis Committee was off to Washington again. They distributed information packets and six hundred members of Congress and staffers joined them for an informational meeting. They followed their trip to the nation's capital with meetings in Iowa with Senator Grassley and various western Iowa business and community organizations and prepared for a statewide "prayer weekend," to be held in the first weekend of September. They continued raising funds for their lobbying efforts, although they were afraid that "big money may win out." On August 10, country star Merle Haggard wrote them a check for $10,000.[73]

September was all about protest and support set to music. On the fifteenth, more than forty musicians performed at an "Iowaide" concert at the Sylvan Theater in Des Moines. The musicians donated all of the funds to the Food Bank of Iowa and PrairieFire's Farm Survival Hotline. As the organizers proclaimed, "REMEMBER: WE'RE ALL IN THIS TOGETHER."[74] Iowaide took place just one week before the fall's main event, the first Farm Aid Concert, held on Sunday, September 22, 1985, in Urbana, Illinois. County star Willie Nelson, in conjunction with rock musicians John Mellencamp and Neil Young, orchestrated the event. The music festival featured performers from different generations and genres, such as Bon Jovi, Foreigner, Roy Orbison, Waylon Jennings, and B. B. King. John Mellencamp wore his FFA jacket for his set, illustrating his personal connection to the cause. Prime time television carried several hours of the programming. The concert drew eighty thousand attendees and raised approximately nine million dollars.

While the effort was impressive, it fell far short of the $50 to $100 million the organizers had hoped to raise. Observers believed that multiple factors led to the disappointing results. July's televised Live Aid concert for Ethiopian famine relief had raised $55 million. Live Aid's organizers benefited from dramatic images of starvation in Africa, something that Farm Aid's organizers lacked. Instead, they had a complex problem, with no easy solutions, and the money they raised would be a drop in the bucket compared to the hundreds of millions of dollars that farmers owed. The intricacies of the farm situation baffled casual observers, and even farmers were confused about the concert's purpose. Many hoped for direct payment of their debts. Unfortunately, the concert's proceeds would not even be enough to pay one day's worth of farmers' loan interest. The organizers funneled the proceeds toward multiple purposes, including food pantries and legal aid. The director of Nebraska's volunteer hotline, however, believed that the concert had a more important purpose. Even though the money would not pay off anyone's debts, it had made it acceptable to talk about the crisis. Farmers who called in seeking funds went away with referrals to food programs, legal aid, and other services.[75]

Support Groups

Participation in advocacy and protest organizations allowed suffering people to do something for their own mental health. It gave them an outlet. Although it was not their stated goal, many of these organizations functioned as support groups. In other cases, such as the group Farmer to Farmer, the purpose of the organization was support rather than any sort of activism. It had its origin in 1983, when Chuck and Joanne Heick, farmers from rural Clarence, went for help to St. Luke's Hospital in Cedar Rapids. Chuck was deeply depressed and suicidal. The couple developed a relationship with one of the hospital chaplains and began receiving counseling. What became clear was that the Heicks were not the only couple in need of support services. In February 1985 the hospital sponsored a conference titled "You Are Not Alone: Hope in a Hopeless Land." About 250 people came to the event. The hospital organized a second conference in November.[76]

The Farmers to Farmers Support Group arose out of the meetings. Although Joanne Dvorak of the Family Service Agency in Cedar Rapids did the initial organizing, the support groups that developed were actually self-help groups, planned and led by farmers. They did not promise therapy. Instead, they offered farm families "the opportunity to exchange 'help for help' in sharing. This is an age-old farm custom." As with the encouragement to take food stamps, organizers cast these measures as new expressions of older traditions of rural neighboring. Farmers listened to each other, provided referrals for those needing professional help, and brought in experts sharing useful information. The group promoted itself with the assertion that "'Farmers to Farmers' will give force and conviction to the belief in the American family farm. We believe in the family farm, the farmer, and the 'individual in transition'!" It was a public/private cooperation that gave families in need access to attorneys, counselors, financial experts, and clergy. The formula struck a chord, and the groups developed and spread throughout northeast Iowa. As one farmer commented, "If I have to go through this [bankruptcy], I don't want to be alone."[77]

These committee meetings, auction disruptions, concerts, and support groups were just a small sampling of the larger body of organizing across Iowa. More than half of the state's ninety-nine counties had Farm Unity groups or Farm Crisis Committees. Meetings that once drew fifty farmers were drawing two hundred. Advocacy, protest, and action came in many different forms. One involved sitting down together in a church basement to talk about worries that farmers had in common and to search for solutions. And over time, the organizations and protests grew to encompass more than simply the agricultural community.

Among their most important allies were rural churches. On the eve of the crisis, roughly 90 percent of farm families attended services, making them a logical place from which to organize aid and advocacy. Although not all churches were oriented toward activism, many pastors and priests counseled their parishioners and opened their facilities to meetings. They rang church bells in support of awareness campaigns and food stamp drives and hosted "Farm Survival Days."[78] Catholic clergy, in particular, were in the forefront of organizing activities, with Bishop Maurice Dingman, Monsignor A. W. Behrens, and Father Frank Cordero leading the charge. As clergy saw the number of their parishioners diminishing and the turmoil they faced increasing, it seemed logical to step in with support.[79]

Federal and State Action

In 1985 the activism took on a particular urgency. Every five years, Congress passes a new farm bill, laying out federal farm policy for the next five-year period. Beleaguered farmers were particularly fearful of what that legislation might look like. Early in the year, as the process of negotiation got underway, there seemed no way to reconcile the Reagan administration's desire for cost cutting and budget balancing with the perceived needs of farmers. As one commentator put it, "It will be a miracle if farmers aren't hurt in the crash." The negotiations ran down to the wire, with everyone unsure of what would emerge until the last moment.[80]

With the outlines of the federal farm program unclear throughout most of the year, farmers turned their attention to state government. Many were concerned that they would not have the funds to plant in the spring. Deep levels of debt meant that many were in the high-risk category, with complicated loan applications. Many lenders were also in financial trouble. PCA offices, too, were in the midst of restructuring and facing their own difficulties. The FmHA was badly backlogged, unable to keep up with loan processing. President Reagan allowed the FmHA to hire extra workers to process loan requests, but Iowa lacked sufficient qualified loan officers to handle the paperwork. At the end of February, Governor Branstad exercised his emergency powers to activate National Guard personnel to help with processing. The state also worked with the FmHA to develop a "last resort" loan program, providing operating loans using the crop in the field as collateral. The FmHA would have the first rights to the harvest, but qualifying farmers would have the wherewithal to get into the fields. These were all temporary measures, but the state hoped to avoid a situation in which large numbers of farmers were unable to plant because they had no way to purchase seed, fertilizer, and fuel.[81]

Some state legislators hoped for more permanent ways to improve the incomes of farmers, including minimum pricing of farm products. Such legislation had been in the air for a while. In essence, it was the same measure that AAM championed in the late 1970s, when asking for parity pricing. This time, however, the request came at the state level, rather than the national.[82] In spring 1985 Iowa's state legislature surprised everyone by doing something no other had done before; both houses voted to set minimum prices for corn and soybeans. The vote came after much wrangling. Republicans in the Senate argued the bill would hurt more than it helped, and that its backers meant it as a wake-up call, rather than a measure that would actually improve the agricultural situation. Indeed, advocates in the House as good as admitted that the action was symbolic rather than practical.[83]

The governor thought carefully before deciding to sign or veto the bill. A number of the state's major farm organizations spoke out against minimum pricing. The governor received a letter from the presidents of four of the state's largest organizations, and secretary of a fifth, asking for a veto.[84] J. Howard Mueller, the chairman of the US Feed Grains Council, also wrote the governor. He commented, "The emotion of the times has obviously clouded the clear thinking supposedly possessed by the decisionmakers we elected to represent us. . . . 'It won't work but it might send a message' is not the thinking of leaders. The Iowa state legislature cannot repeal the law of supply and demand; we must be constantly aware of the realities of the marketplace."[85] Local Farm Bureau chapters registered their displeasure. Erma C. Stewart, legislative chairman of the Grundy County Farm Bureau Women, wrote , "We cannot see how this bill will do anything but injure the chances of a farm recovery. Iowa State University studies show that it would mean a loss of thousands of jobs in agri-industry . . . [elipses in original] and livestock producers would be forced to pay such high prices for feed that they would be driven out of business."[86]

One of the biggest questions on the minds of many in state government was constitutionality. Senators wanted to know if they could expect the passage of the law to result in a long legal battle, culminating in its defeat on the basis of the US Constitution's interstate commerce clause. They asked the attorney general's office for a ruling. The somewhat equivocal and reluctant answer from the legal pundits was—they had no idea. No state had ever done this before, so there was no legal precedent against which to measure the law. The deputy attorney general was uncomfortable making any predictions, noting, "the upshot of this brief research is that we can guarantee neither the constitutionality nor the unconstitutionality of S. F. 32. The simple fact is that the legislation [is] unprecedented in the history of the country and there is no modern case law directly on point."[87] If the attorney general's office had counseled against the measure, everyone would have had an easy out, one that even the most outspoken of the activist groups might have understood. The easy out, however, was not forthcoming.

The letters poured in. Judging from the relative size of the stacks, Iowans opposed the measure roughly two-to-one. The similar wording in many of the letters demonstrated that interest groups were marshalling their forces and providing their members with templates. Other messages were much more personal, and much more effective. Many of those who favored minimum pricing wrote impassioned pleas on behalf of their farms. One from Dennis Wauters of Elberon was short and sweet, penned on the back of a postcard. "*Don't* veto the Parity Bill. You will have your job next year, but will I? I don't want to be a farmer under a corporation take over. I feed the world and *you*."[88] An even more poignant letter came from the Meseck family, written on the back of the notice for their farm auction. Susan Meseck wrote, "I beg you go please sign the minimum pricing bill as my farmer husband will try to keep on farming wether [sic] there is a profit or not & end up working both of us to death." The Mesecks were working in town during the day, and coming home to their farm work at night. "Now whenever we do our farm work we're tired & on edge so there is so much tension & stress causing too much fighting. We just feel like we've worked hard but for what.... we need to have fair prices on the farm so please help us. Sincerely & prayerfully, Mrs. Ronnie Meseck." One of their children added her own addendum, "Dear Gobernor Bramsted, Please help us farmers! Then my Mommy & Daddy will be happy again!"[89] Farmers supporting the measure pointed to their inability to profit with production costs exceeding the prevailing price for corn and soybeans. They wanted better prices, and barring that they wanted the attention the measure would generate. Many of the letters in favor of minimum price legislation were, as much as anything, a desperate cry to the governor to do something—anything—to help.

Those who disagreed were just as adamant. Some argued that the state was not an island. If Iowa set a floor on corn and soybean prices, neighboring states would take advantage of the situation, undercutting the competition. Others saw markets for their crops disappearing because processors would move out of state in order to find cheaper supplies. Bill Rempe, of Montezuma, was sure that the measure would be "devastating" for the Cargill corn syrup plant at Eddyville.[90] Many also were livestock producers and feeders, who saw their interests and those of cash grain producers as fundamentally different, just as they had been during the PIK debacle. One commented, "I like the thought of $4.11 per bu. for corn and $10.24 or more for beans but it spells doom to my hog raising business at current prices."[91] Many simply saw the measure as another insidious government intrusion into agriculture. John Welle, of Newton, was "feeling a real squeeze from the interest rates" but did not see minimum prices as the solution. He wrote, "I feel this bill calls for too much government management of agriculture. I don't think that is the job of our government nor are they capable of doing it. Past history proves my

A cross displayed in front of a piece of equipment at an auction indicated that the farmer still needed it and that attendees should not bid. By permission of Charlie Langton.

point."[92] Many farmers were suspicious of government at all levels and envisioned even more troubles if a minimum pricing bill became law.

Ultimately, the governor vetoed the measure. The grounds he cited were largely those emanating from agricultural economists at Iowa State University. When it had become clear that the state senate might approve the measure, William Meyers, head of the Center for Trade and Agricultural Policy, provided an analysis of the bill. Meyers wrote, "Iowa would very likely lose rather than gain income in the farm and processing sectors as a result of this legislation. The better strategy for Iowa would be to let surrounding states adopt this law so the livestock and processing industries would flock to Iowa."[93] In other words, let other states be so misguided as to adopt this legislation; Iowa would reap the benefits. Branstad agreed. His veto message was long, but the essential points were simply summarized. Yes, Iowa's farmers were in deep financial difficulties, and they needed solutions, but minimum pricing was not the answer. Because Iowa's farmers did not control the market for their grain, they were likely to lose rather than gain. He believed it would reduce farm income and cost jobs in processing. He wrote, "I am concerned that signing this legislation would send the wrong message to Iowa farmers. It could have the impact of giving Iowa farmers the false hope that the prices they receive for their products would be miraculously increased." That, he was sure, would not happen. What farmers did need was the time and space to work out their problems with credit. The governor wanted to keep the pressure on Washington for a strong farm bill, and not distract everyone with an unprecedented and potentially unconstitutional piece of legislation.[94]

Some accepted the decision with relief, while others expressed outrage. An unexpected letter came from the US Farmers Association (USFA), a group that had long lobbied for parity. F. W. Stover, USFA president, wrote,

> This letter is just to express our rather tardy but sincere appreciation for your veto of the Minimum Price Bill. The crucial matter of farm prices requires national action and cannot be effectively dealt with by State legislation. We did not lobby against the Bill because we did not consider it necessary. The vote for it was a surprise to us. So we want to commend you for your veto action.

An aide to the governor attached a note to the missive, "'Gov sez 'Interesting letter' they tend to be a fairly radical group."[95] Radical or not, the USFA did not want state legislation that might send a message but not do the job. They wanted parity on a national level. Theirs was not the only opinion, however. Iowa Citizens for Community Improvement (ICCI), which had strongly backed the bill, led with the issue in their April/May newsletter, under the headline "Branstad Acts against Family Farmers, Vetoes Minimum Pricing." Under a political cartoon featuring the governor and his veto, they wrote, "HEY, GOVERNOR—EITHER LEAD, FOLLOW OR GET OUT OF THE WAY." The veto effectively killed the issue, but some were unwilling to let it go.[96]

The minimum price fight happened in the spring. In the fall, the problems facing farmers were just as intense and Congress was still a long distance from finalizing a farm bill. In the spring, Minnesota's governor Rudy Perpich had gotten tired of waiting for action and declared a state of emergency in every Minnesota county where the unemployment rate exceeded 10 percent, or where agriculture occupied more than 10 percent of the population. He sought similar declarations from other Midwestern governors, hoping to force Washington to act.[97] Branstad was not yet ready to follow his lead, but as fall arrived, the situation changed. Planning papers within the governor's office indicated that the statehouse expected the farm economy to go from bad to worse. The farm bill was coming together very slowly, and in the meantime, conditions were deteriorating. An internal governor's office memo read, "It is important to note that the farm crisis that is facing us this fall and winter will become, in all probability, more serious than that we faced last winter and spring."[98]

The credit situation was disastrous. The FCS was "likely to undertake a significant liquidation program this fall and winter." The federal financing system for farmers was troubled, and as many as 10 percent of their borrowers might face liquidation before the first of the year. As such, the governor's office planned to use the threat of a foreclosure moratorium to try to slow the process and, if necessary, tie up the FCS in litigation. In the meantime, Branstad continued talking with farm groups and leaders and began working on an interest rate buy-down for farmers and farm supply companies. He also pushed the Iowa congressional delegation to include farm credit measures in the farm bill. At the state level, the governor hoped to use funds from the state's new lottery to guarantee operating loans for the spring of 1986. He also planned to push for more diversification and better farm management. Staffers worried about the way in which these problems might play out in families and communities; they planned to work with PrairieFire and law enforcement "to insure [sic] the prevention of violence this fall and winter." Governor Branstad was finally ready to declare a state of emergency, triggering a foreclosure moratorium.[99]

On October 1, the 1985 farm bill expired without a measure to take its place. Branstad chose that moment to sign the executive order allowing a limited farm mortgage foreclosure moratorium. His statement reflected his frustration at the lack of a farm bill and his concerns about potential FCS liquidations. He commented, "I know that FCS officials may challenge the applicability of the moratorium to their operations, but I am prepared to go to court, if necessary, to protect the farmers of Iowa. These farmers need time; it would be a tragedy to lose these farmers simply because the FCS grows tired of waiting for Congress to act." The provisions of the moratorium allowed for a year of grace for farmers in foreclosure, as long as they applied to the courts for a continuance. Farmers would not have an absolute right to relief. If their lender had made a good faith effort to restructure their debt, if state and federal programs had been used in good faith, or if the farmer had failed to pay interest on the debt, then the court could cancel the continuance. The moratorium only covered real estate loans, and not loans on equipment and other property. The measure did not cover FmHA loans, since the federal government had already forbidden FmHA foreclosures. Branstad intended the measure as a wake-up call: "My action today is designed to tell Washington in a loud and clear voice—we need help in the heartland. The time for action is now."[100]

Iowans had mixed opinions about the measure. Peter Brent, who coordinated the IFUC hotline said, "Thank goodness," while the Bruce Meriwether, a Dubuque banker and president of the Iowa Banker's Association, opined that the governor was "simply delaying the inevitable" failure of many of the state's farmers.[101] The letters flowing into the governor's office both before and after the measure's implementation were also divided. A retired farm woman protested that the moratorium was unfair. She and her husband, who had retired because of disability, were trying to sell their farm on contract to a young couple who had gone into bankruptcy. Two harvests had passed since they had seen any payments. She asked, "What is going to happen to us old farmers who sold farms in good faith? What are we supposed to live on with the cost of living going up every day?"[102] A Johnson County farm woman protested, "There is no way to decide who deserves help. If a moratorium is declared on farm closings, etc., we who have managed to stay in farming are going to have to help others through taxes, bank charges, and probably other ways." Those who did not deserve help, in her opinion, included farmers who had "got gready [sic] and purchased ground and machinery to farm more land than they needed for a sufficient living."[103] Larry Wenzl, president of United Bank and Trust, in Ames, argued that the moratorium would only hurt farmers and stated that his bank would respond with reduced agricultural lending. He wrote, "I know your intentions for the farm industry are good," but the moratorium would hurt more than help.[104] On the other hand, a farm manager from Algona chimed in with the thoughts of the farmers he encountered on his rounds: "On my travels around Kossuth County and the surrounding counties [I] have heard many things and would like to give you what seems to be the sentiment on the farm moratorium. It ranges all the way from 'It might not help much' to 'At least the Governor is making some attempt to help the farmers.' My opinion encompasses both those sentiments."[105] This was not a time for elation, but for hoping that something, anything, would help.

Food Security Act of 1985

A farm bill, the Food Security Act of 1985, finally made its way through the US Congress on December 23. The $169 billion act was considerably more generous than anyone had expected, the costliest piece of agricultural legislation to date. The price tag included funds for food stamps, food aid for nations around the world, extension programs and agricultural research, and $85 billion in support payments for farmers. Included in the support payments were $52 billion in price and income supports over the next three years. Following those three years, the government planned to ease back, moving closer to a system governed by market forces. The payments for farm subsidies were greater than the president initially wished. He ultimately conceded this point, he claimed, because "government is responsible for some of the farmer's problems." On the same day, Reagan signed a bill authorizing restructuring of the Farm Credit System, which held a third of the nation's agricultural debt.[106]

The farm bill included some substantial changes to policy. It required that the USDA provide education and counseling grants for farmers affected by the downturn in the agricultural economy. The bill also took aim at the costs involved in supporting the dairy industry. The government had distributed tons of cheddar cheese and dried milk to the poor because of vast oversupplies of milk. The 1985 program included a dairy herd buyout, or "milk production termination," meant to reduce production of milk and other dairy products by paying farmers to sell their animals for slaughter or export. To pay for the buyout, the government cut price support payments for milk. Probably the most important provisions of the farm program were those related to conservation. The sodbuster, swampbuster, and Conservation Reserve Programs helped farmers to remove highly erodible and swamp land from cultivation. Any farmer who produced crops on highly erodible land without employing conservation measures became ineligible for federal farm programs, including crop insurance and disaster loans. The USDA planned to move 40 to 45 million acres out of production by 1990, and more than 6.6 million acres of Iowa's cropland was eligible for this change. The bill required farmers enrolling acreage in the program to plant and maintain suitable cover vegetation on the land for ten to fifteen years.[107] The nation had its farm bill, but its possible impact on the crisis remained unknown. Given that it involved removing land from production, the Conservation Reserve program was likely to aid farmers but undermine rural businesses.[108]

The year ended with shock and grief. On December 9, 1985, Dale Burr lashed out at his wife, his bank, his neighbors, and finally, himself. Four people died that day. Iowans ended 1985 in vehement disagreement about what these deaths meant. The controversy erupted as the national press reported the shootings. The *New*

York Times ran a large story under the headline "Death on the Iowa Prairie: More Victims of the Economy." The article quoted Peter Zevenbergen, an eastern Iowa mental health professional, as saying, "It was bound to happen somewhere." Dan Levitas, of PrairieFire, also talked to the reporter, commenting, "I'm afraid this violence is the beginning of what is to come." The *Chicago Tribune* ran a similar story, as did several small-town papers. In Mellinger, the author of the "Sincerely Yours" column in the *Sun News* concluded with her reflections on the murders, "This week 4 people lost their lives to the farm crisis."[109]

James P. Gannon, editor of the *Des Moines Register*, begged to differ, and strongly. He used most of a page to make his own argument about the meaning of Burr's actions. Referring to Dale Burr as a "crazy man with a shotgun," he objected to those who made him a symbol of disintegration in rural Iowa. He elaborated, "Collectively, the result is to paint a portrait of a state full of desperate men in pickup trucks fingering loaded guns, driving around wondering whom to shoot first, with their friends and neighbors nodding sympathetically in understanding at the terrible financial pressures that have driven poor, old Harold to this tragic end. That's garbage. Furthermore, it's dangerous garbage." Gannon wanted no part of the sympathy or understanding some people expressed for Burr and his situation. He concluded, "Let's tell America: if you think this madness makes sense to most Iowans, you've got us all wrong."[110]

The responses to Gannon's editorial reflected the division within Iowa. Janet McLaughlin, whose own husband had committed suicide, wept in agreement with Gannon's words. She wrote, "Life does go on; let us enable others, rather than destroy or diminish them." Sandy Plagge, of Webster City, agreed, writing, "We Iowans do not think killing is right under any circumstances." Linda Muston, a friend of John Hughes, wrote, "Thank you, Jim Gannon, for telling America that this madness did not make sense!" Mary Helen Severson, of Webster City, however, called Gannon's column "downright crude." "One cannot say that the incident was not precipitated by the economic deflation brought about by the government in Washington. It most certainly was. A person cracking under economic pressure is not evil. He was unprepared for such a crisis in his life, as was pointed out in the news articles."[111]

Iowa's Cooperative Extension Service had its own take on Burr's actions. A small pamphlet, *Lenders: Working through the Farmer-Lender Crisis*, appeared in April 1986. The little publication encapsulated just how dire the situation in rural Iowa had become. Extension intended the pamphlet to educate farm community bankers about empathy and communication skills. In particular, they advised bankers how to spot and respond to farmers showing "Suicide Warning Signs." The pamphlet instructed that it was imperative to "be a good listener." Bankers were at the front line of an economic crisis, and they needed appropriate skills for the fight. They also needed to exercise care. There was an unwritten subtext to this piece of educational material; if bankers neglected their communication skills, the next desperate farmer might be shooting at them.[112] As 1985 struggled to a close, Iowans were far from agreeing on the meaning of the year's most disastrous event. But no matter the interpretation of Dale Burr's actions they favored, they would have agreed that the silent protests with which the year had begun were preferable to the shootings with which it ended.

CHAPTER FIVE

From Fears of Violence to Glimmers of Hope: 1986

On January 17, in the shadow of the events at Lone Tree and Hills, Major W. D. Petersen of the Iowa State Patrol wrote a memo. Governor Branstad planned to attend a community meeting in Cherokee and the state patrol was worried about conditions there. The Cherokee County sheriff was serving foreclosure notices to a number of farmers and the situation was ripe for conflict. Outsiders were also stirring the pot. Tommy Kersey, a Georgia farmer turned radical farm activist, along with several other members of a group identified as the Heritage Foundation or Heritage Library had been in Minnesota and South Dakota, trying to mobilize farmers. Members of the organization believed, among other things, that banks could make no legal claim to a farmers' property and had no right to foreclose. Kersey also advocated armed resistance to foreclosure proceedings. The State Patrol had identified him as one of several men who had thwarted a foreclosure in Georgia by brandishing semiautomatic weapons. Now, he and members of his group were encouraging farmers in the upper Midwest to do the same. After holding meetings in Minnesota and South Dakota, the men headed for Iowa, where they attempted to organize a gathering for farmers in Sioux City but were unable to find a meeting hall. In Holstein, local officials asked them to leave. The state patrol thought they were trying to find a venue in the town of Cherokee, or elsewhere in the county. In the face of what might be a ticklish situation, the Iowa Department of Public Safety increased the security for the governor's trip, but "as unobtrusively as possible." The governor's meetings went ahead, but with care.[1]

Tommy Kersey's meeting would go on, too. On January 18, after officials denied him space in Sioux City and Holstein and locked him out of the community center at Marcus, a gathering of roughly a hundred moved to Hull, a town of less than two thousand in Sioux County. There, Kersey told the crowd that they should resist foreclosure. "If enough farmers do not repay loans and enough farmers and their friends resist foreclosure, there is nothing the banks and the government can do about it," he asserted.² The *Sioux County Capital* reported Kersey as saying that "bankers and federal officials will 'shoot you off your farm' if borrowers cannot make timely payments."³ While one attendee stated that Kersey was reasonable, and the meeting was "about as dangerous as a Tupperware party," others disagreed.⁴ The editor of Orange City's newspaper cast Kersey and other members of his organization as extremists, charlatans, and conspiracy theorists whom Iowans would do best to ignore. Kersey and his like were, in the words of this editor, dangerous men who had been "invited uncomfortably close to our neck of the woods by local yokels (or yokelesses) who should know better."⁵ Kersey and his entourage also showed up in Decorah, advocating armed resistance and causing the editor of the Cedar Rapids paper to complain, "As if the Hills—Lone Tree communities' aberrant triple murder and suicide hadn't shaken Iowans enough."⁶ This kind of extremism worried many, who feared even greater troubles than those that had occurred in eastern Iowa. With tempers short and many deeply discouraged, the emphasis on helping farmers became even more critical.⁷

The emphasis of crisis managers in 1986 became assisting and encouraging Iowans to do what they could to help themselves. In some cases that meant retraining farmers to do new jobs. In other cases, it meant bringing in support teams to help when a bank failed. It could also mean more extensive programming on the part of Extension, designed to help those families in the deepest financial and emotional turmoil. Denying what was happening to farmers and communities was useless. Worse, it could be destructive. The governor chose to acknowledge the situation in his Condition of the State Address, commenting, "1985 was a tough year in Iowa. Yet, we Iowans faced reality with courage. Across the nation, the farm crisis is front-page news from time to time, but in Iowa, we live with it day to day." Given that situation, it was time to extend and implement programs that might, perhaps, reduce the level of pain and suffering.⁸ The number of agencies and individuals embracing this idea would be large and various.

New Assistance Programs

In November 1985 a small ad ran in the *Des Moines Register*, advertising a position at Des Moines Area Community College (DMACC). DMACC needed a director for a new program called FARM/CAP. The college advertised for a specialist with experience in career development or agricultural education to provide "career assessment services to displaced farmers and other agriculturally related workers and their spouses." That person would be Joe Harper, a former vocational agriculture instructor-turned-auctioneer and farmer. When he read that advertisement just before Thanksgiving 1985, he was in a panic; he was having the worst day of his life. Several years earlier, pseudorabies (a viral disease that causes reproductive and respiratory problems) had destroyed his herd of purebred Duroc hogs and hard times had taken two thirds of his auction income. The bank had just informed him that he would be expected to pay off his loan by the first of December or lose his land. The bank wanted more than 20 percent interest to refinance the loan. As frightening as his situation was, it made him the perfect person for FARM/CAP. He had the requisite academic credentials and experience and a load of empathy for farmers in crisis. On the Monday after Thanksgiving, DMACC hired him to direct the program.[9]

Funded by a grant from a large agribusiness, FARM/CAP served families in eleven central Iowa counties. The purpose of the program was to help participants assess their options. In the first half of 1986, eleven FARM/CAP workshops took place around central Iowa. More than two hundred participants attended at least part of a nine-day event. The first week offered career planning services. One of the initial steps in the process was to ask, "Is farming an option for me?" Based on the answer to that question, participants could make the decision to remain on the farm or seek employment or training. The workshops helped those moving out of agriculture to work through "a process of loss including periods of denial, guilt and anger." The second week of the workshop addressed the fundamentals of looking for a job, including filling out applications, preparing resumes and cover letters, and interviewing. Many farmers had never done any of these things. Following the workshop, participants could pursue individual counseling and aptitude testing at a DMACC campus. With the help of a counselor, they could develop a plan for a job search. Counselors also provided referrals to social services and mental health centers.[10]

In the summer of 1986, Harper followed up with all 201 FARM/CAP participants. He wanted to know why they had enrolled, and if the program had in any way helped them. Just over 25 percent participated to "determine my options." The other most important reasons for joining were to "identify my skills," "find a job," and deal with "my financial status." The individuals in the program ranged from eighteen to sixty-seven years in age, with the average being 43.5 years old. Most participants were men (63.7 percent). The balance was farm women, usually spouses of farmers. Only 12 percent had college degrees; 71 percent were high school graduates, while 7.5 percent had not graduated from high school. Out of the 201 participants, 121 looked for jobs once the workshop concluded; 78 found employment. Four became carpenters, four went into construction, and four became farm laborers. There were also truck drivers, an aerobics instructor, and a groundskeeper for the Des Moines Golf and Country Club. The list of jobs was long and diverse. Many found agriculture-related careers, while others left farming altogether, whether working for the state lottery or making doughnuts. Just under half of the attendees planned on future training, particularly with computers. Unfortunately, the job market was just as hard on the older participants as agriculture had been. Harper discovered that "only 33.3% of those over 52 obtained employment while 51.3% of those under 36 have new jobs. The unemployment rate was 12.8% for the older group and 2.6% for the younger group." Even so, 93 percent of the participants found the program either very helpful or helpful.[11]

One of the most important aspects of the program was the support it provided to people in turmoil. At a workshop in Knoxville, a leader asked participants to stand and introduce themselves to the group. He wanted them to give their names and explain why they had signed up for the program. One participant in particular illustrated the need for FARM/CAP. As he stood up, he pulled two envelopes out of the front of his bib overalls. One, he explained, was from his lender. He was in foreclosure. The other was from his wife's lawyer; she was divorcing him. He sat down and began to cry. It was for precisely to help this type of person that DMACC had created FARM/CAP.

The program offered displaced farmers an opportunity to develop constructive approaches to their troubles. In the aftermath, participants wrote to program staff to express their appreciation. One wrote, "I was able to find out things about myself I did not know. I found out that I do have other abilities, and skills, besides farming.... I had my first interview on February 8, my second interview on March 1. I begin work on April 1st." Another, who had been out of school for thirty years, wrote, "Many farmers after losing their life's earnings, feel they don't have much to offer society." The workshop had helped him to overcome those feelings, and find his first nonfarming job. One reflected on the benefits to his mental health: "I got to talk and meet people and realize that some of them have the same kind of problems that I have." The wife of a participant explained what FARM/

CAP had done for her husband. "Butch is more content with his situation now . . . He was really feeling out of place with all the failure he had been handed. It's not easy making someone see that a failure, is only a chance to grow again. Butch is a very special man and just needed someone else to tell him so . . . he will succeed."[12]

FARM/CAP organizers realized that the two weeks they spent working with participants was not enough; nor was the scope of the program broad enough to meet some of their most serious needs. Consequently, the FARM/CAP staff cooperated with Extension to organize a conference they called "Project Hope," which trained interested individuals in the creation of farm family support groups. More than one hundred people from all over Iowa attended. FARM/CAP used the balance of their funding to spread their model to other educational institutions, including Iowa Lakes Community College, Simpson College, and Westmar College in Iowa and Lincoln Land Community College in Illinois. The DMACC Foundation also created a $10,000 scholarship fund to which program participants could apply to further their training at DMACC. Seven participants began community college in the immediate aftermath of FARM/CAP.[13]

FARM/CAP was not the only 1986 initiative for farmers under stress. Extension also launched a new program that they called 14–40, or Taking Charge in Changing Times. While the Rural Concern Hotline and ASSIST generally dealt with farm families in the short term, many needed support services over a longer period of time. Beginning in 1986, the Extension program applied for and received funding from the USDA for long-term programming for distressed farm families. Over the last four years of the 1980s, twenty-two Extension personnel would work with between 2,500 and 3,500 families, with an active case load of 550 to 560 families at any one time. This new program was different than many other Extension programs. Daniel Broshar, who headed the program for ISU, explained this new approach: "For the first time I think in the recent history of Extension, we were not going out as Extension employees and saying: we're here with the solution to your problem. Instead, we were going out and saying: okay, tell us—first of all working to develop a close relationship, a good rapport with those families and saying: tell us about your problems." They would work with "economically and emotionally distressed farm families" to identify problems and work toward solutions. In the program's second year, they added distressed small-town families, affected by the downturn in rural business. The program grew out of Extension's need to develop an approach that was less about cows and plows and more about meeting the mental health needs of families experiencing enormous change. To accomplish this goal, Extension agents wanted new tools. For example, one reported, "Boy, it's difficult for me to address the traditional . . . male farm kinds of issues with the male in the family when he is sitting there at the kitchen table with his child in his lap and maybe even crying." Extension agents arrived at farm homes and discovered a changed world: women at work, men caring for the household, and nobody feeling comfortable with this new situation, including the Extension agent. As Broshar put it, "He is feeling stressed by all of that; she is feeling stressed by going to work, and here is this County Extension person saying, well, let's talk about your herbicide and fertilizer needs and he's going I don't care about that stuff." Extension needed a plan for working with families whose most pressing needs had nothing to do with the crop in the field.[14]

Under the umbrella of Taking Charge in Changing Times, staff went into rural homes and worked with families "on their own turf." It was an intimate, long-term process. As Broshar explained,

> People come in, they listen, they don't judge the families for where they are, they allow the families to vent their anger and their frustration and then begin to help them identify small increments of what can be done. And the families choose their own problems that they want to work on and they break it down into very small steps so that you're sort of guaranteeing some success in small step to small step.

Extension designed the program for families that were "extremely immobilized. They are so emotionally distraught and so economically strapped that they really don't know where to go and what to do to get started." Some families needed to adjust to the idea of a parent going off the farm to work, which required them to take a new approach to the care of their homes and children. For the vast majority, the program would help them to make the transition to a life off the farm, providing practical advice about finding jobs but also helping with intangible needs, such as rebuilding the self-esteem of individuals who were now struggling with life's meaning.[15]

The program also involved education for the wider community. Teachers and principals needed to know why students were struggling. In addition to schools, extension staff also worked with churches; along the way, they discovered that some had failed to care for their congregants. Broshar remarked, "One of the big discoveries we found in working with the people was that families in distress who have maybe been very active in the church, all of a sudden stop[ped] going to their church. They felt real embarrassed and real isolated and the church then didn't necessarily recognize and pick up and support that."[16] Churches were some of the most important institutions in the Iowa countryside, but for the most part, they did not have a long history of working with severely distressed farmers. Some churches classified failure to pay debts as a sin and asked members who were in bankruptcy to surrender leadership positions. More than that: Many ministers simply did not know what to say. They knew how to respond to a death in the family, but not to the loss of a farm, which for many families was as wrenching as any other bereavement. Even congregations with a strong communitarian ethos, like the Mennonites, often did not know how to approach the problem, and farmers did not want to burden their friends and neighbors with their financial concerns. Extension provided resources to ministers and lay leaders to improve relations with suffering families.[17] Extension stepped into the process to provide the necessary tools.

Besides the churches, they worked with lenders, who also had no idea how to deal with distraught individuals. A loan officer for the FmHA told Broshar, "I can't handle it when a family comes in to our office and starts crying in the middle of the interview." Others told him, "I won't look up from the desk, I just stare at the paper until it's over." Embarrassment made working through a family's financial problems more difficult for everyone.[18] In response, Extension developed banker education; indeed, while Extension originated in a desire to help farmers to grow more and better crops, the 1980s required the organization to think more holistically about what rural life and community meant. Without a healthy countryside, and an effective support structure for farm families, there might come a day when there was no further need for Extension.

Taking Charge in Changing Times could only help a limited number of families, but the need for support was great, as the psychological toll of economic troubles and farm loss could be overwhelming. Many of the support groups begun in the previous year continued, and new initiatives developed as communities responded to hurting neighbors. In 1986 Farmer to Farmer turned a year old. By that time, organizer Joanne Dvorak of the Family Service Agency in Cedar Rapids had organized nine adult groups and five youth groups that met on a weekly or biweekly basis. Across northeast Iowa, volunteer facilitators who had received twenty hours of training led the groups. The program also trained peer listeners, who acted both formally and informally as a friendly ear for those in need. For the support groups, there was no typical meeting. Instead, individual groups worked on the problems most perplexing their members. Dvorak rooted her understanding of support groups in the Midwest's long agricultural history: "We want to revive neighborliness. We want to revive the community spirit we had when we had threshing bees in rural Iowa. The threshing bee was the first farmer support group. We want farmers to know they are not alone."[19] In Wilton, a group met regularly around a kitchen table, in part with the purpose of educating struggling farmers, and each meeting included ten to twelve participants. They focused on "getting everybody talking," as opposed to having a formal structure. Sometimes members gathered for fun, making ice cream, but just as often they accompanied each other as they applied for jobs or aid. Even at this late date, many people did not know the number for the Rural Concern Hotline.[20] By late 1986, Farmer to Farmer was expanding its reach, hiring full-time counselor Julie Paulsen, who organized a rural women's support group and provided short-term, in-home counseling for families and individuals whose troubles were too complicated for a self-help group.[21] The program evolved with the needs of families throughout northeast Iowa.

Banks in Troubled Times

Problems within the banking system added to the challenges of farmers in distress. Iowa lost thirty-nine banks to the credit crisis. By contrast, the state experienced only four bank failures in all of the 1970s, and would see only one in the 1990s. While no banks closed in either 1980 or 1981, two closed in 1982, and one in 1983. In 1984, it was three. At the height of the crisis, closings accelerated. In 1985, eleven banks failed, and in 1986, ten. The last banks to fail were six each in 1987 and 1988. There was very little in the way of a pattern in those failures. They happened in thirty-four counties spread all across the state. There were multiple bank failures in Hancock, Cherokee, Butler, Sac, Harrison, and Jasper Counties. Some happened in counties that lost many farms to the crisis, while others happened in areas that lost few. Each of these failures, however, happened in a small place (and sometimes a very small place) with a primarily agricultural population.[22]

When a bank failed, the community experienced turmoil. Bank examiners and representatives of the Federal Deposit Insurance Corporation (FDIC) assessed the situation. They evaluated a bank's assets, as well as individual borrowers' accounts. They scrutinized the actions of the banker and his or her employees to discover what had gone wrong and when. Unlike the bank failures of the early 1930s, depositors were unlikely to lose their assets, because the vast majority were insured.

That was the purpose of the Great Depression–era FDIC—to insure deposits and pay off those who might otherwise lose money in the event of a failure. There might be some long, lean months until the insurance payment came through, but it eventually would.

The issue was different for those to whom the bank had made loans. The FDIC was not in the business of keeping farmers on the land; it insured assets and made sure that those who had assets insured with them received payment in full. The FDIC required farmers to apply to at least three other lenders before helping to find alternate funding. The process could take months and the FDIC did not guarantee that farmers would find new lenders. A failed bank's loans received a great deal of scrutiny, and farmers and other small businesses might find themselves without a source of funds for operating expenses and mortgages if their history was the least bit questionable. In the blink of an eye, a farmer could go from having a secure source of operating capital to none at all.[23]

In 1986 Commercial State Bank in Pocahontas failed. On June 27 the FDIC began the process of taking claims and making payments to depositors. In another week, the bank would have been in business for sixty years. Rodney Amlie, bank president until just weeks before the bank closed, announced through his son and successor that "some mistakes had been made." In a slightly more specific letter to the local paper's editor, Amlie clarified, "A few bad apples caused a lot of problems that together with consistently adverse agricultural economic factors, brought my role to an end." In the meantime, the community would not be left without a bank. Citizens State Bank, which operated out of Carroll County, took over.[24] The FDIC processed approximately eleven hundred claims. It would be weeks before depositors saw their money. In the meantime, FDIC officials warned locals to watch their budgets carefully. Social workers came down to the FDIC's temporary offices and provided information to bewildered depositors about how to apply for food stamps.[25]

Farmers held their breath when a bank failed. Bank examiners worked their way back through the books and classified loans. Those farmers whose loans received an "adverse classification" would struggle to find a new lender. Commercial State Bank was in trouble two years before it closed, and the examiners' comments contained many sad stories. The ghost of the 1970s lurked on some farms, with penciled in notations such as "too rapid expansion of facilities." Many farmers had substantial operating losses and insufficient income. Others had lost significant amounts of money on cattle and hog operations. High interest rates also undermined farms. Particularly damning were underlined comments such as "less than average management ability" and "spends liberally." If there was an off-farm job for husband or wife, an inheritance in the offing, or a sympathetic and prosperous family member willing to assume responsibility for a loan, then the comments became more positive. More often, however, examiners littered the pages with notations such as "Not making any commitments," "Open heart surgery," and "FLB (Federal Land Bank) already turned down," indicating that a foreclosure was likely. In other cases, the decision appeared to already have been made, and the bank examiners recommended sale of all or part of the farmer's land, livestock, and machinery; as one farmer's page in the ledger said, "the sale of remaining assets should wash out the line without further loss to the bank."[26]

In the lead up to the failure, however, the bank had been lenient toward distressed farmers. In the flurry of comment surrounding the bank's closure, a writer for the local paper had editorialized about President Rod Amlie, saying, "He worked hard until the end to keep many struggling farmers in business, and the people here thank him for that."[27] The bank examiners saw the situation differently, unhappy with the position he and his staff took with most loans, which they characterized as an attitude of "Yeah, we'll have to wait 'til after harvest and then take a good look at where we are." The bank staff tended to reserve judgement and continue to work with borrowers despite difficulties. This attitude, the examiners alleged, amounted to borderline negligence: "The fact that some of these overlines are repeat situations and others are relatively clear-cut excesses suggests that not enough attention is being given to lending limits and the monitoring of line totals." The examiners' position was that lenience was a weakness, rather than a strength. When a small-town bank folded, troubled borrowers were unlikely to find another lender that was as willing to extend credit and forbearance, if they found a lender at all.

In light of that reality, the IFUC and PrairieFire stepped in to help borrowers understand the situation when their bank failed. The groups published a flyer for rural communities, laying out in brief how to proceed in such cases. They stressed a proactive approach, especially on the part of those with a loan that was "undersecured, past due, or has serious credit weaknesses." That kind of situation required a farmer to "market" his or her loan and work hard to find another lender. The IFUC admonished borrowers to be "assertive, patient, polite, and persistent!" They also encouraged people to be realistic: "Do not make indebtedness a moral standard! Bankruptcy is not a moral condition, it is a financial condition and should be recognized and treated as such. You, your family, and your community will need support and resources during this particularly difficult time. Use the available resources offered by others. Organize effectively and move quickly from crisis to community!"[28] If all else failed, and a farmer wanted to remain in agriculture, bankruptcy might be the only solution.

In 1985 PrairieFire also created a "Bank Failure Response Team," formalizing its training materials a year later. The team involved farmers, ministers, attorneys, and community leaders. They provided extensive information to individuals, and especially farmers affected by bank closures, reminding them that "when FDIC says 'everything is OK,' they are referring to depositors, not borrowers!" Borrowers needed to plan carefully, make difficult decisions, and move into action. "ACTION," they claimed, "is the key word. Do not wait for FDIC to make the first move; procrastination should not be in your vocabulary." Stranded borrowers needed to know what their family required this week and next, and what resources their livestock and farming operation demanded. They needed to plan to survive the next six months. Ultimately, they might have to face some very hard questions, such as "Do I want to continue this business or 'chuck it in'?" or, "Do I have alternative plans if this doesn't work?"[29] The Bank Failure Response Team could not eliminate the stress of the situation but could alleviate some of the tension and provide borrowers a blueprint for moving ahead.

If borrowers were in trouble, then bankers and other loan officers were, too. The stresses of working day in and day out with people in trouble, often angry, depressed, or distraught, were enormous. In some cases, bankers found themselves in a hole, and in desperation dug themselves in even further. Such was the case of Rodney Amlie, who owned banks in both Pocahontas and Webster City. The failure of the bank in Pocahontas revealed a mess of misappropriation that led to a five-year prison sentence. Amlie pleaded guilty to five felonies, including embezzling $2 million from the bank in Pocahontas, defrauding the FDIC of $485,000, and three counts of falsifying the bank's books to cover his crimes. In an unusual move, the editor of the *Pocahontas Record Democrat* gave Amlie most of the front page of the paper above the fold to explain his actions. It was a recitation of troubles that explained the many ways in which the problems of the decade had pinched bankers—some of them to the point of fraud. Amlie claimed that prior to the events of the spring of 1986, he was "Iowa's largest independent agricultural lender. This was predicated considerably upon livestock lending—and 1985 was a disastrous year for livestock prices." But this was not the only challenge Amlie faced. Cold weather in the previous two years had pushed up the price of feed, making the livestock business even more precarious. The dairy herd buyout further drove down the profitability of cattle. As he was a large livestock feeder on top of his banking business, this did not bode well.[30]

Problems with the agricultural loan business ran even deeper. As Amlie put it, the decline in land prices had led to "farmers with burdensome amounts of debt... being driven to the wall." He also worried that they were being driven into lawyers' offices to file for bankruptcy. Perhaps not surprisingly, all four of the long-time loan officers in the Pocahontas office left their jobs between mid-1984 and mid-1985. Amlie complained, "It was no longer any fun to be constantly embroiled with the credit problems of people who were not making it." With the experienced loan officers gone it became more difficult to manage the bank and get loans repaid. Farmers were no longer working with their long-time loan officers, to whom they might feel a sense of responsibility. At the end of 1984, a major borrower sold livestock in violation of the terms of his mortgage and failed to use the proceeds to pay down his loan. The borrower's father was financially responsible for the loan and went into bankruptcy, creating a large hole in the bank's finances. By February 1986 the bank and its president were on the verge of collapse. Amlie wrote, "I began to take abnormal risks in the commodity markets to effect a quick recovery. I had been in the saddle constantly for several years, and I was totally exhausted from the pain and strain. It was in this environment that I began the chain of misappropriation of funds and false entries. And once the cat was out of the bag, there was no recovery." Amlie used the bank's money to gamble on commodity trading, hoping to recoup the $18 million dollars that his banks lost between 1983 and 1986. The gamble did not pay off. Amlie wrote, "Now I am finished." He provided an explanation but also apologized: "There is no justification for what I did in those final months of virtual panic and turmoil."[31] While it is difficult to tell from a distance exactly what happened at the Commercial State Bank in Pocahontas, Rodney Amlie spun a likely tale of what *could* happen under the conditions existing in 1980s agriculture. Adverse conditions made small-town, agricultural banking difficult to sustain, even when pursued on a large scale.

Farmer-Creditor Concerns

Given the anger and anxiety generated by problems within the banking system, relieving stress between farmers and lenders was a legislative priority in the new year. The Republican governor and Democratic lieutenant governor made a bipartisan plea to the legislature, supported by a number of farm organizations, from the Farm Bureau to the IFUC, to do something about problems between farm borrowers and lenders before more disputes bubbled over into violence. Initially, they asked that the state legislature appropriate $100,000 to help to finance Drake University's farmer/creditor mediation service. Michael Thompson, the program's director, began the service late in 1985 with $25,000 from Pioneer Hi-Bred. It was the first program of its kind. It began as a voluntary service and 99 percent of the requests for mediation came from farmers. One of the initial hurdles was the $50 an hour fee, which many farmers could not afford. Once farmers and lenders were in the room together, the next challenge was getting them to understand each other's language. Farmers, said Thompson, talked "emotionally about the land and about how it's been in the family for generations and what the land means to them." Lenders, on the other hand, "talk about debt-to-asset ratios and cash flows." The mediators facilitated communication.[32]

In the spring, state legislators decided to go a step further and passed a Farmer/Creditor Mediation law. Both Iowa and Minnesota passed laws requiring mediation in the case of a pending foreclosure, while Wisconsin and North Dakota passed voluntary measures. The Iowa law required lenders to request mediation before they could begin foreclosure proceedings on any debt greater than $20,000. Lenders would notify the farmer by mail, giving him twenty-one days to respond. Farmers could waive their right to mediation. Both the farmer and the lender paid a $25 fee for the first hour of mediation and $12.50 per hour thereafter. Mediators encouraged farmers to come to the negotiation with all of their documents, as well as a plan. While workers in Extension's ASSIST program offered to help gather the documents, mediators made no promises: "Mediation is an opportunity for you to negotiate with your lender(s) and possible work out a financial agreement. However, an agreement cannot always be reached because of the circumstances involved. You need to be prepared for the possibility that the results of the meeting might not meet your expectations."[33]

What definitely did not meet the state's expectations was the volume of farmers referred to the program when it went fully into effect in the summer of 1986. In the second week of June, the program received four hundred requests for mediation; the state had expected four hundred cases per month. Over the course of the summer, the FLB referred one thousand cases for mediation. Thompson and his office had already trained ninety-five volunteer mediators by the time the law went

Farmers turned to the law in the hope of finding a solution to their problems with lenders. By permission of David Peterson.

into effect, but they needed more volunteers and more funds.³⁴ The high caseload continued through the summer and fall. In December Thompson requested another $100,000 from the state legislature and predicted that running the program through 1988 would cost approximately $800,000. He also predicted that it would be another four years before the numbers of cases would fall sufficiently to bring the service to a close. Thompson claimed that of the four thousand cases submitted in the second half of 1986, roughly 30 percent did not go to mediation because the farmer chose not to exercise this option. He believed that 55 percent of cases had been "successfully concluded," although he did not define what he meant by that term. Presumably, the lender and the borrower had come to an agreement that both could accept. The mediators could not resolve every case satisfactorily. Many farmers had been ill-prepared for the mediation, and some had unrealistic expectations about what could be accomplished. Nonetheless, it may have defused some potentially explosive situations.³⁵

A new bankruptcy law, whose chief sponsor in the US Senate was Iowa's Republican senator Chuck Grassley, also changed creditor/farmer relationships. Bankruptcy was an increasingly important issue in the state. The number of bankruptcies in Iowa had been growing by leaps and bounds, but on the whole, bankruptcy law was not terribly favorable toward farmers. Nevertheless, Iowa's farmers increasingly chose bankruptcy because of concerns with taxes. If farmers liquidated assets outside of bankruptcy, they often discovered they had a huge tax bill to pay. If a farmer threatened a bankruptcy, a lender might decide to help develop a payment plan to forestall action; if the farmer proceeded, the family would not be left with capital gains taxes. The new bankruptcy law, unlike the existing Chapter 7 or Chapter 11, had provisions written expressly for farmers. The Family Farmer Bankruptcy Act, also called Chapter 12, gave families the opportunity to continue farming while they attempted to reorganize their debts and retain control of their land. As long as they were capable of paying a fair market rent and creating a reasonable repayment plan, they would be able to keep farming. Lenders would not be able to immediately demand a forced sale. While it made bankers unhappy, the law had the approval of farm advocates such as PrairieFire's David Ostendorf, who had worked with Grassley on the contours of the legislation.³⁶

The sponsors intended the law for family farmers who received either more than 50 percent of their income or 80 percent of their debts from agriculture, and whose debts did not exceed $1.5 million. In order to qualify, the farmer needed to have sufficient annual income to repay the debt after reorganization and restructuring. A farmer filing Chapter 12 bankruptcy could remain in possession of and work the land as long as there had been no fraud, gross mismanagement, dishonesty, or incompetency on their part. After a bankruptcy declaration, the law barred creditors from collecting any money from the debtor, unless allowed by the bankruptcy court. One important feature of the law was that lenders could not force farmers to pay for the decline in their land's value due to losses in the land market. A farmer whose property's value had fallen from $1.5 million to $750,000, for example, would not be liable for the $750,000 in value that the land had lost. This significantly improved a family's chances of hanging onto their acres, since the court could not require them to compensate a lender for "lost opportunity costs," something previous bankruptcy legislation allowed.[37] Because of the provisions made to deal with the problem of land values, farmers had a far better chance of emerging successfully from bankruptcy under Chapter 12 than under any other law. The provision's sponsors hoped that it would "stop the displacement" and "stop the bleeding on the farm."[38]

Farmers who chose to go through bankruptcy, however, faced unpleasant conversations with family and neighbors, and much soul searching. Many in the farming community perceived bankruptcy as shameful and wanted to avoid it at all costs. Although a number of advocacy organizations argued that it was a reasonable strategy for those who wanted to remain in agriculture, farmers struggled to accept the idea. In small places, a failure to pay one's debts meant that someone with a face, not some distant corporate entity, was likely to suffer and might lose their business as a result.[39] Declaring bankruptcy also reinforced the shame that economically distressed farmers experienced, forcing them to confront their own guilty feelings about bad decision making. Bankruptcy made private failures very public.[40] When *Successful Farming* ran an article in February 1986 suggesting that bankruptcy was an honorable course for those in extreme financial difficulty, the letters to the editor showed the division on the subject. A North Dakotan wrote about their family situation, "your article said more than we ever could about our sons who are trying to keep the family farm. They are going through Chapter 11, and swear they will pay every cent to their creditors if they can. Thanks for being behind those of us who are trying our best."[41]

Others within the farming community, however, vehemently rejected the idea of bankruptcy. A farmer from Alma, Missouri, sent a blistering note: "Cancel my subscription immediately. Every penny not wasted on magazines like *Successful Farming* will help keep me from following your despicable suggestions to walk away from debt and take bankruptcy 'with all honor and dignity.'" Another asserted that he had paid his bills, had not borrowed excessively, and now would be paying the freight for those who had tried in the 1970s to get big. He wrote, "I'm not saying that lenders should not try to work with farmers who have a chance to survive. They should. But they do not have the obligation to keep an insolvent farmer in business. Bankruptcy should not be a way to continue operating."[42] Chapter 12 might give families an opportunity to keep the farm intact, but the new law would not ease the disdain for bankruptcy that existed in many parts of the rural community.

Stopping the bleeding on farms required more than bankruptcy legislation. In 1986 the state legislature took the unusual move of authorizing interest rate buydowns for distressed farmers. The General Assembly appropriated $5 million to fund and administer the program. Farmers enrolled in the Iowa Agricultural Loan Assistance Program (IALAP) would have a buydown of up to 3 percent on their operating loan for 1986–1987. Other farmers could see their interest rates decline by as much as 7 percent, with a 2 percent contribution from a local lender and 3 percent from the FmHA, which had begun a program to buydown interest rates in March. Only resident farmers qualified, and only for operating loans. There were no net worth restrictions on the loans, but they were unavailable to farmers who were "exiting agriculture" or who were in a "positive cash-flow position." In other words, they were for the struggling, but not-yet failed. Farmers who wanted to participate but were ineligible for FmHA loans had to agree to a farm financial analysis through Extension or another reputable farm financial organization, with the goal of working toward eligibility for FmHA assistance. The program would buy farmers time to improve their operation.[43]

Larry and Mary Beth Mather of Sigourney were the first farmers to qualify for the program. They had been farming for seventeen years but were at the end of their tether. The couple worked four hundred acres, some owned and some rented, and ran a herd of sixty-five cattle. They also purchased feeder pigs to raise to slaughter weight. Under the new law, they qualified for—and could afford—a $45,000 operating loan, which they used largely for feed and fertilizer. The break in interest rates, they hoped, would be enough to keep them going. Without the loan, they believed they were looking at their last year in farming.[44]

The Mathers's good fortune, however, was not good news to everyone. Iowans expressed a vast range of opinion on the interest rate buydown, and whether or not farmers should receive that kind of aid. Some rejected the idea of aid at all. One wrote, "If you wish to continue to make this a growth state, give the breaks to people in this state who can make the growth possible by lowering taxes for new business, not by giving the breaks to the 'problem areas.'" A motel owner in Ames did not object so much to the idea of aid, but to the fact that it was restricted it to farmers. He wanted the same offer: "Since I'm also an owner of a small business (just like a farmer) and my receipts are going down and expenses going up, are you going to do the same for me? Since my mortgage is $750,000, a 4% 'buy down' would sure 'help' me (about $30,000 a year)." Keith Heffernan, the governor's special assistant for agriculture, assured the writer that the governor was not ignoring his troubles, but he may not have been convinced. The state provided no interest rate buydowns for businesses. A widow from the Carroll area was unhappy with the legislation because it did not apply to her situation. Her husband had died of cancer, and rather than farm the land herself she rented it to a farmer. She still owed money on the property and would have benefited from an interest rate buydown, but she did not qualify. She wrote, "I feel all farmers who borrow money should receive cheaper interest, not just a few. Why penalize those who did without, to pay their interest and principal & give the cheap interest to a few." Another farm woman from Charter Oak agreed, writing, "the farmers who always pay their bills are the ones who have to suffer. No one will give them a break on interest rates. Your new bill doesn't help us. We will end up paying in a different way." Instead, she wanted a state usury law, which would hold interest rates down for everyone, farmers, small business owners, and home owners alike.[45] No farm legislation was likely to please everyone, and new measures resolving debt issues were particularly tricky politically since many Iowans associated debt with the idea of profligate behavior, especially during the boom times of the 1970s, whether it was reality or not.

Food Aid Continues

Fighting out of deep loan debt was not the only kind of struggling occurring on Iowa's farms. Problems with hunger in agricultural communities had not resolved themselves and continued to get attention from charities, activist groups, and social services agencies. Sometimes free food arrived unexpectedly. In April 1986 a truckload of free potatoes appeared at the Cargill parking lot in Fonda. As the local paper noted, "This is a Farm Crisis program and anyone who needs potatoes can get them."[46] At other times, local organizations scrambled to take advantage of circumstances. In December 1986 a driver for the Super Value grocery store in

Mapleton missed a curve in the fog and early morning dark and rolled his truck into a ditch, "strewing groceries as it went." Volunteers scurried into action, picking up $5,000 of salvageable food. Some of the food went to emergency pantries in northwestern Iowa. West Central Development in Mapleton also claimed some of the food for use in Christmas boxes for the needy. Super Value, a company that already supported many Iowa food pantries, wrote off the truck and its contents.[47] Monsignor A. W. Behrens, pastor of St. Mary's Church in Mapleton, extended his thanks to area residents who helped with the salvage effort and offered to pay for the labor of all who volunteered for food recovery and distribution.[48]

The push to enroll farmers for federal food aid also persisted. In March 1986 the IFUC continued the food stamp drives. Prior to the event, the organization held a training seminar in Ames and asked that each county send an IFUC member. Organizers wanted to make sure that there were informed people at courthouses for the March 3 event.[49] The Iowa Department of Human Resources also produced new food stamp literature for farmers and self-employed Iowans to help them determine whether they fit income guidelines and to help them understand how bank failures and bankruptcies affected eligibility. For example, "any asset which has been frozen as a result of a bank failure or FDIC takeover is not considered a resource during the time it's frozen." On the other hand, "the equity value of grain being held for higher prices is counted as a resource."[50] Applying for food stamps remained a complicated process.

The March drive had mixed success, with families claiming a smaller than expected number of applications, although some came before or after the event. A representative from the IFUC commented, "One of the things that we have learned in the past is that some people go before and after the drive, because they are not too thrilled about going, and they are afraid the media might be there."[51] This was not how most Iowans wanted to get themselves into the papers or on the evening news. Some families, too, still worried about the embarrassment of accepting and using food stamps. A Chariton, Iowa, woman described to a *Chicago Tribune* reporter driving seventy miles away from home to buy groceries, because "snooty cashiers" in local stores gossiped and spread the stamps across the counter, "like they're playing Monopoly." Using benefits remained painfully public. Nevertheless, she continued using food stamps because she and her husband wanted to save their farm: "If it means we have to go into every kind of government program to get a check to save the farm, then we've got to do it."[52]

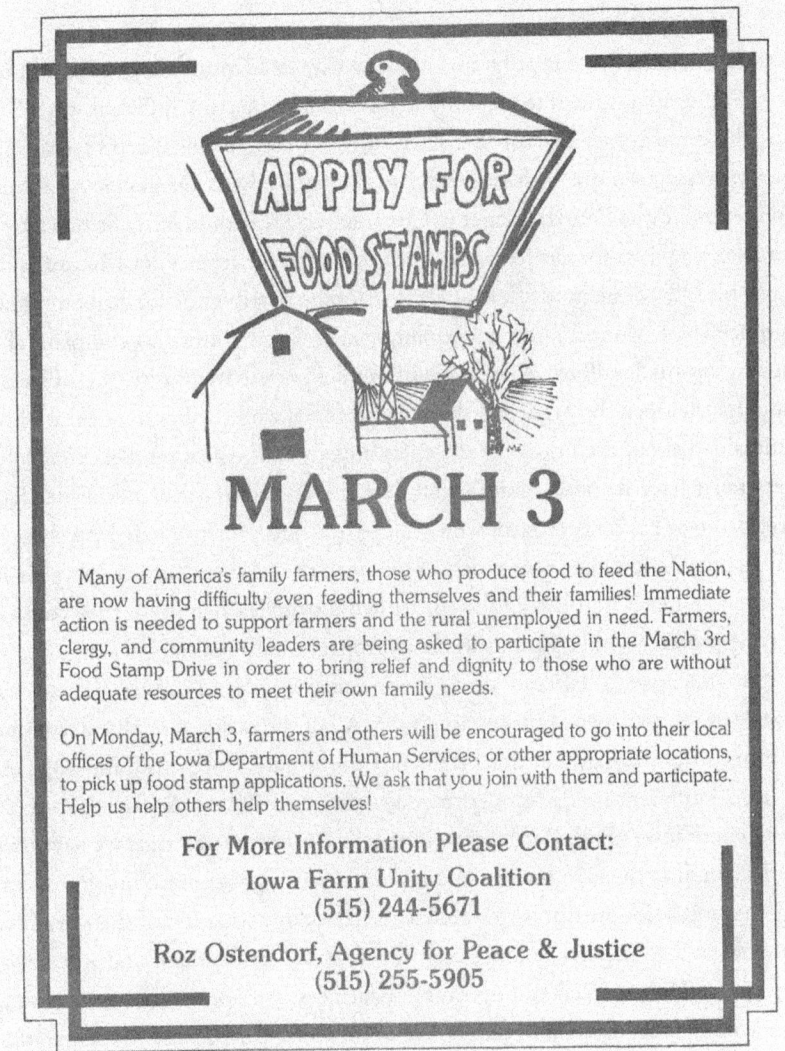

The Iowa Farm Unity Coalition advertised its food stamp enrollment drives with flyers indicating that everyone, eligible or not, should attend. Denise O'Brien Papers, Iowa Women's Archives, University of Iowa Libraries.

Advocacy

Getting into government programs was one way to advocate for oneself and one's farm. Farmers continued to stand up for themselves in many different ways. Some took the opportunity to visit the offices of their congressional representatives to convey messages more-or-less directly to those in power. Democrat Neal Smith represented Iowa's Fourth district in Congress, and his Ames office fielded a steady stream of requests for aid from rural people. A farmer from Pilot Mound, unable to pay his bills, came in to ask for help developing a strip mine for coal on his land. Another Pilot Mound farmer, a tenant, visited Smith's office to complain about gouging by his landlord. A resident of rural Perry chatted with the office staff about his views on the origins of the farm problem, while a man from rural Huxley complained about the impact of the dairy buyout on the beef market. Some of the visits must have worried Smith's staff, like the one from a Roland farmer facing foreclosure of his century farm who seemed "to think violence may help things, or may happen." How they responded to that visit they did not record. Nevertheless, the congressman's staff listened to constituents' troubles, helping as they could and relaying problems and opinions to the appropriate authorities.[53]

Others chose to demand aid in more visible ways, and cooperation seems to have been the watchword throughout 1986. All of the major agricultural commodity groups worked together that year, a rare occurrence, since cattle and hog raisers often had different needs from corn and soybean producers. As Rich VandeHaar, president of Iowa's Pork Producers announced, "this is the first time we have united in one common cause to make a public statement." Eight commodity groups came together to ask for measures to stabilize the economic situation of their producers. They wanted to see less-volatile cash flows, stable land prices, and interest rate buydowns. They wanted to buy time for farmers to improve their situation and were willing to set aside their differences to present a united front to their state and national representatives.[54]

A different kind of unity was also evident in the spring of 1986. Farm groups reached beyond the borders of agriculture to ask for help. The IFUC made common cause with labor unions and social policy groups such as the Iowa Citizen Action Network (ICAN) to plead the case for a program to benefit "all working people in Iowa." IFUC, ICAN, the Iowa Federation of Labor, and the UAW jointly sponsored an "Iowa Solidarity Day" on March 11 in support of family farms, higher wages, tax reform, and an improved human services budget.[55] At the national level, eleven organizations, including the AFL-CIO, to the National Rural Life Conference, the National Educational Association, and the United Auto Workers, issued a joint statement. The groups announced, "It's Everybody's Crisis: No One Is Immune to the Family Farm Collapse" and called for federal government action. Their combined concern arose from the power of the agricultural depression to undermine both rural communities and industrial employment. The organizations blamed the federal government for the troubles in the countryside and demanded action to solve them: "It is the responsibility of those in government to exercise their leadership to alter those policies which perpetuate this economic and social catastrophe." Precisely which policies those were, they failed to mention. Something, however, needed to be done, with farms and jobs at stake.[56]

Making a statement was not just for the adults; as the crisis dragged on into the second half of the decade, more young people worried about their ability to continue in agriculture. A vehement fourteen-year-old, relying on many an exclamation point, laid out his concerns for the governor. Aaron Brodersen came straight to the point: "I am writing due to the Farm Crisis. My parents and I are very concerned. I am a 14 yr. old Iowa Farm boy. I *know* what is going on." He explained to Branstad that "all we need is a price for our grain and our animals we raise. We cannot survive with low markets and high expences [sic]." By way of example, he mentioned what happened when his parents went to the parts store: "They want an arm and a leg for the parts!" He also wanted to see a new president. "President Reagan talks like he is going to be a big help, but he is *all* talk and *no* go! He don't care what is happening on our farms." Broderson knew that he would have to wait for the next election, but "by then for some, it will be too late for help." It was time to appeal to the governor. "I am wondering if you can help us out? There are more and more farm sales every week! It has to be stopped! Soon their [sic] won't be any small farmers left. Only the 'big shots' will be farming.... Maybe you can talk to the president to get us some help.... I invite you to my farm or write, or call me." He signed himself "A concerned farmboy!" His postscript placated the governor, just in case he had been a little too vehement: "I realize you are trying very hard to help us. Keep it up! Thanks A lot!"[57]

Aaron Brodersen was not the only Iowa youngster feeling the pinch of troubled times, looking for guidance and help. Deanna Potter wrote to express her concerns to the governor as well. "What I don't like the most," she wrote, "is that now days [sic] children have to watch while people take away their home and it seems like the family can't do anything about it. The farmers and their families are doing everything they possibly can but some still lose their farms and some people who have the money don't want to help that need it and are just thinking about themselves."[58] Meanwhile, an Adair mother reported to the statehouse what she had learned from her son's teacher: "Our youngest son is in 6th grade. When I attended parent-teacher conferences, his teacher told me almost every day a student comes to school crying because they will lose their farm and have to move. Is this what we want for our children? Is this the best Iowa can offer its young people?"[59] A grandfather from Hubbard mourned his grandson's abandonment of agriculture, writing, "My grand Son is a Sophemor he was going to be a farmer but now no way he says he is going to be a Lawyer he is a student in High Scool. Wat a loss [sic]." His father's situation had discouraged the boy: "Our Son is in debt $150,000. He says shall I quit."[60] Jeff Tilkes, a high-school student from rural New Hampton had noticed the same phenomenon: "The kids my age that always wanted to farm when they were younger don't even think about farming."[61] The exodus from farms troubled Iowans, young and old.

Young people's concerns went beyond issues such as occupational choice. A Silver City boy whose father depended upon the farm economy struggled to understand what was happening and wanted more than a form letter from the governor: "I would like it a little better if a letter was to ME not everybody in one." He explained, "My dad is a Blacksmith in Silver City. He depends on the farmers for business. My dad is the one who brings the food money in, and mom's job does the rest. I guess the reason I am writing you is because I would like to see every farmer come out on top for once."[62] Even youngsters who came from nonfarming families had concerns about the farm economy. A girl from Sioux City wrote, "Every time I hear of a farmer killing himself, his wife, and innocent children, it makes me think of how hard you really are trying to clear up a poor farm economy, and how stubborn the president really is in not passing farm bills."[63] A boy from Rolfe was worried about his classmates: "I have many friends that their mothers and fathers are being handicapped by this ordeal. I can see how this is impairing them so I am asking you to please look into this situation a little farther."[64]

Children needed adults to explain the crisis to them, but many parents struggled to understand their own situations, let alone explain them to children. The alternative, however, was to leave the situation to children's own musings, which could be a terrible decision. As one writer put it, "if we don't talk with them, they can only imagine what terror is changing mom and dad and threatening their home."[65] Given parents' struggles to explain difficult family situations, sometimes someone outside the home needed to initiate the conversation. To that end, elementary schools in Onslow and Monmouth, in eastern Iowa, piloted a program begun by a farm couple who described themselves as casualties of the rural crisis. Called "It Helps to Talk," the program provided children the details of what could happen to a farm when financial troubles hit. The point of the program was not to scare children but to give them the information they needed to understand that they had not caused their families' problems. "It Helps to Talk," in theory, would replace fear, rumor, and misinformation with a foundation of understanding. The schools invited parents to sit in and publicized the program to other area schools.[66]

"It Helps to Talk" was not the only programming originating out of Iowa schools. In Benton County, a school board meeting resulted in a commitment to special programs for students whose parents were experiencing financial difficulties. In the fall, four students from the high school attended a camp organized by a student support group from Vinton. Five different school districts sent a total of twenty-five students. They watched *Country*, listened to speakers, and shared ideas. The Benton students planned to return to their own school and begin a support group. Their district was not alone in considering these issues. The Coon Rapids Parent Council scheduled a series of informational meetings for the 1986–1987 academic year and asked the public to vote on which topics to consider. They suggested a number of programs related to the agricultural downturn: a peer help program, the "Farm Crisis: Impact on Children and Families," "Stress on Students," and stress management. The Mid-Prairie District, near Kalona, held a workshop in February to discuss the farm crisis. Organized by the school counselor and a committee of FFA members, they sponsored the event to "increase awareness of the difficult financial and emotional problems prevailing." They, too, showed *Country* , followed it with a discussion about "dealing with stress," and planned more events for the future.[67]

Extension also turned to the problems of rural children, often in the form of direction for individuals leading 4-H programs (4-H was the USDA's youth development program, managed by Extension). The list of issues that 4-H leaders needed to address in light of the agricultural collapse was daunting, made even more so by the fact that 4-H leaders were volunteers, often farm men and women themselves, facing the same sorts of doubts, uncertainties, and stresses as many across the state. 4-H encouraged both parents and leaders, stressed or not, to pay close attention to the needs of children who were experiencing the Farm Crisis and might be suffering depression, physical illness, and any number of behavioral problems. Adults needed to help children transform their thinking about difficult conditions. As an example, children might be moving off the farm. In that situation, a piece of 4-H advice suggested how youngsters might view that situation: "He has a choice of what he can tell himself about the move. *Negative thoughts*: I'm a farm kid. All my ancestors were farmers. It will ruin my life if we lose the farm." The adults in that child's life had the opportunity to help him rewrite the script: "*Positive thoughts*: I'm proud of my farm background. I would like to farm myself; but I can do other things. Some of these may be more enjoyable and less stressful than farming."[68]

The organization also addressed the practical, day in and day out challenges that a changing economy imposed upon farm families. Circumstances pushed many farm parents to take jobs off the farm, which meant that more farm children would be home alone after school. 4-H leaders, in response, provided skill-building for new "latchkey kids." One way to do this was for adults to encourage children, in a positive way, "to imagine things that can happen. A discussion among a group of latchkey 4-H'ers might turn up a batch of good safety tips." Of course, sending a child to 4-H after school was a great way to keep them occupied and safe while mom and dad were at work.[69] In the 1980s, even in farm country, 4-H was about more than growing the best corn or raising the best pig for the county fair. Leading 4-H required a combination of both new and old approaches. In a world where the unthinkable had happened, and some Iowa farm families were too severely stressed to afford to give a child a pig or a calf for a 4-H project, 4-H leadership meant considering new approaches and projects.[70] The program attempted to provide children a safe space where they could continue to be children, even if their families were living with enormous strain.

Even in the depths of the crisis, there were still young people who wanted to get into agriculture. In 1986 those hopes and dreams could seem very distant. A twenty-one-year-old from Fenton named Scott Alan Looft wrote an impassioned plea to the governor and penciled in across the top of the first page, "Please if some[one] else reads this PLEASE give to the *Governor*." Looft wanted to farm his own land, but he had no idea how he would achieve that goal. While still in high school he had gone to work for a hog operation and "learned the skills of a Hog man." Declining prices had put an end to that job, and he followed it with seasonal work with another farmer, and then a short course at Iowa State. He also took jobs in manufacturing and as a hired man. He wrote, "I make enough to pay the bills but there is no extra money to do anything." He had two years' experience with hogs, two years in manufacturing, and four years as what he called "a decision-making hired man," one with greater responsibility. When he wanted to strike out on his own, however, he could not find a lender. He wrote, "I have the skill and the experience to do anything But don't Have the old Family money Be hind [sic] me. You see my father is in poor financial shape, and probably won't be farming any more in a few years." He wanted a chance to make it on his own: "I won't starve but I can't even feed a family and Have NO Future." Please, he said, "All I need is a start. Then I will begin to feed the world."[71]

Doug Mayland, another young farmer, was in a better position; the state had just approved his application for an IFFDA beginning farmer loan, but the letter he wrote to the governor reflected more than a little insecurity. He had his loan in hand but he was not out of the woods. He wrote, "What happens to those farmers with a 1990's future, a 1970's past and a 1986 debt?" Mayland believed that many of his fellow farmers would have no future without a debt buydown: "We *must* have a debt write off, or *at least* a debt restructuring program that realizes we must have time to move our operations into the new lower priced, lower cost era. We've been made to 'change horses in the middle of the stream.'" He wanted a future for rural Iowa and its farmers, and for the state to help pay the cost. He argued, "The cost is being paid by numerous foreclosures, forced sales, dreams torn apart, familys [sic] broken and yes, even violence. Let the remainder of the cost be paid for by understanding legislation that speaks to those of us caught in the middle. We are a productive hard-working people. By keeping our current farm population intact they can only be an asset to this states future [sic]."[72] Mayland was a hopeful young farmer, but even he was not at all certain that rural Iowa would recover from its current crisis.

Conditions in Rural Communities

Mayland was right to be concerned about rural Iowa; hard times pummeled small communities. A falling—and financially stressed— population meant that Main Streets throughout Iowa's farm country were under pressure and business failures abounded. A survey of bankers in the upper Midwest indicated that there were as many small business failures as there were farm failures, and maybe more.[73] Among the businesses most seriously affected by the downturn were agricultural machinery dealerships. In the first half of the decade, 150 machinery dealerships across the

Tiny communities faced especially tough times as schools and businesses left. By permission of David Peterson.

state folded. These businesses often brought farmers into town, who then turned around and spent money at other businesses. When a machinery dealership died, the town lost an economic anchor.⁷⁴

Businesses were not the only economic anchors in small towns; services also brought people to town and kept them there. They were employers, but also magnets, drawing in residents. They could not keep their doors open without a stable population base. Small-town hospitals were losing patients, seeing 25 percent fewer admissions than in 1983–1985.⁷⁵ Rural schools were also in trouble, losing revenue as families left the countryside. The state provided limited aid and getting cash-strapped farmers to approve bond issues and voluntarily increase their taxes was a difficult business. By the mid-1980s, districts risked losing their schools if they could not find a stronger revenue stream. In 1986 the state began to require school districts to provide "appropriate instructional programs" or pay tuition for students whose parents wanted to enroll them outside the district. If a school could not afford instruction in foreign languages or advanced math and science, it would lose children to other districts, while paying their costs at a larger, better funded school. Dozens of small communities across the state faced difficult questions about the continued viability of their schools.[76]

How to salvage the fortunes of rural communities was unclear. The state began the push to promote small towns to interested businesses, hoping to lure more industry to Iowa.[77] Iowa also accelerated its participation in the Main Street program, a nationwide initiative to bring more business and greater development to the nation's central business districts. In 1986 the state committed money from its lottery to community grants, providing each Main Street participant community a $15,000 grant, with the understanding that the town would raise matching funds. In Marion, for example, local business associations and the Chamber of Commerce pledged more than $50,000 over three years toward the revitalization of the city's downtown. Marion planned to use most of the money to hire a project manager to oversee economic development and improvement efforts. Whether the program would help to stop the bleeding, however, remained to be seen.[78]

Agricultural Conditions

Farmers entered planting season in 1986 feeling very unsure about the health of their farms and those of their neighbors. The spring "Farm and Rural Life Poll" out of Iowa State Extension showed that since the fall of 1984, farmers' concerns had grown, rather than diminished. The crisis that had been relatively new to many in 1984 was by 1986 dragging on. The 1986 numbers, generated by polling a random sample of 3,282 Iowa farmers, were depressing. When asked about the current financial condition of Iowa farmers, only 1 percent believed that there was no problem. The vast majority, 93 percent, believed that the financial condition of people like themselves was a moderately serious (19 percent) or very serious (74 percent) problem. They also believed that the agribusinesses in their area were in trouble, with 37 percent seeing a moderate problem, and 48 percent seeing a very serious problem. They believed that their financial institutions were also in trouble, with 41 percent seeing a moderate problem, and 23 percent a severe one. When it came to the condition of their own farms, 22 percent were mildly concerned, and 41 percent very concerned. Only a tiny minority planned expansion in their farming operation, with most hoping simply to maintain their current level of operation. At this point, 8 percent anticipated a foreclosure in the next year or two, and

10 percent planned to file for some sort of bankruptcy. The poll's respondents were not a cheery group.[79]

Additionally, farmers' reflections on the previous five years and their expectations of the five years to come were grim. When asked about changes in their quality of life over the previous five years, 51 percent believed that it had become somewhat worse, while 23 percent believed it was much worse. Only 1 percent believed that the quality of life for Iowa's farm families would become much better in the next five years; 34 percent believed it would be somewhat worse, and 10 percent much worse. When asked about the economic prospects of farmers in the next five years, 38 percent said they would be somewhat worse, and 25 percent much worse.[80] At this point, the state's farmers were years into a crisis with no end in sight. In terms of their ability to make a living, nothing significant had changed. Farmers' corn fetched $1.83 per bushel, but it cost them $2.45 to grow.[81] There was no new hook upon which to hang an improved future. There were more supports in place for failing farmers, but there was no easy remedy for the conditions producing distress.

The year had begun with the news that landowners had lost even more money on their property in the previous twelve months. For the fourth consecutive year, land values had fallen; they had dropped more than 30 percent in 1985. It was the worst single year drop in the value of land since the most crushing of the Great Depression years, 1932–1933. The average value of all agricultural land in the state stood at $948 an acre, down $409 from the previous year. Corrected for inflation, land values were lower than at any time since the 1960s. Bob Jolly, an Iowa State University economist, was surprised by the situation. He had expected land values to fall by 20 percent, rather than 30. He had no idea when the slide would end and expected that it would increase the stress on farmers in trouble. He told *Wallace's Farmer*, "It makes it harder to dispose of assets to readjust debt burdens." Troubled farmers would be unable to use land sales to offset other expenses. Additionally, because farmers had less collateral they would continue to struggle to get operating loans. There was a bit of grim optimism in the situation. Jolly commented, "It may be one of the best opportunities we have seen in years for a young man to start farming." With land cheap and getting cheaper, anyone capable of scraping up the cash—and that was the kicker—would be able to find bargains.[82]

People, however, were much more cautious than in the past. A *Wallace's Farmer* poll showed that even if land fell to a price low enough to allow the owner to make a profit, few were interested in buying. Answering the question, "If a neighboring or nearby farm should come up for sale within the range you estimate it would begin to cash flow, how interested would you be in purchasing it," 19 percent said they would be "not very interested," while another 43 percent said they would be "not interested at all," a significant change from the 1970s.[83] This lack of interest in expansion reflected the frustrations farmers felt with their financial situation and the way in which the crisis had persisted. A Howard County farmer, discussing his situation with a reporter from *Wallace's Farmer*, spoke for many when he said, "I don't know why I keep at this.... You'd think after I've been hit on the head so many times, I'd quit. I just keep hoping things will get better before the money runs out."[84]

Because of debts, farmers were in no position to think about expansion. A survey of Iowa farmers showed that they were spending 51 percent of their cash income on interest payments, an unproductive expense.[85] Those struggling the hardest were families on midsize farms. Large farmers could spread their risk over more acres. Small farmers either had avoided expansion in the 1970s or were already supplementing their income with outside sources. Many farmers in the middle had to make choices, either to grow bigger or to scale back and take outside jobs. Both of these strategies were evident on Iowa's farms. Farm size was growing, but off-farm employment was growing, too, with $3 of every $10 of farm family income in Iowa coming from off-farm sources.[86] Scrambling for money was a way of life for Iowa families struggling with debt.

But even with the evident gloom, analysts were beginning to use the expression "bottoming out" in reference to the agricultural depression. Interest rates were falling. Fuel prices fell dramatically. The value of the dollar was also falling, which would make American agricultural goods more competitive in world markets. Economists thought it unlikely that land values would decline as much in 1986 as they had in 1985. Cattle and hog prices were also on the rise, after a long slump. Unfortunately, prices for corn and soybeans continued to be depressed, but officials at the USDA hoped this would lead to greater exports. And then, in late summer, the Reagan administration decided to increase agricultural aid. Farm-state Republicans facing tough reelection bids had pressured the president to do something about the farm economy. They worried about losing their seats and the thin Republican majority in the Senate. With the new funds, the government paid farmers to store surplus grain on their farms, a huge benefit to Midwestern farmers who were expecting a bumper crop of corn, wheat, and soybeans. With the government's help, they could hold their grain off the market until prices, hopefully, increased.

The measure included no additional provisions for livestock raisers. The Republicans lost anyway, but those in the know expected that the Democrats in Congress would keep the flow of money going. The optimism generated by increased federal spending slowed the decline in land values. It looked as if the situation finally had the potential to improve, but that improvement was resting on some fragile foundations, such as hopes for continued government funding and hopes for improved markets. Hope was going to have to keep Iowa's farmers afloat for a bit longer.[87]

CHAPTER SIX

From Crisis to Chronic: 1987–1993

On September 22, 1987, Dean Kleckner, Iowan and president of the American Farm Bureau Federation, appeared before the Iowa Banker's Association. The topic of Kleckner's talk was the ongoing relationship between lenders and farmers. Looking for a laugh, he quipped, "I'm sure many of you are pretty weary of several ongoing farm credit relationships—about which you privately know." His main topic, however, was his conviction that the Farm Crisis was, essentially, over, although many did not seem to know it. The "farm income problem," he stated, had taken on "a life of its own. Some have suggested this is being encouraged by those who, for various reasons of their own, cannot bear the thought of the crisis ending." Although he did not name these crisis opportunists, the objects of his scorn were various farm advocacy groups cautioning that farmers were not yet out of the woods. Nevertheless, Kleckner argued, "the current situation is better than a year ago and considerably better than two years ago." A transformation, he claimed, was underway: "Somewhere in mid, or late 1985, the farm economy reached a turning point and started to swing around." Income was up, he said, production expenses were down, and debt was becoming more manageable. Farm equipment manufacturers were rolling out new products, and John Deere would not be making more tractors, he reasoned, if they did not expect to sell them. In his view, all of these developments pointed to recovery.[1]

Kleckner told his audience that it was time to be positive: "Our months of crying—much of it justified—has attracted a lot of the wrong kind of attention. It's the cripples in the herd that bring on the wolves." But Iowa farmers and Iowa agriculture, he argued, were not crippled. It was time to declare an end to the crisis. "I think it's time we declare a victory for the approximate three-fourths of all farmers who have emerged in fair to good shape from the economic crush that has gripped us," he announced. "Then we need to pledge our heartfelt support to the 10 to 15 percent still in deep trouble, while we move ahead with our own, positive program for rural America." Forging ahead with a new and improved attitude, healthy farm operations would reap the benefits. He exhorted his listeners to think positively about the future. "By doing this, we serve notice on politicians—social activists and the professional worriers, that although the pain remains, agriculture is alive and growing in America, even in Iowa." He put his emphasis on that last phrase, "even in Iowa."[2]

The president of the American Farm Bureau Federation had declared the crisis to be over, but did that make it so? Historian Mark Friedberger, who concluded his study of the crisis with 1987, believed that by the end of that year times were still hard, but the worst was over. Those who had flourished during the downturn would continue to do so; as for those at the bottom, some of them would be mired perpetually in trouble, until they, too, were forced out of agriculture. And for young farmers with parents still firmly in the business, the crisis had been a boon. "The lowering of rents, the return to crop sharing, the availability of secondhand machinery—all results of the crisis—made tenure more open than it had been ten years before," he posited. "For the lucky ones, the farm crisis gave them a start." He ended his analysis on a positive note, touting the "basic resilience of the cornbelt farm family."[3] Richard Krumme, editor of *Successful Farming*, was also inclined toward the positive. In an editorial, he compared statements by David Ostendorf, the director of PrairieFire, and David Garst, executive president of the Garst Seed Company. Ostendorf continued to be concerned about conditions in the countryside and claimed that ongoing bankruptcies and poverty proved that the crisis was not yet over. Garst, on the other hand, had commented that four years previously, the farm economy was depressed, but "today, four years later, over 65,000 farmers are planting Garst corn hybrids. We're the nation's third largest seed corn company. Never before have there been so many opportunities for American farmers." Krumme asserted, "I'm with Garst." Adding emphasis, he concluded, "Could it be some activist groups don't want the farm crisis to end? They'd lose their franchise, and their headlines."[4]

Not all of Krumme's readers were as optimistic. Donna Winburn, from Malcom, Iowa, wrote that she "took offense at your assessment of two views of the farm crisis." She accused him of "burying your head in the sand" and asked him to consider his sources. "You are aware, aren't you, that we cannot farm without seed, and Mr. Garst does not ask what we will give him for it?" she asked. "David Ostendorf and his PrairieFire staff make contact with more bona fide farmers in a week than David Garst does in a year." An Arkansas farmer, Harvey Joe Sanner, agreed with Winburn, writing, "How Dave Garst selling seed corn translates into opportunities for farmers escapes me. . . . I think Mr. Ostendorf is much more qualified to assess the rural situation. He recognizes 'happy talk' as being a lot of bull." Leonie Hanson of Garretson, South Dakota, dubious of Krumme's conclusions, decided to investigate. "Since reading your August issue I have been clipping the notices of bankruptcies that have appeared in our local paper. More bankruptcies have been filed in the last three months than all 10 years between 1970 and 1980 in South Dakota."[5]

These farmers were not the only ones who were hesitant to draw a firm line between the difficult days of the 1980s and new beginnings. In particular, people involved with Extension, who worked with farmers every day, remained cautious. They were not willing to claim a victory even as the decade closed. In a 1990 interview, W. John Johnson, assistant dean of University Extension at Iowa State University, opined that the crisis had yet to pass. Too many farmers were teetering at the edge. In his assessment, "It is not over at all. Things are better than they were. Many, many people have worked through it as best they can work through it. But if economic conditions take a turn for the worst—it's not over at all."[6] Elizabeth A. Elliott, interim dean of University Extension and director of Extension at Iowa State, was equally dubious, commenting that "right now there's a feeling that we probably have a large number of families who are not going to make it through this crop season. You know they got a moratorium on their interest and their payments and . . . now it is time to start paying that again and things are really not a lot better than they were before."[7] Joan Blundall, coordinator of consultation and education at the Northwest Iowa Mental Health Center, could not have agreed more. Suffering families were still trooping into her clinic. She noted, "Everyone is sick and tired of the farm crisis. Yet being sick and tired does not change reality."[8]

There was, however, another possibility. Perhaps the state had shifted into a position where problems in the countryside seemed chronic and intractable. Between the beginning of 1987 and the floods of 1993, the state and its rural people would limp along, sometimes up, sometimes down, but always concerned about possible ugly developments waiting around the corner. At some moments, it would appear that recovery was, indeed, underway. At others, as with the drought in 1988 and massive flooding in 1993, it seemed as if the situation would never improve. The state's experiences over the previous six or seven years were never far from the public mind.

The new year began again with unhappy news. The numbers were in, and in 1986, the value of farmland had fallen again. Across the year, the price for an average acre of farmland in Iowa had fallen to an estimated $786. This represented a decrease of 17 percent from 1985 values. The price of land had dropped 63.3 percent since its high point in 1981, and was now (adjusted for inflation) where it had been in the mid-1940s. This meant trouble for all farmers, not just those in debt. For most, land was their primary asset, and as the price of land slid ever lower, so did their wealth. Extension's Mike Duffy explained that for farmers attempting to conduct their businesses, this decline meant "considerable confusion, uncertainty and apprehension." Iowa's farmers began 1987 with a host of concerns beyond low land values: low commodity prices, difficulties with financing, and general pessimism.[9]

Farmers worried about farm income, restructuring debt, and the condition of their rural communities.[10] When they looked beyond the state's borders, the world was still awash in cheap grain, which pushed down prices. Farmers were rebuilding their herds of both cattle and hogs, which would also ultimately mean lower prices. To some analysts, it appeared that improvements in the level of debt resulted from farm liquidation, and rising farm income came from federal farm programs, rather than more profitable crops and livestock.[11] Peter Brent, of PrairieFire, noticed the same problems—low grain prices and government payments keeping farmers afloat. He also noted that the hotline phones kept ringing, although callers wanted to discuss new problems. At present, many calls referenced farm financial difficulties finally coming home to roost, with troubled people needing help with emotional stress, Chapter 12 bankruptcy, and housing—now that they had finally, truly lost the farm. The numbers of calls were down, but PrairieFire volunteers still talked to ten to twenty distressed farmers per day.[12]

There were, however, a few signs of hope. The number of financially stressed farmers appeared to be shrinking and the amount of farm debt was contracting as well. As much as a third of that reduction was due to lending institutions writing off loans. Farmers utilizing the 1985 farm bill and taking land out of production were hoping to improve their incomes and lower surpluses.[13] More and more farm families were reshaping their operations. Aaron Vorthmann, of Carson, Iowa, was taking advantage of lower grain prices and custom feeding twenty-five hundred head of cattle. Darrell Morse of Minden had diversified his operation by opening a feed store in his basement and barn, while Betty and Floyd Van Roekel refurbished their basement to rent out to hunters during the pheasant and deer seasons. Because of falling land prices, Gary and Brenda Thompson of Liberty Center finally bought their own 172 acres, instead of moving from farm to farm as renters.[14] For those not mired in debt, 1987 looked like a promising year for new ventures.

The auctions continued as long-standing credit problems forced families out of agriculture. Photograph by Bill Gillette, by permission of the State Historical Society of Iowa.

Yet even the most optimistic of pundits knew that families continued to stand on the brink of financial disaster. The number of bankruptcies and foreclosures in 1987 was high. Friedberger argued that these bankruptcies and foreclosures represented long-term problems, unresolved for years. Among farmers filing Chapter 12 bankruptcy in Iowa's Northern District in the period from January to May of 1987, average debts totaled more than $600,000, with assets of only slightly over $300,000. Catastrophic debt to asset ratios on this scale did not develop overnight. Friedberger pointed out that "these petitioners had lived in limbo for months, if not years, before they actually filed."[15] New applications for bankruptcy represented old, intractable problems, as did completed foreclosures. The Engelken foreclosure, completed in 1987, was the result of a long, drawn-out battle over the family's organic farm. When Ralph Engelken wrote to the governor for help in 1983, the family was already several years into economic difficulties. The FLB began foreclosure proceedings in 1982; the foreclosure concluded in 1987, more than two years after Ralph's death. Two hundred people, friends, neighbors, and reporters, showed up in support of Rita Engelken.[16] Farm dissolutions long in the works were drawing to a close.

The state continued to try to reduce the pain of families going through financial stress. In April the legislature extended the foreclosure moratorium that began with the governor's disaster declaration in 1985. Neil Harl, the Iowa State University economist to whom the legislature often turned for advice, was in favor of the extension. While farm debt had fallen significantly, he advised, "between 10 and 15 percent of farmers continue to have significant debt problems." Continuing the moratorium, he believed, would have a positive effect on debtor-creditor negotiations.[17] In June, the state legislature clarified the rights of foreclosed families that wanted to redeem a portion of their land. The Iowa Homestead Act gave farmers two years to buy back at fair market value up to forty acres of their land and made the provision retroactive. The IFUC made this part of their legislative agenda for 1987, and while they failed to get everything they wanted, spokesperson Daniel Levitas called it a measure that would enable "thousands of Iowa farmers to retain a foothold in their rural communities."[18] The Iowa Farmer/Creditor mediation service continued into 1987, with the system becoming more successful as farmers became more comfortable with the process. By the spring of 1987, Iowa's attorney general Tom Miller estimated that two-thirds of all mediations had resulted in an agreement acceptable to both parties.[19] Beginning farmers continued to receive aid from the state in the form of low interest loan programs. Borrowers could use the money to buy or make improvements on land or buy farm equipment.[20]

As the year drew to a close, both the US House and Senate approved a bill to bail out the Farm Credit System. The most important feature of the bill was a requirement that federal agricultural lenders ease repayment terms for borrowers if it could be proven that modifying the terms of a loan would cost less than a foreclosure. The law required lenders to restructure loans by lowering interest rates, extending the time for repayment, or other measures, if a borrower could prove that these new terms would allow them to return to profitability. This kind of restructuring was already underway in Iowa but would now have the force of law. While federal lenders had strongly opposed such measures previously, by 1987 they were largely on board and boasting about the number of farms they had saved with restructuring. The new law had other provisions as well, such as allowing foreclosed farmers the right of first refusal when their property went on the market. Under homestead provisions, they would have the right to purchase their home on the property as well as ten acres. Using Iowa as a model, the law also set aside funds for farmer/creditor mediation programs. President Reagan signed the measure into law in the first week of 1988.[21] The federal government was finally acting just as some were pronouncing the end of the crisis.

Provisions were in place to improve the situation of many farmers, but whether or not the deeply indebted could be saved was another issue altogether. Mike Duffy offered advice to the state's farmers as they evaluated their options. Land prices were stabilizing and the market for used machinery was strong. If a farm was still struggling, it was a good time to sell. He concluded his advice with the admonition, "Use this time wisely."[22] This might be the last window of opportunity for a while.

Rural Schools and Rural Communities

By late in the decade, restructuring was happening at every level of the rural community. The same economic conditions that had forced individual farm families to change were transforming communities broadly speaking, including contentious shifts in education. Iowa had a tradition of supporting small rural schools. Because of the long agricultural depression of the 1920s and 1930s, Iowa had consolidated its schools far later than most other states. There had been a few attempts in the first two decades of the twentieth century, but the biggest round of school consolidation occurred in the 1950s, when most of the state's one-room schools finally disappeared. Except for Amish schools, the last one-room schools in Iowa closed on July 1, 1966. At that time, the state mandated that school districts have at least three hundred students. Yet, in the 1980s, depopulation in the countryside meant that more than eighty districts operated with fewer than three hundred pupils. The state predicted that by 1992, the number of underenrolled districts would rise to roughly one hundred. At a time when more students were college bound, and when expectations of what constituted a good education had become more complex, small districts struggled to keep up. Providing the full range of math, science, and language courses was a strain, if not impossible.[23]

Early in the year, the Iowa Department of Education began drafting plans, suggesting possible future directions for schools. Plan A was for minimum enrollment and no district with less than six hundred students. Higher enrollment at the secondary level would make it possible for schools to offer a full range of courses. Most small towns would be able to maintain their elementary schools while sharing middle and high schools. The plan was projected to affect as many as four hundred school districts. Plan B suggested that the state construct school districts around "dominant" communities, with less dominant communities forming "rural coalitions." It was a complicated idea and quickly died. Plan C was by far the most ambitious and called for ninety-nine school districts attached more or less to the ninety-nine counties. There would be fewer elementary schools and far fewer high schools, and the plan would reorganize every district in the state. The issue was a hot potato, and the state legislature delayed its decision, eventually going with a less prescriptive model in which the state required schools to provide a basic curriculum and meet accreditation standards and rewarded with greater funding those schools that took steps to cooperate and consolidate with other districts. The incentives were there to consolidate, but without the contentious size requirements for districts.[24]

The firestorm surrounding the issue was inevitable. Small communities identified strongly with their schools, which were economic and social anchors. Ethnic, cultural, and religious issues often divided neighboring communities from each other, making school consolidation fraught with tension. Additionally, schools often were a community's largest employer, providing reasonably paid jobs with benefits. People came to town for school activities and spent their money. They also hesitated to settle in towns that did not have a full complement of schools, balking at the idea of sending their children on long bus rides. The thought of losing a school, after losing so much else, was anathema. When the legislature began considering House Bill 499, which would have mandated a minimum district size of six hundred students by 1990, the letters poured into the governor's office. Many of the writers believed very strongly that this was yet another blow to already suffering communities. A resident of Aurelia asserted, "Rural Iowans are victims again. Victims of people who neither understand nor care about small schools.... If agriculture wasn't depressed, would someone listen to us. We are facing grim times in rural Iowa. We have no control over the plumiting [sic] farm economy. We insist on having control over the education of our children."[25] In an uncertain world, people demanded control over their local schools. Letters came in from multiple constituencies. Businesspeople wrote in about their fears for the economic health of their communities. Parents wrote in to decry the inconvenience and cost of large-scale busing.[26]

The occasional teenager wrote an impassioned plea for their small school. Christy Bailey, an eighth grader at Murray Community School, threatened to drop out rather than attend a consolidated school. She claimed that long bus rides would force students to forgo extracurricular activities and that consolidation would destroy small towns: "Farmers would be more tempted to move to larger towns to find work and to be closer to the school. So . . . if you like to brag about *Iowa being a place to grow*, I suggest you *help* the small communities, where children can learn in a *peaceful, uncrowded environment.*"[27] Schools had special meaning to people in small communities, and the hard years of the Farm Crisis magnified their attachment. While the occasional person spoke up in favor of consolidation on behalf of a child who wanted to play football with a better team or have the opportunity to take advanced classes, most small-town residents expressed misgivings.

In 1986–1987, the high-school students at Stratford faced the possibility of losing their school. Stratford was a small town, hovering somewhere between seven hundred and eight hundred residents. A picture of the senior class of Stratford High School graced the inside cover of their yearbook, featuring all sixteen students. That year, they titled the publication *The Year of the Comet*. After a hiatus of roughly seventy-six years, Halley's Comet was due to be visible again and the students built the yearbook around this theme. They noted that people in past times believed that the comet was a harbinger of change, either good or evil, and often blamed its appearance for disasters. What, they asked, would the comet bring? In spite of a gloomy and trepidatious introduction, they directed their classmates' attention toward the positive: "Let's remember the good times at Stratford High—the laughs, the talks, the girlfriends and boyfriends, the football games at noon, lounge, and all the rest. Let's not forget the teachers and classes and how the teachers really did care about what we learned." The reason for the emphasis on the comet became evident in a small bit of type, deep in the yearbook. A writer noted that the school board was holding many extra meetings, "making decisions about our school's future." Poised at the top of the page were two fists, one with thumbs up, the other with thumbs down. Although the students never used the words school closing or consolidation, they were aware of the possibility. The yearbook went to press before the school board announced its decision.[28]

The Year of the Comet was Stratford's last yearbook. The town's elementary school remained operational, while the junior and senior high schools closed. The school board made the decision in February 1987, ending three years of deliberation and planning. "Declining enrollments and scarce dollars" forced the closures. In an attempt to stave off consolidation, the district had eliminated physical education teachers at the elementary level and typing and languages at the junior high and high school. Unable to staff schools fully at any level, teachers instructed classes outside of their specialties. Rather than continue, Stratford chose to consolidate with Webster City, seventeen miles north of Stratford and ten times its size. Webster City faced a slight decline in enrollments and happily accepted Stratford's students, even lowering tuition charges to sweeten the deal.[29] In 1988 Stratford's high-school students would appear in Webster City's yearbook, heralded under the banner, "Forty-three new students enroll." This new group was comprised of four foreign exchange students and thirty-nine students from the now-defunct Stratford High School. A writer noted that this meant change: a commute, different lunches, different standards of discipline, and a much bigger school. Seniors who had expected to graduate from their hometown high school now found themselves on unfamiliar ground. They ended the story on a positive note, quoting senior Jennifer Lundberg, "I really like it here!"[30] As might be expected from a high-school yearbook, there was no discussion of those who might have disagreed, or how it felt to be in a completely new, far less intimate learning environment. Webster City, after all, was the larger school, swallowing up the smaller. Many rural people dreaded what had happened in Stratford happening to their own community schools. The common wisdom held that if the school went, the town would be next.

In spring 1988, the Northeast School District Parent Teacher Organization sponsored a "What's so great about Iowa?" contest for pupils. Nearly eight hundred Clinton County students from first to twelfth grade participated, and Mary Farwell, the contest chair, marveled at their enthusiasm. She commented, "Iowa's children have suffered much in the last five years... Despite that, 99% of the essays written expressed great pride and hope in an education in Iowa." She sent a long list of excerpts to the governor's office, so he could enjoy the students' work. The oldest students made the expected contributions about topics such as education and the agricultural work ethic. Lisa Chambers, an eleventh grader, described the state's agricultural ethos: "The feeling you have when you grow things on your own, with your own hands; and when you work to make it produce and knowing at the end that you are helping others at the same time is astounding." The younger students' responses covered an enormous range of topics, reflecting the concerns of children who were just beginning to understand the relationship between their state and the larger world. Fourth grader Christina Witt commented on the state's miles of open fields, saying, "You can have a big, big playground!" Chad La Douceur also chimed in with an environmental observation: "People in Iowa never really notice all the stuff in Iowa besides corn and pigs. Iowa had the largest frog in the United States." Sixth grader Kari Campbell probably elicited a chuckle or two with her reply, "Believe it or not, the people in Iowa are not all totally country pumpkins." Brandi J., a third grader, wrote, "What I really like about Iowa is the people. Some are kind and generous . . . and helpful. But I wish they still had ice cream trucks." Another third grader, Jenny J., wrote, "I wish the whole world was living in Iowa. But it would be really crowded." The children of the Northeast School District were cute and funny and capable of finding something good to say about their home state, even though many of them could hardly remember a time before the Farm Crisis. For them, like many of the Great Depression's children, the situation was not one to lament but rather their own version of normal.[31]

Conditions in Agriculture

For the grown-ups, 1988 began on a more cautiously optimistic note. In 1987, when the state tallied the numbers, it turned out that land values had gone up for the first time since they began their disastrous descent in 1981. The value of an average acre of Iowa land had climbed 11 percent, to $875. Land was beginning to sell and farmers who had made it through the downturn in relatively good shape had cash to spend. Mike Duffy, who released the figures, asked farmers to act as "positive realists." Still, the fact that the numbers were going in the right direction did not mean that Iowa's agricultural economy was entirely healthy. Prices for hogs were down, as were corn and soybeans. Just over a quarter of Iowa's farmers were still in a "critical situation," and these were the people holding nearly half of the state's agricultural debt. One year of improvements did not equal a trend.[32]

There were other signs that things were improving, however. The Iowa Farm and Rural Life Poll showed that the mood on the farm was better than it had been two years previously. Between 1986 and 1988, farmers became much more positive about Iowa's agricultural economy. In 1986, 74 percent of the farmers polled believed that the financial condition of the state's farmers was "very serious." Two years later, just 30 percent were as concerned. Fewer still were seriously worried about their own farms. In 1986, it had been 41 percent, but in 1988 it was 26 percent, although another 23 percent were moderately concerned. People's perceptions of their quality of life were also better; 34 percent believed their quality of life had improved in the last five years, and 40 percent felt their family's quality of life would improve in the coming five years, about double the percentage in 1986. But again, there were elements of caution within the report. The poll showed that while

62 percent of Iowa's farms had manageable debt-to-asset ratios, 38 percent were still in trouble. Life was better, but there was still room for improvement.[33]

As with 1987, no one seemed willing to draw a definite line between the crisis and economic recovery. Both *Successful Farming* and *Wallace's Farmer* were claiming some measure of victory over the crisis, but not completely. While an article in *Successful Farming* described "5 signs that the farm depression is over," the writer still hedged his bets, emphasizing that the situation "appeared" better. Conditions were ripe for a recovery that had not actually arrived. *Wallace's Farmer* touted the remarkable increase in 1988 farm income while warning that more than one in five Iowa farmers remained "stressed."[34] Writers were not overly confident. National publications, such as the *Wall Street Journal*, published stories about young farmers getting into the business, but again, offered a barely positive spin. An April 1988 article featured twenty-six-year-old Robert Koenigsfeld, an eastern Iowan who was leaving factory employment for agriculture. The writer stressed what a rare bird the young man was: "Around these parts, they haven't seen anyone like Robert Koenigsfeld in years." Because of the decline in land prices in the first half of the decade, people like him were able to think about buying or renting land. With used and rented equipment, and with money borrowed from a neighbor, Koenigsfeld planned to rent his father-in-law's land. Between frugal living, his wife's job, and his own off-farm employment, he would have the opportunity to escape the full-time factory work he hated. The writer emphasized the tenuous position of Koenigsfeld and similar individuals, stating, "The basic problem: The first post-farm-crisis generation is struggling to fill a need that doesn't exist. The U.S. already has far too many farmers and produces far more food than it can consume or sell." It was another "yes, but" story, describing a turnabout in farm country that might not actually be a turnabout, given the state of the market.[35]

The news media were not alone in their caution. Activist groups were not ready to allow anyone to claim victory. The IFUC did not believe the fight between farmers and lenders had reached a conclusion. In April their executive committee wrote to Governor Branstad to ask that the state make a supplemental appropriation of $60,000 for legal services for farmers. The governor's office complied.[36] The Catholic Rural Life office continued to publicize and participate in protests against farm foreclosures across the state and in 1988 participated in the production and distribution of a video about a farm foreclosure in Shelby County, entitled *Ending the Silence—Civil Disobedience in the Farm Crisis*. The film told the story of a foreclosure protest the year before in Harlan, at which the sheriff arrested five clergy and one nun for disrupting the sale.³⁷ These protestors, too, believed that victory over the crisis was in the future.

The lingering of the crisis, now as much as a decade old, contributed to the continuation of the mental health problems. Anger and resentment bubbled not far below the surface in many Iowans. When a farmer lost his family's land and business after years of anxiety, negotiation, and legal maneuvering, the passions could be overwhelming. Seething with anger, a farmer from southern Iowa wrote the governor's office. He classified the mediation his family had gone through on the way to bankruptcy as "crooked." The insurance company to which they had lost their farm would soon be taking possession. The farmer promised that when the sheriff came to take his land, he would be waiting on top of his silo with a twenty-foot rope around his neck, ready to hang himself in protest. He planned to call the press to witness the event. The governor's office did not have much to offer, other than to plead with him to seek help from the legal system and to provide a referral back to the Rural Concern Hotline, with which the distressed farmer was already working. By September, having been "stalled" by Rural Concern, he was even more angry and making more substantial threats. He wrote, "I am . . . well-armed waiting for the day for whoever goes tresspassing [sic] on the ground illegally, supposedly taken away from me by the state of Iowa. Traffic is dead on our road anymore, and easy to keep an eye on. I don't want violence but it was unjustly brought upon me." This time, there was no indication that the governor's aide answered the letter; it may have been turned over to the sheriff. As correspondence like this indicated, the mental health crisis generated by the agricultural depression had yet to be satisfactorily resolved. There were other equally angry people who were not in contact with the governor's office.³⁸

The people answering the phones at the Rural Concern Hotline heard from plenty of folks as agitated—or nearly as agitated—as the farmer with the rope and the gun. They were still receiving an average of twenty-five calls a day and many of the callers claimed to be feeling more isolated than ever. A recovery was supposedly underway, and yet they were not a part of it. Rural Concern received fewer questions about legal issues, but three times as many called with family problems, and twice as many with emotional stress. According to hotline coordinator Fran Phillips, people struggled with the pain of living in limbo. Based on a statewide mental health survey, researchers estimated that 21 percent of the rural farm and 24 percent of the rural nonfarm population was either "possibly or probably depressed."³⁹ Joan Blundall saw the same problems at her mental health clinic in northwest Iowa.

The loss of a farm was also the loss of a home. Photograph by Bill Gillette, by permission of the State Historical Society of Iowa.

She claimed that the problems of the average patient had become more severe, rather than moderating with the alleged deceleration of the crisis. Recent visitors to the clinic included a woman in her seventies needing advice about how to find a job, an exhausted farm wife in her thirties working three jobs and getting four hours of sleep per night, and a young child in a highly stressed household who had gone eighteen months without growing. Blundall compared rural Iowa to a veteran experiencing post-traumatic stress disorder.[40] The worst of the crisis might be over but the pain continued.

Fortunately, the help continued as well. The state and Extension continued the Rural Concern Hotline, and PrairieFire continued theirs. Federal aid for mental health continued, too. In 1988 Congress expanded its support for the Rural Crisis Recovery Program Act, the source of funding for the Taking Charge in Changing Times initiative. Iowa was not the only participating state. In addition to funding Iowa's program, the USDA provided grants to Missouri, Kansas, Nebraska, North Dakota, Oklahoma, Vermont, and Mississippi as the states worked to provide education, training, and mental health services to displaced and discouraged farm families.[41] As the FmHA sent out notices late in the year to let delinquent farmers

A farmer being evicted from his home waited with the sheriff outside. Photograph by Bill Gillette, by permission of the State Historical Society of Iowa.

know that it was time to assess their options—and perhaps leave agriculture—Extension encouraged families to make use of the program and to consult with them about their situations.[42]

Drought

When observers predicted the imminent demise of the Farm Crisis, they had not counted on the weather. This was to be a year of severe drought throughout much of the United States. In mid-June, 150 people gathered in Wapello County to pray for rain; unfortunately, their prayers went unanswered. Most talk of a farm recovery died in late June, when the weather suddenly took a very hot and dry turn. In northeast Iowa, the rain stopped in early May, which meant that by July the corn was dying. In other areas, the corn was not dying but neither was it growing. The Midwest was in the midst of the worst drought in fifty years. Rainfall ranged from 50 to 75 percent of normal. Much of what did fall was timed poorly, coming too early or too late. By midsummer, the drought was forcing cattle raisers to send cows and calves to market. Some farmers were selling entire herds because their pastures were dead. While the drought affected much of Iowa, the southeast suffered the most. The harvest would not be a complete disaster, but the corn crop would be the smallest since 1983, also a drought year.[43]

Conditions varied from place to place and from farm to farm. A Clinton County woman, in far eastern Iowa, invited the governor to see what the drought had done to her farm. She offered him iced tea or iced coffee and a shower before he left, "That's *if* our well doesn't run dry." Gardens were dying (it was too expensive to water them) and the drought had also destroyed the supply of hay for the winter. Southeast of Iowa City, the Berry family was feeling the effects. The extreme heat stressed their Duroc hogs and on some 100-degree days the animals needed water every hour. At any one time, there were one thousand hogs on the property and the Berrys evaluated each one regularly for heat stroke. Poor conditions pushed the price of hogs down, so the family's mother, Jan, was cutting coupons and feeding her family as cheaply as possible. Extension personnel and mental health professionals warned families like the Berrys to keep an eye out for stress and anxiety. Even little things, like a summer without tomatoes and sweet corn from a family garden, could add to the sadness and worry people were experiencing. Conditions forced families to scrimp and cut corners yet again as hard times extended into another year.[44]

Still, it was unlikely that the drought would push the state back into the depths of crisis. The drought did not depress land prices as the credit crisis had.[45] Additionally, the state acted on the problem quickly. The governor appeared on *Good Morning, America* to let the nation know about the problems of drought-stricken farmers and went to Washington to talk with the USDA about aid.[46] Congress agreed to a $4 billion drought relief package. Some farmers grumbled that the only reason they were getting anything from Congress was that it was an election year, but nonetheless took their share. Farmers whose crops yielded at least 35 percent less than normal would get payments of $1.90 per bushel of corn lost, and $3.50 per bushel of soybeans lost. Livestock producers whose feed crops the drought destroyed would have access to federal grain supplies at reduced prices or help purchasing feed. The governor commented, "It's not the same as getting a good crop, but it will help some."[47]

Oddly enough, and in spite of the drought, the worst of the food crisis seemed to be over and the number of Iowans using food stamps fell. The *Des Moines*

Register reported that the number of Iowans enrolled in the program declined 12 percent between April of 1987 and April of 1988. Food stamp usage had begun to climb steeply in 1980, increasing every year through 1984. After a slight decline in usage in 1985, and a high of 221,946 Iowans receiving food stamps in 1986, the numbers began to fall, and fall quickly. The number of farm families receiving food stamps also declined from 1,909 in 1987, to 1,202 in 1988. This, state officials announced, reflected a better job market and increases in farm income. The official peak of food stamp use by farm families came in 1986, with 2,316 families receiving aid. The decline in the number of farmers on food stamp rolls had many possible interpretations. Improvements in income might have taken some families off the rolls, but it might also have indicated that families with marginal operations had left agriculture. The growing number of families combining on and off farm employment also may have eased the strain. Some worried, however, that these improvements were temporary. It would not take much to push many families back into poverty.[48]

Other observers pointed to continuing feelings of shame as a possible cause for the decline. David Ostendorf, director of PrairieFire, suggested that the phenomenon might be related to activists' failure to continue food stamp drives. "The primary problem is always the stigma of going in for food stamps," he commented. Kathy Bicking, welfare specialist for Legal Services Corp of Iowa, in Sioux City, claimed that many eligible families refused to take them. They told her, "We're really grateful for the help, but we'll see how we can do without them."[49] Other reflections on the food stamp experience help to explain this desire to avoid their use. Small-town Iowans remained ashamed of their poverty and their neighbors continued to deride food stamp use. Jane Sellers and Kim Gilliland of Bagley, in rural Guthrie County, ran the gauntlet when using food stamps to purchase food for themselves and Sellers's four children. Sellers commented, "I would have been better off having a sack over my head. You know, just the people staring at me." Gilliland elaborated, "It makes you feel like, 'Well, they're nothing but scum, because they need help.'"[50] Improving times might have reduced the number of rural and farm families making using of the food stamp program, but there was also little evidence that a decade of troubles had significantly shifted attitudes about taking food aid even when it was desperately needed.

Small Communities and Economic Change

What rural and small-town Iowans needed was employment. Businesses had suffered during the agricultural downturn and more people than ever wanted jobs. Both farm men and women were looking for off-farm employment at the same time as their nonfarming neighbors were also looking for work. But there were few jobs to be found. Between 1979 and 1986, Iowa lost eighty-four thousand high-wage manufacturing and construction jobs bringing in $20,000 or more per year. The agricultural machinery industry, for example, had suffered catastrophic damage when the farm economy collapsed, and high-paying assembly jobs disappeared. At the same time, the meat packing industry reorganized, and newer companies replaced union wages with dramatically lower-paid positions. The state gained thirty-seven thousand service industry jobs, which paid only $11,500 per year, on average.[51]

Additionally, small town businesses faced a new set of problems with the unanticipated consequences of the 1985 farm program. The Conservation Reserve Program (CRP) promised to take large numbers of acres out of production in parts of Iowa, especially those with hilly and highly erodible land. Farmers who put land into CRP received payments for doing so, in place of selling the crops they would have raised. Idled acres meant farmers making fewer purchases in local stores. In Bloomfield, the owner/operator of a fertilizer business claimed to have lost 20 percent of his business to CRP. The costs of the large-scale land retirement program had yet to be fully measured.[52]

The state had not just lost businesses and jobs, it had lost citizens. In the wake of the drought, the *Wall Street Journal* sounded the death knell for rural Iowa. The population fell by eighty thousand in the midst of the Farm Crisis and the Census Bureau predicted worse to come. By the year 2010, it projected a population of just 2.4 million. The publication predicted that without an infusion of jobs there soon would be no more small towns in Iowa.[53] Even if the governor's office did not agree with the numbers, it did agree that something had to be done. In a National Governor's Association statement about rural development, Branstad commented that there was much work ahead if rural Iowa and rural America were to survive: "Tremendous damage has been done to rural economies, and the recovery will be long and difficult. A fundamental restructuring of the rural economies and many rural institutions will be necessary if rural America is to prosper." The fix, if there was one, was going to be both difficult and expensive.[54]

Not surprisingly, the buzz term for 1988 was "economic development." Iowa's small communities sought to improve their economic climates and to attract more business and dollars. The Algona Area Chamber of Commerce decided to tackle the problem with tourism and assembled, printed, and distributed twenty thousand copies of a visitor's guide throughout Iowa and southern Minnesota. They also organized a "BRAK," or "Bike Ride across Kossuth" County for August. As the vice president for the Chamber of Commerce commented, "Those of us in small communities know that we cannot depend upon the state for help in local tourism efforts."[55] Rolfe, home to seven hundred, rolled out a whole range of improvements. In 1987 the community began an advertising and development program to bring in new businesses and residents. For such a small place, the results were impressive. Rolfe recruited a manufacturer of batteries, employing three full-time and two part-time employees. The city purchased and remodeled a vacant auto dealership and leased it out to two more new businesses, a popcorn processor and a bean seed distributor. The city also purchased a plot on the edge of town for a campground. A local elevator purchased five vacant buildings and converted them into a broiler facility, raising three hundred thousand chickens per year. The list went on from there, including a handful of additional businesses and development initiatives, such as a tourism office.

A shiny brochure beckoned new residents to "Come and see . . . 'the Heart of the Heartland' Rolfe, Iowa."[56] That did not mean, however, that all residents understood the effort or thought that the city officials were going about their plan in the right way. A letter to the newspaper's editor from Marilyn Point lambasted the plans for recruitment, since jobs were still scarce. Point spoke to a young couple who had come to Rolfe, lured in by that shiny brochure. She asked the young man how he found the job situation. "He said, not good. They tell him if you haven't lived here five years it's real hard to find a job." She continued, "When these people call about moving here, why are you making it sound like a booming metropolis? I've travelled 48 states, I know what these depressed city people are thinking. It sounds great but it's not."[57] Jobs were the key to rural economic development, and while a few new jobs had come to Rolfe there were not enough to support large numbers of new arrivals. Additionally, employers were more inclined to hire people they knew than outsiders lured in by advertising.

While small towns worked on creative solutions to their economic dilemmas, the state poured funds from its lottery into the Community Economic Betterment Account (CEBA) and towns vied with each other for funds. Communities competed for lottery money to fund business start-ups or expansions and to lure existing businesses from other states. In return, the businesses pledged to create jobs. In 1988 the program was two years old, and the first reports about job creation were coming in. They were a mixed bag. Five companies that had received $380,000 between them had already folded. The majority delivered far fewer jobs than they promised. Only a few produced more than promised, including two companies in Council Bluffs, Blue Star Foods and IBP. On the whole, larger businesses receiving funds under the program more consistently produced the results they had pledged.[58]

Sometimes things worked out well, as in Red Oak. Red Oak Die Casting Company received a $60,000 grant to open a foundry in the small, western Iowa town. The owners had looked at 150 different sites, but the site in Red Oak came with a cash grant, which was a major factor in the decision to move to Iowa. The business began manufacturing parts for Ford and GM as well as other companies. In turn, they provided employment for thirty residents, many of whom had been unable to find jobs, or well-paying jobs, in the area. The wages were not phenomenal, but at $6.70 an hour plus benefits, they were twice the minimum wage and significantly higher than agricultural wages. In order to qualify for CEBA money, firms had to pay wages at least 75 percent of the average wage in the county where they located.[59]

Many towns wanted to replicate Red Oak's success. Grundy Center asked for $77,000 to fund an expansion project with Goodwill Industries of Northeast Iowa. Iowa Falls was hoping to reopen the closed Farmland Foods plant under a new owner, Steamboat Farms. The superintendent of schools from nearby Hampton wrote the governor to plead Iowa Falls' case. When the plant closed, sixty local residents lost their jobs, badly damaging the town. He wrote, "Our school population has dropped dramatically in the past few years. Many, many houses are vacant and have been listed for sale for several months. We have several vacant buildings in our downtown business district." A reopened plant just eighteen miles down the road could breathe new life into the town. The Chamber of Commerce in Ackley, thirteen miles from Iowa Falls, made the same plea. The city of Audubon had its own plans, and wanted to open an ethanol plant with state funds. Harlan and Lenox were fighting over an egg processing facility, with Harlan (the larger of the towns) attempting to sweeten the pot by pledging not to take state funds. In the search for industry, there would be inevitable winners and losers, and sometimes not the ones expected. The egg processing facility went to Lenox.[60]

The scramble for attention and funds was, to some, worrisome. Millions of dollars were involved, generating concerns about whether or not the money was being put to good use.⁶¹ University of Iowa president Hunter R. Rawlings III believed that the competition among communities was not good for Iowa's quality of life. He pled for "no more communities vying with each other, no more pitting parts against the whole, no more feeling that 'if we can't have it, you shouldn't have it down the road a mile.'"⁶² Some wondered if the jobs paid enough to support a family. R. C. Wahlert, president emeritus of FDL Foods in Dubuque, was not convinced that the change was positive. While meat processors Hormel and Oscar Mayer were leaving the state, taking jobs that paid more than $10 an hour, Excel and IBP were entering, paying a bit over $6 an hour. On top of the obvious problems with trading high wage jobs for lower wage jobs, Wahlert disapproved of funding economic development by way of a lottery: "It's gotten to be a 'me-too' deal; whenever one county gets a quarter-million-dollar grant, the next guy wants the same. A vicious circle!! The truth of it is, the lottery money itself is taken from the 'have-nots' in the first place."⁶³ A member of the United Food and Commercial Workers from Perry also objected to the way in which the state used lottery money to bring in meatpacking companies: "Everytime [sic] I buy a ticket I am driving a nail in my own coffin, putting an end to the rest of the meat packers who are in competition with I.B.P. and now EXCEL."⁶⁴ Concerns about the quality of these new meatpacking jobs would be permanent. Economic development schemes, like the one in Rolfe, might bring a community together, but competition over economic development funds did not promote a vision of a united Iowa.

Continuing Anxiety

The concerns of 1988 bled into 1989. There was more cautious optimism, but it was, indeed, cautious. When *Wallace's Farmer* polled the state's agriculturalists early in the year, they found a somewhat positive outlook. Most respondents thought their farms' financial position was either holding its own or improving slowly. Most also believed that the prospect for their farm in the next five years was either good or fair. On the whole, the younger farmers were the most optimistic, a definite change from the early 1980s.⁶⁵ The Iowa Farm and Rural Life Poll also fell into the more positive category, with levels of stress among farmers on the decline since 1986. The number of farmers feeling very high levels of stress had fallen from 19 percent to 8 percent. Other statistics dampened the mood, however. About 13 percent were still feeling unable to control important elements of their lives fairly often or very often, and 20 percent were feeling nervous and stressed. When asked if they felt that their difficulties were "piling up so high you could not overcome them," 31 percent were in that category at least sometimes.[66] The situation was better but the problems of the era had not been resolved.

The most serious problem of the previous year, drought, had also yet to be resolved. Farmers in the Kalona and Wellman area, in southeast Iowa, had made only one cutting of poor-quality hay in the previous summer. They were happy recipients of a haylift from farmers in Manson who donated seventeen semiloads of hay by way of the Mennonite Disaster Service. The Manson community was returning the favor of aid given following a 1979 tornado. The low levels of moisture in 1988, in many places half or less than half of normal, meant that farmers were going into 1989 planting with inadequate moisture. Even people who normally hated the snow were desperate to see it fall. Although the drought would not be as widespread as in 1988, the spring and summer were very dry in some locations. In northeast Iowa, the soil cracked for lack of moisture. In northwest Iowa, the crop in places was worse than the year before. In some parts of southwest Iowa, the ponds dried up, forcing farmers to sell large numbers of cattle. Families facing a second year of drought adopted a strategy well-known to many farming people: "Watch, wait, pray."[67]

Extending beyond the drought were a network of other issues making the agricultural situation equivocal. Farmers had watched the value of their land climb again throughout 1988. Oddly enough, the drought had boosted land values. Most of the increase in value had come before the drought set in and land had held its value as investors anticipated higher commodity prices due to the drought. Mike Duffy, however, cautioned against being "foolishly optimistic," even though Iowa had experienced the largest gains in land value in the Midwest. Iowa land prices had risen by 20 percent. Land values in Indiana had seen a 14 percent increase, Illinois a 9 percent increase, Michigan 4 percent, and Wisconsin 1 percent. If the drought did not ease, or if the federal government cut payments to farmers (which the USDA estimated made up 18 percent of gross and 70 percent of net farm income), the upward trend could be reversed.[68]

Lingering doubt, unhappiness, and stress meant disruption for Iowa's farm families, particularly within marriages. Many couples had been through long years of upheaval, much of which they had never expected; many were unsure where they were going once the crisis passed. In particular, farm women found themselves in circumstances greatly at odds with their ideals for a farm marriage and wondering what they would do with their lives as their families emerged from the crisis. Paul Lasley taught sociology at Iowa State University and remembered an exchange with a farm woman in one of his classes. He was "lamenting the stories and the hardships families were experiencing," when a student spoke up. "One of my students, young farm wife, maybe 35 or so, said 'Well, I'm back to school to improve myself because I've been working the last three or four years in . . . [an] egg processing plant to make ends meet.'" The change she envisioned, however, went farther than a college degree and more fulfilling employment. He recalled, "She said 'And I am tired of supporting my husband's habit of farming.' . . . She wasn't sure how long she would stay in that marriage. But there were a lot of marriages that failed. Because women went off to work, quote 'temporarily' to make ends meet. And it drug on and on."[69] Many women found themselves off the farm, working to support it, and wondering why. Especially if they were in low-wage work, women taking on additional outside roles became dissatisfied with their marriages and their life on the farm. Their wages contributed to the survival of the farm, but did little to improve their economic position. They were doing jobs that they sometimes did not want to do, often for low wages, to support an enterprise that never seemed to get ahead.[70]

Lasley's student was not the only farm woman having doubts about the advisability or desirability of continuing to support a husband's farming habit. *Successful Farming*'s editors turned to the issue of the farm marriage in 1989 and even sponsored a series of marriage seminars. Out of these came a serious look at farm marriages and the discontents of women in particular. Women complained of husbands who would "eat, drink, and sleep farming" but not pay attention to them. Off-farm jobs added another layer of trouble to managing a home and a farm. Women sometimes felt that working, saving, and scrimping were the sum total of their lives.[71] In the pre–World War II era, farm women had accepted making do and doing without. They expected to have little and stretch their resources as far as was humanly possible. Most of the cultural attachment to frugality, however, had worn thin in the intervening years. Few wanted to continue scrimping when the rest of the country went on a buying spree. Before World War II, sticking with a spouse in spite of problem upon problem had also been an accepted part of farm marriages. Women stayed with difficult and demanding husbands for the sake of the farm and a legacy for their children. Lacking other alternatives, they often repressed their own desires on the farm's behalf. This stance, too, was losing its appeal, especially in a time when the farm was proving to be such a poor provider. Women had more options in the 1980s than in previous decades, and farm women increasingly questioned whether they had an obligation to stick with their husbands, and their husbands' farms, especially as their children chose to leave the land.

Successful Farming gathered information from women across the Midwest and shared anonymously their frustrations with farm marriage. An Illinois woman wrote to express her dissatisfaction with her husband's commitment to the farm, rather than her. Because of financial troubles, she had thrown herself wholeheartedly into the couple's dairy farm, milking in the morning and at night, before and after working full time for a much-needed paycheck. On top of that, she was solely responsible for the housework. Help with household chores would have reduced her stress considerably, as would less verbal abuse from a husband who demanded to be treated as "the boss." She was almost to the point of getting out of the marriage, but "I would not want my husband to lose the farm."[72] Another dissatisfied spouse complained about the claims the farm made on every penny of the family's money: "I feel like a serf around this farm. When we need new farm equipment or tires for the pickup, we get machines and tires. But when we need new curtains in the living room or a new washer, what we get is 'Later. The farm comes first.'" She resented her subservient position, commenting, "I love the farm because it's his dream—but it doesn't make it my farm." She needed something more, including a sense of personal investment in the farm they called home.[73] A Kansas farm woman described her husband as "very demanding and sometimes short-tempered" and commented that she was, in fact, the third wife. About his previous wives, she wrote, "They fell in love with a good, hardworking man, but not necessarily with the farm—which was *his* first love." Because she loved the land, she thought that she would be more capable of handling a man who tended to be "a tyrant about the farm."[74] Not all of the stories were gloomy. A Minnesota woman explained that she had finally gotten stubborn with her husband, "I'm not a doormat anymore. I love me!" She forced her workaholic, dairy farmer husband into regular weekends away and began to assert herself. While she continued to be a supportive wife, "I do speak my piece, make demands, decline to do certain things . . . I stand my ground when I don't think we need a new piece of equipment."[75] In a world where the farm did not always pay, wives felt increasingly empowered to question their husbands' single-minded devotion to the land.

Without the weight of ideology to hold them in place, farm women needed stronger incentives to remain on farms. In past times, women had gathered strength from organizations that brought them together with others in their rural neighborhoods. The crisis had tested their fortitude, but it had also stripped away some of the traditional structures that had added richness to their lives. Women's clubs were another of the casualties of the crisis. Many of them faded away into nothingness at the close of the decade. The Freedom Township Women's Club, begun in 1923, met for the last time on June 2, 1989, when a social worker came to discuss domestic violence. The club secretary penned in the minutes, "The club seems to have died a natural death for lack of interest. One factor in its demise may have been the consolidation of farms into larger units. On one mile in the township where there were four sets of farm buildings, there is now only one."[76] There were fewer and fewer neighbors to provide social support. The Omega Township Women's Club was also dying a slow death. On February 21, 1989, "A letter was received and read from Lanette Person asking to resign because her job is demanding more of her time."[77] Without change, many rural institutions were going to disappear. As a Little Sioux resident commented, "Unless clubs or church groups change meeting times, most young women are automatically excluded."[78] With the rural neighborhood succumbing to depopulation, and farm people increasingly holding jobs in town, the social aspects of farm life suffered.

Neighborhoods and communities were shrinking, and schools faced even more challenges. In 1989 the state moved to allow open enrollment in Iowa's schools. Under this system, families had the option of moving their children between schools within their district and across district lines. Schools could admit new pupils up to their enrollment limits, although families moving students had to provide transportation. To many supporters of small schools, this sounded like another nail being pounded into their coffins. A woman from rural Akron wrote to the governor to protest: "It seems to me when we are fighting in the rural communities to survive that the open enrollment bill is one more way of destroying us. . . . For our school to lose even a small percentage of students is going to make our programs less effective and the loss of staff due to losing students will make a dent in our effective programming." She asked the governor, "You are on record as saving the farms, saving small towns, save small businesses—well, why don't you continue with that and save the 'small school' as well?"[79] Additionally, many Iowans objected to the state allowing homeschooling, which would also reduce the number of students in small districts.

When the *Chicago Tribune* published a 1989 article on the demise of the Midwestern small town, two locations in Iowa made the list, Diagonal and Mount

Ayr. Diagonal's contribution to the story focused on its tiny high school, enrolling only forty-two students, which nonetheless packed in one thousand spectators per home basketball game. As the writer put it, "This is where Diagonal reminds the rest of Iowa that it is still on the map." It was the tiny school, and its winning and strongly-supported basketball team, that kept the town with its three block-long Main Street going. Because of the precarious position of such a small high school, the author opined, "there is a bitterness beneath the surface. Diagonal is a terminal patient. As with hundreds of other small rural communities across the Midwest, its chances of surviving into the 21st Century look bleak." The author would probably be startled to know that in 2020, Diagonal was still alive, slightly bigger than it was in 1989. Unlike many other very small towns surviving and thriving into the twenty-first century, it was not a bedroom community for any significantly larger, neighboring town. Diagonal even still had its own high school. That outcome, however, seemed fanciful in the waning days of the 1980s.[80]

Death of Dixon Terry

On May 28, the death of Dixon Terry, dairy farmer and head of the PrairieFire board, took the wind out of the sails of Iowa's farm activists. Terry was in the fields, baling hay with his father and thirteen-year-old son when lightning struck the thirty-nine-year-old, killing him instantly. Dixon's death was both sudden and sobering. Roughly one thousand people attended his funeral at Greenfield's United Methodist Church, including Iowa Senator Tom Harkin, Missouri congressman Richard Gephardt, and the Reverend Jesse Jackson. The local paper eulogized Terry, as did the *Des Moines Register*, but tributes also appeared in the *New York Times* and on the floor of the US Senate. Speaker after speaker at the funeral noted that although Terry might be remembered most often as a farm activist, he would have wanted to be remembered as a farmer, and that he died doing what he loved.[81]

Linda Terry woke up the morning of May 29 realizing she had forty-five cows to milk, morning and night, and the FmHA to battle. She became the sole provider for a family of three. In addition to trying to keep up with the cows and the crops, she had a part-time job as a waitress. For a while, she and the children continued to milk cows, but before long substituted sheep, which did not have to be milked twice a day. Unfortunately, the farm also carried substantial debt. When Dixon died, the family owed $300,000 on their farm and were at risk of losing it. Various organizations held benefits in Iowa, to help the family pay off the loan. There was also a benefit in Washington, DC, sponsored by Willie Nelson, Governor Branstad, and Illinois congressman Paul Simon. In spite of these efforts, the family was not able to save the entire property. Eventually, Linda Terry worked out an agreement with her lenders, allowing her to keep the forty acres that included the house and the outbuildings and one cow they particularly loved named Jesse, after Jesse Jackson. With the help of her daughter, she put together her first resume and went to work in Tom Harkin's Des Moines office.[82]

Living with Less, Including Expectations

In the fall of 1991, the editors of *Successful Farming* polled their readers to take the pulse of agricultural America. It was a three-page survey, examining attitudes about home, family, and the farm operation. They had done the same thing in 1974 and wanted to gauge what had happened in the meantime. As Farm Issues Editor Cheryl Tevis noted, "Today, 17 years later, agriculture is trying to put behind it the most devastating era since the Great Depression. . . . On many farms, financial stress, bankruptcies and restructuring fractured marriages and killed the dream of passing the farm to the next generation."[83] Hundreds of farmers from across the country returned surveys; the average farmer to answer was between thirty-five and sixty-four years old, a high-school graduate, perhaps with some college courses under his belt, and earned a gross income of $100,000 to $250,000. Among this group, the hardships of the 1980s had changed lives. Far more were scrimping on family living expenses in order to meet the costs of the farm; 74.7 percent were economizing in 1991, compared to only 41.4 percent in 1974. While they were vacationing slightly more than in 1974, they were eating fewer restaurant meals. While 23 percent of farm wives in the 1974 survey had worked off the farm, 46.6 percent did in 1991. Slightly larger numbers of men worked off the farm, 29.8 percent versus 26.6 percent. The number of farmers who hoped to have one of their children take over the farm had also declined, 54.8 percent in 1991 versus 68.8 percent in 1974.[84]

There was, on the whole, less confidence and contentment with life on farms and in rural America. Fewer felt successful—80.2 percent as opposed to 92 percent, and more worried about their future—56.5 percent versus 34.5 percent. Most enjoyed farming less than in the past and were also concerned about the quality of the schools and other institutions in their communities.[85] In an addendum to her family's survey, a farm woman from Iowa, Amy Petersen, explained the equivocal feelings of many farm families. She wrote, "We felt we would have the same growth rate we had seen in the 1970s," but they were mistaken. "As solo operators through the 1980s, we have watched the composition of our socio-economic landscape change dramatically from what we grew up with through the 1970s, to what is a living business reality in the '90s . . . I'm sure we are not alone in having mixed emotions about what we have observed or lived through; for the most part, we are optimistic."[86] While the Petersens were optimistic, most farmers were frustrated. They would do it all over again, but they enjoyed the job less, worried more, and believed they had lost out economically relative to their urban counterparts. One commented, "The decline being felt in rural America is from a system of economics that reduces food to its lowest possible cost without regard to the infrastructure that produces it (and the damage being done to it)."[87]

A survey in rural Iowa, carried out by Joan Blundall, revealed much of the same sense of loss, and worse. The experiences of the previous decade had reinforced the idea that bad things happened to good people. People who had once believed that hard work could take them anywhere no longer believed it: "Many families clearly expressed the fact that experience had taught them that the world is not a fair place. Rain, drought, inflation, and deflation of land values were all seen as external causes that had nothing to do with deservingness." Experience had chipped away at the optimism farmers needed to keep going in the face of the day to day, month to month, and year to year stresses. Even so, most kept right on going, often in defiance of their own experiences. Among her sample, Blundall found that in spite of a growing feeling that "working hard did not pay off . . . they continued to work hard, often at two or three jobs."[88] That was a recipe for unhappiness and discontent, making life on farms an even more unattractive proposition for the next generation.

The gloom that lingered more than likely had something to do with a continuing perception (and for many, reality) that the crisis was not quite over. The Farm Aid concerts continued. The sparring with lenders continued, although the situation seemed to have declined to a low rumble. An agreement worked out with Norwest Bank through pressure applied by ICCI, Catholic Rural Life, and AAM provided more credit to smaller operations. ICCI had successfully threatened Norwest with legal action over federal legislation that required banks to meet the credit needs of their localities, loosening up $16 million in new funds. The hotlines established at the height of the crisis continued to operate, but the calls were fewer.[89]

Iowa's farmers were feeling more optimistic and their finances were improving, but for a stubborn 15 percent, hard times lingered.

While agricultural sales were improving, profitability was not. Expenses continued to gobble up farmers' profits. Farmers who raised grain only saw a bit of improvement in their incomes, but those who were sticking with livestock, and especially beef and dairy cattle, were fighting a losing battle.[90] One measure of the ongoing struggle in agriculture was that parents were telling their children not to go into the family business. Some were taking a relatively passive route and not encouraging their children to take over the family farm. They did not want their children go through the same struggles they had. Others were much more vigorous in their objections, refusing to talk with their children about going into the business. To them, it was too much sweat, poverty, and insecurity. They had no desire to see another generation go through the same pain they had experienced.[91]

Even as times improved, people continued to feel uneasy, with every setback and difficulty reminding them of the hard times they had suffered. People constantly looked over their shoulders, even as they appreciated the way in which their circumstances had improved. *Successful Farming* published a series of portraits of "successful family farms" in the early 1990s, and for most of the Iowans featured success rested on a foundation of near-disaster. The Bensons, farmers from rural State Center, had been through serious financial losses with cattle feeding. While the family eventually settled on corn and beans, the problems with the cattle-feeding operation forced them to sell several hundred acres of land, as well as some of their machinery. Jim Benson's wife, Greta, also took an off-farm job.[92]

The Bradfords, from Guthrie Center, also had a tale of struggle to tell. By the 1990s four of the Bradford children would be away at Iowa State University, but the family's experience of the mid-1980s had almost killed the dream of a college education for their many children. Credit problems made it difficult to buy groceries, the children gathered pop cans from beside country roads for a little extra cash, and the family lost four hundred of its six hundred acres. By giving up the majority of their land, the Bradfords were able to keep their Angus herd. At the worst of times, the Bradfords split up the family to keep money coming in, with Mary taking the six youngest children with her to southeast Iowa where she was able to secure a teaching job. They went home for holidays and weekends.[93] Like the Bensons and Bradfords, many of the families featured had followed a very rocky road to success.

The series editors also chose to feature Dixon and Linda Terry's farm, which was under threat of foreclosure. This was a different kind of success. The article began with the words, "If you're looking for a financial success story, stop right here. Dixon and Linda Terry struggled financially from the day they bought their 160 acre dairy farm until the day Dixon was struck and killed by lightning while bailing hay with his son and father. But if you believe success can be measured in many other ways, read on." While the Terry's dairy farm never managed to pay their debts, Dixon Terry's work with the Iowa Farm Unity Coalition, Farmer's Union, and PrairieFire brought the concerns of small family farmers to the attention of politicians in Iowa and Washington. *Successful Farming* editor Loren Kruse explained how a decade of difficulties had changed his perspective on what it meant for farmers to be successful: "*Success is simply doing the best you can with what you've got.*" Given the disaster that had come with the "go-go, aggressive and often reckless style of farming" in the 1970s, this was, perhaps, a more realistic expectation.[94]

Floods of 1993

While the early 1990s had shown slow, steady upward progress for those who had managed or eluded credit problems, 1993 would be a year to try every Iowan's fortitude. The flooding that spring and summer was the worst in Iowa history—or at least the worst for which the state had accurate measurements. Iowa might have experienced flooding as significant in 1851, but the measurements of that era were crude. What happened in 1993 was relentless and breathtaking. The winter of 1992–1993 was cold, gray, and very wet. As late as March 1, there had been little melting or evaporation and the snowpack was more than two feet deep in some parts of the state. The flooding began in early March as rain fell on deep snow. Rapidly melting snow and heavy rains meant trouble in many parts of the state, especially as ice dams propelled many rivers and streams out of their banks. As the spring wore on, the weather stayed cool and cloudy; the summer continued in the same vein. The sun rarely shone. It was the coolest summer since 1907.

Then, the clouds opened up. It rained, and rained, and rained, and much of it was torrential. Location after location reported storms dumping four and five inches. It got worse. Over the July Fourth weekend, a 250-mile stretch across the state received four to eight inches of rain. Three days later, an uninterrupted band of 275 miles of Iowa received three to twelve inches. The already serious flooding became catastrophic. It affected people in the immediate areas of the storms but also others, as the water surged downstream. The waves of thunderstorms and abnormally low temperatures continued through August. From November 1992 to November 1993, nearly fifty inches of precipitation fell, roughly twenty inches more than normal. This would have been problem enough, but often when it rained, it poured. This was not gentle rain, but rain that came in torrents, making absorption difficult (and after a certain point, absorption was no longer possible). By the time it was over, every county in the state had experienced flooding, and some communities had been through multiple major flood events.[95]

Rural communities had flooded, but so had urban areas. There were small towns, like Carter Lake, where the worst flooding had been from below. Groundwater had risen, inundating basements and destroying the sewer system, sending raw sewage into homes and businesses. In a town of just over three thousand residents, flooding damaged roughly two hundred homes. River and stream flooding knocked out Des Moines's water system for weeks, and seriously damaged both the University of Iowa and Iowa State University. The coliseum at Iowa State filled with fourteen feet of floodwater. So much was happening that the state climatologist could not keep up with his reporting.[96] Of all of the states in the Mississippi and Missouri River basins, Iowa was worst hit by the year's flooding, with 1.1 million acres of land experiencing flooding and 250,000 acres under standing water.[97]

For many farm families, the size of the catastrophe was mind-boggling. Lloyd Weyerholz, of Wapello, watched water claim four hundred acres of his farm. Fortunately, he had only planted one hundred acres before a levee burst and flooded his land. He also had to sell three-quarters of his beef cattle, unable to feed them. A neighbor, Ed Yotter, had ten feet of water covering his four hundred acres. He had already purchased his seed and fertilizer when the flooding hit: "All of my inputs on those acres were paid. And my land taxes go on whether I have a crop or not."[98] In Van Buren County, the Plowmans saw the water drown 140 acres of corn and soybeans. They were able to rescue their young pigs at the last minute, the trailer floating as the truck hauled it to higher ground.[99] One Iowa farmer discovered that the waters had drilled a fifty-foot-deep hole in the middle of his fields, while others had to deal with fields too deeply gullied and banks too deeply undermined for their large machinery.[100] Farm journalist and farm woman Cheryl Tevis reflected on the weight of the summer's events, "The weather is one reason that I never wanted to marry a farmer.... I never have been able to reconcile the fact that a farmer could do everything right, and still end up with a poor crop—due to disastrous weather conditions."[101] John Ley, agricultural extension agent for Kossuth County, commented to a reporter for the *Des Moines Register*, "Just look at that, it's field after field. . . . I just thought we'd break out of this weather pattern, but we never did."[102] The phones at the Rural Concern Hotline, now called the Iowa Concern Hotline, rang nearly as vigorously as they had at the height of the farm crisis, with callers anxious and even suicidal over the new disaster confronting them.[103] PrairieFire opened a Rural Recovery Line and provided information, referrals, and technical assistance for families affected by the floods.[104]

The summer of 1993 was an enormous setback for farmers who had been working toward recovery. The state and federal government hurried flood relief packages into place, but they could not compensate for acres of land left unplanted or destroyed after planting. The flooding reduced the state's soybean and corn crops by more than a third. The state estimated that farmers' losses in their corn crop added up to $835 million, in their soybean crop to $212 million, and in livestock, $278 million. The state received roughly $500 million in disaster payments for farmers.[105] Those who did have crops to sell did not benefit from flood-induced scarcity, since farmers east of the Mississippi enjoyed substantial harvests. The economic conditions on Iowa's farms had been slowly but steadily improving over the previous five years, but 1993 would be a return to hard times for many of the state's agriculturalists. The number of farmers in weak to severely stressed conditions would climb back up to 23 percent, the highest since 1987. Crop losses threatened to push the 40 percent in stable condition into the red zone.[106] It had to have seemed like a never-ending battle, facing off perpetually against the cost-price squeeze and weather conditions that stymied forward progress.

What was different about this particular crisis, as opposed to the long, drawn-out troubles of the eighties, was that this was an obvious disaster. It was visible, it was dramatic, and there was no doubt that nature rather than farmers had caused the problem. In mid-July, even before the state felt the full effects of the flooding, President Bill Clinton declared the entire state a disaster area, opening the way for all manner of support programs.[107] Help came in the form of FmHA disaster loans, FEMA programs, and donations of money and supplies. In an unprecedented move, the government provided unemployment benefits to farmers whose operations had been completely derailed by the floodwaters.[108] Additionally, more than $225,000 in private donations sat in the statehouse in November, ready to be distributed throughout Iowa. The state made that money available to individuals and small businesses that had suffered damage, in addition to funding other initiatives, such as pizza suppers at which counselors mingled with the crowd. Donations paid for truckloads of food for particularly hard-hit towns, such as Chelsea and Hamburg. The state even planned on using the funds to build a bridge for a farmer near Roland, cut off from his fields by damage from the flooding.[109] Unlike a decade before, help came quickly and efficiently, and even while the disaster was still unfolding.

An End to the Crisis?

The floods of 1993 provide a stopping point for this narrative, not because the crisis necessarily ended there but because a pattern had been established. Farmers saw their fortunes improve, they forged ahead, and then disaster came along and halted forward progress. There would be no Great Depression-esque line between the past and the future. At the end of the Great Depression came a world war that boosted incomes radically and reordered every feature of the nation's farms. At the end of the Farm Crisis of the 1980s came more years of up and down and up again. As with the Great Depression, the events of the 1980s for many years shaped the expectations, hopes, and dreams for farm and rural families. Those who lived through the crisis would have a very hard time forgetting. The ongoing uncertainties of agriculture, in addition to the incredible vagaries of nature, were not going to allow the peace of mind that came with an orderly and understandable world.

EPILOGUE

Last-Generation Farmers

By the time Iowa entered the 1990s, the world had shifted.[1] The Farm Crisis had dribbled to a conclusion of sorts, but it was difficult to draw the line between the end of the crisis and the beginning of a new era. For many, this transition was very much an individual matter. For one family, the crisis might have ended when they received final notice that their problems with their lender had been resolved. Maybe it was when they completed their bankruptcy filing and said goodbye to their farm forever. Perhaps the end came when there were jobs in town to go to and the family settled into a new version of normal. The crisis might have ended when the trucks came for the hogs and the cattle and the farm took on a new shape in the face of economic pressures dictating that raising livestock on a small scale would no longer pay, and the family would be raising only corn and soybeans. Or maybe it felt as if the crisis years never quite ended, its ripples shaping life—and even the landscape—for decades to come. It remained visible, in farm houses left vacant until the volunteer fire department burned them to the ground for practice. It remained visible in barns and corn cribs that have been empty for decades, with roofs slowly caving in, waiting for the next big snow or wind to push them over. It remained in the big, blue Harvestore silos, uselessly towering over farms that no longer raised cattle. It was achingly apparent in empty small-town schoolhouses, gathering graffiti and waiting for redevelopment that rarely came, and in business districts pockmarked with empty storefronts: the clothing shop, the gift shop, and the grocery store gone for good. Those who remained noted the absences. Farms, small towns, and the rural landscape no longer looked as busy or vital as they once did.

Families and Change

Landscapes bore visible scars longer than families. Studies undertaken with "displaced" farm families in the late 1980s through the early 1990s suggested that farm

The past and the present continued to live in this farmyard, with the old round barn surrounded by newer structures. Photo by Bob Kisken, by permission of Iowa State University Library Special Collections and University Archives.

couples did, with a little time and effort, remake their lives. Losing the land meant an initial economic shock and emotional disarray, but husbands and wives eventually created new niches for themselves. Those who left farming earlier in the crisis, before 1984, found their feet more quickly. As their economic stress diminished, so did their emotional turmoil. Especially as young people lost farms, they moved on quickly, finding new jobs, often in new locations. Their incomes often increased and their new occupations brought them less stress and more stability. Those who chose to stay in farming often experienced economic stress in the 1990s, as federal support for farms fell, fueling the continuing exodus of families from agriculture. Those who became part-time farmers, at least partially dependent on outside income, often used that income to help themselves stay in place, rather than move ahead. Women who found off-farm employment continued to feel stressed by their choice to work, perhaps because the jobs were difficult, perhaps because they struggled to balance work, farm, and family. Nevertheless, as couples emerged on the other side of the crisis, and as the economic strain on their families decreased, so did the emotional turmoil that marked the hardest years of the downturn.[2]

Children, too, adjusted to this new life. When mothers went to work, children learned to help out more around the house. When facing financial hardship, youngsters found ways to bring money into the family coffers. At the time when a family lost its land, everyone suffered depression and doubt, but five years later, most young people were adjusting. Those who had the hardest time learning to live their new reality were those whose fathers failed to find satisfaction in new occupations. When fathers remained distressed, their children did, too. Rural sociologists attributed the resiliency of Iowa's farm children to the social capital embedded in the environments in which they lived. Many regularly saw grandparents and had access to other concerned adults, such as church or 4-H leaders. Despite a decade of hard times, the schools they attended still provided an excellent education. Researchers concluded that the experience of economic distress, even including the loss of a family farm and mental distress and depression on the part of parents, did not have to ruin a child's life and prospects for the future. The authors of one study commented, "A large number of young people from disadvantaged circumstances ended up doing better than one would predict; they exceeded expectations based on their backgrounds." Again, the social capital with which their families entered the crisis stood youngsters in good stead as they came out on the other side.[3]

Demographic Change in Iowa

The state as a whole also exhibited resilience. In spite of the predictions of the late 1980s, Iowa did not dry up and blow away. There was no stampede of residents out of the state, although the Farm Crisis decade saw the loss of nearly 10 percent of the rural population and almost 5 percent of the state's total population.[4] The 1980s had been staggeringly bad, but the 1990s and 2000s saw a return to a modicum of health. Population growth resumed, although at a modest pace. The population estimate for 2019 was of more than 3.15 million Iowans, up by 3.6 percent since 2010.[5] What was changing more significantly was the balance between urban and rural. In 1970 the state had been 57.2 percent urban; in 1980, it was 58.6 percent urban. In 1990 it was 60.6 percent urban, heading for 64 percent in 2010. Still, even with the downward trend in the rural population, in 2010 only ten states were more rural than Iowa.[6] What was falling more rapidly was the number of farms. In 1978 Iowa had been home to 126,456 farms. Between 1978 and 1992, the number dropped to 96,543, or 24 percent fewer farms than before the crisis. This pattern repeated itself across the Midwest. Minnesota lost 27 percent of its farms, Wisconsin, 24 percent, and Illinois, 29 percent.[7] It is impossible to know exactly how to categorize these disappearances. Some were bankruptcies and forced sales. Some were choices made more or less freely to retire or to leave agriculture for a path that was less uncertain. Some of these losses represented careers in agriculture never begun by young people who chose, happily or not, to do something different with their lives. Although families and individuals bounced back from the crisis, life, and particularly life on farms, was not as it had formerly been.

Old patterns of farm loss continued and intensified. When farms failed, they disappeared into the operations of neighbors, often that third of Iowa's farmers who entered, and left, the 1980s with little debt. It is no surprise that the size of the state's farms grew. Farms of varying sizes experienced the pressures of the 1980s differently. It was not a good decade in which to be a small- to medium-sized operator. The number of small farms, from 50 to 179 acres, fell by 30 percent. Farms from 180 to 499 acres suffered even greater losses, 35 percent. Larger farms, in total numbers and in proportion to the whole, grew. The number of farms from 500 to 999 acres grew by 12 percent. Larger farms grew more. The number of those from 1,000 to 1,999 acres grew by 97 percent, and those larger than 2,000 acres by 94 percent. While most of Iowa's farms were still in the 180- to 499-acre category, they had shown far less resiliency than the larger operations.[8] In 1978 the average Iowa farm was 274 acres. By 1992 the average farm had grown to 325 acres. Twenty years later, in 2012, it was 345 acres. Big farms survived by growing even bigger. Smaller farms survived because their operators took jobs off the farm in order to supplement inadequate farm incomes.[9]

In the 1980s the number of farms disappearing was highly variable by county. The biggest losses came in Hamilton County, in central Iowa, with a 32 percent decline in farms over the decade. In Winnebago County, on the state's northern border, it was 31 percent. The lowest numbers were largely clustered on the eastern border of the state. Dubuque County lost 3 percent; Jackson County, 6 percent, Clayton County, 8 percent, and Delaware County, 9 percent. In far western Iowa, only 8 percent of the farms in Sioux County disappeared. Because of their proximity to larger cities, farmers in these locations had greater access to industrial or other employment to supplement their farm incomes, staving off the loss of their land. The highest concentration of misery came in an eleven-county block running more or less up the middle of the state, along Interstate 35, including Dallas and Polk in the south and Winnebago and Worth in the north. Two other northwestern

Iowa counties, Clay and Calhoun, had losses above 25 percent, as did Harrison, in far western Iowa, and Mills and Fremont in far southwestern Iowa.[10] Mills and Fremont Counties experienced prolonged, severe flooding at several points in the 1980s, which hastened the demise of a number of farms. These variations in numbers of farms lost do not seem to have much, if anything, to do with changes in land values across the 1980s. When the value of farmland came crashing down, every part of the state suffered, and suffered fairly equally. At the least, land values in a few counties, such as Muscatine and Louisa, on the state's eastern border, fell by 60 percent. At the most, land values fell by 67 percent, as they did in Winnebago County, on the state's northernmost border, and Cerro Gordo County, one tier south and one county east of Winnebago County. Across the whole state, land values declined precipitously, and the numbers were remarkably similar.[11]

The patterns apparent in these losses are rather different than the longer-term trends the state experienced. In the long century from 1900 to 2012, 60 percent of the state's farms disappeared. The biggest losses over the long haul have been in the southern tier of the state, with most counties losing in excess of 65 or 70 percent of their farms. As of this writing, the northern border is more stable, with Sioux, Osceola, Palo Alto, Hancock, Mitchell, Howard, and Winneshiek Counties still retaining more than 50 percent of their farms.[12] The lowest losses of all have come in Delaware and Dubuque Counties, hilly territory, marginal for large scale, mechanized agriculture, but just right for Amish farm families looking for inexpensive land upon which to establish modest-sized family farms. Farms in the southern tier of the state have always been poorly capitalized, and smaller. Southern Iowa rolls, which has limited the kind of development that is possible. In general, this has made farms there more susceptible to failure. Those in the flatter north have been better capitalized, and more suitable to large scale, highly mechanized agriculture. Over the long haul, farms in the northern two-thirds of Iowa, and particularly those north of Interstate 80, were better prepared for the agricultural changes of the twentieth century and beyond. This pattern, however, did not hold in the midst of the Farm Crisis.

During the 1980s, there were several important differences between farms in the northern two thirds of the state and the lower third, which resulted in the loss of fewer farms in far southern Iowa. What is most apparent is that the farms in far southern Iowa did not participate in the go-go seventies. There were stark differences between the levels of capital represented by farms in the northern reaches of the state, as opposed to the lowest two tiers of counties. By 1978 the value of land and buildings per acre on Iowa farms averaged a healthy $1,548; far southern

Iowa lagged in the doldrums. Acreage in Monroe County held the lowest value in the state, $650. The average for the southernmost two tiers of Iowa counties was $1,008. In the eleven counties in the middle of the state that experienced some of the worst of farm loss, the average was $2,011, at the high end for the state. The areas that experienced the highest levels of farm loss also had the greatest collateral for extensive agricultural loans in the 1970s and very early 1980s. Southern Iowa, which saw lower losses, did not. Debt had been deadly for many of Iowa's farms, and those farmers with the wherewithal to acquire debt suffered proportionately.[13]

Farmers on low value southern Iowa land also put considerably less money into other capital investments. Those southern Iowa farms had, relative to others, less in the way of machinery and equipment. While the average Iowa farmer had $47,666 worth of machinery and equipment on the place, southern Iowa farmers came in at 20 percent less, at about $38,000.[14] Southern Iowa farmers also made fewer purchases between 1978 and 1982, just as the economy was beginning to falter seriously. While the agricultural census found farmers in the most seriously affected counties making two major purchases (a car, truck, combine or tractor, or similar equipment) during those years, southern Iowa farmers made a more restrained one to one and a half major purchases.[15] The buying and investing that happened on a good number of Iowa farms in the 1970s bypassed the southern part of the state. Those farms were less vulnerable to loss in the face of the credit crunch. Another factor working in southern Iowa's favor, oddly enough, was that its farmers were older than those in the rest of the state. Age could mean stability and greater resistance to the temptations of debt. Young, more vulnerable farmers made up a considerably smaller proportion of farmers throughout the area.[16]

Agriculture Ages

The agricultural downturn affected the age of Iowa's farmers. At its beginning, the average farmer was in his forties and had children at home. The countryside was relatively young, and people expected that at least some of their children would want to remain on the land. The Farm Crisis dramatically aged the agricultural and rural population, falling most heavily on people who were young, innovative, and well-educated.[17] In the mid-1970s the average age of Iowa farmers had actually dropped. In 1969 the average farmer had been 48.5 years old; by 1974 that farmer was 49.3. And then, in 1978, the average age fell, rather surprisingly, to

47.2 years.[18] The 1980s, however, were not good years to be a young farmer. Debt factored heavily, as being a young farmer often meant taking out loans for purchases of land, machinery, and buildings. It was hard to get credit, and the credit that was available came with very high rates of interest. It was better, in these years, to be established rather than an entrant. The youngest cohorts of farmers saw their numbers drop. In 1978 there were 6,339 farmers (5.2 percent of the total) under the age of twenty-five in Iowa. By 1992, the number had dropped to 2,276 (2.4 percent of the total). This shrinkage represented farm failures, but even more so, young people who chose other paths, unwilling or unable to stay on the farm. The cohort that represented their fathers—aged forty-five to fifty-four—also shrank, from 25 percent to 20 percent of the whole. Some farm losses took out multiple generations of farmers; when fathers lost their land, sons and daughters lost opportunities, too. The cohort aged twenty-five to thirty-five shrank, from 16 percent of all farmers to 14 percent. On the other hand, the oldest cohort of farmers, those over the age of sixty-five, grew both in total numbers and in relation to the larger group. In 1978 they numbered 12,577, or 10 percent of Iowa's farmers. In 1992, there were 18,341 of the oldest farmers, 19 percent of the total.[19]

Notably, this oldest cohort would have remembered the Great Depression, probably living through those dark years as children or young adults on farms. Even the youngest of them would have been born in 1927 and would have had many of their attitudes about life, and the accumulation of debt, shaped by that experience. A lifetime to build up stores of land, machinery, and improvements, in tandem with avoidance of debt, would have kept them free of many of the problems that plagued younger farmers in the 1980s. By 1992 the average Iowa farmer was 50.3 years.[20] This aging was not a short-term trend. By 2017 the agricultural census reported that the average Iowa producer was 57.4 years of age. As of this writing, the numbers for Iowa essentially reflected the numbers for the United States; the average agricultural producer nationwide was somewhere between fifty-five and sixty-one years old. Only in Pennsylvania, with its large population of Amish farmers, is the number very slightly lower, at 54.8 years.[21]

Decline of Diversification

At the end of the crisis, farmers were not only older—they had changed the way in which they farmed. Diversification declined considerably. The number of animals

This picture of a Wright County farm, ca. 1950, shows evidence of diversification. There is also a second, smaller house, indicating a multigeneration farmstead. By permission of Steven D. Hill.

on farms was already dropping before the crisis hit but fell even further throughout the decade. In 1959 there had been 174,707 farms in Iowa. Of that number 145,351 kept cattle. More than ninety thousand milked dairy cows. Hogs were nearly as popular, with 134,503 farms raising swine. Families raised chickens on 119,149 farms. In 1992 the total number of farms had fallen to 96,543. Less than half, or 43,610, kept beef cattle. The number of farms with dairy cattle fell even more steeply, to 5,878, with the federal government's whole herd dairy buyout contributing to the decline. Only about a third of Iowa's farms, 31,790, still had hogs. Chickens had gone the way of dairy cattle, with only 2,633 farms left raising them.[22] Farmers focused on corn and soybeans and were less likely to have a mix of crops and livestock as part of their operations. In the wake of unstable prices, grain seemed like less of a gamble and less work. Eliminating the cattle and hogs also meant that a farmer did not have to worry about animals starving if timely credit could not be secured, one less gut-wrenching problem with which to contend. Those who chose to continue with cattle and hogs raised them in larger (often far larger) numbers. Farmers increasingly raised hogs in large confinement buildings, where they lived on concrete floors with hundreds of others. Hog raisers often contracted with processors, guaranteeing a market.[23]

EPILOGUE

Taken in 1996, this view of the farm shows evidence of the demise of animal agriculture. The corn crib and hog barn were gone, and the last seven cattle awaited transportation to a sale. Although the chicken house remained, there were no longer any chickens. The second house had also been removed. By permission of Steven D. Hill.

Some farmers have chosen to walk an independent path, avoiding the either/or proposition of corn and soybeans or large-scale livestock production. Vic and Cindy Madsen, of Audubon County, run a highly diversified farm, far different than the average Iowa operation. The Madsens own 225 acres and rent another 90. They purchased their current property in the 1970s and, despite troubles, made it through the 1980s. The Madsens run the farm with the youngest of their three sons, Eric; their father believes that the Farm Crisis soured the older two on the idea. They belong to the Practical Farmers of Iowa, an organization founded in the 1980s that grew out of the farmer's need to "leave more money in [the farmer's] pocket after ... production costs." For the Madsens, keeping more in their pockets meant making a transition to organic production of corn and soybeans, in rotation with oats, wheat and hay. They also grow aronia berries. Cindy manages the livestock operation, raising chickens, hogs, and cattle. The livestock provide manure for the fields, and Cindy sells chickens, eggs, pork, and beef directly to consumers. Cindy explained the logic of their diversified farm: "When you have grains and livestock, you are busy year-round. Plus, with so many enterprises, we balance the debt-flow during the year. If you have a failure in one area, hopefully the other enterprises will make up for that failure." What they want, in the long run, is for people to "to remember that the farm was organic and sustainable. We tried to improve the soil to pass on to future generations."[24] Theirs is not the usual Iowa farm. It is more like a farm of the 1960s or 1970s than the 2000s.

For most Iowa farmers, diversification came to mean something different: a diversification not of crops but of the family's income stream. Less and less, farming meant sole reliance on income from crops and livestock. Farm women went out to work in large numbers, bringing an income back to the farm. Farm men also worked off their properties. By 1992, 18 percent of Iowa's farmers who worked farms with over $10,000 in sales per year (meaning they were not hobby farms) spent more than two hundred days a year working off the farm. Of course, there was a range, and farmers who lived in close proximity to urban areas had greater access, and greater participation, in this type of income diversification. Farmers in Black Hawk County, near the packing plants and farm equipment manufacturers in Waterloo, had the highest participation in off-farm employment. A full 31 percent worked off the farm more than two hundred days a year, as did 30 percent in neighboring Bremer County. Equally, farmers in Wapello County took advantage of their proximity to Ottumwa, where there was employment in meat packing as well as a John Deere factory and 27 percent were off the farm more than half the working days of the year. If farming could not yield an adequate income, then a mix of agriculture and wages would have to do.[25]

Small Communities in Danger

A shrinking number of farmers live in Iowa's rural places, and a shrinking number of rural residents people the state's hinterland. Rural communities are aging, and the smaller the community, the older the population.[26] A story of persistent losses of the young echoes throughout the agricultural heartland. In the early 2000s, sociologists Patrick Carr and Maria Kefalas researched their book, *Hollowing Out the Middle: The Rural Brain Drain and What it Means for America*, in rural Iowa. Carr and Kefalas examined the experiences of residents of the northeastern Iowa town of "Ellis," to try to understand why it is that small towns are dying and the rural heartland's chief export is its best and brightest young people. Their answer to this question was simple: towns are dying and the best and brightest are leaving because the mothers, fathers, neighbors, and teachers are sending them away, presumably for their own good. The rapid decline in the number of young people is not simply the product of young people's independent decisions, but also the encouragement of adults who push the highest achieving youngsters to go to college and move out of small-town Iowa permanently. They want their children to have more and better opportunities than are currently available in rural places.[27] When questioned about the role that the school and teachers played in increasing the migration out of Ellis, the high school principal replied, "This is the job we set out to do."[28]

Darcy Dougherty Maulsby was one of those rural children who, under the influence of the legacy of the Farm Crisis, left a farm for what looked like better opportunities. She grew up in rural Yetter, a tiny town in Calhoun County, in northwest Iowa. In 1980, on the eve of the crisis, fifty-two people lived in Yetter; in 2020, there were thirty-four. Maulsby's father was a farmer, and while the family managed to keep their land, there was one year during the downturn when the proceeds from the farm were a meager $1,000. Hard times shaped the choices she made. At her rural high school, the teachers encouraged bright young people to find their opportunities elsewhere. Even though Maulsby was active with FFA at Southern Cal (Calhoun County) High School, she plotted a course away from agriculture. After graduation, she headed off to college, eventually ending up at Iowa State University, where she majored in journalism and mass communication and history. She also eventually earned an MBA. She followed her dreams to Des Moines. All of that, however, would come crashing down in the dot.com failure of the early 2000s. She headed back to Calhoun County and evaluated her options. Maulsby made an unusual choice; she decided to stay in the countryside and go into business as a self-employed marketing professional, writer, speaker, and farmer. She meshes planting, cultivating, and harvesting her corn and soybeans with time spent at the computer and on the road, working with businesses, giving speeches, and telling stories about Iowa's past. She has come home.

While relatively unusual, Maulsby's experience is by no means unique, as surprising numbers of Americans with rural backgrounds eventually return to their roots. There are many reasons people make their way back to small places. Aging parents and family crises are often a catalyst, as can be the desire to raise children in a quieter atmosphere. Coming home often means taking a job at lower pay than might be available in a suburb or a city, but the cost of living is usually lower, too. Returnees hope that the sense of community they gain will offset material losses.²⁹ The twenty-first century has seen significant ups and downs for rural populations throughout the Midwest. While the number of people leaving rural areas rose during the recession of 2007–2009 and immediately thereafter, by the late twenty-teens, the number of people moving to rural areas was again growing. While this trend is most obvious in the rural West and the sunbelt where rural growth is happening at a relatively brisk pace, it is also faintly visible in some parts of rural Midwest. Prior to the recession, twenty-eight of Iowa's nonmetropolitan counties showed growth. Since 2010, however, the growth has been more modest, with nineteen nonmetropolitan counties showing population increases. The vast majority of growing counties are within commuting distance of the state's major towns. Population growth in counties more than thirty miles from an urban area is a far rarer situation.³⁰

In the face of changes in agriculture and adverse population trends, Iowa's very small communities face an uncertain future. Nearly forty years beyond the Farm Crisis, Iowa's smallest places have remained more resilient than anyone would have expected. Examples abound, such as one of Shelby County's tiny places, Irwin, which is just north of county seat Harlan. Shelby County, as a whole, was hard hit by the Farm Crisis, especially little places outside of the county seat, like Irwin. Yet, studied by agricultural economists and rural sociologists around 1940 and again in the early 1990s, Irwin survives. At the time of the 2010 census, Irwin's population was roughly the same size as in 1930, although smaller than it had been in the 1980s. Among other businesses, the town boasts an implement dealership, a locker plant that processes meat for hunters and small farmers, a grain elevator, and a BP station that has expanded to include a pizza parlor in addition to its mini mart. The grade school (pre-K–4) is one of two remaining in the IKM-Manning school district. Methodist, Lutheran, and Church of Christ congregations continue to worship there, just as they did in the 1980s. Residents have painted every house and mowed every yard. Against all odds, Irwin appears to be a very small but healthy community.

Irwin is not alone. In 2010 there were approximately two dozen similar communities in rural Iowa, concentrated largely in the northern and western parts of the state. These were small towns of approximately three hundred residents in the 1930s and maintain a very similar size today, though some do so with an influx of immigrants, working in meat packing and other rural industries. In 1930, at the onset of the Great Depression, no one would have predicted their survival into the twenty-first century. At the height of the Farm Crisis, their prospects seemed bleak. But these communities have persisted. Rather extraordinarily, they have defied the odds. They also defy the conventional wisdom. One of the truisms of rural community studies is that when the school goes, so goes the community.[31] Surprisingly, that has not been the case in very small places such as Irwin. Their populations have remained remarkably stable in the face of closing high schools and middle schools, and even with the loss of elementary schools. Irwin, not unlike many Iowa communities, has experienced multiple rounds of school consolidation. Once it was a full-service, kindergarten through twelfth grade community, then the schools served grades kindergarten through eight. In the last round, consolidation reduced the community's offerings to preschool through fourth grade.[32] Either because of shifts in the population, with an older age group predominating, or because of shifts in attitude, the consolidation of schools has not resulted in the dismantling of these communities.

Other assumptions about what is necessary to the survival of a small place also require reconsideration. When sociologist Eric Hoiberg surveyed Irwin's surviving businesses in the early 1990s, there was a meat locker, beauty shop, a small appliance repair shop, three small restaurants, and a pool hall. During the time he studied the community, it lost two restaurants, an insurance agency, a feed store, and its veterinarian.[33] People tend to believe that certain amenities are necessary for a community to survive, given a desire among modern Americans to have what they want, when they want it. Very little of this is available within Irwin today. The locker plant sells meat, and the BP station's mini mart stocks milk and other necessities, but there is no grocery store and no restaurant, beyond the pizza parlor tucked into the back of the same BP station. There are no doctors or dentists. Irwin's residents must drive between fifteen minutes and half an hour through open country to find a town of any size, stocked with many of the necessities that urban and suburban Iowans take for granted. For those under the age of seventy, with reasonable health, an automobile, and money for gas, this probably represents inconvenience rather than a serious problem. For the poor and the older segment of the population, this would seem to be a serious complication, yet the older age group is the one that continues to live in the smallest places. Irwin is persisting in spite of a lack of services that would seem to be necessary to an aging population. Irwin, and many towns like it, survive.

Nevertheless, the challenges facing tiny Iowa towns are real. As discussed previously, at the end of the 1980s, the city planner in Rolfe, in western Iowa, hoped to advertise the town's way out of population decline and bring in new residents. He mailed out shiny blue brochures all across the country advertising Rolfe's version of the good life. Local boosters hoped that the effort would bring families and enhance the community's ability to bid on economic development projects. Empty properties would be full and closure would not threaten the school. The brochure, and the hopes upon which its publication was based, however, did not bear fruit. The town stood at a population of 796 in 1980. By 1990 it had fallen to just over 700. The town entered the new century at 675, and the population was, by 2016, less than 550. The Rolfe Community School District ceased to exist in 1993, after a 1992 measure in which Rolfe residents voted roughly two to one to consolidate with Pocahontas. The Pocahontas Area Community School District reorganized twice in the late 1980s and early 1990s, pulling in students from parts of three different counties.[34] A Lutheran church and the Spanish-speaking Mision Evangelica Monte Sion still welcome worshipers, but in 2018 St. Margaret's Catholic Church closed its doors. The pool and golf course are still there, and the city converted the high-school gym into the RAM Event Center, which provides gym facilities for a fee. An organization of community boosters, Rolfe Betterment Inc., meets the second Monday of each month.[35]

Today's community brochure is a webpage, and although the site does not describe Rolfe as a full-service community, it does tout the town an active place, in the way that many very small towns define activity:

> Area farmers and other folk wanting the latest community news convene at the CO-OP for coffee or simply to talk. Rolfe Heartland is another hub of conversation. It is a convenience store with gasoline pumps. There is only stop light intersection in town. Wednesday mornings find a good variety of citizens at the Rolfe Public Library gathered for conversation and occasional special features. Rolfe Heartland [a program for seniors] provides noontime and evening meals as well as a place to meet up with friends.[36]

Rolfe boasts that although a small town, residents can still check out a book, buy groceries, get a massage, find an attorney, veterinarian, or a local banker, and be embalmed and buried within the city's limits. The town website fails to mention buying a beer at the Rolfe Roadhouse, but that, too, is possible. However, there is no doctor, no dentist, no hospital, details that the website omits.[37] Those services are available in Pocahontas, roughly thirteen miles away, depending upon which country road a driver chooses. Pocahontas is also a very small place, home to just over fifteen hundred people, which raises questions about the long-term viability of its schools and services. It illustrates just how lean the network of amenities is in some parts of the state, especially given the population's age.

The line between a community's health and a precipitous decline can be remarkably thin. Many small towns rely on aging infrastructure, and because of low levels of income and low property valuations, it may not pay to make improvements, or even critical repairs. This can lead to unanticipated problems, ranging from minor to devastating. One such devastating event happened in Ackley, in north central Iowa. In the midst of the troubles of the 1980s, Ackley was staking its future on access to employment in Iowa Falls, roughly thirteen miles due west. In 1980 nineteen hundred people called Ackley home. By 1990 their numbers had fallen to 1,696. A decade later, the number was up to 1,809, but despite being relatively close to Iowa Falls, which has a population of more than five thousand, the town has shrunk ever since. Nevertheless, Ackley has an active Chamber of Commerce, a Rotary Club, a young professionals' group, and several community centers. It also hosts an annual Sauerkraut Days festival that celebrates the town's German roots.[38]

Ackley has a small, aging downtown, but residents hoped eventually to place it on the National Register of Historical Places. Events, however, took a different turn. Early in 2017 a business in the 700 block of Ackley's Main Street suffered a small collapse in a portion of a basement wall. Questions over insurance and the timing of consultation with a structural engineer led to considerable delay. Weeks turned into months of inaction, until in November, two adjoining buildings in the same block suffered a significant structural collapse. In the process of planning demolition, contractors discovered that shared walls made it impossible to demolish the badly damaged structures without the loss of half a block's buildings. It was a crushing blow. The property owners did not have the money for the complicated demolition, and neither did the town. Two years later, a large portion of downtown sat behind a chain link fence, walled off for safety. Losses include several businesses, including the town's only dentist, and much-needed rental housing from the second stories of the downtown block. Residents also struggled with bad feelings over responsibility and blame.[39] It is too early to tell if Ackley will be able to overcome the loss of a substantial chunk of its downtown, but a community that was already coping with depopulation now has an unanticipated struggle with a proportionally massive property loss that endangers its ability to attract and maintain businesses and services. Given low property values and aging buildings in downtowns across the rural Midwest, many Main Streets are a similar situation waiting to happen.

The numbers have led Extension personnel to warn Iowans that the state's loss of population in the countryside is unlikely to stop anytime soon and to opine that "a rural renaissance is unlikely in Iowa and other states in the Corn Belt and Great Plains."[40]

"Shrinking Smart"

Concerned about the future of Iowa's small places and reading unfortunate signs, Extension decided to focus on the importance of helping small towns to "shrink smart." Project personnel have classified Iowa's small communities in (more or less) three ways, as growing smart, shrinking smart, or shrinking poor. The growing communities tend to be clustered in the eastern part of the state, where there is greater population density and more industry. The shrink-smart communities tend to be in west-central Iowa, while the shrink-poor communities are more often found in central Iowa. Extension asserts that shrinking communities can still be healthy ones: "Not all shrinking communities are withering. In fact, some small towns have thrived in terms of quality of life despite shrinking populations." Shrinking but thriving communities have certain characteristics. In terms of average income and the number of jobs available, they are little different from those that are shrinking poorly. Shrink smart communities are different in that they have relatively large numbers of children growing up in two parent families. They are populated by a larger proportion of college-educated adults. These are agricultural communities but have increased the size of their industrial base. Their people are active in their communities; they belong to organizations and take part in local events. Communities are well-kept and their residents view them as both safe and comfortable places. The internal narrative that people tell about their communities is positive, resulting in greater community involvement.[41]

The question, of course, is how to encourage communities in their quest to shrink smart, since the shrinkage is going to happen anyway. The answer, according to Iowa State University architecture professor Kimberly Zarecor and sociology professor David Peters is connection, connection, connection. People must want their communities to thrive in order for the quality of life to remain high in the face of population numbers that drift ever lower. According to Zarecor, this means helping people to build interpersonal relationships that extend across existing divisions of age, class, and race. It means encouraging philanthropy and involvement.

Peters commented that the answer was to "get residents to give more of their time and more of their money to local projects. Get people involved in local organizations, allow new people to take leadership roles, support new leaders in pursuing new ideas and accept that failure will occur but keep trying whatever you do." Zarecor commented, "I think one of the most important messages we want to send is that the growth narrative, that only growth is positive is something that we think some towns have to get past because trends show that it's simply not going to happen."[42] Shrinking smart means encouraging a level of involvement that belies the numbers. People have to be enthusiastic and engaged enough to join in with activities at the schools, churches, community betterment organizations, and food pantries. They must claim their community and its future as their own.

Developing this kind of community engagement becomes even more important as the downward trend in Midwestern rural populations increases. Sociologist Robert Wuthnow, who has intensively studied Midwestern communities, has contended that the Irwins, Rolfes, and Ackleys of the region are on an inevitable path toward extinction. He noted that at the end of the twentieth century, three thousand Midwestern towns were home to five hundred people or fewer and that three-quarters of them were on a steady downward march in population. He agreed with demographers' conclusions that "many of these communities would become ghost towns."[43] Larger towns with more resources, or towns with a "hook," such as close proximity to larger cities, would survive.[44] While Wuthnow imagined a future for towns of five to the thousand residents, places like Harlan and Iowa Falls, he predicted that very small places would disintegrate completely in the twenty-first century.[45] Extension's quest is to stem the bleeding and focus on the health and well-being of those who remain. Instead of launching a campaign to bring the outside world in, their emphasis is on building connections within communities, in order to create a greater sense of contentment and attachment among those who remain.

Contentment and attachment have been, at times, hard to find. People in small places have had to confront issues they did not want or expect. It is perhaps unsurprising that a serious drug problem followed a decade of extraordinarily hard times in the countryside. In the last years of the twentieth century and the beginning of the twenty-first, the rural Midwest became the nationwide center for the production of methamphetamine. The number of small-town drug labs located and raided by authorities grew into the hundreds.[46] There was a reason why the meth crisis, unlike earlier drug crises, erupted in the countryside. Large numbers of empty buildings and a low police presence made finding locations to manufacture the drug easy, and farmers who stored anhydrous ammonia (an important ingredient in meth) without protections against theft unwittingly facilitated production.[47] The prevalence of low-wage jobs in rural communities also made manufacturing and selling meth seem attractive. And people who worked those same low-wage, physically demanding jobs were also a ready-made market for the drug.[48]

In a somewhat coincidental way, the meth story meshed with the Farm Crisis story in the form of the trials of local Raymond resident Levi Knebel, who played the teenaged son in the movie *Country*. In 2013, at age forty-seven, he was sentenced to a ten-year prison term for conspiracy to manufacture meth, possession of the ingredients to cook meth, and possession of the drug. It was not his first jail term. In 2009 he had also been imprisoned on drug charges.[49] Whatever dreams he might have had for life after the movies fizzled out in a story of drug use and drug manufacture that was sadly familiar to postcrisis Iowans. A search of the *New York Times* from 1990 to 2014 found more than one thousand articles referencing both Iowa and either methamphetamine or meth. While the number of meth labs throughout the Midwest fell as state governments made it harder to purchase its raw ingredients, the source shifted to Mexico, and supplies continued to flow into the nation's midsection.[50] Particularly in the immediate aftermath of the agricultural downturn, meth manufacture may have seemed like a surer path to economic security than work in one of Iowa's agricultural industries.

At the same time, the second drug crisis of the late twentieth and early twenty-first century has been far less virulent in Iowa. While rates of opioid abuse and deaths due to overdoses have soared in some parts of the nation's rural midsection, such as in Ohio and West Virginia, there has been less evidence of this scourge in Iowa. While the state has a higher rate of opioid deaths than neighboring Nebraska or South Dakota, it has a far lower rate than other adjacent states such as Minnesota, Wisconsin, and Illinois. Urban Iowans die from opioid overdoses at a rate of 7.4 deaths per 100,000 residents, as compared to a national rate of 13.4. Rural Iowans had an overdose death rate of 3.3 deaths per 100,000 residents, far less than the rate in urban Iowa, or the national rate. In its study of these issues in Iowa, Extension concluded that in those rural counties where there was a growing opioid problem, the causal factors were high unemployment, poverty, dangerous work that caused injuries, low levels of law enforcement, and a lack of civic resolve to fight opioid abuse.[51] As much of this particular drug crisis evolved in the aftermath of the 2008 recession, rural Iowa more than likely benefitted from the recession's relative shallowness in Iowa and the state's fairly quick recovery, a situation very different from Ohio and West Virginia.

The fact that the current rural drug crisis has not yet hit Iowa hard is perhaps attributable to the relative economic health of rural Iowa in the years since 2000, unlike many other spots in the nation. Even though the population is declining, by many of the measures deployed by the USDA, rural Iowa is getting by in reasonable shape. Although the USDA defines a number of Iowa's counties, particularly in the northwest, as "population loss counties," in other ways, the counties are in far better shape than those in other locations in the Midwest or in the South. The USDA found no "low employment" counties in Iowa, let alone rural Iowa, a situation that is replicated in only a handful of other states, and only Kansas and Minnesota in the Midwest. Instead of remaining in place and unemployed, the rural parts of the region tend to "export" their unemployed to larger communities with better job prospects. Researchers also found no "persistent poverty" counties in Iowa, meaning counties where more than 20 percent of the population has lived since 1980 below the poverty line. There is only one "persistent child poverty" county on the southern border of the state. Postcrisis Iowa may not be rich, or growing significantly, but economic indicators suggest that the state as a whole has soldiered on in a comparatively healthy manner, despite the pressures imposed by population decline.[52]

Growing Challenges

Even so, the problems facing Iowa's farmers—and Midwestern farmers in general—are easily visible. Economic stress has affected nearly everyone. Dairy farmers have been losing money on their milk due to depressed prices. Iowa is the tenth largest dairy producer in the United States, with just over one thousand farms. In 2018 alone, eighty of them quit operations. In Toledo, Eric Lyon decided to sell off his 320 cows after three generations of milking. He and his family could not afford to keep on losing money. Fortunately, they would be able to switch to beef production, although selling their purebred Jersey herd was deeply painful.[53] Agricultural problems were not isolated to dairy farmers; corn and soybean farmers watched prices slide, as did livestock producers. By the spring of 2019, Iowa's farmers were facing a credit crunch and worrying about being able to find the money they needed for operating expenses. They also led the nation in terms of total agricultural debt, and in the face of low prices for both corn and soybeans, were unsure where they would find the wherewithal to pay. Government payments meant to offset the cost of trade wars with both Mexico and China were not adequate to overcome their losses, especially for small and midsize farmers. Trade struggles with China, in particular, left corn, soybean, and hog producers with a surplus on hand, and surpluses drive down prices. As in the 1980s, farmers began to sell off chunks of their holdings in order to pay debts. Unlike the 1980s, land prices held steady, making this strategy more successful.[54]

Then in the spring of 2019 the flooding began yet again, and portions of western Iowa along the Missouri River and in eastern Iowa along the Mississippi went underwater. Mike Rosmann, a clinical psychologist who has worked with western Iowa farmers since the 1980s, listened in dismay as the number of farmers calling him in a state of crisis increased. In an interview he commented,

> farmers have been calling me more and more recently because of low farm prices, the prolonged recession in agriculture, and more recently because of the flooding that is occurring in major river systems in the Midwest.... I try to answer all of the requests I get from farmers and ranchers because they're looking for help. But sometimes I have to leave the telephone and answering machine on and not answer and get away.[55]

A poll sponsored by the American Farm Bureau Federation in the spring of 2019 found 45 percent more farmers feeling stressed than the year before.[56] Rosmann would not have been surprised.

As in the 1980s, help has been slower to come than many advocates hoped. Rosmann was part of an effort to get support from Congress for the Farm and Ranch Stress Assistance Network (FRSAN), which would have funded behavioral health services for rural families throughout the nation. FRSAN was part of the 2008 Farm Bill, but despite lip service, Congress left it unfunded.[57] As of spring 2020, action at the federal level on farmer mental health was still pending, awaiting a congressional vote on the Seeding Rural Resilience Act, sponsored by Senator Chuck Grassley (R-IA) and Senator Jon Tester (D-MT), the two remaining farmers in Congress. The bill provides for public service announcements across multiple media, addressing the mental health concerns of farmers and ranchers, as well as research and training programs to reduce the number of suicides among agricultural producers. Grassley's motivation in sponsoring the measure was to keep the events of the 1980s from happening again. Impeachment hearings and the coronavirus pandemic of winter and spring 2020, however, pushed the measure to the back burner.[58]

In the place of federal measures, states have had to fill in with their own programming. Iowa State's Extension and Outreach ramped up its mental health programming, reminding Iowans that its crisis hotline, Iowa Concern (Rural Concern in the 1980s), was still available, providing free counseling and referrals for individuals under pressure. In the late fall and early winter of 2019–2020, specialists provided suicide prevention training at fifty meetings statewide. Additionally, Extension expanded its offerings of an eight-hour course, Mental Health First Aid, meant to provide their staff the skills they needed to meet the needs of Iowans under stress.[59] Each of these efforts was an updated edition of projects undertaken during the 1980s. The lessons of the Farm Crisis reverberated in Extension's call to action in the second decade of the twenty-first century.

Mental health problems have not been the only sign of continuing difficulties in rural Iowa. Another of those manifestations has been the growth of the rural-urban divide in the state. The way in which this is most visible is in voting behavior. While urban Iowa tends to vote for Democratic candidates, rural Iowa is firmly Republican. This was quite evident in the election of 2016, where Democratic candidate Hillary Clinton won Polk, Story, Linn, Black Hawk, Scott, and Johnson Counties, and Republican candidate Donald Trump won all others, by percentages ranging from 46 to 81 percent.[60] One of these counties, Howard County, had voted overwhelmingly for President Barack Obama in 2008 but voted just as overwhelmingly for Trump in 2016. More than eleven thousand people lived here at the start of the 1980s. Today, Howard County is home to just under ten thousand people. There are no large towns. Fewer than four thousand people inhabit county seat Cresco. On the surface, the change in local voting habits between 2008 and 2016 would seem to be a mystery. At the time of the election, unemployment was low. There were not large numbers of people living below the poverty line, but incomes were not robust, either. There was no overwhelming drug crisis. There was no obvious, aching void. There was, however, a feeling of being passed by. The recovery from the recession had come slowly here, and wages remained low. Local residents felt as if, somehow, they had been abandoned.[61]

This feeling of being passed over is shared throughout a large swath of rural America. Farmers are distressed that their concerns seem to have been ignored. People living in small places feel distress, too, as they come to understand the long-term implications of their dramatically shrinking and aging populations. There is a feeling of loss that manifests itself as alienation from urban Americans, whether they live in Des Moines, Minneapolis, or Washington, DC. Rural Americans believe their communities have value. They believe that those communities are good places to live. They want to see the places where they live not just survive, but thrive, but the odds are not in their favor. No one seems to be coming up with good solutions that will allow for rural communities to keep a standard of living equal to urban America, if that standard of living is measured in terms of institutions, such as schools, hospitals, and churches. Robert Wuthnow has described the internal conversation that accompanies such losses: "You tell yourself your community is doing fine. It's a good place to live. It's had problems before and it's always come through. People are strong. The community is resilient. But it makes you mad that people elsewhere, especially in Washington, don't see it that way.... They talk and talk but don't get anything constructive done. Their interests are with people who live in cities and don't look like you."[62] Other communities, urban and suburban, seem to both survive and thrive. The best that people in positions of power can offer rural populations is advice on how to downsize, preferably with grace.

Pandemic Agriculture

As the nation moved into a new decade, the outlook for rural Iowa remained uncertain. In the fall of 2019, Extension was in the process of rolling out a crisis response to help mitigate mental health problems in the countryside. What no one expected at that moment was that more complications for farmers, and indeed the entire population, lurked around the corner. The COVID-19 pandemic of the spring of 2020 almost immediately changed the fortunes of the state's farmers. The effects were far different than those in Des Moines, Ames, or Cedar Rapids. The desire to stop the spread of the virus forced many Iowans for the first time to work from home, or to lose their jobs when bars, restaurants, and retail businesses closed. For farmers, however, the crisis altered their day to day working lives far less. Most of Iowa's agriculture in the twenty-first century is a solitary business, done by an operator working alone behind the wheel of a tractor or combine. As such, the closures that dramatically affected individuals working in retail, education, and many other lines of business did very little to impinge upon the work life of the average corn and soybean producer. The state also defined agricultural operations and agricultural processing as essential businesses, leaving farmers and processing plant employees free to do their jobs. Farmers climbed into their tractors and planted their fields. They went to the confinement unit to check on their hogs, or out to the field or feed lot to care for their cattle. Human beings need to eat, pandemic or not, so a market for their product remained. However, the economic chaos the pandemic caused did farmers no favors. Keeping working in a crisis is one thing; maintaining a processing and distribution system is something else altogether.

The chaos surrounding the pandemic cut into prices and damaged the food and fuel chain. In February and March of 2020, as the crisis set in, hog prices tumbled 31 percent, cattle 25 percent, corn 14 percent, and soybeans 8 percent. Dairy farmers watched prices fall by between 26 and 36 percent. Then they faced a problem they had never imagined. While there were shortages of dairy products in some markets, the shortage was not caused by a lack of milk. Instead, unforeseen problems in the supply chain upended the dairy market. Much of the milk farmers produced went to institutions, such as schools, or to restaurants, and so was packaged in bulk. When schools and restaurants closed or reduced their operations because of the threat of disease, there was no way to repackage their product quickly for sales to individual consumers. Horrified farmers had no other choice than to dump their milk. The shutdown of hotels and restaurants also affected livestock farmers, as most steak, bacon, breakfast sausage, and ham make their way into the American diet through restaurant meals, rather than home consumption. The market for both beef and pork tumbled.[63]

Livestock producers also faced supply chain problems, as processors shut down in response to outbreaks of COVID-19 among packing house workers. When the Smithfield plant in Sioux Falls, South Dakota, suspended operations because of a large number of workers becoming ill (an outbreak so big that Sioux Falls became a nation-wide hotspot for the virus), it affected 550 farmers, many in Iowa, who supplied the meat packer with pigs. Because of the close proximity within which laborers in packing plants worked, the virus spread like wildfire. COVID-19 also closed a Tyson pork processing plant in Louisa County, after nearly two hundred workers tested positive. The Iowa Premium Beef plant in Tama also suspended operations. Processing plant workers sickened in towns small and large across the state.[64] Farmers were then left with animals that could not be slaughtered and processed in a timely manner, for which they had no room on their farms. For the first time ever, Extension began issuing instructions to farmers about how to retard growth in their hogs, as an alternative to euthanizing animals.[65]

Another unexpected result of the measures taken to curb the pandemic was a drastic reduction in automobile travel, and therefore, consumer purchases of fuel. Consequently, farmers who sold their corn for ethanol production suffered a dramatic decrease in their markets. In early April 2020, the nation's largest ethanol producer, with plants in Coon Rapids and Ashton, Iowa, idled plants, leaving farmers with no place to send their corn. The slowing of ethanol production affected farmers in other ways, too. Distillers' grains are a byproduct of ethanol production, and Iowa farmers use that byproduct extensively for animal feed. The scarce supplies of distillers' grains meant that farmers had to purchase more expensive products to feed their animals. While this situation might have benefits for soybean producers, it hurt livestock producers.[66] The only consolation in all of this, if it was any consolation at all, was that this was, to some degree, shared pain. Many Iowans were suffering from the ripple effects of the pandemic. Farmers would not be suffering alone.

The long run effects of the virus on rural Iowa remain to be seen. Its initial spread across the state was relatively slow, with the largest initial outbreak in Iowa City and adjacent areas. In more thinly populated areas, the virus began with a case here, a case there, and a very gradual spread to the most rural counties. A month after its first appearance in the state, roughly a quarter of Iowa's counties had seen no confirmed cases. By two months into the pandemic, however, the virus had expanded across the state, especially affecting nursing homes and meat-packing plants. The spread of the virus underscored the worries of residents of very small places. The populations of rural counties tend to be elderly and medically vulnerable, increasing the likelihood of stricken individuals needing significant care. Their communities, however, are low on medical expertise and medical facilities. Some have no doctors at all, and patients who need attention must be able to travel to clinics in the next largest town. Many of Iowa's rural counties have no hospitals, or if they do, they average roughly twenty-five beds and have little or no capacity to handle patients requiring extended periods of intubation and ventilation, not to mention dialysis. Small hospitals rely on their ability to transfer patients to larger facilities, which presumably will have room for their patients. In a time of crisis, however, this assumption may not hold. When workers from the Tyson plant in Columbus Junction became ill, there was no hospital in Louisa County to treat them. In order to receive care at a hospital with a substantial intensive care unit, residents of Columbus Junction and the surrounding area had to travel to the major university medical center in Iowa City, a forty-five-minute drive, or Davenport, an hour away.⁶⁷ How the pandemic will ultimately affect life in small communities remains to be seen, but it has already illustrated the weaknesses that exist in the rural safety net.⁶⁸

The Last Generation on the Farm?

Rolling crises and uncertain rewards have done little to make remaining in the countryside an attractive option to Iowa's young. Agriculture is, by its very nature, an uncertain business, and the added uncertainties of the early twenty-first century have made agriculture less and less appealing. There is a phrase that Extension personnel in Iowa now use to describe what they are seeing: last-generation farmers. These are older farmers who will be the last of their family to work the land. They raised children on the farm, but those children have left or are leaving for education and job opportunities and will not be returning. The problems of the 1980s accelerated a trend that was already happening in many rural communities. Maynard Hogberg, a retired animal scientist and employee of Iowa State University Extension, worked with farmers through the crisis. About those years, he recalled, "I think part of the best advice that we could give some people is, you need to sell now and try to hang out to whatever you have left, rather than lose it all and not have anything." In that era, being a last-generation farmer meant cutting losses and moving on, whether or not the children wanted to continue to farm.⁶⁹

The attempt in the 1980s to move farmers gracefully out of agriculture has become a rush on the part of the children and grandchildren of farmers to leave that life behind. This response is not equally strong across all areas of agriculture; the most labor-intensive farming, such as dairying, has seen the sharpest increase in the number of last-generation farmers, but these responses are evident across the industry. Hogberg characterized young people's responses as a desire to do something new and different and a desire to see a better return on their efforts than agriculture might provide. This generation of farm-raised Iowans wants to "make a decent living" and "enjoy the same standard of living that all my friends have."⁷⁰ These aspirations may not always mesh with life on the family farm.

Iowa's 2014 Farm and Rural Life Poll confirmed these impressions. Those surveyed had a long history of farming in Iowa; most of their farms were "century farms," which had been in a family for at least one hundred years. The survey revealed an aging population, with farmers over sixty-five making up nearly 30 percent of all of Iowa's farmers. On the whole, the children of these farmers were not farmers themselves. Among respondents, only 31 percent had an adult child who farmed; 51 percent had yet to identify someone who would take over their land upon their retirement. Given these numbers, it is not surprising that farmers under the age of forty-five make up just 18 percent of total farm operators.[71] Unless the children of this youngest group execute a surprising about-face and take up agriculture in far greater proportion than their elders, Iowa's farmers would seem to be on the verge of demographic decline on an epic scale.

Continuing decline in the number of farmers will mean continuing adjustment on the part of rural Iowa. The very smallest towns, relying on the business of farming families for their livelihood, will have to look elsewhere for their futures—but where to look is elusive. There is a limit to how much shrinking a rural community can do, even if that community is "shrinking smart." If Iowa's agricultural future is an amplified version of what has occurred over time, there will be considerably fewer farms, considerably larger than they are now. There may no longer be a need for the feed store, the implement dealer, and the local elevator. And if there is no need for the feed store, implement dealer, and local elevator, there is also very little business for the gas station, the convenience store, the last remaining elementary school, or the church, whether or not the remaining population believes it needs those amenities. While the predictions for the future of Iowa's countryside were grim in 1985, at the height of the Farm Crisis, they remain guarded today. As the Farm Crisis raged, people wondered if family farms should be saved, and how. In the twenty-first century, the questions have multiplied. Is a downward trend in farmer numbers, and an upward trend in farm size, good for agriculture? Are very large farms good for the environment? Is it healthy for a nation to have so much of its food produced by so few? How does a nation balance what is good for farmers against what is good for those who process agricultural products? How is it possible to balance what is good for farmers with what is good for consumers? Can cheap food also be high quality? How can the effects of the demographic change that comes with concentration be weathered by rural America? Do rural places and small towns have value, and if so, what? Given the prospect of radical shrinkage, are there steps that should be taken to save small communities, small schools, and small churches, and is the saving worth the cost? None of these are new questions, and none are easy to answer. In the years since the 1980s, most farm states have postponed the discussion. People can choose to grapple with these issues, or they can let time and inertia take their toll. In the best of all possible worlds, the people of the United States will consider them and take thoughtful action before circumstances deprive them of the ability to shape the future that they want.

Notes

Introduction

1. Mary Murray, "'His Pride Was Broken' Says Brother-in-Law of Killer-Farmer Burr," *Des Moines Register*, December 11, 1985; John Carlson and Wendell Cochran, "Farmer's Wife Knew Something Was Very Wrong," *Des Moines Register*, December 11, 1985; Larry Fruhling, "Burr's Shotgun Blast Heard 'Round the Nations," *Des Moines Register*, December 15, 1985; "4 Dead in Rampage in an Iowa Town," *New York Times*, December 10, 1985; "Burr Buried, DCI Says Financial Documents on Him to Be Released," *Mt. Pleasant News*, December 14, 1985.

2. Murray, "'His Pride Was Broken;" Carlson and Cochran, "Farmer's Wife Knew Something Was Very Wrong;" Frank Santiago, "Hughes Murder Stuns Bankers on the Main Streets of Rural Iowa," *Des Moines Register*, December 11, 1985; Governor Terry Branstad, interview by Pamela Riney-Kehrberg, January 5, 2017; "Help Is Available for Families Coping with the Rural Crisis," and "Feeling Desperate? Call Hotline," *Mellinger Sun-News*, December 26, 1985.

3. Fruhling, "Burr's Shotgun Blast."

4. Robyn Sue Singleton, "A December Morn Shattered," *Iowa City Press-Citizen*, December 10, 1985; Tad Bartimus, "AP Reporter Returns to Missouri Hometown," *Mt. Pleasant News*, December 20, 1985.

5. Bartimus, "AP Reporter Returns"; Singleton, "December Morn Shattered"; "1985 a Bitter Year for Iowa Farmers," *Mt. Pleasant News*, December 30, 1985.

6. "1985 a Bitter Year."

7. United States Department of Commerce, Bureau of the Census, *1992 Census of Agriculture*, vol. 1 (Washington, DC: US Government Printing Office, 1994), 8.

8. Linda Lobao and Paul Lasley, "Farm Restructuring and Crisis in the Heartland: An Introduction," and Daryl Hobbs and Robert Weagley, "The Agricultures of the Midwest and Their Demographic and Economic Environments," in Paul Lasley et al., *Beyond the Amber Waves of Grain: An Examination of Social and Economic Restructuring in the Heartland* (Boulder: Westview Press, 1995), 5, 33.

9. Dirk Johnson, "Death Is as Capricious as Life for Farm Leader," *New York Times*, June 2, 1989.

10. Caroline Bird's classic book, *The Invisible Scar*, provides the best description of the way in which the Great Depression devastated formerly comfortable families (New York: Pocket Books, 1967).

11. Mark Friedberger, *Shake-Out: Iowa Farm Families in the 1980s* (Lexington: University of Kentucky Press, 1989), 24.

12. Paul Lasley, Rand Conger, and Curtis Stofferahn, *Farm Crisis Response: Extension and Research Activities in the North Central Region* (Ames, IA: North Central Regional Center for Rural Development, 1986), 1.

13. Wayne D. Rasmussen, *Taking the University to the People: Seventy-Five Years of Cooperative Extension* (Ames: Iowa State University Press, 1989), 166.

14. Neil Harl, *The Farm Debt Crisis of the 1980s* (Ames: Iowa State University Press, 1990), 40–41.

15. Harl, *Farm Debt Crisis*, 20–41.

16. Lasley, Conger, and Stofferahn, *Farm Crisis Response*, 1.

17. David B. Danbom, *Born in the Country: A History of Rural America* (Baltimore: Johns Hopkins University Press, 1995): 263; Kathleen Beery and Robert W. Jolly, "Extension and Research Programs on Rural Financial Stress in Iowa," in Lasley, Conger, and Stofferahn, 5.

18. Kathryn Marie Dudley, *Debt and Dispossession: Farm Loss in America's Heartland* (Chicago: University of Chicago Press, 2000), 135.

19. Russel Christensen, Royal, Iowa, Testimony given at Senator Grassley's request, September 1985, Office of the Governor, RG 043, Box 90, Miscellaneous Agriculture, Keith Heffernan, 1984–1987, File 90.6, State Historical Society of Iowa, Des Moines (SHSI-DSM).

20. Peter Stearns's description of shame aligns with the emotions expressed by farm people losing their land. Suicide as a means of "coping" with the loss of a business appeared first in the US historical record in 1819. Peter Stearns, *Shame: A Brief History* (Urbana: University of Illinois Press, 2017), 3–4, 89.

21. Friedberger, *Shake-Out*, 73.

22. Emilia E. Martinez-Brawley and Joan Blundall, "Farm Families' Preferences toward the Personal Social Services," *Social Work* 34, no. 6 (November 1989): 513–522.

Chapter 1. The Go-Go Seventies

1. Elizabeth Schwennen to Governor Terry Branstad, January 24, 1986, Office of the Governor, RG 043, Terry Branstad Papers, Box 90, File 90-2, SHSI-DSM.

2. Gerald V. Pedersen to Governor Terry Branstad, June 19, 1984, Office of the Governor, RG 043, Terry Branstad Papers, Box 74, File General Correspondence 1984, P-R, SHSI-DSM.

3. Wesley A. Drahos and Lorna R. Drahos to Governor Robert Ray, March 17, 1982,

Office of the Governor, RG 043, Ray, Robert, Constituent Correspondence, Box 11, Folder Dr.-Du, 1981–1983, SHSI-DSM.

4. Ray and Dorothy Reicherts to Governor Terry Branstad, received March 23, 1984, Office of the Governor, RG 043, Terry Branstad Papers, Box 74, File General Correspondence 1984, P-R, SHSI-DSM.

5. Mrs. Michael Urban to Governor Terry Branstad, May 16, 1984, Office of the Governor, RG 043, Terry Branstad, Box 74, File General Correspondence, 1984, T-Z, SHSI-DSM.

6. Sondra L. Van Der Pol to Governor Terry Branstad, April 5, 1986, Office of the Governor, RG 043, Terry Branstad Papers, Box 90, Agriculture 1984–1987, File 90-1, SHSI-DSM.

7. For a thorough discussion of America's problem with overabundant agricultural production, see R. Douglas Hurt, *Problems of Plenty: The American Farmer in the 20th Century* (Chicago: Ivan Dee, 2002).

8. Hurt, *Problems of Plenty*, 134.

9. J. L. Anderson, *Industrializing the Corn Belt: Agriculture, Technology, and the Environment* (DeKalb: Northern Illinois University Press, 2009), 5.

10. Anderson, *Industrializing the Corn Belt*, 5.

11. For a discussion of the pre–World War II ethos of frugality on Midwestern farms, see Mary Neth, *Preserving the Family Farm: Women, Community, and the Foundations of American Agribusiness, 1900–1940* (Baltimore: Johns Hopkins University Press, 1994).

12. Anderson, 11.

13. Myron Ohrtman to Governor Terry Branstad, July 11, 1983, Office of the Governor, RG 043, Terry Branstad Papers, Box 43, File 43-7, SHSI-DSM.

14. Hurt, 93–96, 137.

15. Danbom, *Born in the Country*, 244–245.

16. United States Department of Agriculture, *1969 Census of Agriculture, Farms: Number, Use of Land, Size of Farm*, vol. 2, General Report (Washington, DC: USDA, 1973), 11.

17. Anderson, 195.

18. "Are There Any Land Bargains Left?" *Successful Farming*, September 1975.

19. Hurt, 132.

20. Eric O. Hoiberg and Wallace Huffman, *Profile of Iowa Farms and Farm Families: 1976* (Ames: Iowa Agricultural and Home Economics Experiment Station and Cooperative Extension Service, Iowa State University, 1978), 42.

21. Hurt, 133.

22. Hurt, 132.

23. Hurt, 134.

24. For some farmers, the most important factor was not getting rich or easing their physical burdens. As John Eicher has noted in his research on Iowa's Mennonite farmers, feeding the world was a significant factor pushing them toward greater mechanization.

Easing hunger around the globe was a central element of the Mennonite farmer's worldview. John Eicher, "'Every Family on Their Own?': Iowa's Mennonite Farm Communities in the 1980s Farm Crisis," *Journal of Mennonite Studies* 35 (2017): 76.

25. "A Profile of Rural America," *Successful Farming*, February 1975, 11.

26. Hurt, 145.

27. Wendong Zhang, "Historical County Farmland Values," Iowa State University Extension and Outreach, Ag Decision Maker, accessed September 5, 2019, https://www.extension.iastate.edu/agdm/wholefarm/html/c2-72.html.

28. Barry J. Barnett, "The U.S. Farm Financial Crisis of the 1980s," *Agricultural History* 74, 2 (Spring 2000): 368, 372.

29. Folke Dovring, "The Farmland Boom in Illinois," *Illinois Agricultural Economics* 17, no. 2 (July 1977): 34–38.

30. Hoiberg and Huffman, *Profile of Iowa Farms*, 11.

31. Friedberger, *Shake-Out*, 45.

32. Friedberger, 45.

33. R. H. Lounsberry to Douglas Stroud, January 21, 1980, Agriculture, RG 4, Executive Correspondence, Box 047, Folder 1980 General, SHSI-DSM.

34. Iowa began its young farmer program several years after Minnesota. The Minnesota legislature created its program in 1976. "First Farmers Get State-Guaranteed Loans," *Farm Journal*, June/July 1977, 20B.

35. Dixon Terry, Save Our Soils Conference Speech, October 6, 1987, 3, Collection on Dixon Terry, MS2014.8, File 1, SHSI-DSM.

36. "Small Farms: Overlooked and Underestimated," *Successful Farming*, September 1975.

37. Barnett, "U.S. Farm Financial Crisis," 370.

38. "Land Values Jump—Again," *Successful Farming*, November 1976, 7.

39. Harl, *Farm Debt Crisis of the 1980s*, 14.

40. Barnett, 371–372.

41. Barnett, 372.

42. "Drought Assistance Funds in Big Demand," *Successful Farming*, August 1977, 8–9.

43. "How to Adjust an Out-of-Balance Debt Load," "Coping with Financial Crisis," and "Drought Assistance Funds in Big Demand," *Successful Farming*, August 1977, 8–9.

44. Advertisements, Kawasaki and Caterpillar, *Successful Farming*, November 1977.

45. Don Muhm, "1977 Iowa Corn Crop Marked by Contrasts," *Des Moines Register*, February 3, 1978; "It Was Our Turn," *Farm Journal*, September 1977, 24.

46. Kent Parker, "Iowa's Record-Breaking Corn Crop to Top 1.4 Billion Bushels—USDA," *Des Moines Register*, November 10, 1978.

47. "Large '78 U.S. Production Spells Gloom," and "Don't Be in a Hurry to Sell Beef," *Successful Farming*, January 1978, 9; "Marketing Section," *Successful Farming*, February 1978, 12.

48. "Farm Purchasing Clout Halved over 5 Years," *Successful Farming*, February 1978, 7.

49. Don Muhm, "Net Income for Farmers Drops to $5,769," *Des Moines Register*, October 24, 1978.

50. "Only 25 Percent of Farmers Will Break Even," *Daily Freeman Journal*, December 1, 1977.

51. Harvestore advertisement, *Farm Journal*, Beef extra, mid-March 1978, BEEF-16-19.

52. Buying from Harvestore ended up being a strategic mistake for a number of farmers. The systems worked poorly, and farmers alleged that spoiled feed led to weight loss and lowered milk production in cattle. In the 1980s the company lost several major lawsuits brought by unhappy farmers. Additionally, the conditions of the 1980s, plus the federal dairy buyout, took many farmers out of the cattle business, leaving them with expensive silos they no longer needed. "Superiority of Harvestore Silos Challenged," *Farm Show Magazine* 9, no. 3 (1985): 1, 4.

53. Joseph Frazier Wall, "The Iowa Farmer in Crisis, 1920–1936," *Annals of Iowa* 47 (1983): 120–121.

54. Dorothy Schwieder, *Iowa: The Middle Land* (Ames: Iowa State University Press, 1996), 255–261.

55. Mark Ritchie, *Loss of Our Family Farms: Inevitable Results or Conscious Policies* (Minneapolis: League of Rural Voters, 1979), 2–10; Committee for Economic Development, *An Adaptive Program for Agriculture: Statement on National Policy by the Research and Policy Committee of the Committee for Economic Development* (New York: Committee for Economic Development, 1962), 7, 11, 42, 59.

56. "N.F.O. Ire Paraded for Ford Dealers," *Des Moines Register*, August 23, 1962.

57. "N.F.O. Vote Launches New Bid for Holding Action," *St. Cloud Times*, August 28, 1962; "Effectiveness of Holding Action Scored at N.F.O. Meet," *Sioux Falls Argus-Leader*, December 13, 1962.

58. For the Porkettes' story, see Jenny Barker Devine, *On Behalf of the Family Farm: Iowa Farm Women's Activism since 1945* (Iowa City: University of Iowa Press, 2013), 113–136.

59. Gary Vincent, "The New Activists: Raising Responsible Hell," *Successful Farming*, November 1978, 24–25.

60. Michael Stewart Foley, "'Everyone Was Pounding on Us': Front Porch Politics and the American Farm Crisis of the 1970s and 1980s," *Journal of Historical Sociology* 28, no. 1 (March 2015): 112.

61. These parity figures are based on a price index set between 1909 and 1914. Foley, "Everyone Was Pounding on Us," 112–113.

62. Gary Vincent, "Farmers Union: 'We Don't Have to Guarantee Cheap Food,'" *Successful Farming*, April 1978, 29.

63. Don Muhm, "NFO Endorses Next Week's Farm Strike," *Des Moines Register*, December 10, 1977.

64. "Farm Bureau against Strikers," *Successful Farming*, February 1978, 4.

65. "Farm Leader Finds Little Strike Support," *Des Moines Register*, December 7, 1977.
66. Lane Palmer, "Appraising the Farm Strike," *Farm Journal*, January 1978, 1.
67. "USDA Opposes Gov.-Regulated Agriculture," *Successful Farming*, February 1978, 4.
68. "Carter: U.S. Trusted Go-Between," *Cedar Rapids Gazette*, December 15, 1977.
69. "Iowa Farm Strike Office Opens in Council Bluffs," *Des Moines Register*, October 27, 1977; "They Rally in Defiance for Proposed Farm Strike," *Des Moines Register*, November 20, 1977.
70. Claudia Waterloo, "Desperate Words at Farmers' Rally," *Des Moines Register*, December 11, 1977; idem., "Lack of Enthusiasm Noted for Today's Farm Strike," *Des Moines Register*, December 14, 1977; "State Dairy Convention Cut Short by Weather," *Cedar Rapids Gazette*, December 10, 1977.
71. Waterloo, "Lack of Enthusiasm."
72. "Ray Aide: 'Parity Unrealistic,'" *Cedar Rapids Gazette*, December 29, 1977.
73. Waterloo, "Lack of Enthusiasm."
74. "Small Iowa Towns Feel Farm Strike," *Des Moines Register*, December 15, 1977.
75. Don Muhm, "Farm Strikers Try to Kindle Iowa's Interest," *Des Moines Register*, March 2, 1978.
76. "Farm Strike *Flops*," *Cedar Rapids Gazette*, May 10, 1978 [italics in original title].
77. Robert J. Dole, "News from U.S. Senator Bob Dole," March 15, 1978, Robert J. Dole Archive and Special Collections, University of Kansas, http://dolearchivecollections.ku.edu/collections/press_releases/780315sen.pdf.
78. Foley, 114.
79. Gary L. Vincent, "The Strike: A Postmortem," *Successful Farming*, October 1978, 21.
80. "Farmers to Government: Leave Us Alone . . . but Stay Close By," and "Farmer Plea: 'Fair Profit; No Excess Regulation," *Successful Farming*, February 1977, 8–9, 28–29, 32.
81. These issues became apparent in hindsight. The *American Journal of Agricultural Economics* only published one article that suggested that the boom was about to go bust. Agricultural economist Barry Barnett suggested that they were too busy with mathematical modeling and insufficiently concerned with both the political and historical contexts within which American agriculture operated. Iowa State University economist Neil Harl provided a different explanation. To the average agricultural economist, the difficulties of the late 1970s may have looked like business as usual. He commented, "One of the reasons for the lack of awareness of the problem was that relatively rapid economic and social change in agriculture is not a new phenomenon." Barnett, 379; Harl, 18–19.
82. Schwennen to Branstad, January 24, 1986; Pedersen to Branstad, June 19, 1984; Drahos to Ray, March 17, 1982: Reicherts to Branstad, received March 23, 1984, SHSI-DSM.
83. Ohrtman to Branstad, July 11, 1983: Van Der Pol to Branstad, April 5, 1986; Urban to Branstad, May 16, 1984, SHSI-DSM.

Chapter 2. From Fencerow to Fencerow to Failure: 1979–1983

1. Forest Louis Winters to Governor Robert Ray, May 14, 1980, Robert Ray Papers, RG 043, Box 11, Folder Agriculture 1980, SHSI-DSM.
2. "Datebook," *Cedar Rapids Gazette*, April 8, 1980, 9.
3. Doug Rossinow, *The Reagan Era: A History of the 1980s* (New York: Columbia University Press, 2015), 84.
4. Harl, *Farm Debt Crisis*, 14–15; Rossinow, *The Reagan Era*, 17–18.
5. Hurt, *Problems of Plenty*, 138–142.
6. Monte Sesker, "Food Is a Weapon in Foreign Policy," *Wallace's Farmer*, January 26, 1980.
7. "Iowa's Farmers Are Angry About Embargo," *Wallace's Farmer*, August 23, 1980.
8. Jim Head, "Farmers Face Most Critical Year," *Wallace's Farmer*, April 26, 1980.
9. "Crisis: The Piggy Bank Runs Dry," *Successful Farming*, June–July 1980, H-18.
10. Production Credit Associations-Federal Land Bank Associations, Advertisement, "How Can I Make Ends Meet When I See No End to Inflation?" *Wallace's Farmer*, March 22, 1980.
11. Head, "Farmers Face Most Critical Year."
12. "Surviving 1980: Can Times Get Better Soon Enough?" *Successful Farming*, June–July 1980, 7–9.
13. "Machinery Costs for Corn Jump One-Third," *Wallace's Farmer*, February 23, 1980.
14. Mrs. Ervin Konz to Governor Robert Ray, April 15, 1980, Robert Ray Papers, RG 043, Box 28, Folder J-L 1980, SHSI-DSM.
15. Food stamps (known today as SNAP, or the Supplemental Nutrition Assistance Program), administered by the USDA, provided food aid for economically distressed families.
16. James Ney, "Iowa Farmers Getting Food Stamps," *Des Moines Register*, April 18, 1980.
17. Monte Sesker, "What Iowa Farmers Like and Dislike about Farming," *Wallace's Farmer*, May 10, 1980.
18. Cheryl Tevis, "STRESS," *Successful Farming*, October 1980, 20–21; Sara Wyant, "Practice Good Stress Management," *Wallace's Farmer*, March 8, 1980; Gregg Hillyer and Sara Wyant, "Stress in Starting Farming," *Wallace's Farmer*, July 26, 1980; "The Stress Connection: Coping with Pressure," *National 4-H News*, November 1980, 23; Randy Weigel, "Helping Farmers Handle Stress," *Journal of Extension* (May–June 1980): 37–40; "Farm Progress Show: New Ways to Manage Farm Stress," *Wallace's Farmer*, August 23, 1980.
19. "Starting to Farm: Finding Land, Financing Are Major Concerns," *Wallace's Farmer*, January 12, 1980.
20. "Iowa's Beginning Farmer Program," *Wallace's Farmer*, October 11, 1980.
21. Memo, November 4, 1981, and Iowa Family Farm Development Authority, "Report for the Period July 1, 1980, to December 31, 1981, Robert Ray Papers, RG 043, Box 46, Family Farm Development Authority folder, 1981–1982, SHSI-DSM.

22. Richard Krumme, "Across the Editor's Desk," *Successful Farming*, October 1980, 4.

23. Terry E. Brandstad, Opening Remarks by the Lieutenant Governor, and Robert Ray, Condition of the State Message, *Journal of the Senate*, vol. 1, January 12–April 30, 1981, January 12, 1981, 1981 Regular Session, 69th General Assembly, 1, 262.

24. Peter Lindert, "Long-Run Trends in American Farmland Values," *Agricultural History* 62, no. 3 (Summer 1988): 83–84.

25. Morris Neighbor to Governor Robert Ray, August 4, 1981, Robert Ray Papers, RG 043, Box 12, Folder N 1981–1983, SHSI-DSM.

26. Press release, July 24, 1981, PrairieFire Records, MS 313, Iowa's Economic Crisis, Correspondence, News Clippings, etc., 1981–1987, SpecColl-ISU; David Ostendorf, interview by Pamela Riney-Kehrberg, October 9, 2019.

27. Estimates of the amount of time farm women devoted to housework per week are drawn from Jane E. Meiners and Geraldine I. Olson, "Household, Paid, and Unpaid Work Time of Farm Women," *Family Relations* 36, no. 4 (1987): 408. Hours of agricultural labor are found in Hoiberg and Huffman, *Profile of Iowa Farms*, 39.

28. For a more thorough discussion of farm women's perceptions of their roles see Devine, *On Behalf of the Family Farm*, ch. 1; Deborah Fink, *Open Country, Iowa: Rural Women, Tradition and Change* (Albany: State University of New York Press, 1986), intro.; and Rachel Rosenfeld, *Farm Women: Work, Farm, and Family in the United States* (Chapel Hill: University of North Carolina Press, 1985), ch. 7.

29. This is approximately $30,000 in 2018 dollars. All conversions done using the Measuring Worth website of EH.net. "Timely Tips," *Wallace's Farmer*, September 24, 1983, 130.

30. Fink, *Open Country, Iowa*, 195–197.

31. Cheryl Tevis, "Women Earn Off-Farm Income," *Successful Farming*, June–July 1981, 14 E; "Wives Make Sacrifices for Off-Farm Jobs," *Farm Wife News*, January 1981, 23, 32; Sara Wyant, "Working Off the Farm Boosts Farm Family Income," *Wallace's Farmer*, March 28, 1981; Cheryl Tevis, "Should Mom Join the Job Market," *Successful Farming*, November 1981, 36-X, 36-Y.

32. Robert Steinke to Governor Robert Ray, August 31, 1981, Robert Ray Papers, RG 043, Box 13, File Sie-Smi 1981–1983, SHSI-DSM.

33. Omega Township Women's Club. Secretary's Book, 1976–1982, Iowa Women's Archives, University of Iowa Libraries, Iowa City (hereafter IWA-UofI).

34. Cheryl Tevis, "Women Cite Stress Conditions," *Successful Farming*, October 1981.

35. M. L. N. to David Ostendorf, PrairieFire Collection, MS 313, Iowa's Economic Crisis, Correspondence, News Clippings, etc., file, 1981–1987, SpecColl-ISU.

36. Iowa Family Farm Development Authority, "Report for the Period July 1, 1980, to December 31, 1981," Robert Ray Papers, RG 043, Box 46, Family Farm Development Authority Folder, 1981–1982, 1–6, SHSI-DSM.

37. Iowa Family Farm Development Authority, Minutes, November 18, 1981, Robert

Ray Papers, RG 043, Box 46, Family Farm Development Authority Folder, 1981–1982, SHSI-DSM.

38. Iowa Family Farm Development Authority, Minutes, November 18, 1981; Leanne Lundt, "Farm Purchase: A Dream Come True," *Maquoketa Sentinel-Press*, December 26, 1981.

39. Robert Ray, Condition of the State Address, January 12, 1982, *Journal of the Senate*, 1982 Regular Session, 69th General Assembly, 17.

40. "Farmers Show Caution in Cash Flow Projections," *Successful Farming*, January 1982, 7.

41. "90,000 Hog Farms Wiped Out in '81 Price Crunch," *Successful Farming*, February 1982, 10-H.

42. Greg Wood, "State of the Farm Economy Annual Report 1982," *Successful Farming*, September 1982, 15–17.

43. "Heartlands Mirror Hard Times with Land Price Decline," *Successful Farming*, April 1982, 10; "Land Prices Will Fall Even Farther," *Wallace's Farmer*, September 11, 1982.

44. Monte Sesker, "Tough Year ahead for Many Farmers," *Wallace's Farmer*, April 24, 1982.

45. John Otte, "Many Farmers Face Financial Problems," *Wallace's Farmer*, September 25, 1982.

46. Dorothy J. Scarpiniti to Governor Robert Ray, June 23, 1982, Robert Ray Papers, RG 043, Box 12, Folder Sa-Sc 1981–1983, SHSI-DSM.

47. John Otte, "Farmers Trim Living Costs to Survive Hard Times," *Wallace's Farmer*, September 11, 1982.

48. John Otte, "Challenge for the 1980s . . . Focus on Survival, not Growth," *Wallace's Farmer*, April 10, 1982; Marlin Pfannkuch, "Making the Most of a Troubled Economy," *Wallace's Farmer*, February 13, 1982.

49. "Strategies for Another Year of Belt Tightening," *Wallace's Farmer*, February 13, 1982.

50. Duane M. Skow to Doug Gross, May 21, 1982, Robert Ray Papers, RG 043, Box 46, Agriculture 1982 File, SHSI-DSM.

51. Duane M. Skow to Doug Gross, May 21, 1982.

52. Daniel Pedersen, "Fred Stover, the Last Apostle of the New Deal," *Des Moines Register*, April 18, 1982; Memo, Iowa Farm Unity Coalition, January 2, 1985, Denise O'Brien Papers, Box 11, Organizational Involvement File, IWA-UofI.

53. Jerry Perkins, "Farms Bemoan Economic Straits," *Des Moines Register*, October 3, 1982.

54. Hotline materials, PrairieFire Collection, MS 313, Farm Crisis-Foreclosure Hotline File, 1982; and Correspondence and Publications File, 1982, SpecColl-ISU; "FmHA Deferral Practice Illegal," *Small Farm Advocate*, Summer 1982, 4–7; "Two More Injunctions Stop FmHA Foreclosures," *Small Farm Advocate*, Winter 1982/1983, 4, 7.

55. Other smaller volunteer hotlines also existed. A Mennonite couple from the Kalona

area who had lost their forty-acre farm operated a hotline and took approximately two calls a day from distressed families. Theirs was a nationwide service. Eicher, "Every Family on Their Own," 89–90.

56. Greene Township Women's Club Minutes, October 27, 1982, IWA-UofI.

57. Flyer, 1982 Iowa Power Farming Show, Terry Branstad Papers, RG 043, Box 87, File 4, SHSI-DSM.

58. News release, National Corn Growers Association, Robert Ray Papers, RG 043, Box 30C, Folder H, 1981–1982, SHSI-DSM.

59. Cheryl Tevis, interview by Pamela Riney-Kehrberg, April 19, 2018.

60. Val Farmer, "Ending the Hurt and Danger of Violent Relationships," *Farm Woman News*, November 1985, 20.

61. Cheryl Tevis, "Where Does SHE Go to Let Off Steam?" *Successful Farming*, October 1979, 22–23.

62. Cheryl Tevis, "Stress," *Successful Farming*, October 1980, 20–21; idem., "Stress," *Successful Farming*, February 1982, 27–42; "Depression: Growing Occupational Hazard for Farmers," *Successful Farming*, January 1984, 30–31.

63. George Anthan, "Democrats Seek to Ease 'Farm Crisis,'" *Des Moines Register*, March 19, 1982.

64. Al Swegle, "'Farm Crisis,' Milk Bills to Panel," *Cedar Rapids Gazette*, June 5, 1982.

65. Don Muhm, "Farm Group Decries 'Crisis Bill' Defeat," *Des Moines Register*, June 25, 1982.

66. Memo, from Doug Gross to Governor Ray, September 21, 1982, Robert Ray Papers, RG 043, Box 31A, Folder L-M, 1981–1982, SHSI-DSM; Ostendorf interview.

67. Mrs. Garrett Schreur to Governor Robert Ray, March 23, 1982, and Douglas E. Gross to Mrs. Garrett Schreur, April 12, 1982, Robert Ray Papers, RG 043, Box 12, File Sa-Sc 1981–1983, SHSI-DSM.

68. Pat Moyer to Governor Robert Ray, October 13, 1982, Robert Ray Papers, RG 043, Box 31A, Folder L-M, 1981–1982, SHSI-DSM.

69. "Ray Negative about Moratorium," *Des Moines Register*, October 1, 1982.

70. Pat Moyer to Governor Robert Ray, October 13, 1982; Charles Bullard, "Lousberry May Be Facing His Toughest Re-Election Battle," *Des Moines Register*, October 20, 1982.

71. David Elbert, "Branstad, Conlin Discuss Farm Problems, but Can't Do Much to Solve Them," *Des Moines Register*, October 25, 1982.

72. David Yepsen and Tom Witosky, "Branstad, Conlin Clash on Job Issue," *Des Moines Register*, October 12, 1982.

73. James Flansburg, "Iowa Vote: A Call for Consensus," *Des Moines Register*, November 4, 1982.

74. Governor Terry Branstad to Robert D. Benton, February 15, 1983, Terry Branstad Papers, RG 043, Box 104, File 104-9, SHSI-DSM; David Yepsen, "Time Is Ripe to Launch

Apple Corps," *Des Moines Register*, March 24, 1983; Agricultural Diversification Task Force, Report, June 28, 1983, Terry Branstad Papers, RG 043, Box 104, File 104-9, SHSI-DSM.

75. Kenneth Nollen to the Office for Planning and Programming, April 12, 1983, and Laura Burrow to Edward Stanek, July 18, 1983, Terry Branstad Papers, RG 043, Box 104, File 104-9, SHSI-DSM.

76. Dennis Juhl to Governor Terry Branstad, July 8, 1983, Terry Branstad Papers, RG 043, Box 43, File 1983 I-K, SHSI-DSM.

77. Don Muhm, "Panel Asks More Diversity in Farm Crops," *Des Moines Register*, June 29, 1983; Lee Aldrich to Edward Stanek, June 29, 1983, and Memorandum, Lynette Broders to Dave Swanson, May 23, 1983, and Memorandum, Lynette Broders to Jack Bailey, July 5, 1983, Terry Branstad Papers, RG 043, Box 104, File 104-9, SHSI-DSM.

78. Claudia Waterloo, "Muddy Midwestern Fields Endanger Cattle, Frustrating Farmers and Driving Up Prices," *Wall Street Journal*, April 15, 1983; "Spring Storms a Disaster for Iowa Farmers," *Des Moines Register*, April 15, 1983; USDA, "Weather Assessment," Terry Branstad Papers, RG 043, Box 43, File 43-11; Briefing paper, Terry Branstad Papers, RG 043, Box 43, File 43-11, SHSI-DSM; Richard Krumme, "Across the Editor's Desk," *Successful Farming*, November 1983, 3.

79. Stephanie Mendenhall to Governor Terry Branstad, December 21, 1983, and R. R. Pim to Governor Terry Branstad, December 27, 1983, Terry Branstad Papers, RG 043, Box 75, File 75--12, SHSI-DSM.

80. Monte Sesker, "Iowa Farmers Like Crop-Swap Idea," *Wallace's Farmer*, February 26, 1983; USDA, *An Initial Assessment of the Payment-in-Kind Program* (Washington, DC: USDA, April 1983).

81. "Famers Bounce Back with PIK," *Successful Farming*, June–July 1983, 8; "Farm Hotlines Still Ringing," *Wallace's Farmer*, July 9, 1983.

82. Sesker, "Iowa Farmers Like Crop Swap Idea."

83. Paul Lasley, *Iowa Farm and Rural Life Poll*, Iowa State University Cooperative Extension Service, Pm-1130, November 1983, 3.

84. "County Agribusiness Loss Estimated at $6.8 Million," *Harlan Tribune*, April 27, 1983; "Hard Times Hit Machinery Dealers," *Successful Farming*, June–July 1982, 36-B-36-D; Governor's Press Release: PIK Disaster Loans (Draft), Terry Branstad Papers, RG 043, Box 102, File 2, SHSI-DSM.

85. "Farmers Bounce Back with PIK," *Successful Farming*, June–July 1983, 8; "PIK Program Draws Fire as Costs Mount," *Successful Farming*, September 1983, 18; "Is PIK Welfare," *Successful Farming*, September 1983, 14; Rod Swoboda, "Life after PIK . . . What Kind of Program Do Crop Farmers Want?" *Wallace's Farmer*, July 9, 1983.

86. Interest Rates Trend Down," *Wallace's Farmer*, January 8, 1983; "Iowa Farmland Values Plunge to 20-Year Low," *Wallace's Farmer*, January 8, 1983; "Farmers Getting 'Go,' 'No Go' Word from Lenders," *Successful Farming*, March 1983, 22; "Rise in FLBA Delinquent Loans

Reflects Trying Times," *Harlan News Advertiser*, September 3, 1983; "Research Shows 944 Auctions in Two Months," *Harlan News Advertiser*, June 25, 1983; "Farm Families Share Plans for 1983," *Wallace's Farmer*, January 8, 1983, 58; "Across the Editor's Desk," and "Recession Over, but Prosperity Comes Slowly," *Successful Farming*, April 1983, 3, 15; Rod Swoboda, "You'll Have to Farm 'Smarter' in 1984," *Wallace's Farmer*, November 12, 1983.

87. "Farm Women Must Speak Up," *Farm Wife News*, January 1983, 32; Press Release, March 4, 1983, Iowa Farm Unity Coalition, PrairieFire Papers, MS 313, Correspondence and Publications File, SpecColl-ISU; "Farmers Protest at Algona Bank," *Des Moines Register*, March 5, 1983; "Algona Bank Denies Loan Despite Protest," *Des Moines Register*, March 10, 1983.

88. "Farm Groups to Sponsor July 13 Meeting in Irwin," *Harlan News Advertiser*, July 9, 1983; "Ecumenical Conference to Focus on 'Rural Crisis,'" *Harlan Tribune*, September 28, 1983; Jack Hovelson, "Iowans Round Up 68 Hogs to Squeal against Reagan," *Des Moines Register*, October 29, 1983.

89. "Farm Group to Lobby Today," *Harlan Tribune*, March 16, 1983; Office for Planning and Programming, "Iowa Farm Foreclosure Moratorium: An Impact Study," April 1983, Terry Branstad Papers, RG 043, Box 86, Folder 86-8, SHSI-DSM; Jerry Perkins, "Branstad Tells Farmers He Won't Declare Foreclosure Moratorium," *Des Moines Register*, April 14, 1983; Iowa Farm Unity Coalition, "The Response of the Iowa Farm Unity Coalition to the Iowa Farm Foreclosure Moratorium Impact Study by the Office of Planning and Programming," May 1983, Terry Branstad Papers, RG 043, Box 86, Folder 86-8, SHSI-DSM.

90. Robert Lindsey, "For Jessica Lange, 'Country' Was an Exercise in Perseverance," *New York Times*, September 16, 1984.

91. Sara Wyant-McNutt, "'Hollywood' Listens to Farm Women," *Wallace's Farmer*, April 9, 1983.

92. Ostendorf interview; News release, "Country," n.d., 1983, PrairieFire Collection, MS 313, Publications and news releases 1983 folder, SpecColl-ISU.

93. Myron A. Ohrtman to Governor Terry Branstad, July 11, 1983, Terry Branstad Papers, RG 043, Box 43, File 43-7, SHSI-DSM.

94. G. H. and L. H. to Governor Terry Branstad, March 29, 1983, and Douglas E. Gross to G. H. and L. H., June 21, 1983, Terry Branstad Papers, RG 043, Box 43, File 43-4, SHSI-DSM.

95. Ralph Engelken to Governor Terry Branstad, February 5, 1983, and Douglas E. Gross to Ralph Engelken, March 1, 1983, Terry Branstad Papers, RG 043, Box 43, File 43-3, SHSI-DSM; Don Muhm, "Iowa Farmer Spreads Message and Manure," *Des Moines Register*, May 23, 1982.

96. Deborah Wiley, "Greeley Widow Loses Fight to Save Family Farm," *Des Moines Register*, July 1, 1987.

97. Leah Tookey, interview by Pamela Riney-Kehrberg, September 7, 2017.

Chapter 3. The Year of Realization: 1984

1. Ken Fuson, "Baffling Questions in Gruesome Barnyard Full of Dead Cattle," *Des Moines Register*, January 8, 1984.

2. Fuson, "Baffling Questions;" Nick Lamberto, "Banker Relates Visit to Inspect 167 Dead Cattle," *Des Moines Register*, April 14, 1984; Barbara Musfeldt, "Farmer's Version of Cattle Deaths: Creditors at Fault," *Des Moines Register*, January 15, 1984; Kenneth Pins, "'No Choice' Left to Wood, Lawyer Claims," *Des Moines Register*, June 27, 1984.

3. Musfeldt, "Farmer's Version;" "Wood Granted Early Release," *Daily Freeman Journal*, January 17, 1986; Louise Beyea-Omvig, "The Horror of Starved Cattle," *Des Moines Register*, January 23, 1984.

4. Smith, "Not Much Sympathy for Farmer Who Let Cattle Die;" United Press International Archives, April 6, 1984, https://www.upi.com/Archives/1984/04/06/Not-much-sympathy-for-farmer-who-let-cattle-die/5182450075600/; "Wife Says Husband's Sentence Cruel," *Iowa City Press-Citizen*, August 13, 1984.

5. The Meisgeiers, for example, whose story is told later in this chapter, struggled to care for their animals and could not afford the feed necessary to get them to market. A poem their daughter wrote referenced feeding "spoiled frozen corn to starving livestock." Deb Bahe, "I Didn't Know," quoted in Joyce Egginton, "Harvest of Tears," *Ladies' Home Journal*, August 1985, 173.

6. "Final 1983 Estimates Show Drought Severity," *Wallace's Farmer*, April 14, 1984.

7. Governor Terry Branstad to John Block, October 22, 1984, Terry Branstad Papers, RG 043, Box 471, File 2, SHSI-DSM; "Shelby County Crop Damage Estimate: Over 80,000 Acres," *Harlan News Advertiser*, June 23, 1984; "Summary of 1983 and 1984 Ag Sector Action," Terry Branstad Papers, RG 043, Box 75, File 15, SHSI-DSM.

8. Ray Hodde to Governor Terry Branstad, July 2, 1984, Terry Branstad Papers, RG 043, Box 75, File 75-12, SHSI-DSM.

9. Dan Boatman to Governor Terry Branstad, June 22, 1984, Terry Branstad Papers, RG 043, Box 75, File 15, SHSI-DSM.

10. Report, "Farm Economy in Iowa" and News Release, March 28, 1984, Terry Branstad Papers, RG 043, Box 86, File 86-4, SHSI-DSM.

11. Daniel Otto, "Iowa Farm Bankruptcies," in *Progress Report: Some Perspectives on Farm Financial Stress*, Department of Economics, Iowa State University, September 1984, Thomas R. Harkin Collection, Political Papers, Box L-5, Folder 25, Special Collections, Drake University Library, Des Moines (hereafter SpecColl-Drake).

12. "Farm Economy in Iowa."

13. Contributors to the report were Emanuel Melichar, William Edwards, Arnold Paulsen, Daniel Otto, Robert Jolly, Roger Ginder, and Neil Harl. "Executive Summary," in *Progress Report*, 3.

14. Robert Jolly, "Survey of Iowa Farm Financial Stress," in *Progress Report*, 39.

15. "ASSIST: An Iowa Farm and Community Financial Management Assistance Program," "Executive Summary," in *Progress Report*, 63–64; "Shelby County 'Assist' Resource Committee Formed," *Harlan News Advertiser*, November 17, 1984; "FarmAID: Financial Counseling for Farm Families," *Wallace's Farmer*, November 24, 1984.

16. Mike Duffy, interview by Pamela Riney-Kehrberg, October 18, 2018.

17. Duffy interview.

18. Interview with Daniel Merrick, May 1, 1990, Dorothy Schwieder Papers, RS 13/12/54, Box 16, File 20, SpecColl-ISU.

19. Claudia Dreifus, "Families Who Need Someone to Care," *Redbook*, December 1988, 108; Joan Blundall, "The Initial Response from a Community Mental Health Center," *Human Services in the Rural Environment* 10, no. 1 (1986): 30; Dennis Farney, "Politics of Despair," *Wall Street Journal*, October 5, 1984.

20. William Edwards and Cynthia Needles Fletcher, *Take Charge in Changing Times: Managing Farm Family Finances*, Iowa State University Cooperative Extension Service, Pm-1173, November 1984.

21. Randy Weigel, Sharon Mays, and Barbara Abbott, *Stress on the Farm. Lesson 1: Stress Management for the Health of It*, Iowa State University Cooperative Extension Service, Pm-1172a, November 1984; Randy Weigel, *Stress on the Farm, Lesson 2: Stress Management—Taking Charge*, Iowa State University Cooperative Extension Service, Pm-1172b, November 1984; Randy Weigle, Jean Hood, and Barbara Abbott, *Stress on the Farm. Lesson 3: Understanding Depression—Yours and Theirs*, Iowa State University Cooperative Extension Service, Pm-1172c, November 1984; Jeanie Trachta, Randy Weigel, and Barbara Abbott, *Stress on the Farm, Lesson 4: Resolving Farm Family Conflicts*, Iowa State University Cooperative Extension Service, Pm 1172d, November 1984; Randy Weigel, Marilyn Schnittjer, and Barbara Abbott, *Stress on the Farm. Lesson 5: From Family Stress to Family Strengths*, Iowa State University Cooperative Extension Service, Pm-1172e, November 1984; Randy Weigel et al., *Stress on the Farm. Lesson 6: Keeping the Farm Family Operating*, Iowa State University Cooperative Extension Service, Pm-1172f, November 1984.

22. Donald J. McLean and Catherine C. McLean to Governor Terry Branstad, May 2, 1984, Terry Branstad Collection, RG 043, Box 74, File General Correspondence M-O 1984, SHSI-DSM.

23. Deb Wiley, "Suicide on the Farm," *Cedar Rapids Gazette*, September 2, 1984.

24. Meisgeier appears to have been one of the farmers in Friedberger's study who committed suicide while he was researching and writing his book. Friedberger, *Shake-Out*, 74.

25. Deborah Bahe, correspondence with the author, November 15 and 17, 2019.

26. Deb Wiley, "Distressed Farmers Reluctant to Seek Help," *Cedar Rapids Gazette*, September 2, 1984.

27. Kathleen Beery and Robert W. Jolly, "Extension and Research Programs on Rural Financial Stress in Iowa," in Paul Lasley, Rand Conger, and Curtis Stofferahn, *Farm Crisis*

Response: Extension and Research Activities in the North Central Region (Ames, IA: North Central Regional Center for Rural Development, 1986), 6

28. Andrew H. Malcolm, "Problems on Farms Take Toll on Family Life," *New York Times*, November 20, 1984.

29. Joyce Swetstka to Governor Terry Branstad, March 10, 1984, Terry Branstad Collection, RG 043, Box 74, File General Correspondence 1984 S, SHSI-DSM.

30. Mrs. M. U. to Governor Terry Branstad, May 16, 1984, Terry Branstad Papers, RG 043, Box 74, File General Correspondence 1984, T-Z, SHSI-DSM.

31. Christopher J. Siebens to Governor Terry Branstad, September 17, 1984, Terry Branstad Collection, RG 043, Box 75, File 15, SHSI-DSM.

32. Rick Walters to Governor Terry Branstad, ca. June 1984, Terry Branstad Papers, RG 043, Box 74, File General Correspondence 1984 T-Z, SHSI-DSM.

33. David Jungers to Governor Terry Branstad, February 2, 1984, Terry Branstad Papers, RG 043, Box 102, File 102-2, SHSI-DSM.

34. For a description of the money-saving strategies used by Midwestern farming families, see Neth, *Preserving the Family Farm*, 17–40.

35. Paul Lasley, interview by Pamela Riney-Kehrberg, April 5, 2018.

36. "Cite O'Brien County Farmer for Promoting Food for Life," *Fonda Times*, June 19, 1986; Freedom Township Women's Club, Secretary's Book, 1960–1989, February 3, 1984, IWA-UofI.

37. Robin Kline, Phyllis Olson, and Diane Nelson, *Take Charge in Changing Times: How to Set up an Emergency Food Pantry*, Iowa State University Cooperative Extension Service, Pm-1179 (rev.), February 1985, 1–2.

38. "33 Million in Free Food for Iowans," *Walnut Bureau*, February 23, 1984; "More Food Available for Area Hungry," *Buena Vista County Journal*, January 23, 1986.

39. "Hundreds of Farmers Seek Food Stamps," *Daily Iowiegian and Citizen*, December 21, 1984.

40. Denise O'Brien, "Memories of the Crisis," *Middle West Review* 2, no. 1 (Fall 2015): 59; 1984 Individual Farm Business Analysis, Denise O'Brien Papers, Biographical and Family, Farm Records 1975–1997, Box 1, IWA-UofI.

41. J. Mark Dominy, April 5, 1984, Arlan Draayer to Iowa Congressmen, March 30, 1984, John A. De Groot, April 7, 1984, Bette Hanson, n.d., Terry Branstad Papers, RG 043, Box 102, File 102-20, SHSI-DSM.

42. Petition, Inwood, Iowa and surrounding communities, Terry Branstad Papers, RG 043, Box 102, File 102-20, SHSI-DSM.

43. Mark Gregory, petition and letter, October 22, 1984, Terry Branstad Papers, RG 043, Box 75, File 15, SHSI-DSM.

44. Mrs. Michael Urban to Governor Terry Branstad, May 16, 1984.

45. N. H. to Governor Terry Branstad, May 31, 1984, Terry Branstad Papers, RG 043, Box 74, File General Correspondence 1984, F-H, SHSI-DSM

46. Joyce Swestka to Governor Terry Branstad, March 10, 1984, Terry Branstad Papers, RG 043, Box 74, File General Correspondence 1984 S, SHSI-DSM.

47. For a description of the extraordinary efforts of Iowa's farm women in the Great Depression, see Deborah Fink and Dorothy Schwieder, "Iowa Farm Women in the 1930s," *Annals of Iowa* 49, no. 7 (Winter 1989): 570–590.

48. For a thorough discussion of the shame and stigma attached to debt in farm country, see Dudley, *Debt and Dispossession*; Mrs. Raymond Anderson to Governor Terry Branstad, June 25, 1984, Terry Branstad Papers, RG 043, Box 74, File General Correspondence 1984 A B, SHSI-DSM.

49. Mrs. Michael Urban to Governor Terry Branstad, May 16, 1984.

50. Joyce Swestka to Governor Terry Branstad, March 10, 1984.

51. Keith Heffernan to Sandra L. Sesker, November 21, 1985. Office of the Governor, RG 043, Terry Branstad, Box 90, Agriculture, 1984–1987, Folder 90-1, SHSI-DSM.

52. R. R. Pim to Governor Terry Branstad, June 20, 1986, Terry Branstad Papers, RG 043, Box 74, File General Correspondence 1984 T-Z, SHSI-DSM; Notation attached to Swestka to Governor Terry Branstad, May 16, 1984, SHSI-DSM; Paul Klauda, "Advocates Lend Advice, Sympathy to Troubled Farmers," *Minneapolis Star Tribune*, April 29, 1984.

53. Barker Devine, *On Behalf of the Family Farm*.

54. William C. Pratt, "Using History to Make History? Progressive Farm Organizing during the Farm Revolt of the 1980s," *Annals of Iowa* 55, no. 1 (Winter 1996): 31–33.

55. Committees for the Luedtke Sale, PrairieFire Collection, MS 313, Papers, News clippings and correspondence, 1984–1986, SpecColl-ISU.

56. "Statement delivered 8:15 AM Mon 6/4/84, Orville and Joane Ludtke farm, Lucas Co., Iowa," PrairieFire Collection, MS 313, Correspondence and articles, 1984, SpecColl-ISU; "Farm Foreclosures Continue," *Successful Farming*, September 1984; Matthew Okerlund, "Iowa Farmer's Friends Are Dismayed by High Bids at Penny Auction," *Des Moines Register*, July 1, 1984.

57. Cheryl Tevis, "Tinsel-Town Goes Country in '84," *Successful Farming*, December 1984, M4-M5.

58. *Country*, produced by Jessica Lange and William Wittliff, directed by Richard Pearce (Burbank, CA: Touchstone Films, 1984).

59. Jane Norman, "*Country* Is True-to-Life, Farmers at Premier Say," *Des Moines Register*, October 5, 1984.

60. Greg Wood, "Farmers Watch Their Story Being Told in *Country*," *Farm Journal*, December 1984, 20-D.

61. Jack Hovelson, "Dunkerton Teen Makes Movie Debut," and Pat Denato, "'Country' Lets Iowans Portray Themselves," *Des Moines Register*, September 23, 1984; Tevis, "Tinsel-Town."

62. Eleanor Jacobs, "'Country:' A Movie for Our Time," *Farm Wife News*, December

1984, 9; Joan Bunke, "Premier Set for Iowa-Made Film," *Des Moines Register*, September 23, 1984.

63. The case was *Coleman v. Block*, and it made possible a national class action suit against the FmHA. The judge in the case found that the FmHA was not allowing farmers to make use of deferral rules that had been put in place in 1978 and was, in effect, "starving out" farm families. Bruce M. Van Sickle, "The North Dakota Nine and the Family Farm," *Litigation* 25, no. 4 (1999): 49–59.

64. Paul Lasley, *Iowa Farm and Rural Life Poll*, Iowa State University Cooperative Extension Service, Pm-1178, December 1984, 12–14.

65. Sara Wyant-McNutt, "These Farmers Seek Lender Accountability," *Wallace's Farmer*, April 14, 1984.

66. Cheryl Tevis, "Tax Pitfalls Lurk behind Solutions to Farm Debt Problems," *Successful Farming*, September 1984.

67. Cheryl Tevis, "Ultraright Activism Grows in rural America," *Successful Farming*, October 1984, 32-H.

68. Richard Krumme, "Across the Editor's Desk," *Successful Farming*, May 1984, 3.

69. "Block Debt Shows Extent of the Financial Problem," *Wallace's Farmer*, June 23, 1984.

70. Philip Britten to President Ronald Reagan, February 10, 1984, Terry Branstad Papers, RG 043, Box 74, Folder General Correspondence A-B, 1984, SHSI-DSM.

71. Donald Albert to President Ronald Reagan, February 9, 1984, Terry Branstad Papers, RG 043, Box 102, File 102-20, SHSI-DSM.

72. David Noller to Charles Shuman, February 12, 1984, Terry Branstad Papers, RG 043, Box 74, File General Correspondence 1984 M-O, SHSI-DSM.

73. Mrs. Michael Urban to Governor Terry Branstad, May 16, 1984.

74. "Bumper Crop of Debt Relief Plans," *Successful Farming*, November 1984, 18.

75. "Major Farm Debt Relief Plans Basically Similar," *Wallace's Farmer*, October 27, 1984.

76. "Farm Flap," *Monticello Express*, July 18, 1984.

77. Display ad, *Harlan Tribune*, October 24, 1984; Remarks of the Honorable Tom Harkin, Roswell Garst Day, Coon Rapids, Iowa, June 23, 1984, Thomas R. Harkin Collection, Box L-O, Folder 24, Spec-Coll-Drake.

78. David Yepsen, "Reagan Romps in Land, Harkin Easily Dumps Jepsen," *Des Moines Register*, November 7, 1984.

79. Dennis Farney, "Politics of Despair," *Wall Street Journal*, October 5, 1984.

80. "A Service of Celebration, Remembrance and Hope for the People of the Land," November 4, 1984, PrairieFire Collection, MS 313, Correspondence, Church, 1981–1990, SpecColl-ISU.

Chapter 4. From Penny Auctions to a Declaration of Emergency: 1985

1. Photograph and Kenneth Pins, "Silent Crowd Protests Nevada Farmland Sale," *Des Moines Register*, January 4, 1985.
2. Ruth Book to Governor Terry Branstad, January 10, 1985, and Douglas E. Gross to Ruth Book, January 23, 1985, Terry Branstad Papers, RG 043, Box 470, File 5, SHSI-DSM.
3. David Yepsen, Tom Witosky, and Dewey Knudson, "Branstad Says He Has an 'Open Mind' on State-Imposed Foreclosure Ban," *Des Moines Register*, January 16, 1985.
4. Douglas E. Gross to Ruth Book; "Who Is Listening?" *Wallace's Farmer*, February 9, 1985; Mike Chapman, *Iowa's Record Setting Governor: The Terry Branstad Story* (Des Moines, IA: Business Publications, 2015), 63; "It's Time to Tough It Out, Block Tells Strapped Farmers," *Chicago Tribune*, January 25, 1985.
5. Iowa was not the only state where these problems erupted. Nebraska experienced a similar conflict. Judith Dye to Governor Kerry, February 8, 1985, Center for Rural Affairs Papers, MS 413, Box 36, Folder 15, SpecColl-ISU.
6. Roz Ostendorf to Governor Terry Branstad, January 3, 1985, Terry Branstad Papers, RG 043, Box 335, File 6, SHSI-DSM.
7. David Ostendorf to Governor Terry Branstad, January 7, 1985, Terry Branstad Papers, RG 043, Box 335, File 5, SHSI-DSM.
8. "The Iowa Farm Unity Coalition and the *Rural Concerns* Hotline," Terry Branstad Papers, RG 043, Box 335, File 6, SHSI-DSM; David Ostendorf, interview by Pamela Riney-Kehrberg, October 9, 2019.
9. Dorothy Schwieder, *75 Years of Service: Cooperative Extension in Iowa* (Ames: Iowa State University Press, 1993), 36–37, 151.
10. Paul Lasley, Rand Conger, and Curtis Stofferahn, eds., *Iowa Farm and Rural Life Poll*, Iowa State University Cooperative Extension Service, Spring 1985, 8.
11. Lasley, Conger, and Stofferahn, *Iowa Farm and Rural Life Poll*, Spring 1985, 9.
12. Memo from Larry Jackson, "Status of Food Banks," February 13, 1985, Terry Branstad Papers, RG 043, Box 471, File 2, SHSI-DSM.
13. William Petrosky, "Food Stamps Becoming Part of Iowa Farm Life," *Des Moines Register*, August 4, 1985.
14. "Cite O'Brien County Farmer for Promoting Food for Life," *Fonda Times*, June 19, 1986. In Creston, the organization distributed two thousand pounds of meat. "Storm Lake Tyson Boosts Food for Life," *Storm Lake Tribune*, May 14, 2018, https://www.storm lakepilottribune.com/story/2512456.html; "Food For Life Accepts Donations of Livestock, Money," October 30, 2018, https://www.crestonnews.com/2-18/1-/20/food-for-life-accepts-donations-of-livestock-money/adkg7wm/.
15. Ronna Lawless, "Loaves and Fishes Depends on Volunteers, Community Support," *Ames Tribune*, December 30, 2016.

16. Rev. Victor Vriesen to President Ronald Reagan, October 25, 1985, in Governor Terry E. Branstad Papers, Box 90, Folder 90-1, SHSI-DSM

17. Flyer, "Iowa Rural Crisis Fund," Denise O'Brien Papers, Organizational involvement, Iowa Farm Unity Coalition 1985 Folder, Box 11, IWA-UofI.

18. "FarmAid Distributes $900,000," *New York Times*, November 10, 1985.

19. Letter from John Nicholls, Superintendent, September 3, 1985, Farm Crisis Committee, MS 482, Correspondence 1984–1985, SpecColl-ISU.

20. William Petroski, "Food Stamps Becoming Part of Iowa Farm Life," *Des Moines Register*, August 4, 1985.

21. Petroski, "Food Stamps."

22. Petroski, 6.

23. V. Jane Jorgenson, "Farm Income and the Food Stamp Program," Bureau of Economic Assistance, January 24, 1985, Denise O'Brien Papers, Organizational involvement, Iowa Farm Unity Coalition 1985 Folder, Box 11, IWA-UofI.

24. Petroski, 7.

25. "Food Stamps Indicate Farm Crisis," *Des Moines Register*, August 11, 1985.

26. Sister Margaret Mary O'Gorman, "How Can Farmers Be Hungry?" *Catholic Rural Life*, September 1986, 10.

27. Schwieder, *75 Years of Service*, 76–82.

28. Louise Rosenfeld, quoted in Schwieder, *75 Years of Service*, 82.

29. "Farmers Tired of Hearing about the Bad Old Days," *Des Moines Register*, August 18, 1985.

30. "Farmers Tired."

31. "Farmers, Food Stamps: A Message," *Des Moines Register*, August 25, 1985.

32. "Iowa's Three Top Leaders'—Farmers' Food Needs," Terry Branstad Papers, RG 043, Box 471, File 2, SHSI-DSM.

33. Friedberger, *Shake-Out*, 125.

34. Schwieder, *Iowa: The Middle Land*, 270–271.

35. Although this example comes from Nebraska, it is illustrative of the hesitations and refusals surrounding the use of food aid throughout rural America. Carol Fanta to Judith Dye, October 1, 1986, Center for Rural Affairs, MS 413, Box 36, File 14, SpecColl-ISU.

36. Carol Fanta to Judith Dye, October 1, 1986.

37. Dawn Hoffman Price, "An Empty Breadbasket: Studies Document Hunger's Grip," *Catholic Rural Life*, September 1986, 17.

38. Lois [no last name] to Denise O'Brien, September 21, 26, [1985], Denise O'Brien Papers, Box 8, Correspondence, 1967–1988, IWA-UofI.

39. O'Brien was a long-time activist, whose interest in social justice extended back into her college years. See O'Brien, "Memories of the Crisis."

40. Kent Parker, "Besieged Farm Women Seek Ways to Fight Crisis," *Cedar Rapids*

Gazette, January 12, 1986; Prairiefire Collection, MS 313, Iowa's Economic Crisis clippings file, 1981–1987, SpecColl-ISU.

41. Joyce Egginton, "Harvest of Tears," *Ladies' Home Journal*, August 1985, 50.

42. Egginton, "Harvest of Tears," 173.

43. Roz Ostendorf, "Seeking to Break the Silence," *Church Woman*, Fall 1985, 33.

44. Ostendorf interview.

45. For an analysis of the limits of working from home, see Christina E. Gringeri, *Getting By: Women Homeworkers and Rural Economic Development* (Lawrence: University Press of Kansas, 1994).

46. Virginia Molgaard and Jeanene Miller, *Take Charge in Changing Times: Landing a Job: Strategies for Farm Wives*, Iowa State University Cooperative Extension Service, Pm-1234a, December 1985, 2.

47. Molgaard and Miller, *Landing a Job*, 2.

48. T. G., "Life After Farming," Terry Branstad Papers, RG 043, Box 86, Folder 86-7, SHSI-DSM.

49. Virginia Molgaard and Barb Abbot, *Take Charge in Changing Times: Moving on: Getting an Off-Farm Job*, Iowa State University Cooperative Extension Service, Pm-1234c, September 1987.

50. Mr. and Mrs. Dan H. Witt to Governor Terry Branstad, November 26, 1985. Office of the Governor, RG 043, Terry Branstad, Box 90, Agriculture, 1984–1987, Folder 90-1, SHSI-DSM.

51. "Growing Up Afraid: Farm Crisis Is Taking Subtle Toll on Children in Distressed Families," *Wall Street Journal*, November 7, 1985.

52. The *Harlan News-Advertiser* and *Harlan Tribune* confirm the depth of the crisis facing the community. The number of homes and farms for sale in the county was staggering.

53. Beth Ellsworth, interview by Pamela Riney-Kehrberg, September 27, 2016.

54. *Harpoon* (Harlan, IA: Harlan Community High School, 1985), 3.

55. *Harpoon*, 4.

56. *Harpoon*, 7.

57. *Harpoon*, 147.

58. Ellsworth interview.

59. Sara Wyant, "When Financial Problems Occur . . . Should You Tell Your Children," *Wallace's Farmer*, April 27, 1985.

60. Virginia Molgaard, *The Rural Crisis Comes to School: Teacher Handout for Videotape*, Iowa State University Cooperative Extension, August 1985; *The Farm Crisis: Rural Stress and Its Impact on Youth, A Report from a Think Tank Convened in Rural Iowa, October 15 and 16, 1985*, Rural Coalition Papers, MS 368, Youth 1985–1987 File, SpecColl-ISU; Mindy McClintock, "Three-Phase Program Initiated; Support Group Formed at WHS," *Viking Voice*, November 29, 1985, PrairieFire Collection, MS 313, Correspondence and Articles 1986, SpecColl-ISU.

61. "FFA Members Help with Bingo," *Mapleton Press*, May 9, 1985; "Peers Are Working," *Tiger's Tale, The Newspapers of Benton County*, December 11, 1985; News note, *Walnut Bureau*, December 19, 1985.

62. "Reagan Dismissed Farm-Quip Fuss," *Des Moines Register*, March 26, 1985.

63. Monte Sesker, "Bad Joke, Poorly Told," *Wallace's Farmer*, April 13, 1985.

64. James Risser, "Stockman: America Has Too Many Farmers," *Des Moines Register*, February 14, 1985; "Stockman's Outburst has DC Abuzz," *Des Moines Register*, February 7, 1985.

65. Mrs. E. Garoutte, to Governor Terry Branstad, Terry Branstad Papers, RG 043, Box 75, File 13, SHSI-DSM.

66. G. J. Danhoff to David Stockman, February 12, 1985, Terry Branstad Collection, RG 043, Box 75, File 13, SHSI-DSM; W. G. Meinen to Frank Fahrenkopf, July 9, 1985, Terry Branstad Collection, RG 043, Box 470, File 470-2, SHSI-DSM; Wayne and Miriam McDonald to David Stockman, February 12, 1985, Terry Branstad Collection, RG 043, Box 75, File 13, SHSI-DSM; Ronald J. Hall to David Stockman, n.d., Terry Branstad Papers, RG 043, Box 75, File 75-13, SHSI-DSM.

67. "Farm Meeting to Be Held Jan. 16," *Mapleton Press*, January 10, 1985; "Western Iowa Farm Crisis Committee Is Organized," *Mapleton Press*, January 24, 1985; Eldridge Drury, Letter to the Editor, *Mapleton Press*, October 3, 1985; "Farmers, Union Members Cheer, Clap, Sing as Auction Is Called Off," *Des Moines Register*, January 31, 1985.

68. "Buses Will Leave Wednesday for Farm Rally," *Mapleton Press*, February 21, 1985; Frank Holdmeyer, "Farm Crisis Rally, A Sleeping Giant Has Awakened!" *Wallace's Farmer*, March 23, 1985; State of Iowa Executive Department Proclamation, February 19, 1985, Terry Branstad Papers, RG 043, Box 470, File 7, SHSI-DSM.

69. Eileen Ogintz, "15,000 Farmers Rally for Aid," *Chicago Tribune*, February 28, 1985; Holdmeyer, "Farm Crisis Rally."

70. "Area Churches to Ring Bells," *Mapleton Press*, February 28, 1985; "Lawyers Do Chores to Farmers Can Testify," *Adair County Free Press*, March 13, 1985; "Reagan Rejects Help for Farmers," *Des Moines Register*, March 7, 1985; Flyer, "Ag Day Action: Foreclose on the Federal Building," Iowa Farm Unity Coalition, Collection on Dixon Terry, MS 2014.8, Folder 1, SHSI-DSM.

71. Memo, Women's Farm Crisis Committee, April 5, 1985, Farm Crisis Committee Papers, MS 482, Correspondence 1985 File, SpecColl-ISU.

72. Tim Wrage to Sally Field, April 30, 1985, and Lyle Scheelhaase to Jessica Lange, April 14, 1985, Farm Crisis Committee Collection, MS 482, General Information, Correspondence, Articles 1985, SpecColl-ISU; Christopher Drew, "Stars Shine Tearfully in Plea for Farm Aid," *Chicago Tribune*, May 7, 1985. For a detailed analysis of the cultural meaning of the stars' testimony, see Rebecca Stoil, "Desperate Farm Wives: Gender, Activism, and Traditionalism in the Farm Crisis," *Middle West Review* 2, no. 1 (Fall 2015): 33–50.

73. "Farm Crisis Expo," *Mapleton Press*, June 13, 1985; Editorials, *Wallace's Farmer*, July

13, 1985; Richard Pearce to David Ostendorf and Daniel Levitas, February 15, 1985, Prairie Fire Collection, MS 313, Correspondence, Various Offices 1985, SpecColl-ISU; "Hoping to Help the American Farmer," *Mapleton Press*, July 18, 1985; "Farm Crisis Committee Returns Home," *Mapleton Press*, July 25, 1985; Farm Crisis Committee, Minutes, August 20, 1985, Farm Crisis Committee Papers, MS 482, Board Meeting Minutes and Agendas, 1985–1987, SpecColl-ISU; Tim Wrage to Merle Haggard, August 5, 1985, and check, Farm Crisis Committee Collection, MS 482, Correspondence 1984–1985, SpecColl-ISU.

74. Iowaide flyer, PrarieFire Collection, MS 313, Correspondence 1985, SpecColl-ISU.

75. "The Groups, the Times," *Des Moines Register*, September 22, 1985; "Farm Aid Cause Has Tough Row to Hoe," *Chicago Tribune*, September 22, 1985; "FarmAid Was a Success for This Former Farm Wife," *Successful Farming*, November 1985, 14; "FarmAid Distributes $900,000," *New York Times*, November 10, 1985; "Farm Aid to Provide Legal Assistance," *Wallace's Farmer*, November 23, 1985; Mr. and Mrs. Doyle Robinson to Governor Terry Branstad, September 21, 1985, Terry Branstad Papers, RG 043, Box 90, File 90-2, SHSI-DSM; Judith Dye to Carolyn Mugar, November 6, 1985, Center for Rural Affairs, MS 413, Box 36, File 15, SpecColl-ISU.

76. "You Are Not Alone—II: Hope in a Hopeless Land Suicide Intervention in Rural America," Farm Crisis Collection, Msc 32, Box 4, Special Collections, Rod Library, University of Northern Iowa (hereafter SpecColl-UNI).

77. "Introduction to 'Farmers to Farmers' Support Group," and Farmer to Farmer Pamphlet, Farm Crisis Collection, Msc 32, Box 1, Farmer to Farmer, SpecColl-UNI.

78. "Scotch Grove Church Would Like to Help," *Monticello Express*, December 4, 1985.

79. "A Profile of Rural America," *Successful Farming*, February 1975, 28; Eileen Ognitz, "Hardships Pulling Farm Belt Together," *Chicago Tribune*, March 11, 1985; Lauren Cohen, "Farmer Protests Gaining Steam as Crisis Worsens," *Chicago Tribune*, January 27, 1985.

80. Monte Sesker, "Financing for Spring," *Wallace's Farmer*, February 9, 1985.

81. Press release, January 17, 1985, Terry Branstad Papers, RG 043, Box 335, File 6, SHSI-DSM; Press release, February 28, 1985, Terry Branstad Papers, RG 043, Box 470, File 2, SHSI-DSM; Press release, March 18, 1985, Farm Crisis Committee Papers, MS 482, Terry Branstad News Release File, 1985, SpecColl-ISU.

82. Denise O'Brien to Governor Terry Branstad, July 5, 1984, Terry Branstad Papers, RG 043, Box 75, File 15, SHSI-DSM.

83. Tom Witosky, "Heavy GOP Flak Blocks Senate Farm Price Bill," *Des Moines Register*, March 2, 1985; Dewey Knudsen, "Minimum Farm Price Bill OK'd by House," *Des Moines Register*, March 13, 1985.

84. Erma C. Stewart to Governor Terry Branstad, March 13, 1985, Terry Branstad Records, RG 043, Box 119, Folder 119-4, SHSI-DSM.

85. J. Howard Mueller to Governor Terry Branstad, March 13, 1985, Terry Branstad Papers, RG 043, Box 119, Folder 119-5, SHSI-DSM.

86. Erma C. Stewart to Governor Terry Branstad, March 13, 1985, Terry Branstad Papers, RG 043, Box 119, File 119-2, SHSI-DSM.

87. Earl M. Willits, Deputy Attorney General to Senators Small and Welsh, March 4, 1985, Terry Branstad Papers, RG 043, Box 119, File 119-1, SHSI-DSM.

88. Dennis Wauters to Governor Terry Branstad, postmarked March 19, 1985, Terry Branstad Records, RG 043, Box 119–2, Folder 119-4, SHSI-DSM.

89. Susan Meseck and Kasey Meseck to Governor Terry Branstad, Marc 20, 1985, Terry Branstad Records, RG 043, Box 119, Folder 119-2, SHSI-DSM.

90. William Rempp to Governor Terry Branstad, received March 14, 1985, Terry Branstad Records, RG 043, Box 119, Folder 119-4, SHSI-DSM.

91. H. Oliver Hill to Governor Terry Branstad, March 13, 1985, Terry Branstad Records, RG 043, Box 119, Folder 119-4, SHSI-DSM.

92. John Welle to Governor Terry Branstad, March 13, 1985, Terry Branstad Records, RG 043, Box 119, Folder 119-4, SHSI-DSM.

93. William H. Meyers, "Probably Impacts of Senate File 32," February 12, 1985, Terry Branstad Papers, RG 043, Box 119, File 119-1, SHSI-DSM.

94. Governor Terry Branstad to Lieutenant Governor Robert Anderson, March 22, 1985, Terry Branstad Papers, RG 043, Box 119, File 119-1, SHSI-DSM.

95. F. W. Stover to Governor Branstad, April 8, 1985, Terry Branstad Papers, RG 043, Box 470, File 2, SHSI-DSM.

96. Iowa CCI News, April/May 1985, Terry Branstad Papers, RG 043, Box 470, File 470-2, SHSI-DSM

97. Rudy Perpich, 1985 Agriculture Assistance Program, and Rudy Perpich to Governor Terry Branstad, March 6, 1985, Terry Branstad Papers, RG 043, Box 470, File 2, SHSI-DSM.

98. "Draft memo regarding the Branstad plan for dealing with the farm problem this fall," Terry Branstad Papers, RG 043, Box 471, File 1, SHSI-DSM.

99. "Draft memo."

100. Governor Terry E. Branstad Statement on the Farm Mortgage Foreclosure Moratorium, October 1, 1985, and Farm Moratorium Fact Sheet, Terry Branstad Papers, RG 043, Box 86, File 1, SHSI-DSM.

101. "Branstad Calls Moratorium on Foreclosures," *Cedar Rapids Gazette*, October 2, 1985.

102. Mrs. Robert Sjostrand to Governor Terry Branstad, January 16, 1985, Terry Branstad Papers, RG 043, Box 470, File 5, SHSI-DSM.

103. Beverly J. Mueller to Governor Terry Branstad, n.d., Terry Branstad Papers, RG 043, Box 470, File 5, SHSI-DSM.

104. Larry Wenzl to Governor Terry Branstad, October 28, 1985, Terry Branstad papers, RG 043, Box 90, Folder 90-1, SHSI-DSM.

105. Oliver S. Carlson to Governor Terry Branstad, October 3, 1985, Terry Branstad Papers, RG 043, Box 90, File 90-4, SHSI-DSM.

106. George Anthan, "Reagan Signs 5-Year, $169 Billion Farm Bill, Most Costly in History," *Des Moines Register*, December 24, 1985.

107. Lewrene K. Glaser, *Provisions of the Food Security Act of 1985*, Agriculture Information Bulletin Number 498 (Washington, DC: Economic Research Service, USDA, 1986), 1–3, 46–52, 62.

108. Danbom, *Born in the Country*, 266.

109. Andrew H. Malcolm, "Death on the Prairie: More Victims of the Economy," *New York Times*, December 11, 1985; Ann Marie Lipinski, "A Farming Legacy Wiped Out," *Chicago Tribune*, December 11, 1985; "Chet Says," *Kalona News*, January 2, 1986; Sally Taylor, "Sincelely Yours," *Mellinger Sun News*, December 12, 1985.

110. James P. Gannon, Editorial, *Des Moines Register*, December 15, 1985.

111. "Analyzing Hills Tragedy," *Des Moines Register*, December 22, 1985.

112. Ruth I. Harmelink, *Lenders: Working through the Farmer-Lender Crisis* (Ames: Cooperative Extension Service, Iowa State University, 1986); "4 Dead in Rampage in an Iowa Town," *New York Times*, December 10, 1985.

Chapter 5. From Fears of Violence to Glimmers of Hope: 1986

1. Memorandum, Major W. D. Petersen to Colonel Frank Metzger, January 17, 1986, Memo from Gene W. Shepard, and Division of Criminal Investigation notice, Terry Branstad Paper, RG 043, Box 470, File 470-2, SHSI-DSM; William E. Schmidt, "Armed Men Delay Eviction of a Georgia Farmer," *New York Times*, November 16, 1985; "Farm Crisis Resolution, January 14 and 15, 1986," PrairieFire Collection, MS 313, Correspondence December 1985, Box 1, File 16, SpecColl-ISU.

2. "About 100 Hear Farm Activist Kersey," *Sioux Center News*, January 22, 1986.

3. "Area News: Hull," *Sioux County Capital*, January 30, 1986.

4. Jack Salzman, "Media Information Misleading," *Sioux County Capitol*, February 13, 1986.

5. Melvin List, "Square Snide Lines," *Sioux County Capital*, February 6, 1986.

6. A farm crisis group had invited Kersey to Decorah, before realizing that he and the members of his organization advocated violence, at which point they withdrew their invitation. "Betrayed, Isolated," *Cedar Rapids Gazette*, January 24, 1986.

7. Despite the noise they generated, people like Kersey were relatively unsuccessful nationwide, and particularly unsuccessful in Iowa. For an explanation of this result, see Mary Summers, "From the Heartland to Seattle: The Family Farm Movement of the 1980s and the Legacy of Agrarian State Building," in Catherine McNicol Stock and Robert D. Johnston, editors, *The Countryside in the Age of the Modern State: Political Histories of Rural America* (Ithaca: Cornell University Press, 2001), 304–326.

8. Text of Condition of the State Address, *Des Moines Register*, January 15, 1986.

9. Interview with Joe Harper, December 19, 2019; Director, "FARM/CAP," *Des Moines Register*, November 17, 1985.

10. Joe Harper, "FARM/CAP Program Status Report, December 1, 1985 to June 30, 1986," Des Moines Area Community College, Ankeny, Iowa, 3–14, by permission of Joe Harper.

11. Harper, "FARM/CAP Program Status Report," 14–33.

12. Harper interview; Harper, "FARM/CAP Program Status Report,," 50–54.

13. Harper, "FARM/CAP Program Status Report," 1–2.

14. Interview with Daniel Broshar, May 10, 1990, Dorothy Schwieder Papers, Box 16, Folder 22, SpecColl-ISU; see also Schwieder, *75 Years of Service*, 207, 221–222.

15. Broshar interview; Interview with Elizabeth A. Elliott, May 10, 1990, Dorothy Schwieder Papers, Box 16, Folder 23, SpecColl-ISU; Virginia Molgaard, *Rebuilding Self-Esteem—Ideas for Farm Men and Women*, Iowa State University Cooperative Extension Service Pm-1276, September 1986.

16. Broshar interview.

17. Judith Dye to E. E. Bridwell, May 12, 1987, Center for Rural Affairs Papers, MS 413, Box 36, File 24, SpecColl-ISU; Eicher, 87–89.

18. Broshar interview.

19. Al Swegle, "Farmer to Farmer Celebrates 1st Anniversary," *Cedar Rapids Gazette*, March 9, 1986.

20. "Support Group Strengthens Ties with Friends," *Advocate-News* (Wilton, Durant), March 20, 1986.

21. Newsletter, Farmers Helping Farmers, Family Service Agency, Cedar Rapids, Iowa, Fall 1986, Farm Crisis Collection, Msc 32, Box 4, SpecColl-UNI.

22. Iowa Division of Banking, "Failed Banks List," accessed January 4, 2020, https://idob.state.ia.us/bank/Docs/applica/bank/Iowa%20Failed%20Bank%20List.pdf; Federal Deposit Insurance Corporation, Bank Failures and Assistance Data, accessed January 5, 2020, https://banks.data.fdic.gov/explore/failures?aggReport=detail&displayFields=NAME%2CCERT%2CFIN%2CCITYST%2CFAILDATE%2CSAVR%2CRESTYPE%2CCOST%2CRESTYPE1%2CCHCLASS1%2CQBFDEP%2CQBFASSET&endFailYear=1979&selectedStatesAlpha=%2CIA&sortField=FAILDATE&sortOrder=desc&startFailYear=1970.

23. Ellen Huntoon, "Bank Failures—The Iowa Experience," in Peter Brent et al., "PrairieFire Bank Failure Response Team & FDIC Training Manual," October 14–15, 1986, 2, Msc 32, Box 4, Farm Crisis Collection, SpecColl-UNI; "Mediation Aims to Continue Farmer-FDIC Communication," *Cedar Rapids Gazette*, April 27, 1986, 75.

24. "Commercial State Bank Closed; New Bank Reopens," and "Citizens State Bank formed," *Pocahontas Record Democrat*, July 2, 1986; Public notice, *Pocahontas Record Democrat*, July 23, 1986; Rod Amlie, Letter to the Editor, *Pocahontas Record Democrat*, July 2, 1986.

25. "900 Borrowers Work with FDIC Locally," *Pocahontas Register Democrat*, August 13, 1986.

26. Report of Examination, Commercial State Bank, Pocahontas, Iowa, August 3, 1984, RG 10, Box 88-29, SHSI-DSM.

27. Glenn Schreiber, "Poking around Pocahontas," *Pocahontas Record Democrat*, July 2, 1986.

28. PrairieFire and the IFUC distributed the same PrarieFire authored pamphlet. "What to Do When Your Bank Has Failed," *Iowa Farm Unity News*, n.d., Msc 32, Box 4, Farm Crisis Collection, SpecColl-UNI; PrairieFire, "From Crisis to Community: What to Do When Your Bank Has Failed," Box 1, PrarieFire File, Msc 32, Box 1, Farm Crisis Collection, SpecColl-UNI.

29. Brent et al., "PrairieFire Bank Failure Response Team."

30. "Amlie Pleads Guilty to Charges" and "Amlie Gives His Version of Default," *Pocahontas Record Democrat*, November 25, 1987. The bank examiners' report confirmed that Amlie's bank was operating on a very large scale and that Amlie was heavily involved in his cattle feeding operation. Report of the Examiners, Commercial State Bank, page A, "Supervisory Section."

31. "Amlie Gives His Version."

32. "Farm Loan Mediation Beginning to Catch On," *Des Moines Register*, April 13, 1986.

33. Sonja Trom Eayrs, "Protecting America's Farmers under State Mediation Laws and Chapter 12: Who's Being Protected?" *Marquette Law Review* 72, no. 3 (Spring 1989): 468; Rural Communications Research Project, School of Journalism and Mass Communication, University of Iowa, "Farmer/Creditor Mediation Have You Puzzled?" Msc 32, Box 3, Farm Crisis Collection, SpecColl-UNI; "New Iowa Program Aims to Solve Famer-Creditor Disputes," *Wallace's Farmer*, July 12, 1986.

34. "Mediation Service Swamped," *Cedar Rapids Gazette*, June 20, 1986.

35. "Farmer-Creditor Mediator Seeks Aid," *Des Moines Register*, December 11, 1986.

36. "Bankruptcy Offers Limited Haven for Family Farms," *Successful Farming*, March 1986, P2; "Farm Bankruptcy Code Becomes Law," *Chicago Tribune*, October 29, 1986; "Washington Watch: Bankruptcy Law Change," *New York Times*, November 3, 1986; "Reagan Signs Bankruptcy Law Giving Farmers Foreclosure Aid," *Cedar Rapids Gazette*, October 28, 1986; interview with David Ostendorf, October 9, 2019.

37. "Guide to Chapter 12 Bankruptcy," *Small Farm Advocate*, Fall 1986, 3–4.

38. "Guide to Chapter 12 Bankruptcy," 4–6; "Reagan Signs."

39. Friedberger, *Shake-Out*, 99.

40. Dudley, *Debt and Dispossession*, 116–117.

41. "Letters," *Successful Farming*, May 1986, 5.

42. "Letters," 5.

43. Iowa Agricultural Loan Assistance Program, Program Guide, Terry Branstad Papers, RG 043, Box 470, File 1, SHSI-DSM; "Rules Issued for $5 Million State Interest Rate

Plan," *Des Moines Register*, March 26, 1986; Monte Sesker, "FmHA Program Could Aid Many Farmers," *Wallace's Farmer*, April 12, 1986.

44. "New Iowa Buydown Program Makes First Loan," *Des Moines Register*, April 5, 1986.

45. Steven K. Irwin to Governor Terry Branstad, received May 5, 1986, RG 043, Box 90, File 90-2; John R. Willey to Governor Terry Branstad, January 22, 1986, and Keith Heffernan to John R. Willey, February 12, 1986, RG 043, Box 90, Folder 90-1; Peggy J. Pithan to Governor Terry Branstad, received January 30, 1986, RG 043, Box 90, File 90-3; Joan Willenborg to Governor Branstad, February 28, 1986, RG 043, Box 90, File 90-1, SHSI-DSM.

46. "Potatoes Here Today," *Fonda Times*, April 24, 1986.

47. "Truck Accident Benefits the Needy," *Mapleton Press*, December 18, 1986.

48. "Thanks to Area Residents," *Mapleton Press*, December 18, 1986.

49. "Coalition Update–February 1, 1986," Iowa Farm Unity Coalition, Denise O'Brien Papers, Box 11, Organizational Involvement, Iowa Farm Unity Coalition, 1986–1995, IWA-UofI.

50. Iowa Department of Human Resources, "Food Stamps for Farmers and Self-Employed Iowans," Comm. 34 Rev. 9/86, Msc. 32, Box 4, Farm Crisis Collection, SpecColl-UNI.

51. "Food Stamp Drive Results Mixed," *Des Moines Register*, March 4, 1986.

52. Christopher Drew, "The Farmer's Last Straw: Food Stamps," *Chicago Tribune*, April 13, 1986.

53. Ames Mail Log, January–December 1986, Neal Smith Congressional Papers, Political Papers Collection, SpecColl-Drake.

54. "Commodity Groups Unite to Solve Crisis," *Wallace's Farmer*, March 8, 1986.

55. "Iowa Solidarity Day," PrairieFire Collection, MS 313, Box 20, File 6, SpecColl-ISU.

56. The full list of the groups involved includes the AFL-CIO, Consumer Federation of America, National Catholic Rural Life Conference, National Consumers League, National Council of Churches, National Council of Senior Citizens, National Education Association, National Farmers Organization, National Farmers Union, United Auto Workers, and Women Involved in Farm Economics. AFL-CIO et al., "It's Everybody's Crisis: No One Is Immune to the Family Farm Collapse," Farm Crisis Collection, Box 1, AFL-CIO file, SpecColl-UNI.

57. Aaron Brodersen to Governor Terry Branstad, February 13, 1986, Terry Branstad Papers, RG 043, Box 90, File 90-4, SHSI-DSM.

58. Deanna Potter to Governor Terry Branstad, March 25, 1986, Terry Branstad Papers, RG 043, Box 90, File 90-2, SHSI-DSM.

59. Adella Vogl to Governor Terry Branstad, April 10, 1986, Terry Branstad Papers, RG 043, Box 90, Folder 90-1, SHSI-DSM.

60. G. F. Eller to Governor Terry Branstad, March 22, 1986, Terry Branstad Papers, RG 043, Box 90, File 90-4, SHSI-DSM.

61. Jeff Tilkes to Governor Terry Branstad, received March 28, 1986, Terry Branstad Papers, RG 043, Box 90, Folder 90-1, SHSI-DSM.

62. Lohn Roenfeld to Governor Terry Branstad, January 10, 1986, Terry Branstad Papers, RG 043, Box 90, File 90-2, SHSI-DSM.

63. Micki Brummel to Governor Terry Branstad, received January 23, 1986, Terry Branstad Papers, RG 043, Box 90, File 90-4, SHSI-DSM.

64. Steve Struve to Governor Terry Branstad, received February 13, 1986, Terry Branstad Papers, RG 043, Box 90, File 90-2, SHSI-DSM.

65. Margaret Foth, "Your Time," *Kalona News*, April 17, 1986; "Help Farm Kids Cope with Stress," *Wallace's Farmer*, July 26, 1986.

66. "Fearful Farm Youth Grasp at Uprooted Life," *Des Moines Register*, February 17, 1986.

67. Jim Magdefrau, "Sour Grapes," *South Benton Star-Press*, March 19, 1986; "Four from BC Attend Farm Support Program," *Newspapers of Benton County*, November 12, 1986; "Coon Rapids Parent Council Seeks Parental Input," *Coon Rapids Enterprise*, October 23, 1986; "Rural Crisis Workshop," *Kalona News*, March 13, 1986.

68. "Surviving the Crisis: Helping Youngsters Cope with Stress," *4-H Leader* 63, no. 10 (January 1986): 14–15.

69. Kathryn Ring, "Making the Most of the Latchkey Life," *4-H Leader* 64, no. 7 (October 1986): 22–23, 26–27; Cooperative Extension Service, *On Their Own and Ok: A Guide for Parents with School-Agers Who Are Home Alone*, Iowa State University Cooperative Extension Service, Pm-1259, July 1986.

70. Kathleen Beery and Robert W. Jolly, "Extension and Research Programs on Rural Financial Stress in Iowa," in Lasley, Conger, and Stofferahn, *Farm Crisis Response*, 10–11. While Beery and Jolly did not indicate what these "alternative options" for 4-H projects were, it is likely they were projects such as cooking, baking, room remodeling and furniture refinishing, which required considerably smaller infusions of capital.

71. Scott Alan Looft to Governor Terry Branstad, January 1986, Terry Branstad Papers, RG 043, Box 90, File 90-3, SHSI-DSM.

72. Doug Mayland to Governor Terry Branstad, received January 16, 1986, Terry Branstad Papers, RG 043, Box 90, File 90-4, SHSI-DSM.

73. Cheryl Tevis, "The Fight to Keep Main Street Doors Open," *Successful Farming*, August 1986.

74. Dave Mowitz and Charlene Finck, "A Cold Winter for the Machinery Industry," *Successful Farming*, February 1986, 15–18.

75. "Fewer Patients Mean Transition for Iowa Hospitals," *Monticello Express*, June 18, 1986.

76. Cheryl Tevis, "The Fight to Keep Rural School Bells Ringing," *Successful Farming*, April 1986.

77. Cheryl Tevis, "Small Towns Scramble for New Jobs," *Successful Farming*, March 1986.

78. Diane Graham, "Cities Urged to Lay Base for Downtown," *Des Moines Register*, June 18, 1986; "Marion Gung-Ho on Downtown Revival," *Cedar Rapids Gazette*, February 6, 1986; Conference program, "Future of the Iowa Community," March 24–26, 1986, collection of the author.

79. Paul Lasley, *Iowa Farm and Rural Life Poll, Spring 1986 Summary*, Iowa State University Cooperative Extension Service, Pm-1262, June 1986, 4–6.

80. Lasley, *Iowa Farm and Rural Life Poll, Spring 1986*, 9–10.

81. Ag Decision Maker, "Iowa Cash Corn and Soybean Prices," Iowa State University Cooperative Extension Service, accessed January 13, 2020, https://www.extension.iastate.edu/agdm/crops/pdf/a2-11.pdf; Ag Decision Maker, "Historical Costs of Crop Production," Iowa State University Cooperative Extension Service, accessed January 13, 2020, https://www.extension.iastate.edu/agdm/crops/pdf/a1-21.pdf.

82. Monte Sesker, "Iowa Farmland Values Dropped 30% in 1985," *Wallace's Farmer*, January 11, 1986.

83. Monte Sesker, "What's Land Worth? Are Farmers Ready to Buy?" *Wallace's Farmer*, February 22, 1986.

84. Monet Sesker, "Farm Losses Reaffirm That Aid Is Needed," *Wallace's Farmer*, April 12, 1986.

85. Rod Swoboda, "Profitable Advice for 1987," *Wallace's Farmer*, December 1986. idem., "Farm Smart in These Tough Times," *Wallace's Farmer*, January 25, 1986.

86. Danita Allen et al., "Strategies for Middle-Sized farms," *Successful Farming*, November 1986, 11–13; "Farmers Make Adjustments," *Wallace's Farmer*, March 8, 1986.

87. Christopher Drew, "At Long Last, a Kernel of Hope," *Chicago Tribune*, March 30, 1986; "Sunnier Days Ahead," *Wallace's Farmer*, April 26, 1986, 14; George de Lama, "Reagan to Increase Farm Aid," *Chicago Tribune*, August 12, 1986; Christopher Drew, "Hope Sprouts among Farmers," *Chicago Tribune*, November 6, 1986.

Chapter 6. From Crisis to Chronic: 1987–1993

1. Dean Kleckner, "Remarks before the Iowa Banker's Association", September 22, 1987, American Farm Bureau Federation Papers, MS 479, President's Remarks, 1987, SpecColl-ISU.

2. Kleckner, "Remarks."

3. Friedberger, *Shake-Out*, 160, 165–166, 168.

4. Richard Krumme, "Across the Editor's Desk," *Successful Farming*, August 1987, 3.

5. "Letters," *Successful Farming*, November 1987, 34; "Letters," *Successful Farming*, December 1987, 6.

6. Interview with W. John Johnson, assistant dean of University Extension, February 20, 1990, Dorothy Hubbard Schwieder Papers, RS 13/12/54, Box 16, File 16, SpecColl-ISU.

7. Interview with Elizabeth A. Elliott, interim dean of University Extension and

Director of Extension, May 10, 1990, Dorothy Hubbard Schwieder Papers, RS 13/12/54, Box 16, File 16, SpecColl-ISU.

8. "When the Crisis Is Chronic," *Farm Aid Update* 1, no. 1 (Winter 1990–1991): 2, Joan Blundall Papers, Box 1, IWA-UofI.

9. Frank Holdmeyer, "Iowa Farmland Values Decline Again," *Wallace's Farmer*, January 10, 1987.

10. Monte Sesker, "Farmers Say the Economy Is Iowa's Major Problem," *Wallace's Farmer*, September 12, 1987.

11. Gil Gullickson, "Foreclosures . . . Watch Second Wave Warns Economist," *Wallace's Farmer*, November 1987; "Is Farming on the Mend?" *Successful Farming*, September 1987, 11.

12. "Hotlines Remain Open for Crisis Assistance," *Wallace's Farmer*, October 1987.

13. Gullickson, "Foreclosures"; "Is Farming on the Mend," 11.

14. Danita Allen, Gene Johnston, and Cheryl Tevis, "Opportunities Abound," *Successful Farming*, November 1987, 9–15.

15. Friedberger, 160–161.

16. Debora Wiley, "Greeley Widow Loses Fight to Save Family Farm," *Des Moines Register*, July 1, 1987.

17. "Statehouse Briefing," *Des Moines Register*, April 21, 1987; Neil E. Harl to Mr. Jim Carney, January 25, 1987, Terry Branstad Papers, RG 043, Box 453, File H, SHSI-DSM.

18. "A Positive Step in Foreclosure Reform," *Wallace's Farmer*, June 1987. Jerry Perkins, "Farm Coalition Sets '87 Lobbying Agenda," *Des Moines Register*, January 7, 1987.

19. "Mediation Valuable to Farmers, Lenders," *Wallace's Farmer*, April 11, 1987.

20. Don Muhm, "New Tax-Free Bonds Help Farmers Buy Land," *Des Moines Register*, December 18, 1987.

21. David Westphal, "Farm Credit Bailout: The Activists Win," *Des Moines Register*, December 13, 1987; "Reagan Signs Bill Rescuing Rocky Farm Credit System," *Des Moines Register*, January 4, 1988.

22. Mike Duffy, "Ag. Policy Update," no. 50, October 30, 1987, 2.

23. "99 School Districts Best," *Des Moines Register*, August 23, 1987; "Nebraska Holds Dear One-Room Schools," *Des Moines Register*, December 27, 1987.

24. Memo, Draft of Plans for Restructuring Local School Districts, Iowa Department of Education, Terry Branstad Papers, RG 043, Box 446, File 446-4, SHSI-DSM.

25. Mrs. Joe Lageschulte to Governor Terry Branstad, received March 24, 1987, Terry Branstad Papers, RG 043, Box 446, File 3, SHSI-DSM.

26. Deloma Decker to Governor Terry Branstad, March 20, 1987, and Eugene Hess to Governor Terry Branstad, March 20, 1987, Terry Branstad Papers, RG 043, Box 446, File 3, SHSI-DSM.

27. Christy Bailey to Governor Terry Branstad, March 20, 1987, Terry Branstad Papers, RG 043, Box 446, File 3, SHSI-DSM.

28. Annual Staff, Stratford High School, *The Year of the Comet*, 1987.

29. "Stratford Will Poll Students on District Choice," *Daily Freeman-Journal*, January 13, 1987; "Stratford 7–12 Grades to WC," and "Webster City School Officials Say Decision Will Help All Students," *Daily Freeman-Journal*, February 18, 1987.

30. Webster City High School Torch, *Making Our Mark*, 1988, 4.

31. Mary Farwell to Governor Terry Branstad, April 8, 1988, Terry Branstad Papers, RG 043, box 453, File F, SHSI-DSM.

32. "Iowa Land Values Climb 11%," *Wallace's Farmer*, January 12, 1988.

33. Paul Lasley, *Iowa Farm and Rural Life Poll: 1988 Summary*, Iowa State University Cooperative Extension Service, Pm-1298, October 1988, 5–7.

34. "5 Signs That Farm Depression Is Over," *Successful Farming*, January 1988; Monte Sesker, "Iowa Farm Income up $13,300," *Wallace's Farmer*, June 21, 1988.

35. Scott Kilman, "Fledgling Farmers: Some Young People Go Back to the Land despite Big Obstacles," *Wall Street Journal*, April 11, 1988.

36. Executive Committee, Iowa Farm Unity Coalition to Governor Terry Branstad, received April 5, 1988, Terry Branstad Papers, RG043, Box 456, File 1, SHSI-DSM.

37. Barry Kesler, "Video of Harlan, Iowa Protest Highlights Plight of Small Farms," *Northern Sun News*, February 1988, 10, Farm Crisis Collection, Msc. 32, Box 3, Folder 1, SpecColl-UNI; "Nun, Clergymen among 19 Arrested at Sheriff's Sale," *Carroll Daily Times Herald*, February 24, 1988.

38. Douglas Gross to G. B., March 17, 1988, Douglas Gross to G. B., May 1, 1988, and G. B. to Douglas Gross, April 30, 1988, Terry Branstad Papers, RG 043, Box 452, File 1988 B, SHSI-DSM; G. B. September 22, 1988, Terry Branstad Papers, RG 043, Box 459, File 459-7, SHSI-DSM.

39. "Stress Lingers for Farm Families," *Wallace's Farmer*, April 26, 1988; Memo to Doug Gross from Charles M. Palmer, on behalf of the Division of Mental Health, October 21, 1988, Terry Branstad Papers, RG 043, Box 459, File 459-4, SHSI-DSM.

40. Dennis Farney, "In Iowa, Mental Anguish Still Racks Families, Taxes Social Workers, Even as Farm Crisis Abates," *Wall Street Journal*, May 18, 1988.

41. "Congress Extends 'Rural Crisis' Program," *Wallace's Farmer*, April 26, 1988.

42. "Borrowers Urged to Respond to FmHA Letters," *Extension News*, December 1988, Terry Branstad Papers, RG 043, Box 459, File 459-9, SHSI-DSM.

43. Michael Tackett, "Drought in Hot Pursuit of Iowa Recovery," *Chicago Tribune*, July 10, 1988; Rob Swoboda, "Prayin' for Rain," *Wallace's Farmer*, July 12, 1988; "Drought '88," *Successful Farming*, August 1988, 12–15; "Lingering Drought in Iowa Could Hurt Spring Crops," *Iowa City Press Citizen*, November 9, 1988; "Corn Crop Estimates for Iowa, Nation Are Raised," *Des Moines Register*, November 10, 1988; "Cow Herd Liquidations Begin in Iowa," *Wallace's Farmer*, July 12, 1988.

44. Mrs. Wayne Schepers to Governor Terry Branstad, July 9, 1988, Terry Branstad Papers, RG 043, Box 455, File 5, SHSI-DSM; Amy L. Edwards, "Family Adjusts to Drought," *Iowa City Press Citizen*, September 20, 1988; Delight Bobilya Wier, "Blessings in the Midst

of Drought," *Wallace's Farmer*, September 13, 1988; Amy L. Edwards, "Farming Women Must Cope with Husband's, Own Stress," *Iowa City Press Citizen*, September 20, 1988.

45. "Will Drought Bring Back Farm Crisis," *Successful Farming*, November 1988, 27; "Iowa Values Up, but Pace Slows," *Successful Farming*, December 1988, 8.

46. Doug Gross to Rich Williamson, July 29, 1988, Terry Branstad Papers, RG 043, Box 456, File 4, and Richard Lyng to Governor Terry Branstad, August 1, 1988, Terry Branstad Papers, RG 043, Incoming Letters Reviewed by Governor 1988, August 1-August 15, 1988, SHSI-DSM.

47. "How Do You Spell (Drought) Relief?" *Successful Farming*, October 1988, 19; "How Uncle Sam Spells Drought Relief," *Wallace's Farmer*, September 13, 1988; "On First Day of Sign-Up, Iowans Stay Away in Droves," *Des Moines Register*, October 4, 1988.

48. William Petroski, "Iowans Using Food Stamps Down by 12%," *Des Moines Register*, May 20, 1988; idem., "Number of Iowa Farm Families Getting Food Stamps Falls," *Des Moines Register*, June 4, 1987.

49. Petroski, "Number of Iowa Farm Families."

50. Jane Schorer, "The Quiet Desperation of Iowa's Struggling Needy," *Des Moines Register*, December 11, 1988.

51. Cheryl Tevis, "The Frantic Courtship for New Jobs," *Successful Farming*, May 1988.

52. "CRP Will Help Most Rural Towns, Not All," *Successful Farming*, February 1988, 27; "Voice of the Farm," *Wallace's Farmer*, January 12, 1988.

53. Dennis Farney, "Losing Ground: In Iowa, the Drought Might Seal the Fate of the Smallest Towns," *Wall Street Journal*, August 30, 1988.

54. Terry Branstad, Chairman's Summary, National Governors' Association Report of the Task Force on Rural Development, "New Alliances for Rural America," 1988, 1, Terry Branstad Papers, RG 043, Box 459, File 459-9, SHSI-DSM.

55. LaVon Schiltz to Governor Terry Branstad, April 25, 1988, Terry Branstad Papers, RG 043, Box 455, File 6, SHSI-DSM.

56. David A. Jochims to Governor Terry Branstad, received March 23, 1988, and Brochure, "Come and See . . . 'the Heart of the Heartland, Rolfe, Iowa," Terry Branstad Papers, RG 043, Box 454, File 2, SHSI-DSM.

57. Marilyn Point, "Letter to the Editor," *Rolfe Arrow*, April 13, 1989.

58. Thomas A. Fogarty, "When Lottery Grants Fail to Produce Jobs, Iowa Left Holding the Bag," *Des Moines Register*, October 23, 1988.

59. Thomas A. Fogarty, "Success Stories Sprinkled among Lottery Funded Losers," *Des Moines Register*, October 25, 1988; Thomas A. Fogarty, "Big Business Lottery Grants Have Some Officials Spooked," *Des Moines Register*, October 26, 1988.

60. John F. Stilwell to Governor Terry Branstad, December 6, 1988, Terry Branstad Papers, RG 043, Box 455, File 5; James R. Alexander to Governor Terry Branstad, October 3, 1988, Terry Branstad Papers, RG 043, Box 452, File 1988A; Ackley Chamber of Commerce

to Terry Branstad, October 10, 1988, Terry Branstad Papers, RG 043, Box 452, File 1988B; James C. DeBower to Governor Terry Branstad, March 14, 1988, RG 043, Box 453, File D; J. C. Salvo to To Whom It May Concern, December 19, 1988, Terry Branstad Collection, RG 043, Box 453, File S, SHSI-DSM.

61. The *Des Moines Register* published a series of articles about the program in fall 1988. See endnotes 58 and 59.

62. Hunter Rawlings, "How to Preserve Iowa's Quality of Life," *Des Moines Register*, October 14, 1988, 15. For further discussion of the quality of life for workers in meatpacking jobs, see Deborah Fink, *Cutting into the Meatpacking Line: Workers and Change in the Rural Midwest* (Chapel Hill: University of North Carolina Press, 1998).

63. Robert C. Wahlert to Governor Terry Branstad, October 14, 1988, Terry Branstad Papers, RG 043, Box 456, File 4, SHSI-DSM.

64. Bill Conroy to Governor Terry Branstad, January 19, 1988, Terry Branstad Papers, RG 043, Box 452, File 1988C, SHSI-DSM.

65. Monte Sesker, "Farm Financial Situation," *Wallace's Farmer*, March 14, 1989.

66. Paul Lasley, *Iowa Farm and Rural Life Poll, 1989 Summary*, Iowa State University Cooperative Extension Service, Pm-1369, July 1989, 8–9.

67. Mick Kreidler, *Wallace's Farmer*, January 10, 1989; "Don't Risk Another Dry Year," *Wallace's Farmer*, April 11, 1985; "Across the Editor's Desk," *Successful Farming*, January 1989, 3; "Drought a Second Year for Some," *Wallace's Farmer*, August 8, 1989; Mick Kreidler, "Hunkering Down and Holding On," *Wallace's Farmer*, May 9, 1989.

68. Monte Sesker, "Land Prices Soar 20% Despite Drought," *Wallace's Farmer*, January 10, 1989; "Land Values Up in Corn Belt," *Successful Farming*, January 1989, 12.

69. Paul Lasley, interviewed by Pamela Riney-Kehrberg, April 5, 2018.

70. Heather MacDonald and Alan Peters, *Farm Women in the New Rural Labor Markets of the West North Central Region*, Proceedings of the Conference on the Rural Family, the Rural Community and Economic Restructuring" (Ames, IA: North Central Regional Center for Rural Development, March 1992), 53, 70.

71. Betsy Freese, "For Better, for Worse," *Successful Farming*, June 1989, 47–50.

72. "Can Their Problem Be Solved?" *Successful Farming*, November 1989, 60.

73. "Can Their Problem Be Solved," *Successful Farming*, August 1989, 52.

74. "Can Their Problem Be Solved?" *Successful Farming*, November 1989, 60.

75. "Can Their Problem Be Solved," *Successful Farming*, mid-March 1989, 48.

76. Dorothy Place, "Freedom Township Women's Club, History," 1998, IWA-UofI.

77. Omega Township Women's Club, Secretary's Book, 1984–1991, IWA-UofI.

78. "Cheryl Tevis, "Family," *Successful Farming*, mid-March 1992, 45.

79. Wanda Philips to Governor Terry Branstad, February 28, 1989, Terry Branstad Papers, RG 043, Box 466, File 466-2, SHSI-DSM.

80. Tom Hundley, "Small-Town Blues," *Chicago Tribune*, January 29, 1989.

81. Michael Tackett, "Lightning Fells Farm Activist," *Chicago Tribune*, June 2, 1989; Dirk Johnson, "Death Is as Capricious as Life for Farm Leader," *New York Times*, June 2, 1989.

82. Richard A. Gephardt, "In Memory of Dixon Terry, Farmer," May 31, 1989, Collection on Dixon Terry, MS 2014.8, Folder 2, SHSI-DSM; Curt L. Sytsma, "The Cottonwood Still Stands," *Des Moines Register*, June 8, 1989; Chuck Grassley, "A Tribute to Dixon Terry, Iowa Agricultural Leader," and Patrick Leahy, "Dixon Terry," *Congressional Record*, Senate, 135, 70, June 1, 1989; "Dixon Terry Memorial Event Held in Washington, D.C.," *Adair County Free Press*, August 2, 1989; Rich Fee, "Successful Family Farm," *Successful Farming*, August 1992, 58–60; Linda Terry, interviewed by Doris Malkmus, October 7, 2001, IWA-UofI.

83. Cheryl Tevis, "What's Happening to Life in Rural America?" *Successful Farming*, October 1992, 58.

84. "Diminished Expectations: An Exclusive Survey Report from *Successful Farming* readers," *Successful Farming*, mid-March 1992, 9–11.

85. "Diminished Expectations," 10–14.

86. "Diminished Expectations," 15.

87. "Diminished Expectations," 15.

88. Emilia E. Martinez-Brawley and Joan Blundall, "Whom Shall We Help? Farm Families' Beliefs and Attitudes about Need and Services," *Social Work* 36, no. 4 (July 1991): 315–321.

89. ICCI successfully threatened Norwest with lawsuits if the bank did not begin to provide increased credit to farmers, and particularly small farmers, in their banking area. The details can be found in the Farm Credit Organizing files, 1988–1989, ICCI, Spec Coll-Drake. "Farm Crisis Lingers into the 1990's," *Successful Farming*, April 1990, B4.

90. "Farm Finances Show Dramatic Turnaround," *Wallace's Farmer*, March 13, 1990; "On the Brink of Disaster," *Successful Farming*, August 1992, 18–20.

91. "Can Their Problem Be Solved," *Successful Farming*, mid-February 1992; "Can Their Problem Be Solved," *Successful Farming*, March 1992, 59.

92. "Successful Family Farm," *Successful Farming*, September 1991, 48–50.

93. "Successful Family Farm," *Successful Farming*, August 1991, 67–68.

94. "Successful Family Farm," *Successful Farming*, August 1992, 58–60; Loren Kruse, "Across the Editor's Desk," *Successful Farming*, February 1991, 1.

95. "Special Climate Summary: The Great Iowa Floods of 1993," Terry Branstad Papers, RG 043, Box 180, File 180-8, SHSI-DSM; Harry Hillaker, State Climatologist, Iowa Department of Agriculture and Land Stewardship, "Preliminary Monthly Weather Summary, July 1993," Terry Branstad Papers, RG 043, Box 180, File 180-8, SHSI-DSM.

96. Hillaker, "Preliminary Monthly Weather Summary."

97. "Special Climate Summary"; Gerald Waltrip to Lane Palmer, August 23, 1993, Terry Branstad Papers, RG 043, Box 320, File 320-3, SHSI-DSM; Steven Phillips, *The Soil Conservation Service Responds to the 1993 Floods* (Washington, DC: USDA, 1994), 121.

98. "Wild Weather Everywhere," *Successful Farming*, August 1993, 1.

99. "A Year When Nothing Grew in Iowa Except Frustration," *Des Moines Register*, August 22, 1993.

100. "The Year the Skies Opened Up," *Successful Farming*, September 1993, 12.

101. Cheryl Tevis, "Family," *Successful Farming*, September 1993, 37.

102. "A Year When Nothing Grew."

103. Iowa State University Cooperative Extension, "Iowa Concern/Rural Concern Narrative, August 1993," Terry Branstad Papers, RG 043, Box 180, File 180-7, SHSI-DSM.

104. "PrairieFire Prepared to Begin Rural Flood Recovery Program," *Cedar Rapids Gazette*, August 5, 1993.

105. "Disaster Not Over in Iowa," *Cedar Rapids Gazette*, October 24, 1993.

106. "A Year When Nothing Grew"; "Flood Aggravates Weakened Farm Finances," *Iowa Press Citizen*, September 25, 1993.

107. Dale Kueter, "Iowa's Worst Disaster," *Cedar Rapids Gazette*, July 14, 1993.

108. "Unemployment Pay for Some Flooded Farmers," *Cedar Rapids Gazette*, August 5, 1993.

109. Memo to Governor Terry Branstad and staff from Bob Furleigh and Bobbie Finch, November 17, 1993, Terry Branstad Papers, RG 043, Box 180, File 180-9, SHSI-DSM.

Epilogue: Last-Generation Farmers

1. Some parts of this epilogue were previously published as Pamela Riney-Kehrberg, Presidential Address, "Persistence, Change, and Thinking Big about Small Places: Some Thoughts about the Practical Applications of Rural and Agricultural History," *Agricultural History* 88, no. 1 (Winter 2014): 3–17.

2. Frederick O. Lorenz et al., "After Farming: Emotional Health Trajectories of Farm, Nonfarm, and Displaced Farm Couples," *Rural Sociology* 65, no. 1 (March 2000): 67–69; F. Larry Leistritz, "Impacts of Rural Economic Restructuring: Characteristics and Experiences of Displaced Families in North Dakota," in *The Rural Family, the Rural Community, and Economic Restructuring*, ed. Ken Root et al. (Ames, IA: North Central Regional Center for Rural Development, March 1992): 132–133. While the data for the previous article is specific to North Dakota, the experiences reflected in the North Dakota research are essentially those of families in Iowa.

3. Glen H. Elder Jr. and Rand D. Conger, *Children of the Land: Adversity and Success in Rural America* (Chicago: University of Chicago Press, 2000), 25–26, 221–230.

4. David J. Peters, *Iowa Population over 100 Years*, Iowa State University Cooperative Extension Service, Pm-3010, February 2011, 3https://lib.dr.iastate.edu/cgi/viewcontent.cgi?article=1008&context=extension_communities_pubs.

5. United States Census Bureau, "QuickFacts: Iowa," accessed March 4, 2020, https://www.census.gov/quickfacts/IA.

6. Iowa Cooperative Extension Service, Community Indicators Program, Urban Percentage of Population for the States, Historical, accessed March 4, 2020, https://www.icip.iastate.edu/tables/population/urban-pct-counties.

7. US Department of Commerce, Bureau of the Census, *1992 Census of Agriculture*, vol. 1 (Washington, DC: US GPO, 1994): part 15, Iowa, 8–9; part 23, Minnesota, 8–9; part 49, Wisconsin, 8–9; part 13, Illinois, 8–9.

8. *1992 Census of Agriculture*, vol. 1, part 15, Iowa, 8–9; part 23.

9. *1992 Census of Agriculture*, vol. 1, part 15, Iowa, 8–9; part 23; Iowa State University Cooperative Extension Service, Iowa Community Indicators Program, Average Farm Size in Acres, accessed March 27, 2020, https://www.icip.iastate.edu/tables/agriculture/avg-farm-size; F. Larry Leistritz and Katherine Meyer, "Farm Crisis in the Midwest: Trends and Implications," in Lasley et al., *Beyond the Amber Waves of Grain*, 216.

10. US Department of Commerce, Bureau of the Census, *1978 Census of Agriculture*, vol. 1, part 15, Iowa (Washington, DC: US GPO, 1981), 118–120; *1992 Census of Agriculture*, vol. 1, part 15, Iowa, 245–257.

11. Wendong Zhang, Iowa State University Cooperative Extension Program, Historical Iowa Farmland Value Survey by County, Ag Decision Maker, File C-2 72, accessed April 3, 2020, https://www.extension.iastate.edu/agdm/wholefarm/pdf/c2-72.pdf.

12. Iowa State University Cooperative Extension Service, Community Indicators Program, Number of Farms by County, 1900–2012, accessed April 3, 2020, https://www.icip.iastate.edu/tables/agriculture/farms-by-county.

13. US Department of Commerce, Bureau of the Census, *1982 Census of Agriculture*, vol. 1, part 15, Iowa (Washington, DC: US GPO, 1984), 120–132.

14. *1982 Census of Agriculture*, 232–244.

15. *1982 Census of Agriculture*, 232–244.

16. *1982 Census of Agriculture*, 192–204.

17. Linda M. Lobao and Paul Lasley, "Farm Restructuring and Crisis in the Heartland: An Introduction," in Lasley et al., 7.

18. *1978 Census of Agriculture*, vol. 1, part 15, Iowa, 3.

19. *1982 Census of Agriculture*, vol. 1, part 15, Iowa, 192; *1992 Census of Agriculture*, vol. 1, part 15, Iowa, 330.

20. *1992 Census of Agriculture*, vol. 1, part 15, Iowa, 8.

21. US Department of Commerce, Bureau of the Census, *2017 Census of Agriculture*, State Data, Selected Operation and Producer Characteristics, https://www.nass.usda.gov/Publications/AgCensus/2017/Full_Report/Volume_1,_Chapter_2_US_State_Level/st99_2_0045_0045.pdf.

22. *1992 Census of Agriculture*, vol. 1, part 15, 8.

23. Maynard Hogberg, interview by Pamela Riney-Kehrberg, September 28, 2018; for a historical account of the evolution of hog production, and especially the rise of large

confinement operations, see J. L. Anderson, *Capitalist Pigs: Pigs, Pork, and Power in America* (Morgantown: University of West Virginia, 2019).

24. Vic and Cindy Madsen, "A More Complete Farm," in *The Future of Family Farms: Practical Farmers' Legacy Letters Project*, ed. Teresa Opheim (Iowa City: University of Iowa Press, 2016), 66–73; Notice, Practical Farmers of Iowa, 1985, Practical Farmers of Iowa Papers, MS 449, Folder 1, SpecColl-ISU.

25. *1992 Census of Agriculture*, vol. 1, part 15, 317–329.

26. Robert Wuthnow, *The Left Behind: Decline and Rage in Rural America* (Princeton: Princeton University Press, 2018), 35.

27. Patrick J. Carr and Maria J. Kefalas, *Hollowing Out the Middle: The Rural Brain Drain and What It Means for America* (Boston: Beacon Press, 2009), 24, 30, 42–43.

28. Carr and Kefalas, *Hollowing Out the Middle*, 139.

29. Robert Wuthnow, *Small-Town America: Finding Community, Shaping the Future* (Princeton: Princeton University Press, 2013).

30. United States Department of Agriculture, Economic Research Service, Population map, 2001–2008, accessed April 7, 2020, https://www.ers.usda.gov/webdocs/charts/57700/popmap0108.png?v=1583.7; and Population map, 2010–2017, accessed April 7, 2020, https://www.ers.usda.gov/webdocs/charts/57704/popmap1017.png?v=3470.3.

31. See Leah Fran Tookey, "Maintaining *Gemeinschaft* during a Century of Change: Rural School Consolidation in Iowa, a Case Study" (MA thesis, Iowa State University, 2003).

32. Eric Hoiberg, "Irwin, Iowa: Persistence and Change in Shelby County," in A. E. Luloff, and R. S. Krannich, eds., *Persistence and Change in Rural Communities: A 50-year follow up to Six Classic Studies* (New York: CABI, 2002), 59–62.

33. Hoiberg, "Irwin, Iowa," 57.

34. Pocahontas County Board of Supervisors, Notice, *Pocahontas Record Democrat*, August 25, 1992; "Polls Will Be Open Sept. 14 for Schoolhouse Levy Vote," *Pocahontas Record Democrat*, September 14, 1993.

35. City of Rolfe, Community website, accessed March 11, 2020, http://rolfeiowa.com/.

36. City of Rolfe, Community website, https://rolfeiowa.com/.

37. City of Rolfe, Community website.

38. Dustin Ingram, "For Sale or Rent: Preventing Demolition by Neglect in Iowa's Downtowns," Creative Component, Master's in Community and Regional Planning, Iowa State University, 2019.

39. Ingram, "For Sale or Rent."

40. Peters, "Iowa Population over 100 Years," 10.

41. Iowa State University Extension and Outreach, Rural Sociology, "Shrink-Smart Small Towns: Communities Can Still Thrive as They Lose Population," November 2017, 1–2, accessed March 10, 2020, https://store.extension.iastate.edu/product/Shrink-Smart-Small-Towns-Communities-can-still-thrive-as-they-lose-population.

42. Jeremy Hobson, "In Iowa, Small Towns with Declining Populations Learn how to 'Shrink Smart,'" interview on *Here and Now*, WBUR Boston, December 16, 2019, https://www.wbur.org/hereandnow/2019/12/16/iowa-towns-shrink-smart.

43. Robert Wuthnow, *Remaking the Heartland: Middle America since the 1950s* (Princeton: Princeton University Press, 2011), 167.

44. Wuthnow, *Remaking the Heartland*, 165–168.

45. Wuthnow, *Remaking the Heartland*, 257–259.

46. Wendy Haight et al., *Children of Methamphetamine-Involved Families: The Case of Rural Illinois* (Oxford: Oxford University Press, 2009), 9.

47. Haight et al., *Children*, 27.

48. See Nick Reding, *Methland: The Death and Life of an American Small Town* (New York: Bloomsbury, 2009), 15–18; Fink, *Cutting into the Meatpacking Line*, 35, 64–65.

49. "Former Actor Sentenced to Prison on Drug Charges," *Courier*, July 12, 2013, https://wcfcourier.com/news/local/former-actor-sentenced-to-prison-on-drug-charges/article_c13615c8-ead3-11e2-8942-0019bb2963f4.html.

50. Kate Zernike, "Potent Mexican Meth Floods in as States Curb Domestic Variety," *New York Times*, January 23, 2006.

51. David J. Peters, *Understanding the Opioid Crisis in Rural and Urban Iowa*, Iowa State University Extension and Outreach, January 2019, 3–4, 11.

52. United States Department of Agriculture, Economic Research Service, Description and Maps, County Economic Types, 2015 edition, accessed April 14, 2020, https://www.ers.usda.gov/data-products/county-typology-codes/descriptions-and-maps/.

53. "Iowa Dairies Closing Doors," *Des Moines Register*, November 4, 2018.

54. "More Iowa Farmers Face Credit Crunch," *Des Moines Register*, April 14, 2019.

55. Mike Rosmann as told to Emily Atkin, "I Work with Suicidal Farmers. It's Becoming Too Much to Bear," *New Republic*, April 22, 2019, https://newrepublic.com/article/153604/work-suicidal-farmers-its-becoming-much-bear.

56. American Farm Bureau Federation, "Farm Bureau: Seeding Rural Resilience Act Will Help Farmers and Ranchers," October 16, 2019, https://www.fb.org/newsroom/farm-bureau-seeding-rural-resilience-act-will-help-farmers-and-ranchers.

57. "Why Are America's Farmers Killing Themselves in Record Numbers?" *Guardian*, December 6, 2017, https://www.theguardian.com/us-news/2017/dec/06/why-are-americas-farmers-killing-themselves-in-record-numbers.

58. "Grassley Bill Aims to Curb Suicide among Farmers," *Des Moines Register*, November 11, 2019, A 6; H.R. 4820, Seeding Rural Resilience Act, 116th Congress, 2019–2020, current legislation, Congress.gov, accessed April 17, 2020, https://www.congress.gov/bill/116th-congress/house-bill/4820?s=1&r=7.

59. John Lawrence, "Addressing Mental Health and the Farm Economy," Iowa State University Extension and Outreach, October 10, 2019, https://blogs.extension.iastate.edu/didyouknow/tag/mental-health/.

60. Iowa Results, Election 2016, *New York Times*, week of November 8, 2016, updated February 2017, https://www.nytimes.com/elections/2016/results/iowa.

61. David Wasserman, "The One County in America That Voted in a Landslide for Both Trump and Obama," ABC News, *FiveThirtyEight*, November 9, 2017, https://fivethirtyeight.com/features/the-one-county-in-america-that-voted-in-a-landslide-for-both-trump-and-obama/.

62. Wuthnow, *The Left Behind*, 161.

63. "Wisconsin Farmers Forced to Dump Milk as Coronavirus Slams a Fragile Dairy Economy," *USA Today*, April 3, 2020, https://www.usatoday.com/story/money/2020/04/03/coronavirus-forces-dairy-farmers-dump-milk-wisconsin-covid-19/2939959001/; Dermot J. Hayes et al., "The Impact of COVID-19 on Iowa's Corn, Soybean, Ethanol, Beef, and Pork Sectors," CARD Policy Brief 20-PB 28, April 2020, https://www.card.iastate.edu/products/policy-briefs/display/?n=1301.

64. News release, "Smithfield Foods to Close Sioux Falls, SD Plant Indefinitely amid COVID-19," April 12, 2020, https://www.smithfieldfoods.com/press-room/company-news/smithfield-foods-to-close-sioux-falls-sd-plant-indefinitely-amid-covid-19; "Columbus Junction Pork Processing Plant Hit Hard by Coronavirus with 186 Cases," *Des Moines Register*, April 14, 2020, https://www.desmoinesregister.com/story/news/2020/04/14/testing-rural-iowa-covid-19-coronavirus-tyson-food-pork-processing/2989203001/.

65. Steven Lonergan, correspondence with the author, April 21, 2020; "'Horrible Choices': Iowa Livestock Producers May Have to Euthanize Pigs as Packing Plants Struggle," *Des Moines Register*, April 21, 2020, https://www.desmoinesregister.com/story/money/agriculture/2020/04/21/coronavirus-meatpacking-slowdown-force-iowa-pork-producers-euthanize-pigs-covid-19/5164368002/.

66. "POET Idles Ethanol Plants; Corn Farmers Lose Home for 110 Million Bushels," *Successful Farming*, April 7, 2020; Hayes et al., "The Impact of COVID-19."

67. "Health Care Facilities in Rural Iowa," map, *Cedar Rapids Gazette*, September 30, 2019, https://www.thegazette.com/data/rural-health-care.

68. Megan L. Srinivas, "Rural America Is Not Ready for COVID-19," *Des Moines Register*, April 7, 2020, https://www.desmoinesregister.com/story/opinion/columnists/2020/04/07/rural-america-not-ready-covid-19/2952724001/.

69. Hogberg interview.

70. Hogberg interview.

71. Gordon J. Arbuckle Jr., *Iowa Farm and Rural Life Poll: 2014 Summary Report*, Iowa State University Extension and Outreach, August 2015, 2–6.

A Note on Sources

This book is informed by a wide variety of sources, both published and unpublished. I rely heavily on documents from Iowa State University's Cooperative Extension Service, newspapers from across Iowa, both small and large, oral histories, organization records, and state government records. I intend to home the oral histories with the Special Collections at Iowa State University. There are significant collections of Farm Crisis materials in the Special Collections at Iowa State University, including the records of farm organizations and the Cooperative Extension Service. The University of Northern Iowa's Rod Library houses a Farm Crisis collection, including a great deal of information from activists and mental health professionals in eastern Iowa. The records at the Iowa Women's Archives, part of the University of Iowa Libraries, also house important documents from women's groups and various activists, such as Denise O'Brien, Carol Hodne, and Joan Blundall.

The most important of the research materials have been the papers of Governors Robert Ray and Terry Branstad. Policy papers from inside both administrations helped me tease out what was happening in the statehouse during these difficult years. These collections also include thousands of letters from Iowans. I have used these letters liberally, but with care. In the case of materials in which an individual discussed their own mental health or that of a family member, I have identified them in my citations only with initials, and without mentioning their hometown or county. I have done the same for detailed discussions of family finances. In cases where a family's situation was widely known due to newspaper coverage, such as those of Ralph and Rita Engelken or Kenneth Meisgeier, I have not anonymized information about their finances and physical and mental health conditions. At the time I wrote this book, Terry Branstad's gubernatorial papers had yet to be processed. They may never be: there are thirteen hundred boxes of records, and the State Historical Society of Iowa has a limited budget. If they are eventually processed, my footnotes may cease to be useful to researchers.

The Farm Crisis has only recently become history in the way that historians think of the term, which means the secondary literature is fairly thin. The only full-length treatment of the Farm Crisis written by a historian, Mark Friedberger's book, *Shake-Out: Iowa Farm Families in the 1980s*, was researched early and mid-decade and published in 1989, while the crisis was still playing out. It remains a useful, intensive study of farmers in several central Iowa counties and how they and their farms weathered the crisis. Anthropologist Kathryn

Marie Dudley authored her valuable work, *Debt and Dispossession: Farm Loss in America's Heartland*, another farm crisis story, about a single Minnesota county. She has examined in depth the burden of shame and embarrassment that debt and farm loss imposed on farm families. Glen H. Elder and Rand Conger's *Children of the Land: Adversity and Success in Rural America* provides analysis of childhood experiences during and immediately after the crisis. Rural sociologist Robert Wuthnow, in his books *Remaking the Heartland: Middle America Since the 1950s*, *In the Blood*, and *The Left Behind*, helps to explain the possible demographic results of long-term change in the countryside, as well as the impact of that change on the attitudes and beliefs of rural people. A very helpful multidisciplinary work is *Beyond the Amber Waves of Grain: An Examination of Social and Economic Restructuring in the Heartland*. Edited by Paul Lasley, F. Larry Leistritz, Linda M. Lobao, and Katherine Meyer, the book gathers together analysis from agricultural economists, sociologists, rural sociologists, and home economists. It provides a statistically dense study of the ways in which the crisis affected farm families all across the Midwest, changing their lives. I look forward to the publication of Rebecca Stoil Shimoni's dissertation, *Tied to Their Country: Agrarian Mobilization, Rural Politics, and the Farm Crisis of 1977–1987*. Her work focuses on political activism and mobilization across the United States.

For those who want to delve into the moral and ethical dimensions of the shape of American agriculture, I strongly recommend Gary Comstock's edited work, *Is There a Moral Obligation to Save the Family Farm?* Published in 1987, the book contains a number of essays on the topic, from multiple perspectives. Many of the most important participants in Iowa's Farm Crisis story contributed pieces to this work, including Denise O'Brien, Paul Lasley, and Bishop Maurice Dingman.

Bibliography

Primary Sources

Archival Collections

Iowa Women's Archives, University of Iowa Libraries, Iowa City, Iowa (IWA-UofI)
    Joan Blundall Papers
    Franklin Township Farm Bureau Women, O'Brien County
    Freedom Township Women's Club Secretary's Book
    Greene Township Women's Club, Iowa County
    Mahaska County Farm Bureau Women, Annual Reports
    Denise O'Brien Papers
    Omega Township Women's Club, O'Brien County
    Sharon Township Farm Bureau Women's Club
Political Papers Collection, Drake University Archives and Special Collections, Des Moines, Iowa (SpecColl-Drake)
    Harkin, Thomas R. Political Papers
    Iowa Citizens for Community Improvement Papers
    Neal Smith Papers
Robert J. Dole Archive and Special Collections, University of Kansas
    Dole Digital Collections
Ruth Lilly Special Collections and Archives, Indiana University—Purdue University, Indianapolis
    FFA Organization Records
Special Collections, Parks Library, Iowa State University, Ames, Iowa (SpecColl-ISU)
    Center for Rural Affairs. MS 413.
    Farm Crisis Committee. MS 482.
    Government of the Student Body. Farm Crisis Scholarships, Box 14, Folders 8-9, 1986-1987.
    Iowa Farm Bureau Federation. MS 105.
    Iowa Organization of Women for Agriculture. MS 318.
    National Crisis Action Rally. MS 435.

National Family Farm Coalition. MS 548.
North American Farm Alliance. MS 501.
People United for Rural Education. MS 300.
Practical Farmers of Iowa. MS 449.
PrairieFire Rural Action Records. MS 313.
Rural Coalition. MS 368.
Schwieder, Dorothy Hubbard Papers. RS 13/12/54.
Special Collections, Rod Library, University of Northern Iowa, Waterloo, Iowa (SpecColl-UNI)
Farm Crisis Collection
State Historical Society of Iowa, Des Moines, Iowa (SHSI-DSM)
Banking Records, State of Iowa. RG 010.
Terry Branstad, Governor's Papers. RG 043.
Iowa Department of Agriculture and Land Stewardship. RG 04.
Robert Ray, Governor's Papers. RG 043.
Dixon Terry Collection. MS 2014.8.

Iowa Cooperative Extension Documents

Barranti, Chrystal. *Take Charge in Changing Times: Encouraging a Friend to Seek Professional Help*. Pm-1214. July 1985.

———. *Take Charge in Changing Times: Growing Together—Improving Family Communication*. Pm-1200. April 1985.

———. *Take Charge in Changing Times: Support for Friends Who Are Depressed*. Pm-1219. September 1985.

Bultena, Gordon, Paul Lasley, and Eric Hoiberg. *Educational, Occupational, and Residential Patterns of Iowa Farm-Reared Youth*. Pm-1108. July 1983.

Cooperative Extension Service, Iowa State University. *ASSIST: Helping Iowans Deal with Farm Financial Problems*. Pm-1260. June 1986.

———. *Building Family Strengths*. Pm-1122a. 1984.

———. *Family Economic Stability and Security*. Pm-1122b. 1984.

———. *Managing Family Finances*. Pm-1232a-d. 1986.

Duffy, Mike, and Joy Banyas. *FarmAid—Farm Financial Analysis . . . Free and Confidential*. Pm-1272. 1986.

Edwards, William, and Cynthia Needles Fletcher. *Take Charge in Changing Times: Managing Farm Finances*. Pm-1173. November 1984.

Fletcher, Cynthia Needles. *Family Living Expense Planning for Farm and Business Families*. Adapted for Iowa use. Pm-1243. January 1986.

———. *Take Charge in Changing Times: Dealing with Creditors*. Pm-1195. February 1985.

Harmelink, Ruth I. *Lenders: Working through the Farm-Lender Crisis*. Pm-1244. April 1986.

Hoiberg, Eric O., and Wallace Huffman. *Profile of Iowa Farms and Farm Families: 1976* (Ames: Iowa Agricultural and Home Economics Experiment Station and Cooperative Extension Service, Iowa State University, 1978).

Iowa Cooperative Extension Service. Community Indicators Program. Accessed March 4, 2020. https://www.icip.iastate.edu/tables/.

———. Rural Sociology, "Shrink-Smart Small Towns: Communities Can Still Thrive as They Lose Population." SOC 3038, November 2017. Accessed March 10, 2020. https://store.extension.iastate.edu/product/Shrink-Smart-Small-Towns-Communities-can-still-thrive-as-they-lose-population.

Jones, Ron, and Barbara Abbott. *Helping Families Cope with the Stress of Change.* Pm-1025. December 1981.

Kline, Robin, Phyllis Olson, and Diane Nelson. *Take Charge in Changing Times: How to Set up an Emergency Food Pantry.* Pm-1179 (rev.). February 1985.

Labensohn, Dorothy, Carol Hans, and Barbara Abbott. *On Their Own and OK: A Guide for Parents with School-Agers Who Are Home Alone.* Pm-1259. July 1986.

Lasley, Paul, Rand Conger, and Curtis Stofferahn, eds. *Farm Crisis Response: Extension and Research Activities in the North Central Region.* 1986.

———. *Iowa Farm and Rural Life Poll.* 1983–1993.

Lasley, Paul, Rand Conger, Curtis Stofferahn, and Willis Goudy. *Changes in Iowa Agriculture, 1978–1982.* Pm-1152. April 1984.

Molgaard, Virginia. *Depression: Causes, Effects and Treatment.* Pm-1230. November 1985.

———. *Family Stress. Dealing with Blame: Help for Families in Crisis.* Pm-1224. October 1985.

———. *Family Stress: Dealing with Blame: Help for Farm Families in Crisis—Leaders Guide.* Pm-1223. October 1985.

———. *Family Stress in the Middle Years.* Pm-1246. April 1986.

———. *Family Stress. Perception. A Key Variable in Family Stress Management.* Pm-1247. April 1986.

———. *The Rural Crisis Comes to School: Teacher Handout for Videotape,* August 1985.

———. *Self-Help Groups: Guidelines for a Self-Help Group.* Pm-1221c. October 1985.

———. *Self-Help Groups: The Role of Organizer in a Self-Help Group.* Pm-1221a. October 1985.

———. *Self-Help Groups: What They Are and How They Can Help You.* Pm-1221b. October 1985.

———. *Take Charge in Changing Times: How to Help "When You Don't Know What to Say".* Pm-1273. September 1986.

———. *Take Charge in Changing Times: Rebuilding Self-Esteem—Ideas for Farm Men and Women.* Pm-1276. September 1986.

Molgaard, Virginia, and Barb Abbott. *Take Charge in Changing Times: Moving on: Getting an Off-Farm Job.* Pm-1234c. September 1987.

Molgaard, Virginia, and Joy Banyas. *ASSIST: Coping with Stress and Finding Personal Support*. Pm-1278. September 1986.

Molgaard, Virginia, and Jeanene Muller. *Take Charge in Changing Times. Landing a Job: Strategies for Farm Wives*. Pm-1234a. December 1985.

Otto, Daniel. *Analysis of Farmers Leaving Agriculture for Financial Reasons: Summary of Survey Results from 1984*. Pm-1207. June 1985.

Peters, David J. *Iowa Population Over 100 Years*. Pm-3010, February 2011. Accessed March 27, 2020, https://lib.dr.iastate.edu/cgi/viewcontent.cgi?article=1008&context=extension_communities_pubs.

———. *Understanding the Opioid Crisis in Rural and Urban Iowa*. SOC 3088, 2019.

Pitzer, Ronald. *Helping Persons Cope with Change, Crisis and Loss*. Pm-1220. September 1985.

Trachta, Jeanne, Randy Weigel, and Barbara Abbott. *Stress on the Farm. Lesson 4: Resolving Farm Family Conflicts*. Pm-1172d. November 1984.

Weigel, Randy. "Helping Farmers Handle Stress," *Journal of Extension* (May–June 1980): 37–40.

———. *Let Go of Your Depression. Adapted for Iowa Use*. Pm-1154 (rev.). May 1985.

———. *Stress on the Farm—An Overview*. Pm-988. March 1981.

———. *Stress on the Farm—Skills for Stress Management*. Pm-988d. March 1981.

———. *Take Charge in Changing Times: Your Best Friend Is You*. Pm-1191. 1985.

Weigel, Randy, Catherine Hoag, Marilyn Schnittjer, and Barbara Abbott. *Stress on the Farm. Lesson 6: Keeping the Farm Family Operating*. Pm-1172f. November 1984.

Weigel, Randy, Jean Hood, and Barbara Abbott. *Stress on the Farm. Lesson 3: Understanding Depression—Yours and Theirs*. Pm-1172c. November 1984.

Weigel, Randy, Sharon Mays, and Barbara Abbott. *Stress on the Farm. Lesson 1: Stress Management for the Health of It*. Pm-1172a. November 1984.

———. *Stress on the Farm. Lesson 2: Stress Management—Taking Charge*. Pm-1172b. November 1984.

Weigel, Randy, Marilyn Schnittjer, and Barbara Abbott. *Stress on the Farm. Lesson 5: From Family Stress to Family Strengths*. Pm-1172e. November 1984.

Other Government Documents

99th Congress, 2d Session, Joint Economic Committee, Congress of the United States. *New Dimensions in Rural Policy: Building upon Our Heritage*. Washington, DC: US Government Printing Office, 1986.

Center for Rural Health Research. Annual Reports, 1980–1990.

Glaser, Lewrene K. *Provisions of the Food Security Act of 1985*, Agriculture Information Bulletin no. 498. Washington, DC: Economic Research Service, United States Department of Agriculture, 1986.

Iowa Department of Public Instruction. Biennial Reports, 1980–1990.
Iowa Mental Health Authority. Biennial Reports, 1980–1990.
Phillips, Steven. *The Soil Conservation Service Responds to the 1993 Floods*. Washington, DC: Soil Conservation Service, 1994.
United States Census Bureau. "QuickFacts: Iowa." Accessed March 4, 2020. https://www.census.gov/quickfacts/IA.
United States Department of Agriculture. *An Initial Assessment of the Payment-in-Kind Program*. Washington, DC: US Government Printing Office, 1983.
———. *1969 Census of Agriculture, Farms: Number, Use of Land, Size of Farm*, vol. 2, *General Report*. Washington, DC: USDA, 1973.
United States Department of Agriculture, Economic Research Service. Description and Maps, County Economic Types, 2015 edition. Accessed April 14, 2020. https://www.ers.usda.gov/data-products/county-typology-codes/descriptions-and-maps/.
United States Department of Commerce, Bureau of the Census. *1978 Census of Agriculture*, vol. 1. Washington, DC: US Government Printing Office, 1981.
———. *1982 Census of Agriculture*, vol. 1. Washington, DC: US Government Printing Office, 1984.
———. *1987 Census of Agriculture*, vol. 1. Washington, DC: US Government Printing Office, 1989.
———. *1992 Census of Agriculture*, vol. 1. Washington, DC: US Government Printing Office, 1994.

Published Primary Sources

Committee for Economic Development. *An Adaptive Program for Agriculture: Statement on National Policy by the Research and Policy Committee of the Committee for Economic Development*. New York: Committee for Economic Development, 1962.
Comstock, Gary, ed. *Is There a Moral Obligation to Save the Family Farm?* Ames: Iowa State University Press, 1987.
Dovring, Folke. "The Farmland Boom in Illinois." *Illinois Agricultural Economics* 17, no. 2 (July 1977): 34–38.
Harper, Joe. *FARM/CAP Status Report, December 1, 1985 to June 30, 1986*. Des Moines: Des Moines Area Community College, 1986.
Madsen, Vic, and Cindy. "A More Complete Farm." In *The Future of Family Farms: Practical Farmers' Legacy Letters Project*, edited by Teresa Opheim, 66–73. Iowa City: University of Iowa Press, 2016.
Martinez-Brawley, Emilia E., and Joan Blundall. "Whom Shall We Help? Farm Families' Beliefs and Attitudes about Need and Services." *Social Work* 36, no. 4 (July 1991): 315–321.
———. "Farm Families' Preferences toward the Personal Social Services." *Social Work* 34, no. 6 (1989): 513–522.

O'Brien, Denise. "Memories of the Crisis." *Middle West Review* 2, no. 1 (Fall 2015): 51–68.
Ritchie, Mark. *Loss of Our Family Farms: Inevitable Results of Conscious Policies*. Minneapolis: League of Rural Voters, 1979.

Periodicals/Journals/Newspapers

Adair County Free Press
Advocate-News (Wilton/Durant, IA)
Akron Register-Tribune
Ames Tribune
Battle Creek Times
Benton/Iowa County Farmer
Buena Vista County Journal
Catholic Rural Life
Cedar Rapids Gazette
Chicago Tribune
Chronicle (Odebolt, IA)
Coon Rapids Enterprise
Courier
The Cyclone
Daily Freeman Journal
Daily Iowegian (Centerville, IA)
Des Moines Register
Elgin Echo
Farm Aid Update
Farm Journal
Farm Show Magazine
Farm Wife News/Farm Woman News/Country Woman
Fonda Times
4-H Leader
Guardian (UK)
Hamilton County Freeman Journal
Harlan News-Advertiser
Harlan Tribune
Hartley Sentinel
High Flyers (Fonda Community School)
Iowa City Press-Citizen
Iowa Farm Outlook
Journal of the Senate (State of Iowa)
Kalona News

Kingsley News Times
Ladies' Home Journal
LeMars Daily Sentinel
Madisonian (Winterset, IA)
Mapleton Press
Maquoketa Sentinel-Press
Mellinger Sun-News
Minneapolis Star Tribune
Monticello Express
Mount Pleasant News
National 4-H News
National Future Farmer
New Republic
Newspapers of Benton County
New York Times
NFO Reporter
Pocahontas Record Democrat
Redbook
Rolfe Arrow
Rural Development News
Saint Cloud Times (MN)
Sioux Center News
Sioux County Capital
Sioux Falls Argus-Leader (SD)
Small Farm Advocate
South Benton Star-Press
South Hamilton Record-News (Jewell, IA)
Successful Farming
Storm Lake Tribune
USA Today
Wallace's Farmer
Wall Street Journal
Walnut Bureau
Washington Post
WIFE Line

Yearbooks

Bomb Yearbook (Iowa State University)
Boone Scroll

Harlan Harpoon
Stratford Yearbook
Webster City Torch

Oral Histories

Brandstad, Terry. Governor
Ellsworth, Beth
Grassley, Charles (Chuck). Senator
Harper, Joseph
Hoberg, Maynard
Hunter, Edith
Lasley, Paul
Ostendorf, David
Sapp, Stephen
Terry, Linda. Voices of the Land Collection. Iowa Women's Archives, Iowa City, IA.
Tevis, Cheryl
Tookey, Leah

Secondary Sources

Adams, Jane, ed. *Fighting for the Farm: Rural America Transformed*. Philadelphia: University of Pennsylvania Press, 2003.

Anderson, J. L. *Capitalist Pigs: Pigs, Pork, and Power in America*. Morgantown: University of West Virginia, 2019.

———. *Industrializing the Corn Belt: Agriculture, Technology, and Environment, 1945–1972*. DeKalb: Northern Illinois University Press, 2009.

Anderson, J. L., ed. *The Rural Midwest since World War II*. DeKalb: Northern Illinois University Press, 2014.

Barker Devine, Jenny. *On Behalf of the Family Farm: Iowa Farm Women's Activism since 1945*. Iowa City: University of Iowa Press, 2013.

Barnett, Barry J. "The U.S. Farm Financial Crisis of the 1980s." *Agricultural History* 74, no. 2 (Spring 2000): 366–380.

Bird, Caroline. *The Invisible Scar: The Great Depression, and What It Did to American Life, from Then until Now*. Philadelphia: D. McKay, 1966.

Blundall, Joan. "The Initial Response from a Community Mental Health Center," *Human Services in the Rural Environment* 10, no. 1 (1986): 30

Carr, Patrick J., and Maria J. Kefalas. *Hollowing Out the Middle: The Rural Brain Drain and What It Means for America*. Boston: Beacon Press, 2009.

BIBLIOGRAPHY

Chapman, Mike. *Iowa's Record Setting Governor: The Terry Branstad Story*. Des Moines: Business Publications, 2015.

Danbom, David B. *Born in the Country: A History of Rural America*. Baltimore: Johns Hopkins University Press, 1995.

Dudley, Kathryn Marie. *Debt and Dispossession: Farm Loss in America's Heartland*. Chicago: University of Chicago Press, 2000.

Eayrs, Sonja Trom. "Protecting America's Farmers under State Mediation Laws and Chapter 12: Who's Being Protected?" *Marquette Law Review* 72, no. 3 (Spring 1989): 466–493.

Eicher, John. "'Every Family on Their Own?': Iowa's Mennonite Farm Communities and the 1980s Farm Crisis." *Journal of Mennonite Studies* 35 (2017): 75–96.

Elder, Glen H. *Children of the Great Depression: Social Change in Life Experience*. Chicago: University of Chicago Press, 1974.

Elder, Glen H., and Rand Conger. *Children of the Land: Adversity and Success in Rural America*. Chicago: University of Chicago Press, 2000.

———. *Families in Troubled Times: Adapting to Change in Rural America*. Hawthorn, NY: Aldine de Gruyter, 1994.

Fink, Deborah. *Cutting into the Meat Packing Line: Workers and Change in the Rural Midwest*. Chapel Hill: University of North Carolina Press, 1988.

———. *Open Country, Iowa: Rural Women, Tradition and Change*. Albany: State University of New York Press, 1986.

Fink, Deborah, and Dorothy Schwieder. "Iowa Farm Women in the 1930s." *Annals of Iowa* 49, no. 7 (Winter 1989): 570–590.

Foley, Michael Stewart. "'Everyone Was Pounding on Us': Front Porch Politics and the American Farm Crisis of the 1970s and 1980s." *Journal of Historical Sociology* 28, no. 1 (March 2015): 104–124.

Friedberger, Mark. *Farm Families & Change in 20th-Century America*. Lexington: University of Kentucky Press, 1988.

———. *Shake-Out: Iowa Farm Families in the 1980s*. Lexington: University of Kentucky Press, 1989.

Gringeri, Christina A. *Getting By: Women Homeworkers & Rural Economic Development*. Lawrence: University Press of Kansas, 1994.

Haight, Wendy, Teresa Ostler, James Black, and Linda Kingery. *Children of Methamphetamine-Involved Families: The Case of Rural Illinois*. Oxford: Oxford University Press, 2009.

Haney, Wava G. "Women." In *Rural Society in the U.S.: Issues for the 1980s*, edited by Don A. Dillman and Daryl J. Hobbs. Boulder: Westview Press, 1982.

Harl, Neil E. *The Farm Debt Crisis of the 1980s*. Ames: Iowa State University Press, 1990.

Hurt, R. Douglas. *American Agriculture: A Brief History*. Ames: Iowa State University Press, 1994.

———. *Problems of Plenty: The American Farmer in the Twentieth Century*. Chicago: Ivan Dee, 2002.

Ingram, Dustin. "For Sale or Rent: Preventing Demolition by Neglect in Iowa's Downtowns." Creative Component, Master's in Community and Regional Planning, Iowa State University, 2019.

Lasley, Paul, F. Larry Leistritz, Linda M. Lobao, and Katherine Meyer. *Beyond the Amber Waves of Grain: An Examination of Social and Economic Restructuring in the Heartland.* Boulder: Westview Press, 1995.

Lindert, Peter H. "Long-Run Trends in American Farmland Values." *Agricultural History* 62, no. 3 (1988): 45–85.

Neth, Mary. *Preserving the Family Farm: Women, Community, and the Foundations of Agribusiness, 1900–1940.* Baltimore: Johns Hopkins University Press, 1995.

Pratt, William C. "Using History to Make History? Progressive Farm Organizing during the Farm Revolt of the 1980s." *Annals of Iowa* 55, no. 1 (Winter 1996): 24–45.

Rasmussen, Wayne D. *Taking the University to the People: Seventy-Five Years of Cooperative Extension.* Ames: Iowa State University Press, 1989.

Reding, Nick. *Methland: The Life and Death of an American Small Town.* New York: Bloomsbury, 2009.

Reedy, Tyler. "Radicals in the Heartland: The Farm Crisis, Immigration, and Community Organizing." MA thesis, Iowa State University, 2013.

Riney-Kehrberg, Pamela. "Children of the Crisis: Farm Youth in Troubled Times." *Middle West Review* 2, no. 1 (Fall 2015): 11–25.

———. "Object Lesson: The High School Yearbook." *Journal of the History of Childhood and Youth* 10, no. 2 (Spring 2017): 159–167.

———. "Persistence, Change, and Thinking Big about Small Places: Some Thoughts about the Practical Applications of Rural and Agricultural History." *Agricultural History* 88, no. 1 (Winter 2014): 3–17.

———. "A Terrible and Special Irony: Hunger on Iowa's Farms in the Agricultural Crisis of the 1980s." *Annals of Iowa* 78, no. 4 (Fall 2019): 384–413.

Riney-Kehrberg, Pamela, editor. *Routledge History of Rural America.* New York: Routledge, 2016.

Root, Ken, ed. *The Rural Family, the Rural Community, and Economic Restructuring.* Conference Proceedings. Ames: Iowa State University, 1992.

Rosenfeld, Rachel. *Farm Women: Work, Farm, and Family in the United States.* Chapel Hill: University of North Carolina Press, 1985.

Rossinow, Doug. *The Reagan Era: A History of the 1980s.* New York: Columbia University Press, 2015.

Sachs, Carolyn E. *The Invisible Farmers: Women in Agricultural Production.* Totowa, NJ: Rowman and Allanheld, 1983.

Schwieder, Dorothy. *75 Years of Service: Cooperative Extension in Iowa.* Ames: Iowa State University Press, 1993.

———. *Iowa: The Middle Land.* Ames: Iowa State University Press, 1996.

Stearns, Peter. *Shame: A Brief History*. Urbana: University of Illinois Press, 2017.

Stock, Catherine McNicol, and Robert D. Johnston, eds. *The Countryside in the Age of the Modern State: Political Histories of Rural America*. Ithaca: Cornell University Press, 2001.

Stoil, Rebecca. "Desperate Farm Wives: Gender, Activism, and Traditionalism in the Farm Crisis." *Middle West Review* 2, no. 1 (Fall 2015): 33–50.

Tookey, Leah Fran. "Maintaining *Gemeinschaft* during a Century of Change: Rural School Consolidation in Iowa, a Case Study." MA thesis, Iowa State University, 2003.

Van Sickle, Bruce M. "The North Dakota Nine and the Family Farm." *Litigation* 25, no. 4 (1999): 49–59.

Wall, Joseph Frazier. "The Iowa Farmer in Crisis, 1920–1936." *Annals of Iowa* 47, no. 2 (1983): 116–127.

Wuthnow, Robert. *In the Blood: Understanding America's Farm Families*. Princeton: Princeton University Press, 2015.

———. *The Left Behind: Decline and Rage in Rural America*. Princeton: Princeton University Press, 2018.

———. *Remaking the Heartland: Middle America since the 1950s*. Princeton: Princeton University Press, 2010.

———. *Small Town America: Finding Community, Shaping the Future*. Princeton: Princeton University Press, 2015.

Index

Ackley, Iowa, 182, 210–211
activism, farm, 11, 23, 28–33, 36, 43, 50–52, 54, 60–62, 81, 120, 152–154, 163–164, 174–175, 192
Adair, Iowa, 154
Adair County, Iowa, 117
advertising, 26, 27–28
Advisory Committee on Commodity Foods and Shelter, 98
advocacy. *See* activism, farm
AFL-CIO, 153
agrarianism, 121, 138–139
agricultural economists, 22, 34, 70, 123, 125, 160, 168, 228n81
Albert, Donald, 92
alcoholism, 9
Algona, Iowa, 32, 60, 128, 181
Allamakee County, Iowa, 21
American Agricultural Movement, 30–33, 50, 116, 122, 190
American Agri-Women (AAW), 60
Ames, Iowa, 45, 47, 128, 149, 152
Amish, 200
Amlie, Rodney, 140–143
Andersen, Marvin, 66
Anderson, J. L., 17–18
Anderson, John, 42
Anderson, Mrs. Raymond, 83–84
Anderson, Robert T., 55, 116, 144
Anderson, Tom, 47
animal cruelty, 66–67

Arkansas, 164
Arlington, Iowa, 74
Ashby, Hal, 62
Ashton, Iowa, 219
ASSIST, 70, 136, 144
Atlantic, Iowa, 47, 50
auctions, farm, 59, 60, 63, 85–87, 88–89, 96, 125, 167
Audubon, Iowa, 182
Audubon County, Iowa, 64–65
Aurelia, Iowa, 170

Bagley, Iowa, 179
Bahe, Deborah, 74
Bailey, Christy, 170
bankers, 1–2, 26, 43, 81, 130–131, 139–143, 157, 256n89
bankruptcy, 69, 74, 121, 138, 141–143, 146–148, 150, 165, 167
banks; rural, 7, 39, 65, 66–67; failures, 139–143, 150
Barnett, Barry, 25
Bedell, Berkley, 53
Bedford, Iowa, 82
Behrens, A. W., Monsignor, 121, 150
Belle Plaine, Iowa, 36
Benson, Jim and Greta, 191
Benton County, Iowa, 58, 155
Bergland, Robert, 31, 42
Berry, Jan, 178
Beyer, Nancy, 52

277

Bicking, Kathy, 179
bipartisanship, 105–106, 115, 144
Black Hawk County, Iowa, 89, 205, 216
Block, John, 53, 57, 82, 93, 97–98,
Bloomfield, Iowa, 32, 180
Blundall, Joan, 72–73, 75, 165, 175–176, 190
Bode, Iowa, 66–67
Bon Jovi, 120
Book family, 96, 98
Boone County, Iowa, 17, 21, 23, 51, 83
bovine tuberculosis, 28
Bradford family, 191
Branstad, Terry: as governor, 1, 3, 9, 55–56, 61–63, 84–85, 96–98, 105, 116, 122–128, 132, 144, 174, 178, 180, 189; as lieutenant governor, 42, 55
Bremer County, Iowa, 205
Brent, Peter, 128, 166
Bristow, Iowa, 14
Britten, Phil, 79
Broderson, Aaron, 153
Broshar, Daniel, 136–138
Buchanan County, Iowa, 57
budgets, farm, 49
Burr, Dale, 1–2, 129–131, 133
Burr, Emily, 1
Burrows family, 55
Businesses, rural, 58, 81–82, 157–158, 180, 196, 208–211, 221
Butler County, Iowa, 139
Butz, Earl, 20

Cairns, Mickie, 45
Calhoun County, Iowa, 200, 206
Campbell, Kari, 172
Campo, Colorado, 33
capital investment, 200–201
Cargill Corporation, 124, 149
Carpenter, Cy, 93
Carroll, Iowa, 140, 149
Carson, Iowa, 166
Carter, Jimmy, 31, 33, 38–39, 42, 92
Carter Lake, Iowa, 193
Caterpillar, 97
Catholic Rural Life, 50, 61, 79, 100, 116, 174, 190
Cedar County, Iowa, 39
Cedar Rapids, Iowa, 47, 120–121, 133, 138
Center for Trade and Agricultural Policy, 125
Cerro Gordo County, Iowa, 200
Chambers, Lisa, 172
Chariton, Iowa, 116, 150
Charter Oak, Iowa, 149
Chelsea, Iowa, 194–195
Cherokee, Iowa, 15, 62–63, 132
Cherokee County, Iowa, 132, 139
children and youth: care of, 45, 84, 108 156, 191, 198; comments by, 124, 153–154, 170–171, 172–173; and food, 102; leaving farms, 205–206, 220–221; mental health, 75–76, 111–114, 154–156, 176, 198; place on farms, 185–186, 189, 202
China, 215
Chrysler Corporation, 97
churches, 11, 75, 95, 102, 105, 108, 115, 119, 121, 137–138, 217, 221; Roman Catholic, 11, 51, 95, 115, 118, 121, 150, 174
Citizens Organizing Acting Together (COACT), 85
Citizen's State Bank, 140
Civil Works Administration (CWA), 104
Clarence, Iowa, 120
Clay County, Iowa, 199
Clayton County, Iowa, 200
Clear Lake, Iowa, 103
Clemons, Iowa, 115
Clinton, Bill, 194
Clinton, Hillary, 216

Clinton, Iowa, 110
Clinton County, Iowa, 172, 178
Coleman v. Block, 89, 239n63
Columbus Junction, Iowa, 219
Commercial State Bank, 140–143
Committee on Economic Development (CED), 29
commodities, surplus, 78–79, 129, 161–162
commodity groups, 152
Community Economic Betterment Account (CEBA), 181–183
confinement, hogs, 14, 196, 203
Congress, US, 168, 176, 178, 215
Conlin, Roxanne, 55
Conservation Reserve Program (CRP), 129, 180
consumers, 21, 27, 40, 59, 70, 89, 219
Coon Rapids, Iowa, 155, 219
cooperation, rural/urban, 61
Cooperative Extension Service, Iowa State University, 6, 11, 41, 70–73, 78, 79, 81, 98–100, 104, 109–110, 113, 130–131, 136–139, 144, 155–156, 159–160, 165, 176, 211–213, 216, 218, 220
Cordero, Frank, Father, 121
corn, bushels produced, 17
coronavirus, 216–219
cost-price squeeze, 16–17, 19, 27, 40, 46, 48–50, 88, 161, 191
Council Bluffs, Iowa, 31, 60, 182
Council on Wage and Price Stability, 33
Country, 4, 61–62, 88–90, 113, 119, 155, 213
COVID-19, 216–219
Cow War, 28
credit crisis, 44, 126–127, 190–191, 214
Cresco, Iowa, 75, 83
crop prices, 27, 33, 38, 47–48, 58, 122–125, 160–161, 215, 218
crops, surplus, 18, 48

cross, as symbol of farm loss, 10, 86, 96–97, 116–117, 125
Culver, Larry, 2

dairy buyout, 129, 143, 152, 203, 227n52
dairying, 58, 107, 129, 214, 217, 220
Davenport, Iowa, 21, 219
dealerships, agricultural machinery, 58, 70, 157–158
debt, 1–2, 4–5, 12, 18, 23–24, 25, 34, 39, 48, 50, 62–63, 64–68, 70, 74, 81, 88–89, 94, 98, 104, 108, 117, 120, 122, 157, 166, 168, 173–174, 188–189, 201, 214–215; restructuring, 168
Decatur County, Iowa, 22
Decorah, Iowa, 133
DeGroot, John, 81
Delaware County, Iowa, 199–200
Denison, Iowa, 115
depopulation, rural, 7, 11–12, 19, 28–29, 69, 81–82, 111–112, 154, 169–170, 187–188, 197–199, 205–214, 217
Des Moines, Iowa, 31, 43, 49, 51, 94–95, 103, 117, 119, 193, 206, 217
Des Moines Area Community College (DMACC), 133–136
Diagonal, Iowa, 187–188
Dingman, Bishop Maurice, 51, 95, 116, 121
Dircks, Robert, 39
disaster declaration, 68, 194
disaster relief, 57–58, 82, 178, 194–195
diversification: agricultural, 17, 55–56, 127, 202–204; of income stream, 166, 205
divorce, 65, 135, 184–185
Dole, Robert, 33, 58–59, 97
domestic abuse, 9, 53
Dominy, J. Mark, 81
Dovring, Folke, 22
Draayer, Arlan, 81
Drahos family, 14, 34

Drake University, 144
drought, 26, 56–58, 67–68, 103, 165, 177–178, 185
Dubuque County, Iowa, 199–200
Dudley, Kathryn, 8
Duffy, Mike, 71–72, 166, 169, 173, 184
Dunkerton, Iowa, 4, 62, 89
Dvorak, Joanne, 121, 138–139

economic development, 181–183
Eddyville, Iowa, 124
efficiency, agricultural, 16–17
Ehmcke, Paul, 78
Elberon, Iowa, 124
elections, 42, 53, 92–94, 161–162, 216
electrification, rural, 16
Elk Horn, Iowa, 79
Elliott, Elizabeth A., 165
Ellsworth, Beth, 112
embargoes, 38–39, 42
employment, off-farm, 8, 11, 15, 20, 37, 44–45, 47, 48, 63–64, 65, 84, 105, 108–110, 124, 137, 141, 161, 176, 179–180, 185, 188–190, 197, 205
Engelken family, 63–64, 167
Erickson, Susan, 103–104
ethanol, 32, 219
Excel, 183
exports, agricultural, 4, 20, 24, 34, 38
Extension. *See* Cooperative Extension Service, Iowa State University
extremism, 91, 132–133, 246n6

faith, 46, 95, 225–226n24
Family Farmer Bankruptcy Act (Chapter 12), 146–148
family relations, 64, 71–72, 111, 135, 154–155, 184–186, 196–198
Family Services Agency, 121
Farm Aid, 70–71

Farm Aid concerts, 3, 119–120, 190
Farm and Ranch Assistance Network (FRSAN), 215
Farm Bill (1985), 122, 126–128, 166. *See also* Food Security Act of 1985
Farm Bill (2008), 215
Farm Bureau, 28, 30, 76, 78, 99, 100, 116–117, 123, 144, 163–164
FARM/CAP, 133–136
Farm Credit System (FCS), 7, 127, 129
Farm Crisis, origins of, 16
Farm Crisis Bill, 53
Farm Crisis Committees, 115–116, 118–119, 121
Farmer, Val, 52–53
farmers: average age of, 201–202; older, 48, 72, 74, 128, 135, 202, 220–221; young, 22–23, 41–42, 47, 48, 55–56, 64–65, 76–77, 135, 156–157, 160, 164, 168, 174, 183, 201–202
Farmers Home Administration (FmHA), 7, 15, 26, 39, 51, 57, 62–64, 88–89, 91, 93–94, 122, 127, 138, 148, 176–177, 194, 239n63
Farmer's Union, 28, 30, 50, 116, 192
Farmer to Farmer, 120–121, 138
farm income, 20
farming, organic, 63–64, 204–205
farm losses, 5, 199, 200; emotional toll of, 7–8, 19, 137–138
farms, large, 7, 19, 199
farms, number of, 19, 220–221
Farm Security Administration (FSA), 104
farm size, 19, 199
farm succession, 14–15, 74–75, 202, 204, 219–221
Farm Survival Hotline, 51–52, 99, 119, 128, 166, 190
Farwell, Mary, 172
Federal Deposit Insurance Corporation (FDIC), 7, 139–143, 150

Federal Emergency Management Agency (FEMA), 194
Federal Land Bank Association, 14, 15, 39, 44, 59, 63, 96, 167
Federal Reserve, 34, 82
Fenley, Linda, 2
Fenton, Iowa, 156
fertilizer, 20
Field, Sally, 88, 118–119
Fink, Deborah, 45
floods, 56, 68–69, 200, 215; of 1993, 165, 192–195
Foley, Michael Stewart, 30
Fonda, Iowa, 149
Fonda, Jane, 119
Food costs, 21, 40
Food for Life, 78, 101
food insecurity, 62–63, 77–79, 101–109, 149–151
food pantries, 78, 101–102, 105–106, 120
Food Security Act of 1985, 128–129. See also Farm Bill (1985)
food stamps, 11, 40, 79, 81, 103–109, 121, 128, 140, 150–151, 178–179
Forbes, Keith, 2
Ford, Gerald, 20, 38
Ford Motor Company, 29
foreclosure and forced sales, 38, 44, 60–61, 64–65, 69, 82, 85–87, 89, 96–97, 132–133, 141, 167–168, 174–175, 177, 191–192
foreclosure moratorium, 53–55, 61, 63, 94, 97, 127–128, 168
Foreigner, 120
Fort Dodge, Iowa, 29
4-H, 41, 111, 155–156, 198
14–40 (Taking Charge in Changing Times), 136–138, 176–177
Freedom Township Women's Club, 187
Fremont County, Iowa, 200
Friedberger, Mark, 22, 106, 164, 167

fuel costs, 21
Future Farmers of America (FFA), 111, 114, 155, 206

Gannon, James P., 129
gardening, 102–103, 105
Garretson, South Dakota, 165
Garst, David, 164
gender roles, 137
Gephardt, Richard, 4, 188
Gergen, Dave, 40
Gibson, Iowa, 46
Gibson, Mel, 88
Gilbert, Iowa, 101
Gilliland, Kim, 179
Goody, Richard, 1
government, attitudes toward, 34
Grange, 116
grasshoppers, 103–104
Grassley, Chuck, 105, 119, 146–148, 215–216
Great Depression, 4–5, 25, 37, 42–43, 47, 49–50, 51, 53, 61, 69–70, 83, 85, 88, 103–104, 106, 140, 160, 169, 173, 202, 207, 224n10
Greeley, Iowa, 63
Greene County, Iowa, 48
Greene Township Women's Club, 52
Greenfield, Iowa, 188
Gridiron Club, 114
Gross, Douglas, 98
Grundy County, Iowa, 59, 182
Grundy County Farm Bureau Women, 123

Haggard, Merle, 119
Hall, Ronald, 115
Halley's Comet, 171
Hamburg, Iowa, 68–69, 195
Hamilton County, 199
Hampton, Iowa, 182

Hancock County, Iowa, 139, 200
Hanson, Bette, 81
Hanson, Leonie, 165
Harkin, Tom, 36–37, 53, 94, 105, 188–189
Harl, Neil, 94, 168
Harlan, Iowa, 111–112, 182, 207
Harms, Leon, 59
Harper, Joe, 134–136
Harrison County, Iowa, 139, 200
Harvestore, 27–28, 196, 227n52
Heffernan, Keith, 84–85, 149
Heiar family, 47
Heick family, 120
Helms, Jesse, 119
Henley, Don, 3
Hills, Iowa, 1–2, 4, 133
Hodde, Ray, 68–69
Hogberg, Maynard, 220
hogs, total raised, 17
holding actions, 29
Holstein, Iowa, 132
Hormel, 183
hospitals, rural, 158, 217, 219
Hotz family, 2
House Democratic Caucus (US), 119
Howard County, Iowa, 200
Hubbard, Iowa, 154
Hughes, John, 1
Hull, Iowa, 132
Humboldt County, Iowa, 66–67
Hupp, Bev, 45
Hurt, R. Douglas, 16–17
Huxley, Iowa, 152

IBP, 182–183
Ida Grove, Iowa, 115
identity, 7–8
Illinois, 136, 184, 186, 213
impeachment, 216
improvements, agricultural, 6, 14, 22

income, agricultural, 24, 25–27, 44, 174
Indiana, 184
Indianola, Iowa, 94
industry, agricultural, 7, 69–70, 97, 116, 125, 153, 180
inflation, 24, 25, 33, 37–38, 43
infrastructure, 210–211
inheritance, farm, 189, 191, 202, 204, 220–221
interest rates, 6, 12, 25, 34, 37–39, 40, 41–43, 47, 50, 59, 69, 81–82, 97, 117, 127, 140–141, 161; buy downs, 148–189, 152
International Harvester, 97
Inwood, Iowa, 81
Iowa Agricultural Loan Assistance Program (IALAP), 148–149
Iowa attorney general, 123, 168
Iowa Banker's Association, 128, 163
Iowa Bureau of Economic Assistance, 102
Iowa Christmas Tree Growers' Association, 56
Iowa Citizen Action Network (ICAN), 51, 152
Iowa Citizens for Community Improvement (ICCI), 51, 126, 190, 256n89
Iowa City, Iowa, 178, 219
Iowa Concern Hotline. *See* Rural Concern Hotline
Iowa Corn Growers, 27
Iowa Department of Education, 169
Iowa Department of Human Services, 78–79, 103, 106, 150–151
Iowa Department of Public Safety, 132
Iowa Development Commission, 56
Iowa Falls, Iowa, 23, 182, 210
Iowa Family Farm Development Authority (IFFDA), 41, 47, 157, 168
Iowa Farm and Rural Life Poll, 91
Iowa Farm Unity Coalition (IFUC),

50–52, 57–58, 61, 79–81, 87, 96–98, 100, 107–109, 116–117, 121, 128, 141, 144, 150–152, 168, 174, 192
Iowa Federation of Labor, 152
Iowa Grain and Feed Association, 81
Iowa Homestead Act, 168
Iowaide concert, 119
Iowa Inter-Church Agency for Peace and Justice, 51, 102
Iowa Inter-Church Forum, 61, 102
Iowa Interfaith Human Needs Council, 98
Iowa Lakes Community College, 136
Iowa National Guard, 122
Iowa Office for Planning and Programming, 55
Iowa Pork Producers, 29, 152
Iowa Rural Crisis Fund, 102
Iowa State Legislature, 53–54, 170
Iowa State Patrol, 132
Iowa State University, 28, 70, 116–118, 123, 125, 165, 168, 191, 193, 206, 211
Iowa Supreme Court, 53–54
Iowa United Autoworkers, 51
Irwin, Iowa, 60, 207–208

Jackson County, Iowa, 199
Jackson, Jesse, 4, 188–189
Jacobs, Eleanor, 89
Janesville, Iowa, 47
Jasper County, Iowa, 139
Jepsen, Roger, 94
Jesup, Iowa, 45
jobs: creation, 181–182; training, 133–136
John Deere, 7, 66, 163, 205
John Paul II (pope), 95
Johnson, W. John, 165
Johnson County, Iowa, 128, 216
Jolly, Robert, 70, 160
Juhl, Dennis, 55–56

Kading, Stanley, 117
Kalona, Iowa, 155, 184
Kanawha, Iowa, 54
Kansas, 31, 176, 186, 214
Kersey, Tommy, 132–133, 246n7
Kimballton, Iowa, 65
King, B. B., 120
Kleckner, Dean, 30, 163
Knebel, Levi, 89, 213
Koenigsfeld, Robert, 174
Kossuth County, Iowa, 181, 193
Krumme, Richard, 42, 164–165
Kruse, Loren, 192

labor unions, 100
La Douceur, Chad, 172
Lake City, Iowa, 115
land: meaning of, 7–8, 74–75; sales, 7, 25, 166; values, 4–5, 6, 12, 21–24, 34, 38, 43, 48, 59, 69, 147, 160, 162, 165–166, 169, 173, 178, 184, 200–201, 215
Lange, Jessica, 3, 61–62, 88–90, 118–119
Larchwood, Iowa, 81
Lasley, Paul, 77, 91, 100, 185
Lawler, Joseph, 66
Lawrence, Kathleen, 94
Leach, Jim, 36, 53, 93
Ledyard, Iowa, 101
legal aid, 120
Legal Services Corporation of Iowa, 101, 179
Legislature, Iowa, 122–123, 143–144, 148, 168
lenders, 7, 14–15, 23, 26, 39, 51, 54, 104, 122, 127, 130–131, 138–145, 166, 168, 190
Lenox, Iowa, 182
letters, constituent, 3–4, 9, 46–47, 49, 54, 62–63, 68–69, 73–77, 81–85, 92–93, 110, 115, 123–124, 128, 148–149, 153–154, 170–171, 175, 178, 183

Levitas, Daniel, 130, 168
Ley, John, 193
Liberty Center, Iowa, 166
liens, common law, 91
Lincoln Land Community College, 136
Linn County, Iowa, 48, 216
Little Sioux, Iowa, 187
Live Aid concert, 120
livestock producers, 43, 58, 66–67, 93, 140–143, 162, 178, 191, 196, 203–204, 218–219
Living History Farms, 95
Loaves and Fishes, 101
Looft, Scott Alan, 156–157
Lone Tree, Iowa, 1–2
Lottery, Iowa, 127, 181–183
Louisa County, Iowa, 200, 219
Lounsberry, Robert, Iowa Secretary of Agriculture, 2, 23, 32, 54, 69
Luedtke, Orville and Joan, 87
Luse, Brian, 41
Lyon, Eric, 214

Macksburg, Iowa, 88
Madsen family, 204–205
Main Street Program, 159
Malcolm, Iowa, 164
Manson, Iowa, 184
Mapleton, Iowa, 115–116, 118, 150
Maple Valley Concerned Citizens, 117
Marckmann, Bob, 31
Marion, Iowa, 159
masculinity, 7–8, 109–110, 137
Mather family, 148
Maulsby, Darcy Dougherty, 206
Mayland, Doug, 157
McClintock, Patrick, 101
McDonald, Wayne and Miriam, 115
McLaughlin, Janet, 130
McLean, Donald and Catherine, 73

meat packing, 180, 182–183, 205, 218–219
mediation, farmer/lender, 143–144, 146, 168
Meisgeier, Kenneth and Betty, 74–75
Mellencamp, John, 3, 119–120
Mellinger, Iowa, 130
Mennonites, 138, 184, 225–226n24
mental health, 1, 7–9, 11, 40–41, 46, 51–53, 65, 71–77, 88, 120–121, 129–130, 133–139, 175–178, 183–184, 190, 215–217
Merrick, Daniel, 72
Meseck family, 124
methamphetamine (meth), 212–213
Mexico, 215
Meyers, William, 125
Michigan, 184
Miller, Tom, 168
Mills County, Iowa, 200
Minden, Iowa, 166
Minimum Price Bill, 122–125
Minnesota, 57, 85, 87, 126, 144, 186, 213–214
Mississippi, 176
Mississippi River, 193, 215
Missouri, 147, 176
Missouri River, 68–69, 193, 215
Mitchell County, Iowa, 200
Moline, Illinois, 116
Mondale, Walter, 93–94
Monmouth, Iowa, 155
Montezuma, Iowa, 124
Moravia, Iowa, 41
Morningside College, 114
Morrow, Charles, 95
Morse, Darrell, 166
Mount Ayr, Iowa, 187
Mount Vernon, Iowa, 14
movies, 88–90
Mueller, J. Howard, 123
Murray, Iowa, 170
Muscatine County, Iowa, 200

INDEX

National Agricultural Press Association, 91
National Crisis Action Rally, 116
National Education Association (NEA), 153
National Farmers Organization (NFO), 29, 33, 50
National Farmers Union, 93
National Governor's Association, 180
National Rural Life Conference, 153
Nebraska, 120, 176, 213
Neighbor, Morris, 43
Neighbor Helping Neighbor, 102
Nelson, Willie, 3, 102, 119, 189
Neola, Iowa, 40
Nevada, Iowa, 51, 96,
New Deal, 51, 100
New Hampton, Iowa, 14
Newton, Iowa, 124
1970s, 4–5, 6, 14–35, 48, 83, 128, 140, 149, 161, 200–201
Nixon, Richard, 20, 38
Nollen, Kenneth, 55
Noller, David, 92
North American Farm Alliance, 90
North Dakota, 89, 144, 147, 176
Northeast School District, 172
Northwest Iowa Community Health Center, 72, 175–176
Norway, Iowa, 114
Norwest Bank, 190, 256n89

Obama, Barack, 216
O'Brien, Denise, 79–81, 107–109
O'Brien County, Iowa, 78
Office of Planning and Programming, 61
Ohio, 214
Ohrtman, Myron, 18, 34–35, 62
oil embargo, 20
Oklahoma, 176
Omega Township Women's Club, 46, 187

Onslow, Iowa, 155
opinion polls, of farmers, 39, 41, 48–49, 57–58, 91, 159–161, 173–174, 183–184, 189–190, 215, 220–221
opioids, 213–214
Orange City, Iowa, 40, 133
Orbison, Roy, 120
orchards, 55
Oscar Mayer, 183
Oskaloosa, Iowa, 15
Ostendorf, David, 44, 46, 58, 95, 97, 99–100, 148, 164–165, 179
Ostendorf, Roz, 98, 151
Osterkamp, Jim, 89
Ottumwa, Iowa, 205
overproduction, agricultural, 16–18, 26–27, 53, 57–59

Palmer, Charles, 78–79
Palo Alto County, Iowa, 200
Parity, 30–33, 122, 126
Paulsen, Julie, 139
Payment-in-Kind Program (PIK), 57–59, 67, 93
Pedersen, Gerald, 14, 34
Pella, Iowa, 55
penny auctions, 11, 85–87
Perpich, Rudy, 126
Perry, Iowa, 152, 183
Person, Lanette, 187
Peters, David, 211–112
Peters, Karen, 103
Petersen, Amy, 190
Petersen, W. D., 132
Peterson, Suzanne, 95
petitions, 36, 82
Phillips, Fran, 175
Phipps, Wynn, 103–104
Pilot Mound, Iowa, 152
Pioneer Hi-Bred Seed Company, 144

Plagge, Sandy, 130
Plains, Georgia, 31
Pleasantville, Iowa, 103
Plowman family, 193
Pocahontas, Iowa, 140, 142, 209–210
Pocahontas County, Iowa, 101
Point, Marilyn, 181
politics, farm, 99–100, 109, 117, 119
Polk County, Iowa, 199, 216
population, 180, 198–199
Porkettes, 29
Potter, Deanna, 153
Practical Farmers of Iowa, 204
PrairieFire, 4, 51, 97, 116, 119, 127, 130, 141–142, 146, 164, 166, 176, 179, 188, 192, 194
Pratt, William, 85
prices, 27, 33, 38, 47–48, 58, 122–125, 160–161, 215, 218
price supports, 18, 129
production, cost of, 49–50, 124, 161
production controls, 57–59
Production Credit Association (PCA), 7, 15, 39, 59, 91, 116, 122
Project Apple Corps, 55
Project Hope, 136
protest, 11, 51, 60–61, 96–97

Quad Cities Unemployed Association, 54

Ralston, Iowa, 32
Ramsey, John, 2
Randalia, Iowa, 92
Rath Company, 61, 97
Rawlings, Hunter R., III, 183
Ray, Robert, 3, 31–32, 36, 40, 42–43, 47, 54
Reagan, Ronald, 42, 51, 75, 92–94, 96–98, 101, 103, 114–115, 116–117, 122, 129, 153, 161, 168

recession, 37, 42–43, 47
Red Oak, Iowa, 182
Reichert family, 14
Reinsche, Mary Ann, 45
religion, 46, 95. *See also* churches; faith
Rempe, Bill, 124
Reno, Milo, 28
Republican National Committee, 92, 115
Riordan, James, 51, 54
Roberts, Darrah, 23
Roland, Iowa, 101, 152, 195
Rolfe, Iowa, 181, 183, 208–209
Rosenfeld, Louise, 104
Rosmann, Mike, 215
Rouw, Verlan, 88
Rural America, 33, 43, 51, 58, 62, 87, 90, 95, 99, 116. *See also* PrairieFire
Rural Concern Hotline, and Iowa Concern Hotline, 98–100, 136, 139, 175–176, 190, 194, 216
Rural Crisis Recovery Program Act, 176–177
Rural Iowa, 50
Rural Recovery Line, 194
rural/urban divide, 216–117
Rutland, Iowa, 14
Ryan, Chuck, 79

Sac County, Iowa, 48, 139
Sanner, Harvey Joe, 164–165
Schleswig, Iowa, 118
schools, rural, 137, 170–171, 172, 188, 189, 196, 217, 221; consolidation of, 7, 111–112, 158–159, 169–172, 207–209; homeschooling, 187; open enrollment, 187
Schruer, Mrs. Garrett, 54
Schwennen family, 14, 34
Scott County, Iowa, 21, 216
Sears, Roebuck and Company, 29

Seeding Rural Resilience Act, 215
self-sufficiency, 103–105
Sellers, Jane, 179
Senate Agriculture Committee (US), 119
Severson, Mary Helen, 130
shame, 8–9, 46, 73–75, 77–79, 87, 102, 105–108, 137–138, 147, 150, 179
Shelby County, Iowa, 68, 111–112, 174–175, 207
"Shrink Smart," 211–212, 221
Siebens, Christopher, 76
Sigourney, Iowa, 92, 148
Silver City, Iowa, 154
Simon, Paul, 189
Simpson College, 136
Sindt family, 102–103
Sioux City, Iowa, 114, 132, 154, 179
Sioux County, 40, 132, 199
Sioux Falls, South Dakota, 218
Sioux Feed Company, 81
Skow, Duane, 49
Smiley, Jane, 3
Smith, Neal, 152
South Dakota, 117, 213
Spacek, Sissy, 88, 119
Staley, Oren Lee, 30
standard of living, 105, 217, 220
Stanek, Edward, 55–56
State Center, Iowa, 191
Steinke, Robert, 46
Stockman, David, 98, 114–115, 116, 118
Storm Lake, Iowa, 47
Story County, Iowa, 45, 51, 96, 101, 216
Stover, F. W., 126
Stratford, Iowa, 171–172
Stratford High School, 171–172
stress, 41, 46, 67, 72–75, 101, 133–139, 174, 183–184, 190, 215
strike, farm, 28, 30–33, 36
subsidies, farm, 129

suicide, farmers and, 1, 8–9, 53, 72, 74–75, 88, 129–131, 154, 175, 215
Super Value Stores, 149–150
Swestka, Joyce, 83

Tabor, Iowa, 32
Take Charge in Changing Times, 73, 78
Taking Charge in Changing Times (14–40), 136–138, 176–177
Tama, Iowa, 218
taxes, 22, 24, 91, 146–148, 158
technological change, 16–18, 19, 22
Terry, Dixon, 4, 23, 50–51, 117, 188–189, 191–192
Terry, Linda, 188–189, 191–192
Tester, Jon, 215
Tevis, Cheryl, 46, 52–53, 189, 193
Thompson family, 166
Thompson, Michael, 144, 146
Tilkes, Jeff, 154
Tiller, Jim, 112
Toledo, Iowa, 214
Tookey, Leah, 64–65
tornado, 68
tourism, 181
towns, small, 7, 32, 81–82, 153, 157–159, 180, 196, 205–213, 217, 221
Tractorcade, 31
trade wars, 215
tradition, rural, 121, 138–139
Traer, Iowa, 73
tree farming, 55
Trump, Donald, 216

unemployment, 37, 135, 194, 213–214, 216
Union County, Iowa, 57
United Auto Workers (UAW), 61, 100, 116, 152–153
United Central Bank, 60
United Food and Commercial Workers, 183

United States Department of Agriculture (USDA), 6, 12–13, 18, 20–21, 57–59, 78–79, 94, 100, 129, 176–177, 214
University of Iowa, 183, 193
University of Wisconsin-Stout, 53
Urbandale, Iowa, 95
Urban family, 15, 35, 84
US Farmer's Association, 50, 59, 126
US Feed Grains Council, 123
USSR, 20, 38

Van Buren County, 193
VandeHaar, Rich, 152
Van Der Pol family, 15, 35
Veenstra, Wilbur, 87
Vermont, 176
Vinton, Iowa, 113, 155
violence, 1, 4, 28, 73, 87, 127, 129–131, 132–133, 144, 152, 154, 175
Vogl, John, 117
Volcker, Paul, 12, 37, 97
Vorthman, Aaron, 166
Vriesen, Victor, Rev., 101

wages, 180, 182–183
Wahlert, R. C., 183
Wapello County, Iowa, 177, 193, 205
Washington, DC, 116–117
Washington, Iowa, 47
Waterloo, Iowa, 89, 205
Wauters, Dennis, 124
Webster City, Iowa, 45, 130, 142, 172
Wefald, Jon, 166
Weigel, Randy, 41
Welle, John, 124
Wellman, Iowa, 184
Wenzel, Larry, 128
Westbrook, Minnesota, 85
West Central Development, 150

Westmar College, 136
West Virginia, 214
Weyerholz, Lloyd, 193
Wilton, Iowa, 139
Winburn, Iowa, 164
Winnebago County, Iowa, 199–200
Winneshiek County, Iowa, 200
Wisconsin, 144, 184, 213
Witt, Christina, 172
Witt, Mrs. Dan H., 110
Wittliff, Bill, 62
women: advocacy, 29, 60, 82–85, 96, 119; and marriage, 184–186, 197; mental health, 52–53, 72–73, 88–90, 176; organizations, 187; roles on farms, 8, 44–45, 46, 48, 62, 71, 88–90, 106–108, 109–110, 137, 185–186, 189, 197, 205
Women in Farm Economics (WIFE), 60, 116, 119
Wood, Warren, 66–67
Woodbury, Iowa, 102
Woodbury County, Iowa, 119
Works Progress Administration (WPA), 104
Worth County, Iowa, 199
Wright County, 203–204
Wuthnow, Robert, 212, 217

yearbooks, high school, 111–112, 172–173
Yetter, Iowa, 158, 206
Yntema, Theodore O., 29
Yotter, Ed, 193
Young, Neil, 119

Zarecor, Kimberly, 211–212
Zeimet family, 60
Zevenbergen, Peter, 130
Zwingle, Iowa, 47

Printed in the USA
CPSIA information can be obtained
at www.ICGtesting.com
CBHW050321051224
18479CB00006B/9